"TAKE HOLD OF THE ROBE OF A JEW"

HERBERT OF BOSHAM'S CHRISTIAN HEBRAISM

STUDIES IN THE HISTORY
OF
CHRISTIAN TRADITIONS

FOUNDED BY HEIKO A. OBERMAN †

EDITED BY

ROBERT J. BAST, Knoxville, Tennessee

IN COOPERATION WITH

HENRY CHADWICK, Cambridge
SCOTT H. HENDRIX, Princeton, New Jersey
ERIC SAAK, Indianapolis, Indiana
BRIAN TIERNEY, Ithaca, New York
ARJO VANDERJAGT, Groningen
JOHN VAN ENGEN, Notre Dame, Indiana

VOLUME CXXVI

DEBORAH L. GOODWIN

"TAKE HOLD OF THE ROBE OF A JEW"
HERBERT OF BOSHAM'S CHRISTIAN HEBRAISM

"TAKE HOLD OF THE ROBE OF A JEW"

HERBERT OF BOSHAM'S CHRISTIAN HEBRAISM

BY

DEBORAH L. GOODWIN

BRILL

LEIDEN · BOSTON

2006

Cover illustration: Herbert of Bosham presenting his edition of Peter Lombard's Psalms commentary to Archbishop William of Sens, from folio 1 of *Prima Pars Pslaterii Glosati secundum Herbertum de Bosham*, MS. B.5.4, Trinity College Library, Cambridge, England. The image is reproduced by kind permission of the Library.

This book is printed on acid-free paper.

Library of Congress Cataloging-in-Publication Data

Goodwin, Deborah L.
  Take hold of the robe of a Jew : Herbert of Bosham's Christian hebraism / by Deborah L. Goodwin.
    p. cm. — (Studies in the history of Christian traditions, ISSN 1573-5664 ; v. 126)
  Includes bibliographical references and index.
  Contents: The life of a twelfth-century intellectual—Herbert of Bosham's Psalterium cum commento—Twelfth-century Christian hebraism in context—Colonizing the territory of Scripture—The linguistic and cultural horizons of Herbert's hebraism—Herbert's hermeneutics of the literal sense—Herbert as expositor : the faithful synagogue.
  ISBN 90-04-14905-8 (alk. paper)
  1. Herbert, of Bosham, 12th cent. Psalterium cum commento. 2. Bible, O. T. Psalms—Commentaries. 3. Herbert, of Bosham, 12th cent. 4. Christianity and other religions—Judaism. 5. Judaism—Relations—Christianity. 6. Rashi, 1040-1105. Perush Rashi le-sefer Tehilim. I. Title. II. Series.

BS1429.H47G66 2006
223'.206092—dc22

                                                                            2005054238

            ISSN   1573-5664
            ISBN   90 04 14905 8

PRINTED IN THE NETHERLANDS

"Many peoples and strong nations shall come to seek the Lord of hosts in Jerusalem, and to entreat the favor of the Lord. Thus says the Lord of hosts: In those days ten men from the nations of every tongue shall take hold of the robe of a Jew, saying, 'Let us go with you, for we have heard that God is with you.'"

Zechariah 8:22–23

TABLE OF CONTENTS

LIST OF ABBREVIATIONS

AK	*The Archaeology of Knowledge*
BC	*The Becket Conflict and the Schools*
CCCM	*Corpus Christianorum Continuatio Medievalis*
CCSL	*Corpus Christianorum Series Latina*
CSEL	*Corpus Scriptorum Ecclesiasticorum Latina*
DCD	*De civitate Dei*
DDC	*De doctrina christiana*
Mats.	*Materials for the History of Thomas Becket, Archbishop of Canterbury*
PL	*Patrologia Latina*
RTAM	*Recherches de Théologie Ancienne et Médiévale*
SBMA	*The Study of the Bible in the Middle Ages*, 3rd edition
DDC	*De doctrina christiana*

ACKNOWLEDGMENTS

This book is an expansion and substantial revision of my doctoral dissertation, "A Study of Herbert of Bosham's Psalms Commentary (c. 1190)," completed at the University of Notre Dame in 2001. The members of my dissertation committee—John C. Cavadini, Brian M. Daley, Michael A. Signer, and Joseph P. Wawrykow—were unfailingly helpful and astute; they have continued to be generous senior colleagues as my work on this manuscript and related projects has progressed. The University of Notre Dame's Theology Department, Graduate Student Union, and Graduate School funded travel to conferences to present portions of the dissertation and a research trip to England. While there, Raphael Loewe kindly gave me his notes on Herbert; his prodigious erudition has been an inspiration.

Subsequent research has been supported by Gustavus Adolphus College. Its Faculty Development program has funded additional trips to conferences and to England, where I benefited from very useful discussions with my colleague in Herbert studies, Eva De Visscher, and Richard Gameson's graciously bestowed expertise. The staff of the Chapter Library at Saint Paul's Cathedral, most notably Joseph Wisdom, have been exceptionally helpful and accommodating, as have their counterparts at London's Guildhall Library, Lambeth Palace, and the University of Nottingham's manuscript collection.

The Library of Trinity College, Cambridge, in the person of Joanna Ball, generously responded to my many queries and made available the image from another of Herbert's works which has been used as the cover illustration.

I have benefited greatly from the interest, support, and challenging questions proffered by my associates in the field of medieval biblical scholarship, especially Matilda Bruckner, Boyd Taylor Coolman, Theresa Gross-Diaz, Robert Harris, Deeana Klepper, E. Ann Matter, Joseph Pearson, Joy Schroeder, Lesley Smith, and Grover Zinn. Likewise, my colleagues at Gustavus Adolphus College have contributed valuable advice as this book took shape. I am endebted to Laura Behling, Darrell Jodock, Gregory Kaster, Mariangela Maguire, Matthew Panciera, Rebecca Taylor, Robert Weisenfeld, and Kate Wittenstein for their comments and suggestions. John Cha, Mark Dennis, and Mary Gaebler have been companionable, and often uproarious, fellow travelers in the world of theory. The College's library staff, particularly Interlibrary Loan librarian Kathie Martin and her assistants, have been unfailingly helpful and accommodating.

Portions of this work appeared previously in *Traditio*; I am grateful to its editors for granting permission to reprint that material. Brill's *Studies in the History of Christian Thought* series editor Robert Bast has provided me with prompt and encouraging responses; the anonymous reader who reviewed the entire manuscript meticulously in its earlier form offered many valuable suggestions. Finally, any student of the Bible in the Middle Ages must acknowledge her debt to the late Beryl Smalley, whose insights continue to inspire and stimulate my own work, and in whose footsteps I follow unevenly indeed.

All of the people mentioned above have done much, in many ways, to improve this work. Its remaining shortcomings are wholly my responsibility. Only my family knows how much they have sacrificed to allow me to pursue my dreams; only they can imagine my gratitude. I dedicate this work to them, to the memory of my father and mother, and most of all to Rebecca: "Wie du warst! Wie du bist!"

INTRODUCTION

Until the 1950s, Herbert of Bosham was known—if he was known at all—as a member of Thomas Becket's episcopal household. An ardent polemicist for the archbishop's cause during Becket's life, Herbert swelled the ranks of his hagiographers after the murder in the cathedral in 1170. But Herbert was also Becket's 'master of the sacred page,' and his accomplishments as an exegete were studied first by Beryl Smalley and then by her colleague Raphael Loewe in a series of articles starting in 1951.[1]

The exegetical work that captured their attention was Herbert's commentary on the Book of Psalms, probably dating from the 1190s. Smalley ratified Herbert's own claim that the work is unique: a commentary on the literal sense of the Hebraica psalter—the version of the psalms Jerome presumably translated directly from the Hebrew, not the Gallican version usually discussed by interpreters in the Christian tradition. No other Latin Christian exegete contemporary with Herbert had attempted to interpret the psalms literally.

Herbert's commentary exists in a single manuscript, now housed at Saint Paul's Cathedral library.[2] Loewe edited and published three excerpts from the manuscript in 1953. Until now, his analysis of these excerpts and Smalley's discussion of Herbert's career have formed the basis for subsequent scholarly appraisal of Herbert's accomplishments as a linguist and exegete. In Loewe's opinion, Herbert was the most competent 'Christian hebraist' in any generation from Jerome to Reuchlin. In Smalley's judgment, Herbert's sophistication in dealing

---

[1] For discussion of Herbert's life and career as an exegete, see Beryl Smalley, "A Commentary on the *Hebraica* by Herbert of Bosham," *Recherches de Théologie Ancienne et Médiévale* 18 (1951): 29–65, the second and third editions of her *The Study of the Bible in the Middle Ages* (Notre Dame: University of Notre Dame Press, 1978), and *eadem*, *The Becket Conflict and the Schools* (Totowa, NJ: Rowman and Littlefield, 1973). Raphael Loewe's study of the commentary is foundational: "Herbert of Bosham's Commentary on Jerome's Hebrew Psalter," *Biblica* 34 (1953): 44–77, 159–192, 275–298.

[2] Saint Paul's MS 2, catalogued by N.R. Ker, *Medieval Manuscripts in British Libraries I: London* (1969), 241.

with Scripture's literal sense exceeded that of his mentors at the school of Saint Victor. This book is the first full-length study of the commentary and its author.[3]

Beryl Smalley calculated that Herbert was born *circa* 1120.[4] His toponym refers to a village in Sussex on England's southeastern coast. Herbert was educated as a theologian in Paris and claimed Peter Lombard as his principal teacher. In 1157, he was in the service of Henry II of England. Five years later, Herbert accompanied Thomas Becket to the latter's consecration as Archbishop of Canterbury. From 1162 until Becket's assassination in 1170, Herbert was Thomas's constant companion and closest advisor, never leaving Becket's side unless to do battle for him in the international arena of ecclesiastical and royal politics. Missing from the scene of Becket's murder in Canterbury cathedral on December 29, 1170, Herbert made up for his absence by becoming a vigorous contributor to the Becket 'industry': his life of the martyr is the longest and most prolix of the many versions produced by Becket's circle. Neither Herbert's literary efforts nor his eventual reconciliation with Henry II yielded any settled preferment in England. His attempts to find a patron led him back to France where eventually he found refuge at the Cistercian monastery of Ourscamp in the diocese of Arras. Urged by the local bishop, Peter of Arras, to occupy himself as either a teacher, monk or writer, Herbert chose the last as best suited to his talents. His commentary on the Hebraica, probably written in the early 1190s, was the result. Herbert disappeared from public view after 1194.[5] Chapter One sets out Herbert's life and career against the background of twelfth-century political and intellectual currents and then explores how those currents, at first glance unrelated, converged around him.

After examining the context for Herbert's activities, Chapter Two presents an overview of his working methods in the psalms commentary, those methods' relationship to the academic training he had probably received, and the commentary's relationship to other works, both

---

[3] The present work is adapted from my Ph.D. dissertation, "A Study of Herbert of Bosham's Psalms Commentary (C. 1190)," (University of Notre Dame, 2001). See also *eadem*, "Herbert of Bosham and the Horizons of Twelfth-Century Exegesis," *Traditio* 58 (2003). The commentary is the subject of another recent doctoral thesis, that of Eva De Visscher, "The Jewish-Christian Dialogue in Twelfth-Century Western Europe: Herbert of Bosham's *Commentary on the Psalms*" (Ph.D. thesis, University of Leeds, 2003.)

[4] Smalley's biographical essay in *The Becket Conflict and the Schools* outlines succinctly the current state of knowledge regarding Herbert's life and works.

[5] Smalley, *Becket Conflict*, 74.

Christian and Jewish. My approach has involved examining the psalms commentary to identify Herbert's chief areas of interest, then extracting a representative sampling of his comments on various pericopes for detailed analysis and discussion. The materials selected focus on the dialogical relationship of Herbert's psalms commentary to that of the late eleventh-century Jewish scholar, R. Solomon ben Isaac of Troyes (d. 1105), often referred to by the acronym Rashi. This prolific exegete's commentary was not only Herbert's chief source of data regarding Jewish scriptural interpretation but also guided Herbert's theological reflections on the relations between Jews and Christians.

Why and how was Herbert so affected by the experience of working through Rashi's psalms commentary while writing his own? This study tries to answer those questions by locating Herbert both as a scholar—in which regard he may have been more typical of his age than otherwise—and as a polemicist for Thomas Becket's cause. This latter role especially sheds light on Herbert's character: as we shall see, he was impetuous, courageous, supremely self-confident, and no respecter of persons. Herbert exhibited similar qualities in the scholarly arena even before embarking on his idiosyncratic psalms commentary. He defended his old teacher, Peter Lombard, against charges of heresy by producing a painstaking edition (one might almost call it a 'critical' edition) of Lombard's commentaries on Psalms and the Pauline Epistles. At a time when the Lombard's stock was at its lowest, Herbert extolled his merits as a theologian to the very people charged with condemning that theology.[6] Herbert's activities crossed many of the boundaries by which the intellectual and religious lives of medieval people are customarily delimited. In Chapters Three and Four, along with a discussion of the historical background of the phenomenon of Christian hebraism, the significance of Herbert's particular variety of hebraism is considered. He seems to have been a hebraist with a unique agenda. To the extent that he is unclassifiable, he may help us to rethink existing classifications. Chapter Four, in particular, examines current scholarship that seeks to explicate the relationships between Judaism and Christianity in the twelfth century, and suggests some new methodological approaches to the study of these relationships.

While the studies by Smalley and Loewe focused chiefly on establishing the range of Herbert's ability to read and understand Hebrew

---

[6] See the discussion in Chapter 1.

texts on his own, this work has a different goal. Chapter Five considers two issues related to Herbert's knowledge of Hebrew. Firstly, it
examines where and how Herbert might have learned Hebrew. Secondly, the chapter considers in some detail how his linguistic expertise
(whether great or small) contributed to his singular interpretive stance
regarding the psalter. The chapter tries to determine how Herbert's
encounters with Hebrew texts and with Jewish interlocutors reshaped
his exegetical horizons. Herbert's interest in the Hebrew language and
Jewish exegesis was not unique; as we shall see, he followed the leads of
other Christian exegetes in the twelfth century. I argue that Herbert not
only mined Jewish exegesis for the nuggets of historical data prized by
his Christian contemporaries, he also discerned the trajectory of Jewish eschatological expectations encoded in Rashi's psalms commentary.
This encounter opened the horizons of his own interpretations of the
psalms such that he read them not only as predictive of Jesus Christ but
also understood them to speak of a Messiah whom his Jewish contemporaries still awaited.

Equally striking is Herbert's apparent decision to abandon a tradition of psalms commentary with which he was intimately familiar in
order to comment on the psalter's literal sense. Historically Jews and
Christians have read the psalms as prophecy of a Redeemer; each tradition regards the psalms as a reservoir of comfort and assurance, even
in the darkest of times. For these reasons, the history of psalms interpretation is particularly charged. Beginning in the New Testament, Christians interpreted some of the psalms spiritually or allegorically as messianic prophecies fulfilled in Jesus Christ. Rabbinic Judaism developed
a comparable tradition, relating some of the psalms to prophecies to
be fulfilled by the Messiah. In terms of method, Herbert's project had
affinities with the works of Hugh and Andrew of Saint Victor, yet neither of the Victorines ever commented on the psalms. Herbert applied
aspects of the Victorine method to a 'non-Victorine' text—further evidence of his independence and originality.[7] Herbert was both a master
of traditional exegesis as encapsulated in Lombard's commentaries and
at the forefront of the new movements arising from the Abbey of Saint
Victor. He pursued an independent approach, however, despite his allegiance to these schools of thought. Chapters Six and Seven are devoted

---

[7] Hugh regarded the psalter as second only to the Song of Songs in terms of its
allegorical depth; he counseled exegetes to approach such texts with caution and only
after lengthy study; see the discussion in Chapter 2.

to close readings of his commentaries on a series of psalms, all of which demonstrate his independence.

In her foundational studies of Herbert's commentary, Beryl Smalley sketched the affinities between his exegetical practices and those of Andrew of Saint Victor. I contend that while Herbert certainly shared many of Andrew's interests and methods, he may have had more in common with Andrew's teacher, Hugh of Saint Victor. Herbert, like Hugh, was fascinated with the historical narrative chiefly because it described the arc which swept humanity from its fallen beginnings to its redeemed end. Herbert learned from his Jewish interlocutors that there were other ways of imagining that end. He learned, in other words, that his Jewish contemporaries were not merely "stationary in useless antiquity," as Christians since Augustine had argued, but that they looked to a future restoration in the land of Israel in an age of justice and peace.

This orientation to the future, powerfully evoked in Rashi's commentary on the psalms, roused Herbert to reflect anew on aspects of Christian eschatology. The future which seemed so secure, which in fact was already realized according to some triumphalist-minded Christians, demanded rethinking. If the Messiah's coming should usher in a world of peace, what empirical evidence could Christians adduce to prove that this event had happened?[8] This study suggests that Herbert helped to reframe the old topic of Christian-Jewish disputation, 'Is Jesus the Messiah?', in new terms, namely: 'Is Jesus the Messiah whom the Jews expect?' Because of his close study of Rashi's commentary, Herbert was unusually well-informed about the content of Jewish messianic thinking. He was more likely than most Christians to recognize the discrepancies between the Messiah revered by Christianity and the Messiah awaited by the Jews of his time, to be troubled by those discrepancies, and to try to resolve them.

Evidence from the commentary suggests that Herbert formulated a new understanding of Christian messianic expectations that subsumed, but did not eradicate, those of Judaism. This novel formulation resulted from his acceptance of Rashi's critique of Christianity embedded in

---

[8] Gavin Langmuir has studied the effects of what he has termed "rational-empirical doubt" on medieval Christians. See "Religious Doubt," *History, Religion, and Anti-Semitism* (Berkeley: University of California Press, 1990), 232–251 for an overview of his theory of classification and "Doubt in Christendom," *Toward a Definition of Anti-Semitism* (Berkeley: University of California Press, 1990), 100–133 for its application in a medieval context.

the latter's psalms commentary, coupled with his awareness of Rashi's message of comfort to the Jews of Northern Europe. Herbert became a reader of two traditions, best understood in Paul Ricoeur's terms of Tradition as a body of narrative that escapes the dogmatic endeavor to impose a predetermined meaning.[9] The pattern of Christian super-sessionism, which read the Psalter allegorically as predictive of Christ, was interrupted for Herbert by his appropriation of, and reflection on, Rashi's commentary.

As a consequence of his dialogue with Rashi's psalms commentary (which may have taken place through the mediation of a Jewish inter-locutor), Herbert read the psalms as both messianic *and* Christological. He allowed the two traditions to stand in tension with one another. Far from adhering to the Christian practice of using allegory to domesticate the psalter's message, Herbert opens his own tradition to what Gerald Bruns has termed satire: "the discourse of the Other against the Same: counterallegory. Satire explodes the conceptual schemes or mechanical operations of the spirit by which we try to objectify and control things, including all that comes down to us from the past."[10]

For a medieval exegete to be termed a satirist, even in Bruns's particular sense of the term, may seem eccentric. Yet Herbert's work can readily be regarded as a "discourse of the Other," in this case, the Jewish commentary tradition embodied by Rashi, against the 'Same': the Christian allegorical and 'spiritual' psalter commentaries. As Beryl Smalley pointed out long ago, Herbert treated Rashi's text much as he would treat any Christian *auctoritas*. Rashi is cited by name but more often anonymously; his *dicta* are regarded as both authoritative and open to question and revision. Herbert marshals excerpts from Rashi's commentary in whatever ordering suits his (Herbert's) exegetical goals, thus creating a whole new text in the process of commenting on the psalms and upon the two traditions of commentary.[11]

The process of selective addition and subtraction of authoritative texts in the service of constructing a central exegetical or polemical point is recognized as hallmark of medieval authorial activity. What at

---

[9] See generally Paul Ricoeur, *Essays in Biblical Hermeneutics*, ed. Lewis A. Mudge (Philadelphia: Fortress, 1980) and most recently, "Toward a Narrative Theology: its Necessity, its Resources, its Difficulties," trans. David Pellauer, *Figuring the Sacred: Religion, Narrative, and Imagination* (Minneapolis: Fortress, 1995), 236–248.

[10] Gerald L. Bruns, "What is Tradition?" *Hermeneutics Ancient and Modern* (New Haven: Yale University Press, 1992), 204.

[11] Although Rashi is Herbert's most frequently used source, Herbert also incorpo-

first glance may look like chaotic *pastiche* in fact has order, purpose, and even purposeless chaos—such as the inclusion of inferences that direct the reader to look away from the text to entertain new lines of speculation.[12] Herbert's academic training in the Paris schools would have prepared him for this mode of interacting with authorities and with his readers. While other Christians would have directed their intertextual 'play' into accustomed allegorical streambeds, he carved a new, satirical (in Bruns's sense) channel. He was, after all, no respecter of persons.

Another task that this study undertakes, then, is to consider how Herbert was alike and yet different from his contemporaries. Herbert's decision to produce a commentary that showcases his knowledge of the Hebrew Bible and Jewish traditions raises questions about Herbert the author, such as: How did a man who pursued an admittedly hybrid career as a wealthy magnate's 'house' theologian develop a profound interest in an apparently esoteric area of research? Was Herbert's career unusual or typical? It is a truism of the history of twelfth-century education and intellectual life that men prepared for high office by studying law or theology in cathedral schools and the nascent universities, but how well or poorly does Herbert fit this model? Did his interests in Hebrew language and literature somehow qualify him for his position, or were they extraneous and merely personal? The study tries to situate Herbert in all the *milieux*—intellectual, religious and social—of twelfth-century life which informed his scholarship and contributed to his unusual path.[13] The very difficulty inherent in fixing Herbert in any category will help to refresh our thinking about the role of the intellectual in the twelfth century, the interactions that were possible between Christians and Jews, and the horizons of speculation, disputation, and dialogue that those interactions opened up. As a figure on the boundary between Christianity and Judaism, Herbert's career invites us to consider anew the dynamics of attraction and repulsion—of ambivalence—that mark Christianity's encounters with

---

rated material derived from Peter Lombard and other Christian exegetes as he deemed appropriate.

[12] For a provocative and fruitful analysis of medieval compositional practices, see Mary Carruthers, "Memory and Authority," *The Book of Memory: A Study of Memory in Medieval Culture* (Cambridge: Cambridge University Press, repr. 1993), 189–220.

[13] Fifty years ago, Beryl Smalley urged that Herbert of Bosham be studied "'in the round' as a twelfth-century man of letters." Smalley, "A Commentary on the *Hebraica* by Herbert of Bosham," *RTAM* 18:65.

its parent religion. It also invites us to reexamine the narratives that modern historians have constructed in order to explicate that painful and, in Christianity's case, often shameful record.

Finally, a rationale should be advanced for studying such a singular work. Can we gauge Herbert's importance from his posterity? No. Herbert's project was unique, although recent investigations indicate his commentary's connections to other mid-twelfth century Christian investigations of Hebrew language and literature.[14] Still, no devoted community copied and circulated his psalms commentary. Whether in defense of Becket or in a wholly new approach to Christian psalms exegesis, his career as a 'public intellectual' was marked by courage, determination, and painful failure. He earned few rewards for his troubles. His efforts on Becket's behalf failed. His psalms commentary, a work of striking erudition, daring, and subtlety, was ignored for centuries. Herbert's importance derives from the counter-witness he provides. Even without successors who emulated his work, Herbert's example enlarges and complicates our understanding of how medieval people might have thought. His career and works transgressed the categories by which we customarily describe medieval intellectual life. Most importantly, he engaged with the lived reality of people deemed extraneous at best, threatening at worst, by the world around them.

Paul Ricoeur has argued that to let the biblical text speak, we have to free it from doctrinal determinism and be shaken by its arresting, discontinuous aspects—those "peripeties" may be the voice out of the whirlwind.[15] This is the kind of encounter that Herbert had with the Psalms, mediated by his Jewish interlocutors. Perhaps it will serve as a model for future encounters.

---

[14] See now Eva S. DeVisscher, "The Jewish-Christian Dialogue in Twelfth-Century Western Europe: Herbert of Bosham's *Commentary on the Psalms*." (Ph.D. thesis, University of Leeds, 2003).

[15] Ricoeur argues that a "Christian pattern" that "claims to be the universally chronological schema of the 'history of salvation'" has abolished "the peripeties, dangers, failures, and horrors of history for the sake of a consoling overview provided by the providential schema of this grandiose narrative ..." He continues, "The question, then, is whether the so-called biblical narrative is not a culturally motivated reduction of the rich interplay of temporal qualities that are displayed by the different literary genres encompassed in the canonical Scriptures. If this diagnosis is true, one of the tasks of a narrative theology would be to liberate the biblical narratives from the constraints of the 'Christian pattern' and ultimately the multiplex network of biblical narratives from the univocally chronological schema of the history of salvation." "Toward a Narrative Theology," 238.

CHAPTER ONE

THE CAREER OF A
TWELFTH-CENTURY INTELLECTUAL

Herbert of Bosham's career might be visualized as a set of concentric circles, each describing an intellectual, political, and cultural milieu, seemingly unconnected but for the trajectory of Herbert's activities. This chapter examines intersections among Herbert of Bosham and the twelfth-century intellectual, religious, and political *milieux* in which he circulated. It also attempts to bring concord out of the discordant elements of Herbert's life and career. Some of the questions posed in the Introduction regarding the seemingly unrelated aspects of his activities will be addressed here. How did medieval men translate their academic experience into public careers, and how did men who pursued public careers also maintain their academic interests?[1] Where among all Herbert's activities did his interests in Hebrew language and literature fit?

Questions about Herbert's scholarly qualifications for his public career and his seemingly unusual aptitude in Hebrew may, in fact, be related. There was a preponderance of Englishmen among twelfth-century scholars who had, or were credited as having, knowledge of Hebrew.[2] Did such claims originate as a way of publicizing their excep-

---

[1] Beryl Smalley summarized the situation thus: "The growth of bureaucracy in the twelfth century offered dazzling prospects to the graduate. Popes and prelates, abbots, princes, kings and queens employed masters as secretaries, advisers and diplomats. The wave flowing into government from the schools began about the third decade of the [twelfth] century and spread unevenly ... but inexorably." Smalley, *The Becket Conflict and the Schools* (Totowa, NJ: Rowman and Littlefield, 1973), 11 [hereafter, *BC*]. See also R.W. Southern, "The Schools of Paris and the Schools of Chartres," *Renaissance and Renewal in the Twelfth Century*, ed. Robert L. Benton, Giles Constable, and Carol D. Lanham (Toronto: Medieval Academy Reprints for Teaching, 1991), 134–135.

[2] 'Anglo-Normans' would be more precise than 'English.' J.W. Baldwin has noted the disproportionately high percentages of English scholars among the Paris masters of the late twelfth century; "Masters at Paris from 1179 to 1215: A Social Perspective," *Renaissance and Renewal in the Twelfth Century*, ed. Robert L. Benton, Giles Constable, and Carol D. Lanham (Toronto: Medieval Academy Reprints for Teaching, 1991), 148–150; 153–157. Perhaps the number of Anglo-Norman hebraists is a feature of a general trend. These hebraists will be discussed at greater length in subsequent chapters.

tional learning? Was knowledge of Hebrew the mark of first-rate, thoroughly *au courant* scholarship and thus distinguished these men who
might otherwise be considered provincial?[3] If so, would men from the
Anglo-Norman lands have had either a peculiar need to learn Hebrew,
or any special facility for doing so?[4] In short, was 'hebraism' somehow
linked to a twelfth-century form of careerism? A close consideration
of Herbert's career will help to argue this case in the affirmative. This
chapter traces the probable course of his early education, his contacts
with eminent scholars and centers of study, and his career as a 'public
intellectual,' first in the service of England's Henry II and later as an
advisor to Henry's friend-turned-enemy, Thomas Becket.

Although English-born, Herbert of Bosham spent much of his adult
life in France and seems to have preferred it to his native land. We
know that he was educated in Paris. His modern discoverer, Beryl
Smalley, calculated that he was a student of Peter Lombard around
1150.[5] Where he studied before this is unknown. Twelfth-century
schooling in England was largely informal. His father may have super-
vised his early education, if indeed Herbert was the son of a priest,
an accusation hurled at him by Henry II.[6] Besides priests who conducted classes in their parishes, some of the great monasteries maintained schools that admitted external pupils. Opportunities for instruction were scarce otherwise, despite the efforts of Lanfranc, the first
Norman archbishop of Canterbury, to institute a network of cathedral
schools after 1079. Herbert's native Sussex region seems not to have
had a cathedral school until the thirteenth century.[7] In the absence of

---

[3] In his essay, "The Place of England in the Twelfth Century Renaissance," Richard
Southern contended that English scholars labored under various disadvantages compared to their French contemporaries; *Medieval Humanism and Other Studies* (New York:
Harper, repr. 1970). Rodney Thomson has argued persuasively that Southern's findings
should be revised in light of new understandings of the cultural continuities between
those parts of England and France which were successfully integrated under Angevin
rule; "England and the Twelfth-Century Renaissance," *England and the Twelfth-Century
Renaissance* (Aldershot, U.K.: Variorum, 1998), 3–21.

[4] The unique opportunities which arose in the Anglo-Norman realm will be discussed further in Chapter 4.

[5] This is the date proposed by Smalley, based on a personal communication from
Ignatius Brady; see *BC*, 62.

[6] This incident is discussed below.

[7] Nicholas Orme notes the existence of a cathedral school at Chichester in the
thirteenth century. That city was about five miles from Bosham in Sussex. Winchester,
twenty-five miles distant, boasted a school dating from the twelfth century. *Education and
Society in Medieval and Renaissance England* (London: Hambledon, 1989), 1–21.

opportunities available at home or in a local institution, a promising young man such as Herbert may have been taken into a noble household and tutored with its sons.

Despite pockets of excellence in some towns, twelfth-century England lacked schools which could confer training in the higher reaches of the liberal arts, theology, law, or medicine. Like many enterprising scholars in the period, Herbert eventually made his way to Paris. In addition to its international appeal, scholarly life in Paris exercised a particularly powerful attraction for Englishmen.[8] Since the Conquest, the English—especially members of the upper classes—functioned within the cultural ambit of Northern France. This influence was apparent even in rudimentary levels of education. Pre-Conquest Anglo-Saxon England had been literate in *English*; only the advent of Norman rule initiated a widespread use of Latin for official documents. Latin was most commonly taught by schoolmasters trained in France who used French as their language of instruction. A young man of talent and ambition necessarily learned French along the way to becoming a *litteratus*.[9] Once proficiency in French and Latin had been attained, he was ready to start an academic career in one of the great French schools.[10]

Evidence from biographical comments and the rules and charters of cathedral schools suggests that this higher training began when a boy was fourteen or fifteen.[11] Herbert's colleague in the Becket household, John of Salisbury, arrived in Paris at that age and spent the next twelve years sampling the magisterial talent on offer—ranging from Peter Abelard to Bernard of Chartres to William of Conches.

---

[8] See Stephen Ferruolo, *The Origins of the University* (Stanford: Stanford University Press, 1985), 11–44 for a discussion of the material and political conditions that contributed to the Paris schools' preeminence.

[9] Orme, *Education and Society* ..., 10. Julia Barrow has suggested that the prevalence of a cash economy in England and Northern France also fueled the ease with which scholars traversed the two countries in search of training and preferment; "Education and the Recruitment of Cathedral Canons in England and Germany 1100–1225," *Viator* 20 (1989), 117–137.

[10] Or rather, to begin a career with a master or series of masters in Paris, since the schools in the mid-twelfth century were still largely the product of an individual teacher's magnetism. John of Salisbury's career, related in his *Metalogicon*, is evidence of this, as was that of Peter Abelard, recounted in his *Historia calamitatum*; see also the discussions in G. Paré, A. Brunet, and P. Tremblay, *La Renaissance du XIIe Siècle: Les Écoles et L'Enseignement* (Paris: Vrin, 1933), 35–38; 56–75 and Philippe Delhaye, "L'organisation scolaire au XIIe siècle," *Traditio* 5 (1947): 211–268.

[11] Philippe Delhaye, "L'organisation scolaire au XIIe Siècle," 240.

Becket himself took an abbreviated tour of the Paris schools while in his early twenties.[12] By contrast, Herbert stayed long enough to merit the title *magister*.[13] The title's definition remained relatively fluid throughout the century: it might designate a schoolmaster (of low or high degree); a scholar who had completed some years of higher training, including training in theology or law; or a scholar who had been approved by a cathedral's chancellor and had been awarded a *licentia docendi*—a license to teach fee-paying students.[14] In Herbert's case, he had certainly received advanced training and very likely held the *licentia docendi*.[15]

Herbert's *itinerarium studii* does not survive, if it ever existed. In the prologue to his edition of Peter Lombard's commentaries on Psalms and the Pauline Epistles, Herbert reports that the Lombard was "chief among his teachers."[16] If, as Beryl Smalley concluded, Herbert was a student of Peter's in 1150, then he probably attended the cathedral school at Notre Dame de Paris, the latter's academic home from 1145 to 1159. Herbert also seems to have had contact with the scholars of the Abbey of Saint Victor.[17] At the start of his own Paris career, Peter Lombard himself had been warmly recommended to Gilduin, the first abbot of Saint Victor, by Bernard of Clairvaux. The Lombard may

---

[12] On John of Salisbury's education, see his *Metalogicon*, trans. Daniel McGarry (Berkeley: University of California Press, 1962), 1.24, 67–71 and 2.10, 95–101. For Becket, see William of FitzStephen, *Vita Sanctae Thomae, Materials for the History of Thomas Becket, Archbishop of Canterbury*, Vol. 3, ed. James Craigie Robertson (London: Longman et al., 1877), 14 [hereafter, *Mats.*].

[13] The distinctive role of the title *magister* for Englishmen seeking promotion outside an academic milieu, as opposed to their German or French contemporaries, is discussed by Julia Barrow in "Education and the Recruitment of Cathedral Canons in England and Germany 1100–1225," *Viator* 20 (1989): 117–137.

[14] On the title *magister* and the conditions surrounding its award, see Delhaye, "L'organisation scolaire ..."; Barrow, "Education and the Recruitment of Cathedral Canons ..."; Paré, Brunet, Tremblay, *Les Écoles et L'Enseignement*, 59, 66–69.

[15] After Becket's death, he secured the support of Pope Alexander III in his efforts to start his own school in France. In that period, Herbert would have needed a *licentia docendi* if he wished to teach in Paris. Gaines Post, "Alexander III, the *Licentia Docendi*, and the Rise of the Universities," *Anniversary Essays in Medieval History*, ed. C.H. Taylor (Freeport, NY: Books for Libraries, repr. 1967), 255–278.

[16] "... meus in hac doctrina institutor precipuus," Prologue to the *Magna Glosatura* on Psalms; H.H. Glunz, *A History of the Vulgate in England* (Cambridge: Cambridge University Press, 1933), 343:58–59.

[17] On the characteristics of instruction at Saint Victor, see Jean Châtillon, "La vie des communautés de chanoines réguliers de la fin du XIe siècle au début du XIIIe," *Le Mouvement Canonial au Moyen Age: Réforme de l'église, spiritualité, et culture*, ed. Patrice Sicard, Bibliotheca Victorina 3 (Paris: Brepols, 1992), 73–97.

actually have resided at Saint Victor for some years and studied with Hugh (d. 1142), its most eminent scholar, with whose works he displayed considerable familiarity.[18] Herbert's contact with the abbey might have originated through his connection with Peter Lombard, or vice versa.[19]

In an article published in 1951, Beryl Smalley adduced textual evidence for Herbert's connections with the Victorine exegetes. She published the dedicatory letter addressed to Peter of Arras which accompanies Herbert's psalms commentary. Smalley noted verbal parallels between Herbert's letter to Peter and Andrew of Saint Victor's preface to his commentary on Isaiah, suggesting that Herbert may have been a student of the Victorines—Andrew's aptest pupil, in fact.[20] Other parallels between Herbert's interests and activities and Andrew's will be considered in later chapters, as will Herbert's considerable intellectual debts to Hugh of Saint Victor.[21]

It is especially likely that Herbert knew the exegete and mystical theologian Richard of Saint Victor. Richard was very active on Becket's behalf during the archbishop's exile in France in the 1160s. In fact, Herbert's contact with Richard might have preceded the exile.[22] In 1158 the then-Chancellor Becket made an elaborate state visit to Paris and entertained the English scholars in residence there; Andrew and

---

[18] Marcia L. Colish, *Peter Lombard*, 2 vols. (Leiden: E.J. Brill, 1994), 1:16–18. Ferruolo suggests that the Lombard came to Paris with the explicit intention of studying with Hugh of Saint Victor; *The Origins of the University*, 28.

[19] Herbert does not mention any of his other teachers by name; his praise of Lombard is lavish. This suggests that his contact with Saint Victor originated with Lombard rather than the reverse.

[20] Smalley, "A Commentary on the *Hebraica* by Herbert of Bosham," *Recherches de Théologie Ancienne et Médiévale* 18 (1951): 42 ff, [hereafter *RTAM*]. Frans van Liere argues that we should regard Andrew's commentaries as "school texts," containing as they do features likely derived from a classroom setting; F.A. van Liere, "Andrew of Saint Victor's Commentary on Samuel and Kings: Edited with a Study of Sources and Methods" (Ph.D. diss., Groningen, 1995), lxiii–lxix.

[21] If Herbert was born around 1120, as Smalley suggests, he may have met or studied with Hugh before the latter's death. Since it seems likely that Herbert remained in Northern France for much of his adult life, he may also have known Andrew of Saint Victor personally. Andrew shuttled between France and England, serving as abbot of Saint Victor's daughter house at Wigmore, Herefordshire from 1147 to 1154 and then again from 1161 (or 1163) until his death in 1175. Andrew returned to Paris in the interval between 1154 and the early 1160s. Herbert could have studied with him in the 1140s or met with him occasionally in the late 1150s.

[22] There is even an echo of Richard's accusation that Andrew was a judaizer in Herbert's commentary on the Hebraica. At Psalm 67[68], he condemns *judaizantes nostri*. This is further evidence that Andrew was not the sole, nor necessarily the most important, Victorine influence on Herbert (*pace* Smalley's position).

Richard were English or Scots.[23] Richard was head of the school at
Saint Victor, Andrew a notable scholar, and their abbey was patronized
by the French royal family—the very people whom Becket went to Paris
to impress. Becket's entourage may have included Herbert, eager to
renew old acquaintance with his mentors.

One other fragment of knowledge about Herbert's early life, previously alluded to, can be gleaned from an acrimonious exchange
recorded between Herbert and King Henry II, after Thomas Becket's
and Herbert's exile from England.[24] In 1166, some of Becket's circle in
exile approached the king in an effort to retrieve their property seized
by the Crown and to explore the possibility that they might eventually be restored to royal favor. Herbert, John of Salisbury, and Philip
of Calne obtained an audience with the king at Angers. But instead
of furthering his own cause, Herbert hot-headedly defended his master
and in the process managed to insult not only Henry but also the king's
occasional ally, Frederick Barbarossa. "The king cried out in his fury
that this 'son of a priest' was disturbing the peace of his realm. Herbert
denied being the son of a priest. His father had taken orders only after
his birth."[25]

Insult or not, to be the son of a priest was not unusual in England
in the twelfth century. A married clergy, able to pass its benefices on
to the next generation, had been an aspect of the Anglo-Saxon church.
The Norman clerics installed after the Conquest in 1066 curtailed this
practice, however, as part of a general movement of reform modeled
on Gregorian precedents.[26] It seems possible that by the mid-twelfth
century, a segment of England's educated male population found itself
at loose ends. It included men whose upbringing and family connections had led them to expect employment as parish priests, with the

---

[23] William FitzStephen described the embassy in his *Vita Sancti Thomae*: "Qualiter
eum dominus rex Francorum et nobiles illi Franci honoraverunt; qualiter ipse vicissim
eos; et praeterea qua comitate susceperit scholares Parisienses et magistros scholarum,
et cives scholarium Angligenarum creditores, dicere non sufficio." *Mats.* 3, 32.

[24] A detailed discussion of Herbert's role in the Becket controversy follows, below.

[25] Smalley, *Becket Conflict*, 63. The exchange was recorded in William FitzStephen's
Vita; the relevant passage includes the following: "Rex ait: 'Proh pudor! magna siquidem indignatio. Quid hic filius sacerdotis regnum meum perturbat, et pacem meam
inquietat?' Herbertus: 'Ego minime; sed neque filius sum sacerdotis, quia non fui geni-
tus in sacerdotio, licet postea sacerdos fuerit pater meus; neque filius regis est, nisi quem
pater rex genuerit.'" *Mats.* 3, 101.

[26] C.N.L. Brooke, "Gregorian Reform in Action: Clerical Marriage in England,
1050–1200," *Cambridge Historical Review* 12 (1956): 1–21.

likelihood of augmenting their incomes by serving in the chapter of their local cathedrals. Perhaps Herbert was among those men to whom this avenue was now closed. Aelred, the eminent Cistercian abbot of Rievaulx, and Herbert's contemporary, certainly was.[27] Some displaced sons of priests carved out careers in the new, reformed religious orders; in Aelred's case, the Cistercians. Another, scarcer option for men like Herbert was a career in the Parisian schools.[28] Fortunately for Herbert and other Anglo-Normans, the rapidly expanding bureaucracy of Angevin England opened up new prospects. Our earliest reference to Herbert occurs in this setting. In 1157, he was sent by Henry II on a delicate mission to Frederick Barbarossa. The Emperor sought the return of an important relic (the arm of Saint James—Santiago) which Empress Matilda, widow of Emperor Henry V and daughter of King Henry I, had brought with her to England from Germany in 1126. Henry had already given the relic to a religious foundation. His chancery composed a lengthy letter, padded with diplomatic obscurantism. *Magister* Herbert accompanied it, vested with the responsibility of conveying the king's refusal orally.[29] Given his title, Herbert had presumably completed the full course in liberal arts and followed it by studying theology. Serving Thomas Becket would call on all of Herbert's training, especially his ability to express himself in fulsome Latin oratory, written or spoken, in defense of a recalcitrant master.

It is not known when or how Herbert of Bosham came into royal service. Frank Barlow, one Thomas Becket's modern biographers, assumed that Herbert was either already at the chancery or recruited by Becket soon after the latter's promotion to chancellor in 1155.[30] Smalley noted simply that Herbert was in the king's employ in an unknown

---

[27] Marsha L. Dutton, "The Conversion and Vocation of Aelred of Rievaulx: A Historical Hypothesis," *England in the Twelfth Century: Proceedings of the 1988 Harlaxton Symposium*, ed. Daniel Williams (Woodbridge, UK: Boydell Press, 1990), 31–49.

[28] This career choice would be valid, of course, even if he were not a suddenly unbeneficed son of a priest. Despite a life spent in and around monks and monasteries, Herbert never evinces any interest in taking up that life and openly eschews the opportunity when it is proposed to him by Peter of Arras (as he records in the dedicatory letter accompanying his commentary); see Smalley, *RTAM* 18:31–32.

[29] Smalley, *BC*, 60.

[30] Frank Barlow, *Thomas Becket* (London: Guild, 1986), 42. See also Anne Duggan's more recent *Thomas Becket* (London: Arnold; distributed by Oxford University Press, New York, 2004), in which she takes issue with a number of Barlow's hypotheses, particularly those connected with Thomas's motives for his eventual resistance to Henry II.

capacity when he was sent to Germany in 1157.[31] If Herbert was a func-
tionary in Becket's chancery, or in any form of continuing service to the
king, the chances are good that he spent most of the period between
1155 and 1162 in France—as did Becket and Henry.[32] The time spent in
France would have enabled Herbert to maintain his connections both
to the schools of Notre Dame and Saint Victor and, possibly, to Jewish interlocutors with whom he studied Hebrew as a youth.[33] As noted
above, Andrew of Saint Victor, one of Herbert's probable mentors, was
in Paris in that period. His old teacher, Peter Lombard, was active
at Notre Dame until his elevation to Bishop of Paris in 1159. Peter
Comestor, another of the Lombard's pupils whose scholarly interests
were akin to Herbert's, was also in residence at Notre Dame around
this time.[34]

The details of Herbert's training and early career can only be guess-
ed at, however. Aside from his diplomatic assignment in 1157, Herbert's
activities remained obscure until 1162. His record of the life of Thomas
Becket begins in that year, when he accompanied Becket to Canterbury
for the latter's consecration as archbishop. From that time, he was
a member of Becket's episcopal household (*familia*); his role as the
archbishop's "master of the sacred page" is attested by at least one
source independent of his own biography of the martyr.[35] Smalley

---

[31] Smalley, *BC*, 59–60.

[32] Barlow, 48–49; for a breathless and possibly eyewitness account of the embassy,
see William FitzStephen's *Vita, Mats.* 3, 29–33.

[33] In his letter to Peter of Arras, Herbert claims to have studied Hebrew since
his youth. Concerning the background for his work on the psalter commentary he
wrote "… que a primis adolescentie annis, aliis pandentibus latinorum, grecorum seu
hebreorum magistris accepi, explanationi necessaria interserere curavi, nisi forte michi
sedenti interdum quid revelaverit Dominus." Smalley, *RTAM* 18:32.

[34] The chronology of Comestor's activities and whereabouts is contested; Ignatius
C. Brady argued convincingly that Comestor was probably teaching in Paris in the
1160s, not in Troyes as others have suggested; "Peter Manducator and the Oral Teachings of Peter Lombard," *Antonianum* 41 (1966): 454–490. Other *magistri* in Paris whom
Herbert might have known in this period included the Englishmen Robert of Melun, a
student of Hugh of Saint Victor who taught both John of Salisbury and Thomas Becket
(Becket would consecrate Robert bishop of Hereford in 1163), Robert Pullen, and Adam
of Balsham whose school on the Petit Pont lasted from the 1130s until 1175. On these
teachers and their activities, see David Knowles, *Episcopal Colleagues of Archbishop Thomas
Becket* (Cambridge: Cambridge University Press, 1951), 28–30; Ferruolo, *The Origins of
the University*, 16.

[35] William FitzStephen referred to Herbert as "divina pagina magister" in his *Vita*;
Mats. 3, 58: "Interim silentio ait archiepiscopo suus in divina pagina magister Herbertus
…"

details Herbert's role as Becket's most choleric and impolitic of advisers, a role also well-attested by his contemporaries. Before considering the nature of the services Herbert rendered to the archbishop, let us briefly consider the man whom he served.

In 1155, Thomas Becket was promoted to the office of royal chancellor from the household of Theobald, Archbishop of Canterbury. Henry II had recently been crowned England's king, succeeding to the throne after a civil war between his mother, the Empress Matilda (grandaughter of William the Conqueror and daughter of Henry I) and King Stephen (grandson of the Conqueror, who seized power from Matilda in 1135). Archbishop Theobald had actively promoted Henry of Anjou's claims to England's crown. In turn, by sponsoring Becket's service to the new king, he ensured the influence of an 'English' presence—and one closely allied with church interests—in the Angevin court.[36]

Chancellor Becket was a close associate of Henry II. As the king's chief ecclesiastical servant, his duties included the maintenance and supervision of the chapel royal and its scriptorium. The chancellor directed a secretariat and had charge of the royal archives. He traveled with the king on his frequent trips to his French holdings. As a member first of Archbishop Theobald's household and then as chancellor, Becket's subsequent transition to the next step of his career, the see of Canterbury, should have been smooth. But as is well-documented even in the hagiographical accounts of his life, this was far from the case. Chancellor Becket's career had been distinguished by its worldliness and luxury, regarded by some as unseemly even for a high court official. In 1158, during renewed hostilities with France's Louis VII, he made the unusual choice to command troops in the English siege of Toulouse personally. The chancellor distinguished himself in this campaign, which was funded by his levy of new taxes on English dioceses. This did little to endear him to the ecclesiastical establishment. When the king nominated Becket as Archbishop of Canterbury, he was widely regarded as an unsuitable candidate. Anxious, however, to preserve good relations with the king, the bishops charged with electing Becket opted to ratify the king's choice.

The king's initial plan had been for Becket to retain his office as chancellor while serving as archbishop, effecting a consolidation of sec-

---

[36] Avrom Saltman, *Theobald: Archbishop of Canterbury* (London: Athlone Press, 1956), 168.

ular and ecclesiastical power.[37] But sometime in 1162, after his election as archbishop and return to England, Thomas renounced the chancellorship. Perhaps Becket no longer needed the revenues or the prestige that accrued to the chancellor.[38] But while the new archbishop enjoyed material prosperity in abundance, he had other deficiencies to remedy.[39] The son of a London merchant, Becket had spent only a year studying in Paris. His distinctions were not chiefly literary or intellectual; they were personal: "such ease, such manners!" to paraphrase a later English writer.[40] To equip him for the spiritual as well as the temporal tasks of his new position, Archbishop Becket gathered around him a circle of scholars and diplomats. Herbert's later *Life of Becket* offers us a catalog of his *eruditi*.[41]

Becket himself had once been a member of an even more illustrious household: that of Archbishop Theobald. That circle had included John of Salisbury; John of Canterbury, eventually bishop of Poitiers; Bartholomew who became bishop of Exeter; and Ralf of Diss, archdeacon of London and a chronicler of the period.[42] The magnitude of the

---

[37] Such a consolidation was achieved later in Henry's reign: Hubert Walter, royal justiciar and chancellor, became Archbishop of Canterbury in 1193. See Robin Mundill, *England's Jewish Solution: Experiment and Expulsion, 1262–1290* (Cambridge: Cambridge University Press, 1998); C.R. Cheney, *Hubert Walter* (London: Nelson, 1967).

[38] Barlow, 82–83.

[39] Anne J. Duggan disputes Barlow's assessment of Becket's education. She notes (as Barlow did) that Archbishop Theobald had sent Becket to study canon law in Bologna and Auxerre, despite Becket's short tenure in the Paris schools. She points out that Becket's supposed deficiencies in Latin were reported by one—and only one—of his detractors. Further, she argues that John of Salisbury's *Policraticus* and *Entheticus*, works of subtlety and erudition by one of the age's premier rhetoricians, were written for Becket's delectation. *The Correspondence of Thomas Becket, Archbishop of Canterbury 1162–1170*, Vol. 1 (Oxford: Clarendon Press, 2000), xxv–xxvi. On Becket's study of canon law, see William FitzStephen's *Vita*, *Mats.* 3, 17.

[40] Herbert's *Vita Sancti Thomae* was divided by its author into books and subsections. References are to his divisions of the text and the page numbers on which they appear in the *Materials for the History of Thomas Becket, Archbishop of Canterbury*, Vol. 3, but the text also appears in the Patrologia Latina 190. In this instance see Book 2.1 in *Mats.* 3, 164–166. See Jane Bennet's description of Mr. Bingley, "I never saw such happy manners! so much ease, with such perfect good breeding!" in Jane Austen, *Pride and Prejudice*, The Oxford Illustrated Jane Austen, Vol. 2 (Oxford: Oxford University Press, 1988), 14. See also the discussion of Becket's personal qualities as those of the model courtier in Stephen Jaeger, *The Envy of Angels: Cathedral Schools and Social Ideals in Medieval Europe* (Philadelphia: University of Pennsylvania Press, 2000).

[41] Book 7 of Herbert's *Vita* is entitled *De catologo eruditorum Thomae* and discusses the archbishop's closest associates in order of their later fame—and their loyalty to Becket.

[42] Avrom Saltman discusses the caliber of Theobald's personnel in "The Archiepis-

difficulties faced by Archbishop Theobald had demanded that he sur-
round himself with the cream of England's young scholars. The church
and the country were recovering from two decades of civil war. By
contrast, the men around Becket were not so much intellectuals as
'careerists:'

> ... [I]t is clear that [Thomas] looked for men skilled in ecclesiastical
> administration rather than for pure scholars, for usefulness rather than
> holiness. Many of his recruits were, like him, careerists, and Herbert,
> by classifying [the *eruditi*] according to their future achievements, tacitly
> accepts this standard. Herbert does not mention specifically the arch-
> bishop's chaplains and confessors or assign monks an important place in
> the daily round.[43]

Clearly, theological training such as Herbert's did not disqualify one
from becoming a careerist in either secular or ecclesiastical administration in this period. Barlow, Becket's biographer, notes: "A basic feature of medieval life was man's servitude, and the constant aim of the
careerist was to find a more important lord."[44] The most important
lords were the pope and the king. As these powers were intertwined
and their interests often in conflict, disputes that arose between them
were contested as much in theological as in political terms. Also, Herbert's theological training in Paris was the capstone of the traditional
arts curriculum. Like other academic careerists who obtained positions
with influential figures, he would have mastered grammar, rhetoric, and
dialectic:

> The basic and elementary arts of the trivium provided these men with
> the requisite tools—grammar for drafting letters and other documents,
> rhetoric for polemic and persuasion, and dialectic for argument and
> debate. The first of these was essential for the daily business of any
> government; the others could be called into service in times of disputed
> claims and rights ... Few periods have looked so bright for those with an
> education in the liberal arts.[45]

Herbert exhibited consummate—if intemperate—mastery of all these
skills throughout his tenure as Becket's closest advisor and companion. Becket's master of the sacred page was indirectly responsible for

---

copal Household," *Theobald: Archbishop of Canterbury* (London: Athlone Press, 1956), 165–
177.

[43] Barlow, 79.
[44] Barlow, 47.
[45] Ferruolo, *The Origins of the University*, 94.

Becket's transformation from political opportunist to martyr and saint, at least according to Herbert.

Becket's biographers, medieval or modern, share a common difficulty: how to explain the evolution in Becket's character which led him to reject the role envisioned for him, a 'mediator' between the claims of *regnum* (secular power, embodied by the king) and *sacerdotium* (ecclesial power, embodied by the priesthood)?[46] What spurred his reckless opposition to Henry Plantagenet, his friend, patron, and king?

Herbert's version of Becket's life depicts a man who was transformed from the moment of his consecration in Westminster Abbey. The unction of office, bestowed in the sacrament, worked a change in Becket almost immediately, according to Herbert.[47] Alluding to Pauline themes, Herbert proclaimed that the old man had become new, that Becket had put aside the trappings of wealth and high office in exchange for a hair-shirt, the better to imitate the crucified Christ. This pious explanation is difficult to reconcile with Herbert's own account of Thomas's subsequent triumphal tour of the continent, *en route* to the ecclesiastical Council of Tours in 1163. The magnificence of Thomas's

---

[46] That Becket was envisioned as such a mediator is noted by Herbert in his *Vita*, and quickly dismissed by Herbert as an obvious impossibility, in Book 3.5, "Qualiter Cancellarius Electus": "Regis autem voluntate et petitione cito post cancellarii adventum in sancto illo et religioso sanctae Cantuariensis Ecclesiae conventu et episcoporum quibusdam accitis super cancellarii promotione declarata, mox ut solet varia diversorum fertur sententia. Et praesertim in sacro illo monachorum conventu utpote quos prae caeteris contingebat negotium: asserentibus his quod hoc fieri bonum, aliis vero contra imo malum. Hi regis gratiam allegabant et per hoc tam gratioso inter regnum et sacerdotium mediatore Ecclesiae deinceps pacem futuram sicut securam ita et prosperam; aliis vero e diverso illam regis gratiam non profuturam, sed plurimum eo ipso Ecclesiae obfuturam opponentibus; eo quod officiales Augusti et praesertim quotquot aulici, pontifice non de ecclesia sed de aula assumpto, in Ecclesiae bona liberius grassarentur ..." *Mats.* 3, 182–183.

[47] *Vita*, 3.6: "Thomas ergo noster, non jam officialis aulae, non electus Ecclesiae, sed jam Ecclesiae consecratus, omnino supra omnium spem mox deposito cancellario, antistitem vivens in spiritus de coelo subito advenientis vehementia quo in illis unctionis diebus unctus mox fuit repletus, totum veterem hominem adeo concussit, excussit, et expulit ut jam vetustatis nec compareret vestigium. Unde et novus quidam homo, quem supra pro tempore veteris hominis habitu opertum magis quam oppressum a veteri diximus, discoopertus, et in unctione dati spiritus magis robur accipiens, mox totum se exerit et haud segniter strenue se accingit ad opera, ea praesertim quae novum tunc decebant pontificem." *Mats.* 3, 192–193. Anne Duggan notes that most of Becket's hagiographers expatiated on this theme. The rapidity of Becket's transformation from worldly chancellor to devout cleric is likewise contested by his modern biographers; *Thomas Becket*, 25–26.

train and the splendor of his person reduced onlookers to envious stupefaction. Herbert reports that even the Pope fawned on Thomas.[48]

That incongruity aside, the transforming grace of consecration was affirmed by Thomas's new way of life, which centered around the study of Scripture with his master of the sacred page, Herbert of Bosham. Again, the 'new man' theme is prominent in Herbert's account:

> ... he embraced the holy image-bearing Scriptures with deep attention and devotion, in order that by his new learning he should shake off the old ignorance, which long commerce with the world had brought, so that he, a new bishop, should be reformed to the new image of a bishop.[49]

Herbert rehearses a similar theme in his panegyric to Thomas, the *Liber Melorum* which followed his biography. Here, too, he extols the power of the 'divine eloquence' to remake Thomas, its student; Scripture is at once the mold to which the new image conforms and the mirror in which the new man first perceives his transformation.[50] Thomas's encounter with Scripture, Herbert argues in this passage, transformed him inwardly. Theologians became learned by studying Scripture but in Thomas, as in other *theodocti*, divine revelation communicated through Scripture worked its own changes. The result was a superior form of God-given wisdom, through which the recipient was remade in the image of truth (*figura veritatis*).[51]

As recounted by Herbert, this transformation of Becket's life and values did not happen altogether miraculously, nor entirely alone. His companion in study verified the new archbishop's understanding of

---

[48] *Vita*, 3.20, *Mats.* 3, 254–255.

[49] *Vita*, 3.11, *Mats.* 3, 204; translation by Smalley, *Becket Conflict*, 35. The notion of being transformed by the text of Scripture is indebted to Augustine but its more immediate source is probably the didactic works of Hugh of Saint Victor. See the discussion in Stephen Jaeger, *The Envy of Angels: Cathedral Schools and Social Ideals in Medieval Europe* (Philadelphia: University of Pennsylvania Press, 2000), at 259 ff.

[50] The passage is from Herbert's *Liber Melorum*, a panegyric written after the *Vita*; see Smalley, *BC*, 79. "Sacra quippe Scriptura ipsa quasi figura veritatis, quasi umbra lucis, et quasi resultantis imaginis speculum. Per parabolas enim, per figuras et aenigmata in mysticis Scripturarum eloquiis, quasi imaginibus quibusdam in speculo, veritas nobis resultat. Unde et tanquam imago in speculo, Deus in eloquio sacro, et ipsa sacra eloquia Scripturae dicuntur imaginariae, in quibus resultat nobis velut quaedam veritatis imago magis quam ipsa veritas. Propterea et nobis, qui in umbra fidei vivimus, et in imagine pertransimus, iste qui per imaginarias scripturas fit manifestationis modus, multo nobis familiarior est, utpote sicut bonis et etiam malis communis, altero illo qui per inspirationem fit bonorum duntaxat non malorum." Patrologia Latina [hereafter, PL] 190:1362C.

[51] Ibid.

Scripture's plain meaning and guided him through its darker obscurities. In Herbert's highly-charged account of these conferences, Becket emerged with the qualities that Hugh of Saint Victor had outlined as essential to the study of Scripture in his meditation on teaching and learning, the *Didascalicon*.[52] Becket was humble; he was discerning (he sought Herbert's advice and instruction, so as not to fall into error); he was ardent with love for the Scriptures; he meditated alone for hours over their meaning; he prayed while reading, read while praying; and he desired more than anything to be freed from worldly concerns in order to recoup his misspent youth by fruitful study. Describing their late-night sessions of study, talk, and prayer, Herbert compared Becket to the Ethiopian eunuch of Acts 8. Having turned his path into the way of sacred study (*via sacrae eruditionis*), he wanted to pursue its course with a single heart. Herbert emphasizes Becket's fervor and his rapid growth in virtue and discernment, while minimizing his own role. But Herbert's seeming self-effacement is coupled with strategically suggestive quotations. Comparing Thomas to the eunuch in Acts forces the reader to recall that the Ethiopian was converted only after the apostle Philip instructed him how to interpret Scripture. Similarly, Herbert habitually refers to himself as "the disciple who bears witness to these things, and who has seen and written these things" (*discipulus qui testimonium perhibet de his, et vidit et scripsit haec*), a self-conscious echo of the conclusion of the Gospel of John (21:24). Herbert saw himself as more than a political hack or a hired rhetorical gun. He was the Christ-like Becket's Beloved Disciple; his lord's growth in virtue flowed directly from his encounter with Scripture, helpfully mediated by a master of the sacred page.[53]

The new Becket portrayed by Herbert is on fire with idealism, seeking to detach the church from the tawdry confines of secular politics. The Thomas created in Herbert's account is a man who found more than a conscience: his whole being seems illuminated by a noble purpose. Page after page of Herbert's biography is devoted to Becket's stirring speeches which rally his household's flagging commitment. His

---

[52] See *Vita* 3.11 at *Mats.* 3, 204–206 and compare Hugh of Saint Victor, *Didascalicon de studio legendi*, ed. Charles H. Buttimer (Washington: Catholic University Press, 1939); *The* Didascalicon *of Hugh of Saint Victor*, trans. Jerome Taylor (New York: Columbia University Press, repr. 1991), 3.13–17; 5.9.

[53] Moreover, such a master would probably exemplify Hugh of Saint Victor's belief that the fruit of sacred reading is virtue, not knowledge for its own (or ambition's) sake. See *Didascalicon* 5.6.

disciple Herbert is always on hand to urge him on. Herbert's favorite advice to Becket was "*Agite viriliter!*" dispensed even on the eve of the entourage's ill-starred return to England.[54] Thomas's other advisors did not trust the king; they were persuaded Becket would die in England. "What do you say?" Thomas asked the *discipulus qui scripsit haec.*

Herbert replies with typical fervor. If Thomas does not return to England now, it will be as though he had fled twice, not just once, in ignominy. The Archbishop can either retreat once more in disgrace, or advance boldly, acting manfully. Herbert grants that an advance means certain danger from the hands of brutal, evil, and mendacious men. But such, he says, will be the sufferings of the church at the end of days. So if Thomas is to be a martyr, how happy to be among the first-fruits of the end-time! Herbert closes his peroration by urging Thomas to avoid Moses' fate. Whatever the outcome of the journey, Thomas should not die without entering the promised land.[55]

Herbert's self-portrait as Thomas's cheerleader-in-chief is confirmed by contemporary witnesses. John of Salisbury was particularly dismayed by Herbert's imprudence.[56] Becket's other biographers also routinely portray Herbert as an extremist. Herbert scuttled more than one reconciliation between archbishop and king with a whisper in Thomas's ear. In these and other circumstances, Herbert shows himself as no respecter of persons. For the sake of his master and the principles they shared, Herbert defied kings, prelates, and popes. His audacity even won the admiration of his enemies.[57] In short, Herbert was a dangerous man. An intellectual gifted with physical courage; an idealogue with a ready wit; fearless, combative, and voluble, he was probably the least suitable person to advise a proud and reckless cleric in his combat against a proud, unyielding king.

---

[54] Cf. David's commissioning of Solomon in 1 Chron. 28:20: "Viriliter age et confortare et fac ne timeas et ne paveas ..." and Psalm 26[27]:14: "expecta Dominum viriliter age et conforetur cor tuum et sustine Dominum." Hugh of Saint Victor urges the just man who studies Scripture likewise to "Act manfully!," *Didascalicon* 5.9: "Via est operatio bona, qua itur ad vitam. Qui viam hanc currit, vitam quaerit. Confortare et viriliter age."

[55] *Vita*, 5.5, *Mats.* 3, 473–476.

[56] John of Salisbury was distressed by Herbert's temper and its effect on Becket. In a letter to Becket in 1166, he counseled Thomas to bring only a few prudent and wise clerks to a projected meeting, "if you have any," John adds sarcastically. Letter 179, *Letters of John of Salisbury*, Vol. 2, ed. W.J. Millor and C.N.L. Brooke (Oxford: Clarendon Press, 1979), 191.

[57] Smalley notes that one of Henry II's barons admired Herbert's gumption; *BC*, 63.

The transformation in Becket's allegiances, however it was effected, inevitably led to conflict with the king. After his first year in office, capped by a visit to the Council of Tours in 1163, discord arose between the two friends over rights to tax levies. Becket, who had been eager to tax ecclesiastical incomes while chancellor, now refused to surrender any archiepiscopal revenues to the king. This dispute between Archbishop Thomas and King Henry was mere prelude to the larger issues that severed their alliance in 1163–1164. The chief point of contention that arose between Becket and the royal party (which eventually included most of his fellow bishops) concerned 'criminous clerks': members of the clergy who committed felonies but who escaped royal justice by demanding to be tried in ecclesiastical courts. More generally, Henry resented Becket's unwillingness to conduct his relations with the crown according to 'ancient customs.' Starting with a royal council at Westminster Abbey in October 1163, the king tried to persuade Becket and the English bishops to ratify these customs (as yet unspecified in detail). When Becket refused, Henry took his complaints to Pope Alexander III, then in exile in France. Henry sought the pope's support for the customs.

In response, Pope Alexander deployed influential ambassadors to mediate between Henry and Thomas. In 1163, he had sent Philip, Cistercian abbot of Aumône (Blois), who had been prior during Bernard's abbacy at Clairvaux, together with Robert of Melun (once England's most prominent theologian in Paris, now Bishop of Hereford) to urge moderation on both parties but especially on Becket. The combined influence and interest of Parisian theologians and Cistercians would figure significantly in Becket's—and Herbert's—life in France.

Becket remained intransigent, and Henry decided to convene another council, this time at Clarendon. There, Henry demanded "all bishops should give their assent, expressly, absolutely and unconditionally, to the customs and privileges which his ancestor, Henry I, and his barons had observed."[58] Not just Becket but his fellow bishops were distressed by this sweeping demand. In the end, however, the archbishop capitulated. The customs were written down and handed over to Becket, who pleaded for time to study them. But his physical acceptance of the document technically constituted assent to its contents; therefore, when Becket subsequently repudiated the so-called 'Consti-

---

[58] Barlow, 97–98.

tutions of Clarendon,' he lost the support of his fellow bishops who viewed him as duplicitous, naïve, or both.[59]

Relations between the king and archbishop continued to deteriorate over the course of 1164. The nadir was reached in October of that year, when Thomas was put on trial before a council of barons and bishops at Northampton. Thomas was charged with contempt for the king, a blanket indictment for various misdeeds which included alleged obstruction of justice and misappropriation of funds. The bishops refused to rally behind him and the barons were eager to convict him. The council ended in confusion but for this outcome: the king was convinced of Thomas's guilt and Thomas was in fear of his life. He decided to flee to France. John of Salisbury, the most famous of Becket's *eruditi*, had departed for France earlier in the year, presumably to pave Becket's way with King Louis VII and the pope. After the debacle at Northampton, Herbert of Bosham was dispatched to Canterbury to gather cash and valuables to fund their escape.[60]

After arriving in France, Becket took his case to Pope Alexander III, himself a refugee because of the papal schism instigated by Germany's Frederick Barbarossa. For the next six years, Becket's case would be subsumed within the larger concerns of European politics. His presence was especially problematic for the pope, who relied on the loyalty of France's Louis VII but who also needed the friendship of Henry II, Louis's feudal underling but sometime rival in continental politics. (For strategic purposes, Henry occasionally threatened to side with Frederick and his anti-Pope.) Alexander pursued a protracted policy of equivocation, sometimes placating Becket, sometimes his king, in an effort to maintain himself until Barbarossa was driven out of Italy. Alexander's divagations earned him the displeasure of Becket's supporters, notably Herbert and John of Salisbury, who urged him to act decisively against Henry II.[61]

After a brief sojourn in Paris at the Abbey of Saint Victor, Becket and his entourage were directed by the pope to retire to the Cistercian abbey at Pontigny. In the mid-twelfth century, Pontigny is estimated

---

[59] William FitzStephen, *Mats.* 3, 66–67; Herbert, *Vita* 3.29, *Mats.* 3, 288.

[60] Herbert, *Vita*, 3.38, *Mats.* 3, 312–313.

[61] They urged the pope to excommunicate the king and place all of his lands, British and continental, under interdict; see Letters 213 and 219 by John of Salisbury, *Letters of John of Salisbury*, Vol. 2, 347 ff. and 371 ff.; also, Herbert's letter to the Pope in Thomas's name, PL 190:1451 C ff.

to have housed 100 monks and 300 *conversi* or claustral brothers.[62] Its
attraction for Thomas was two-fold, location and ambience:

> In discussions with the pope and curia [Thomas] and his clerks expressed
> a preference for the Cistercian order and, in particular, for Pontigny, the
> second daughter of Cîteaux, situated in the duchy of Burgundy, some 55
> kilometres south-east of Sens. Founded in 1114 by Theobald IV, count
> of Blois, the brother of King Stephen and Henry, bishop of Winchester,
> patronized by Louis VII and with Hugh, count of Macon, as its first
> abbot, it no doubt had an aristocratic tone which Thomas found conge-
> nial. Outside both the royal French demesne and Angevin territory ... it
> was not too distant from the papal court and the courier routes.[63]

For his part, Herbert affected to loathe Pontigny, bemoaning it as
a "wooded solitude between monks and stones."[64] With 400 inhabi-
tants, it is questionable whether Herbert's life at Pontigny was solitary.
Its population grew even larger after Henry II exiled the families of
Becket and his retainers.[65] As he had in Canterbury, Herbert apparently
divided his time in exile between attending to the archbishop's spiritual
welfare and enjoining his master to maintain unwaveringly his position in favor of the church's liberty.[66] Becket renewed his youthful study
of canon law at Pontigny in the hope of furthering his defense, despite
John of Salisbury's despairing counsel that he devote himself to meditat-
ing on the Book of Psalms and the Pauline Epistles.[67] Still, John's advice
to Becket might have sparked one of Herbert's projects at Pontigny.
At Herbert's direction, the monks prepared for Becket an 'edition' of

---

[62] Robert-Henri Bautier, "Les premières relations entre le monastère de Pontigny et
la royauté anglaise," *Thomas Becket: actes du colloque international de Sédières, 19–24 août 1973*,
ed. Raymonde Foreville (Paris: CNRS & Beauchesne, 1975), 42.

[63] Barlow, 123–124.

[64] Herbert's initial description of the Archbishop's choice noted its convenient location: "Et inter caetera ordinis monasteria unum praeelegimus in Burgundia situm,
quod Pontintur: insignis vero et praeclara illius monasterii religio habebatur. Quod
et praefatae civitati Senonis, in qua dominus papa propter schisma morabatur tunc,
vicinum erat, solum per duodecim leugas distans." *Mats.* 3, 357. But after the archbishop's party arrived in Sens, Herbert rhapsodized about that city's 'civilized' attrac-
tions; *Mats.* 3, 403–404.

[65] Herbert's was the only sustained account of Becket's exile; none of Becket's other
hagiographers remained with him for its duration.

[66] At least one potential reconciliation between king and cleric was scuttled by
Herbert's intemperate interference. See Barlow, 179–181.

[67] On Becket's earlier study of canon law, see William FitzStephen's *Vita, Mats.* 3, 17.
As John put it, "Who ever rises contrite from the study of civil or even canon law?"
John of Salisbury, Letter 144, *The Letters of John of Salisbury*, Vol. 2, ed. W.J. Millor and
C.N.L. Brooke (Oxford: Clarendon Press, 1979), 31–37.

Peter Lombard's glosses on the psalms and epistles, known by the corporate name of the *Magna Glosatura*.[68] This splendidly decorated series of volumes was completed only after Becket's death. Herbert eventually donated them to the library of Christ Church, Canterbury.[69]

Becket's sojourn at Pontigny ended in 1166. His retirement 'among the stones and monks' was cut short by Henry II's threat to turn the Cistercians out of his lands, English and continental, if they continued to shelter his refractory archbishop. His warning was conveyed to the General Chapter of the Order meeting at Cîteaux in September 1166. Becket's support in the order was shaky; its leaders recognized the justice of his cause but regretted his intransigence.[70] Abbot Gilbert of Cîteaux, an Englishman, conveyed their dilemma to the archbishop, who took the hint. Thomas reluctantly withdrew to the Abbey of Sainte Colombe, a Benedictine house close to Sens.[71] Herbert of Bosham described the scene when the Canterbury contingent departed from Pontigny for Sens:

> On the day we left, the grieving and lamenting monks ran after the archbishop, coming and going, taking leave of him again and again, demanding his blessing, begging for it again, pleading with him to return over and over and crying to him: Father, why are you parting from us? To whom do you abandon us, in our desolation?[72]

---

[68] Christopher de Hamel disputes the theory of C.R. Dodwell that Herbert's editions of Peter Lombard's works were executed at Pontigny, arguing instead that they were made in Paris in the 1170s from combined exemplars of Lombard's glosses and Herbert's notes and emendations. He concedes, nevertheless, that Herbert probably did most of his research for the editions in Pontigny's well-equipped library. "The So-Called 'Pontigny' School of Illumination," *Glossed Books of the Bible and the Origins of the Paris Book Trade* (Dover, NH: D.S. Brewer, 1984), 38–54. Herbert's edition of the *Magna Glosatura* was broken into two parts at a later date. The commentaries on the epistles and the first half of the psalter are in Trinity College Cambridge MSS. B 5,6,7 and B5.4; the second half of the psalter is in Bodleian Library MS Auct. E infra 6.

[69] Smalley, *BC*, 82, on the donation to Canterbury; and C.R. Dodwell, *The Canterbury School of Illumination* (Cambridge: Cambridge University Press, 1954), 104–109.

[70] See Martha G. Newman, *The Boundaries of Charity: Cistercian Culture and Ecclesiastical Reform, 1098–1180* (Stanford: Stanford University Press, 1996), 209–218, for this reading of the Cistercians' dilemma.

[71] Alexander III, displeased with the Chapter's apparent disloyalty to Becket, to the Cistercian ideal of *caritas*, and to himself, suspended the award of papal privileges to the Order, excepting only Pontigny. See Terryl N. Kinder, "Architecture of the Cistercian Abbey of Pontigny: The Twelfth-Century Church," ("Ph.D. diss., Indiana University, 1982), 20.

[72] "Die vero recessus nostri videres fratres moestos et ejulantes, post archipraesulem currere, discurrere, festinare, salutantes et resalutantes et benedictionem iterum et

Numbered among the distraught monks of Pontigny probably was Peter, future abbot of the house, later abbot of Cîteaux, and ultimately bishop of Arras—Herbert's last patron in exile.

From Pontigny and then from Sens, Herbert launched a barrage of letters, in his own name, in Thomas's, or in the name of Thomas's allies, advocating the archbishop's cause with the Pope, papal legate William of Sens, King Louis of France, and other notables.[73] The letters are characterized by unremitting attacks on Thomas's enemies (chiefly Gilbert Foliot, bishop of London and Roger, archbishop of York) and denunciations of Henry II's ambition and cupidity. The king is usually referred to disparagingly under the cloak of Old Testament analogues such as Jeroboam or Ahab, idolaters and reprobates. By contrast, Thomas Becket earned the pseudonym Elijah, a prophet unflinching in the face of adversity.[74]

Over the course of their wanderings in exile, Herbert seems to have undergone a transformation of his own. By his account, the master of the sacred page and his student Thomas traded places during their long bout of adversity. Herbert recounts how troubles turned Thomas philosophical. This change happened, according to Herbert, soon after Becket's arrival in France. In a reversal of their roles, the first of many, the archbishop expounded a verse from Job for Herbert's benefit.[75] Subsequently, among the Cistercians at Pontigny, isolated from everything Herbert considered necessary to civilized society, Thomas's ardor for study exceeded that of all his studious companions. The books of psalms and epistles scarcely left his hands, Herbert writes.[76] Once a man of the world, the high-living chancellor who commanded the siege of Toulouse, Thomas became a *vir apostolicus*, transformed first inwardly

---

iterum postulantes, et iterum et iterum videre et alloqui cupientes recedentem, interdum conclamantes: 'Pater, cur nos deseris, aut cui desolatos nos relinquis?'" Herbert's *Vita*, 6.20, *Mats.* 3, 404.

[73] Approximately 24 letters date from the exile and were gathered by J.A. Giles in 1845 in his edition of materials relating to Becket; they were reprinted in PL 190. In all likelihood, some of the other letters gathered in PL 190 and attributed to Thomas of Canterbury himself were also written by Herbert.

[74] Not only Herbert but also John of Salisbury adopted names and characterizations derived from the Hebrew Bible to dramatize the struggle between Henry and Thomas. Avrom Saltman, "John of Salisbury and the World of the Old Testament," *The World of John of Salisbury*, ed. Michael Wilks (Oxford: Basil Blackwell, 1984), 343–363.

[75] *Vita*, 4.6, *Mats.* 3, 329.

[76] *Vita*, 4.14, *Mats.* 3, 379.

and at last outwardly by his encounter with Scripture.[77] In the mean-time, his master of the sacred page had become a man of action.

One letter from this period illustrates the intersection of Herbert's scholarly and political interests. Beryl Smalley identified its intended recipient as Henry 'the Liberal' of Blois, Count of Champagne.[78] Henry was a patron of letters; his court was the home of Chrétien de Troyes.[79] Henry had an interest in scriptural studies, too. He solicited John of Salisbury's opinion on the authorship of various biblical books, and he corresponded regularly with Peter of Celle, John of Salisbury's host in exile.[80] Henry's secretary, Nicholas of Clairvaux, prepared exegetical treatises for the count which he had cribbed from the works of Hugh of Saint Victor and Bernard of Clairvaux.[81] The count had also commis-sioned a canon of Saint Victor, Simon Chèvre d'Or, to compose poetic epitaphs of his father, Count Theobald of Blois, and the Cistercian luminaries whose abbeys Theobald had patronized.[82] Henry engaged Herbert to get to the bottom of a legend that had attained scholarly legitimacy in some circles. Herbert furnished his answer in a letter writ-ten in Sens, dating from sometime after Becket and his entourage had left Pontigny in 1166.

The letter deals with an exegetical issue that vexed some Christians in the mid- to late-twelfth century: whether the Salome mentioned in the Gospel of Mark was a man or a woman.[83] Some exegetes, Peter Lombard notably, held that this individual was a man, contrary to the traditional opinion. The legend that arose in tandem with this misattri-bution of gender maintained that Anne, the mother of the blessed vir-

---

[77] In 1165, John of Salisbury commented in a letter to Bartholomew of Exeter that he felt the archbishop was benefitting from his exile, both in terms of his education and his disposition (*ad litteraturum et mores*); Letter 150, *Letters of John of Salisbury*, vol. 2, 48–49.

[78] The addressee is absent from the version reprinted in Migne; Smalley found a fragment of the same letter in an MS and was able to correlate the two based on the *incipit*. *RTAM* 18:37.

[79] John L. Benton, "The Court of Champagne as a Literary Center," *Speculum* 36 (1961): 556 *et passim*.

[80] Avrom Saltman, "John of Salisbury and the World of the Old Testament," 343–363.

[81] John L. Benton, "The Court of Champagne as a Literary Center" 555–557.

[82] Benton, 570.

[83] See Mark 15:40 and 16:1. M.R. James suggested that the belief that "Salome" was a man arose in the eleventh century in Normandy or England. Evidently by the twelfth century it had attained enough stature and currency for Peter Lombard to consider it as possible; "The Salomites," *Journal of Theological Studies* 35 (1934): 287–297.

gin Mary, had had three husbands and children by each.[84] In his epistolary treatise written for Count Henry, Herbert regrets Peter's error, made in the margin of the latter's Gloss on the Epistle to Galatians. But notwithstanding this mistaken view of *magistri mei suavis recordationis Petri Parisiensi episcopi*, Herbert asserts that Peter was a theologian without equal in modern times. For his own part, Herbert attacks the 'Salomites.' He marshals evidence from patristic authors ranging from Jerome to Bede, and complains that he was unable to consult a text by John Chrysostom which might have helped his argument, as it was not available to him at Sens.[85]

Herbert wrote his letter to Henry of Blois and worked on his revisions to Peter Lombard's glosses on the Psalms and Epistles for his edition of the *Magna Glosatura* at a time when his former teacher's reputation was suffering. Peter had died in 1160. Soon thereafter, some of the positions he outlined (but did not espouse) in his *Sententiae* were attacked as heretical by opponents of the growing 'scholastic' movement—most prominently by Gerhoch of Reichersberg, the monastic theologian and exegete.[86] The Lombard was accused of supporting a position known as Christological nihilianism, which maintained that Jesus Christ according to his humanity was 'not a thing' (*non est aliquid*). Even if Peter Lombard had taught that Christ according to his humanity was not *aliquid*, this would not be the same as maintaining that he were nothing

---

[84] This pious fiction was intended to preserve the belief in Mary's perpetual virginity, by dealing with the gospel passage that attributed 'brothers' to Jesus. A long-standing explanation of this phrase, given by Jerome, was that these brothers were actually Jesus' cousins. A source for these cousins had to be generated, since Scripture does not indicate that Anne and Joachim (Mary's parents) had other children. By linking Anne's name to a succession of three husbands (Joachim, Cleophas and Salome), the problem was solved. Or made more complicated. A third view maintained that Salome was identical with the 'third Mary' at the Crucifixion. Herbert's letter to Henry mentions his meeting with a monk at the Benedictine abbey of Saint Denis near Paris who reported that a church in Syria commemorated Salome as one to the three Maries. Smalley identified the monk as William le Mire, whose letter on obscure Greek terms Herbert included in the prefatory material to his edition of the Lombard's Gloss on the Pauline epistles. *RTAM* 18:37–39; *BC*, 79, 81.

[85] This suggests that the letter was written after Becket's entourage had left Pontigny for Sens; the text is printed in PL 190:1418.

[86] Gerhoch initially attacked the Christological teachings of Peter Abelard and Gilbert of Poitiers and their disciples in his *Liber de novitatibus huius temporis*, addressed in 1156 to Pope Hadrian. See *Letter to Pope Hadrian on the Novelties of the Day*, ed. Nikolaus M. Häring; Studies and Texts 24 (Toronto: Pontifical Institute of Medieval Studies, 1974). Subsequently he tarred Peter Lombard with the *habitus* brush in his *De gloria et honore Filii hominis 7.3*, PL 194:1097B.

(*nihil*)—a position even farther from the Lombard's actual stance.[87] In Book Three of the *Sententiae*, Peter had discussed the prevailing attempts to explain the union of the divine and human in Jesus Christ: the *homo assumptus*, subsistence, and *habitus* theories.[88] He found them all lacking to a greater or lesser degree. But under the influence of Gilbert of Poitiers' recent efforts to revitalize the traditional categories of nature, person, and substance, the Lombard contributed his own synthesis of new ideas with the old *habitus* theory.[89]

In 1163, Pope Alexander III convened a council at Tours to examine Christological nihilianism among many other topics. Peter Lombard was not singled out by name in the discussions on that occasion. Although the Council concluded without issuing a definitive statement, John of Cornwall and Walter of Saint Victor, two opponents of nihilianism, left the council convinced that their side was in the ascendant.[90] This impression was confirmed by a letter from the Pope to William of Sens in 1170. The Pope urged William, France's papal legate, to convene a meeting at Paris in order to refute the erroneous doctrine that Christ according to his humanity *non est aliquid*, now attributed to Peter Lombard by name.[91] Hoping for an outright condemnation of the Lom-

---

[87] Walter H. Principe, *William of Auxerre's Theology of the Hypostatic Union* (Toronto: Pontifical Institute of Medieval Studies, 1963), 201 n. 50.

[88] Colish, *Peter Lombard*, 1:417–438; Principe, *William of Auxerre's Theology of the Hypostatic Union*, 1:9–12, 64–70.

[89] Peter Lombard's version of the *habitus* theory maintained that Jesus Christ had a human body and a human soul; he had, therefore, a human *nature*. But his human nature did not exhaust the possibilities of his substance, since, after all, a divine nature was joined to his human nature. The Lombard argued, therefore, that Jesus Christ was not a human person, in the sense that a person could be defined as an "individual rational substance," a definition derived from Boethius. For Peter, Christ's human nature was a reality (it was not nothing). But Jesus Christ was not a human person. Rather, the second Person of the Trinity took on human nature. The integrity of the divine Person was thus maintained, as was the unity of God with humans in Jesus Christ. Colish notes, "Peter points out that it is only the proponents of the Boethian definition of *persona*, who conflate person and substance in the human Christ, who are constrained to answer that one has denied to Christ a human substance if one denies to Him a human person. It is they who are forced to make of His humanity a *non-aliquid*." Colish, *Peter Lombard*, 1:424.

[90] See Robert Somerville, *Pope Alexander III and the Council of Tours (1163): A Study of Ecclesiastical Politics and Institutions in the Twelfth Century* (Berkeley: University of California Press, 1977) for an overview of the council's transactions. For a discussion of the *non est aliquid* question, see 60–62.

[91] PL 200:685B: "Cum in nostra olim esses praesentia constitutus, tibi viva voce injunximus ut, suffraganeis tuis Parisiis tibi ascitis, abrogationem pravae doctrinae Petri

bard's teachings at the Third Lateran Council, John and Walter each circulated skewed analyses of Peter's Christology from 1177 until 1179.[92]

Herbert of Bosham entered into the fray on behalf of his former teacher indirectly, by editing his Scripture commentaries. In his prologue to the Lombard's gloss on the psalter, Herbert notes that his teacher had lectured on his glosses but had died before putting them in finished form: moreover, Peter had intended only to elucidate the brevity and obscurity of Anselm of Laon's gloss of the psalter.[93] Herbert wants to ensure that the reputation of this "luminary eminence of the church not be shrouded by shadows of ignorance or negligence"; a possible dig at those critics who had attacked Peter Lombard by deliberately misquoting him. Herbert claims he writes at Becket's behest. The late archbishop (by now *neomartyr noster sanctus thomas*) had wished him to make the Lombard's glosses available so that they might be fairly judged.[94]

Herbert's version of Peter Lombard's commentaries on the psalter and epistles was a landmark of twelfth-century book design and technology.[95] Well aware that Peter's exegesis had consisted in adducing various authorities and resolving the contradictions between them—and

---

quondam Parisiensis episcopi, qua dicitur quod Christus, secundum quod est homo, non est aliquid, omnino intenderes, et efficacem operam adhiberes."

[92] Colish, 429; 432. In the interval between these two councils, the debate over Christological nihilianism was also kept alive by two of the Lombard's pupils, Peter of Poitiers and Adam of Saint Asaph. They espoused a Christology that, in the words of Marcia Colish, accented "more strongly than [Peter Lombard] does the *habitus* theory, seen at the time as the likeliest link with nihilianism …" *Peter Lombard*, 436.

[93] "Nam cum hec opera scriberet, nequaquam, sicut ipsomet referente didici, ipsi venit in mentem, quod in scolis publicis legerentur; solum ob id facta, ut antiquioris glosatoris, magistri videlicet anselmi laudunensis, brevitatem elucidarent obscuram." H.H. Glunz, *A History of the Vulgate in England* (Cambridge: Cambridge University Press, 1933), 343:63–67. Theresa Gross-Diaz cites an anonymous late twelfth-century commentator who reported that the psalms commentary of Gilbert of Poitiers was similarly an attempt to expand on Anselm of Laon's telegraphic lecture notes. *The Psalms Commentary of Gilbert of Poitiers: From* Lectio Divina *to the Lecture Room* (Leiden: E.J. Brill, 1996), 130.

[94] It seems that Becket's interest in this project extended beyond the grave. Herbert writes that he "armed himself" against Lombard's detractors by recalling the words of Ps. 118:134, "Deliver me from the calumnies of humans, so that I may keep your commandments." He reports that *post gloriosum transitum suum*, Saint Thomas appeared to him in a vision quoting these same words. Glunz, *History of the Vulgate*, 344:100–106.

[95] Richard and Mary Rouse, "*Statim Invenire*: Schools, Preachers, and New Attitudes to the Page" *Renaissance and Renewal in the Twelfth Century*, eds. Robert L. Benson and Giles Constable with Carol D. Lanham (Toronto: Medieval Academy Reprints for Teaching, 1991), 208–209.

conscious that this technique had landed the Lombard in trouble with readers (or hearers) who confused Peter's reports of unorthodox opinions with Peter's own—Herbert ensured that the design of his edition minimized the possibility of misattribution. He added to the Lombard's text of the psalter and accompanying glosses three columns of marginalia: one provided references to the patristic sources excerpted by Peter; the next provided cross-references to sources employed in multiple locations; the last gave clear indications of contrary opinions cited by Peter and his solutions of those contradictions.[96] Contradictions among the ancient authors are highlighted pictorially: Augustine, Cassiodorus and Jerome are represented in the manuscripts as part of its apparatus, "hold[ing] a banderole on which is written a warning such as 'Ego non probo' or 'Hic michi caveat' or 'Non ego.'"[97] The reader is thus prevented—or at least discouraged—from misattributing the Fathers' or Peter Lombard's opinions.

In addition to providing the text of the Gallican psalter on which the Lombard had commented, Herbert completed his edition by giving the Hebraica version of Jerome's translation. He notes in his prologue that the many textual variants in the psalms sung or said in the churches had laid Christians open to criticism by the Jews (an echo of Jerome's prologue to the Hebraica and his justification for Hebrew studies generally). Herbert maintains that he has collated 'verse by verse' many variants of the psalms while preparing the manuscript, and has provided the best examples of Jerome's two translations that he can muster so that the reader can compare discrepancies between them.[98]

Herbert's decision to produce these extraordinarily careful versions of the commentaries in the period when Peter Lombard's reputation was under attack highlights Herbert's independent spirit and intellectual integrity. The timing was unpropitious. He started the project while Becket was in exile and living under the protection of Pope Alexander III and William, Archbishop of Sens. As we have seen, in the year of Becket's murder (1170), Alexander wrote to William asking him to investigate Peter Lombard's Christology.[99] Herbert, undeterred, opted

---

[96] Glunz, *History of the Vulgate*, 226.

[97] As described by Mary J. Carruthers, *The Book of Memory* (Cambridge: Cambridge University Press, 1992), 216.

[98] Glunz, *History of the Vulgate*, 344:112–115.

[99] The pope reaffirmed his condemnation in 1177; see Principe, 68. The efforts to condemn Lombard's Christological teaching at the Third Lateran Council in 1179 failed, however, as his defenders mounted a successful rebuttal to his detractors' con-

to dedicate the completed version of the commentaries to William of Sens—as if to emphasize the falsity of charges against the Lombard derived from his *Sententiae* by producing, just at that moment, a scrupulous edition of his scriptural exegesis. It was a daring move for a man who was friendless in his native country and utterly dependent on his French patrons.

The drama involving his former teacher, and even the achievement represented by the edition of Peter's scriptural commentaries, would have engaged only part of Herbert's attention in the late 1160s. Between 1166 and 1170, several attempts were made to bring about a reconciliation between Henry II and Becket, sponsored mainly by Pope Alexander III. At least one of these efforts employed as intermediaries Richard of Saint Victor and his confrere, Richard of Warwick.[100] The two canons were present at an abortive round of negotiations aimed at reconciling the king and the archbishop in February 1169. This negotiating session collapsed after Herbert of Bosham urged Becket to hold fast to his principles. After what proved to be the penultimate negotiations between Henry and Becket stalled, Thomas traveled to Paris to seek the French king's intervention. While there, he stayed at the Abbey of Saint Victor and preached to the Chapter on the text "His place is made in peace," (Ps. 75:3).[101]

Both parties remained intransigent until 1170. Becket, worn down by the slow-grinding gears of papal diplomacy, and Henry, distressed by threats of excommunication and inconvenienced by unfilled episcopal sees in England (no archbishop being available to consecrate new bishops), finally patched up an uneasy truce at Fréteval in July 1170. Henry assented to Becket's return to England, but—an ominous note—refused to seal their pact with the kiss of peace.[102] The archbishop and his followers returned to England in November 1170. *En route* to Canterbury, Becket was sheltered by an old friend and

---

fused and misleading case. Lombard was thoroughly rehabilitated by the Fourth Lateran Council in 1215; Colish, 1:429–434.

[100] These two Richards may also have collaborated on a letter to Pope Alexander III, in which they warned that the curia's waffling on the Becket conflict had 'scandalized' the French church and, more to the point, the French royal family. PL 200:1443Dff.

[101] Unfortunately, Becket's homily does not survive. J. Châtillon, "Thomas Becket et les Victorins," *Le Mouvement Canonial au Moyen Age: Réforme de l'église, spiritualité, et culture,* 109–110.

[102] Barlow, 208–209, notes that Herbert produced three different accounts of this meeting, including a letter ghost-written for William of Sens and addressed to the pope.

ally, Abbot Simon of Saint Albans, a scholarly Benedictine who corresponded with Richard of Saint Victor. False reports reached Henry II, still on the continent, that Becket was raising an army against him. The archbishop was hounded to Canterbury by royal agents and kept under close watch. On December 26, Becket sent Herbert to France to solicit help from King Louis VII and William of Sens. As a result, Herbert was absent from the archbishop's murder in the cathedral on December 29, 1170.

Herbert remained in France after Thomas's assassination: he feared Henry's wrath too much to return home. He refused, moreover, to submit to the loyalty oath Henry had demanded of Becket's followers.[103] Evidence from his letters indicates that Herbert was consulted by various French clerics on theological matters, but no settled preferment nor income came Herbert's way.[104] He spent some part of the next decade in Paris, as is attested by his presence as an assessor appointed by the papal legate, Cardinal Peter of Pavia, sometime between 1174 and 1178. He was also acquainted with William le Mire, who was Abbot of Saint Denis near Paris from 1172 until 1186. It seems that he wanted to stay in Paris to set up a school of his own. Smalley writes:

> … Alexander III wrote to Richard, archbishop of Canterbury and papal legate, ordering him to allot Master Herbert of Bosham his revenues for three years, since Herbert wished to teach theology and should be helped to do so. The letter is undated, but it must have been sent to Archbishop Richard after he received the papal legateship, 28 April 1174.[105]

Once again, there is no evidence that Alexander's charitable intervention was successful.

After a conciliatory interview with Henry II on the continent, Herbert returned to England from 1184–1186, to work on his life of the *neo-martyr* who had been canonized in 1173. Herbert's was the last of many memorials written by Becket's intimates and seems to be independent of the other narratives' sources. Certainly it is unmatched in its prolixity: roughly three times the length of other *Vitae*. Herbert followed his biography with the *Liber Melorum*, a panegyric which celebrates Thomas

---

[103] Smalley, *BC*, 70.

[104] The pope himself described Herbert as "famous for learning and worth," in a letter to Henry, Bishop of Troyes; the letter is printed in *Mats.* 5, 241. The pope commended Herbert to the cathedral chapter at Troyes, suggesting that they make him provost (a sinecure recently surrendered by William of Sens) in 1165. Smalley reports that there is no evidence this recommendation was accepted; *BC*, 65.

[105] *BC*, 71.

as Christ's perfect warrior. But his life in England proved unsatisfactory. Others in Becket's circle had landed on their feet: John of Salisbury, prudent and restrained where Herbert was hot-headed and adamant, found a place in the household of Bishop Bartholomew of Exeter.[106] By contrast, Herbert was an albatross, morbidly nursing his grievances.[107] He briefly enjoyed the patronage of William Longchamp, Bishop of Ely, who became royal chancellor after the accession of King Richard I in 1189. But this association did not last. A letter from William to Herbert dating from 1190 or 1191 discusses William's political difficulties (he was deposed as chancellor) and seeks word of Herbert's current project, his commentary on the psalms.[108] This inquiry is further evidence that Herbert's patrons were well-aware of his scholarly activities. It also indicates that Herbert's reputation for Hebrew scholarship and his active public career were significantly related.

By that point, Herbert was back in France, probably at the Cistercian house at Ourscamp in the diocese of Arras.[109] Smalley judged it likely that Herbert died sometime after 1194, when a debt charged to

---

[106] As young men, Bartholomew and John had, like Becket, served in the household of Archbishop Theobald of Canterbury. Bartholomew, despite his friendship with John, had been one of Becket's opponents and was even the diocesan primate of William de Tracy, one of the archbishop's murderers. For a study of his career, see Adrian Morey, *Bartholomew of Exeter, Bishop and Canonist* (Cambridge: Cambridge University Press, 1937).

[107] Barlow comments: "The clerk [Herbert] was an unwelcome reminder of everything that the post-martyrdom world wanted to forget. Thomas had been disarmed, purified, mythified, transformed. Herbert, bitter, dissatisfied and irreconcilable, attracted all the odium and none of the solaces of the affair. He had become, in every sense, an exile." 263.

[108] PL 190:1474C–D: "Et praeterea noveritis quod desiderio intimo desideravimus ut opusculum super psalmos ab Hebraica veritate a Patre Hieronymo translatos vestra discretio complevisset, impedimento non esset quidquam ulterius, quin vestra praesentia et optatis colloquiis uteremur." See also David Balfour, "The Origins of the Longchamp Family," *Medieval Prosopography* 18 (1997): 73–92 for details of William's career.

[109] As noted earlier, he addressed the dedication of his *opusculum* on the psalms to Peter, bishop of Arras from 1184 until 1203. Peter had been a monk and then Abbot of Pontigny, and then Abbot of Cîteaux, before being elevated to the bishopric. Peter was one of many Cistercian abbots raised to episcopal dignities in this period. The dedicatee of Herbert's *Vita Sancti Thomae* was Baldwin of Forde, a Cistercian who became Archbishop of Canterbury in 1180. According to Rene Crozet, "L'épiscopat de France et l'Ordre de Cîteaux au XIIe siècle," *Cahiers de civilisation médiévale* 18 (1975): 263–268, the first Cistercian who became a bishop was Peter, abbot of La Ferte, who became bishop of Moutiers in 1124. He was followed by Godefroi de la Roche-Vanneau (1138, Langres), Samson of Igny (1140, Rheims), Peter (1141, Tarentaise). A considerable number of bishops also became Cistercians on their deathbeds; the first example is William of Champeaux, founder of the Abbey of Saint Victor and later bishop of Chalons-sur-Marne (d. 1121).

him disappeared from the Pipe Rolls.[110] Whether he died in England or France is unknown. Local legend says that an unmarked grave in the parish church at Bosham, Sussex, is his.[111] Such obscurity seems to be history's final insult to a man once at the center of so many interconnected events and spheres of influence.

The preceding summary of Herbert's career indicates the close ties that existed among the intellectuals of Becket's circles (his *eruditi*, as Herbert called them) and members of two of the most successful and highly esteemed religious orders borne of the Gregorian reform: the canons regular of the Abbey of Saint Victor and the 'new monks' of Cîteaux and its affiliated houses.[112] The summary also notes in passing Herbert's connections to the wider networks of patronage and influence that engaged Saint Victor and Pontigny, emanating from Paris and the county of Champagne, respectively. Delving deeper into this web of connections clarifies the multifaceted aspects of Herbert's career as a "twelfth-century man of letters."[113] His interests as a scholar and exegete seem incongruous with his activities as Becket's publicist *par excellence*. Closer study suggests there is less incongruity than first appears. Shared sympathies in politics, scholarship, and modes of discourse united him to a wide circle of acquaintance, including factions typically thought of as opposed to each other in this period.

In the case of the Abbey of Saint Victor's most influential members, a set of mutual interests seems to have coalesced between them and Becket's circle. The canons were an outgrowth (and advocates still) of the reform movements of the late eleventh century, promulgated by Pope Gregory VII. In particular, the Victorine view of the right relationship between *regnum* and *sacerdotium* lent support to Becket's unrepentant opposition to his king. Smalley, in *The Becket Conflict and the Schools*, discussed Hugh of Saint Victor's political philosophy which upheld the superiority of the ecclesiastical power to that of the secular arm. According to Smalley, Hugh maintained that:

---

[110] Smalley, *BC*, 74.

[111] J.C. Robertson, "Introduction," *Mats.* 3, xxiii.

[112] Constance Hoffman Berman, *The Cistercian Evolution: The Invention of a Religious Order in Twelfth-Century Europe* (Philadelphia: University of Pennsylvania Press, 2000), disputes the credence lent to chronology associated with the 'primitive documents' of Cîteaux and whether one can in fact speak of a "Cistercian Order" before the late twelfth century.

[113] Smalley's phrase from "A Commentary on the *Hebraica* by Herbert of Bosham," *RTAM* 18:65.

The Church establishes, judges, blesses, and 'forms' or instructs the temporal power. Hugh defended clerical immunities as a corollary. His teaching lived on at Saint Victor and was put in practice. The Chronicle of Wigmore Abbey illustrates it. Wigmore was a daughter house of Saint Victor on the Welsh border. The canons kept in close touch with the Paris abbey in the early years; there was an exchange of personnel and journeying to and fro. The canons of Wigmore refused to pay taxes to their secular baron on grounds of principle and would defend their property rights by appeal to the Roman Curia [sometime between 1148–1161].[114]

Jean Châtillon, in an article published almost simultaneously with Smalley's volume, speculated that Becket might have been influenced, more or less directly, by Hugh's teachings and by the English Victorines' example of resistance to secular power.[115] Herbert of Bosham was the most forceful advocate for the superiority of *sacerdotium* to *regnum* in Becket's circle. He discusses the conflict between Thomas and the king in these terms repeatedly in his *Vita* and letters, far more often than any of Becket's other biographers. Given Herbert's other intellectual debts to Saint Victor, it seems altogether likely that Herbert was the vehicle through which these views (and this sympathetic reading of events at Wigmore) were disseminated to Becket.

Hugh of Saint Victor defended his views of the primacy of the priesthood within the framework of salvation history's unfolding restoration of fallen humanity.[116] But less high-minded factors also contributed to the Victorines' support for Becket. Smalley commented that "[i]nterest fused with conviction to persuade masters of the holy page that they ought to defend the papacy and the *sacerdotium*."[117] She noted that the reformed canons had enjoyed the patronage and sponsorship of the papacy since the eleventh century. In an ironic twist, the house of Saint Victor had been lavishly endowed by the late French King, Louis VI, to manifest his support of the papally-sponsored reform movement—a program he had once resisted.[118] The Victorines' position *vis à vis*

---

[114] Smalley, *Becket Conflict*, 29–30.

[115] Jean Châtillon, "Thomas Becket et les Victorins," *Thomas Becket: actes du colloque international de Sédières, 19–24 août 1973*, ed. Raymonde Foreville (Paris: CNRS & Beauchesne, 1975), 101.

[116] See his *De Sacramentis*, Book 2, 2–8, PL 176:417–422, trans. R.J. DeFerrari, *Hugh of Saint Victor on the Sacraments of the Christian Faith* (Cambridge: Medieval Academy of America, 1951), 254–259.

[117] Smalley, *Becket Conflict*, 30.

[118] Robert-Henri Bautier, "Les origines et les premiers développements de l'abbaye

Becket would also have enhanced their relationship with the French monarchy, insofar as support for Becket injured Henry II's continental ambitions. Interest and conviction—church reform, royal patronage, and the old school tie—bound the Victorines to Becket.[119]

Another connection linking Herbert and the Becket circle to the Victorines and the Paris schools was Robert of Melun, a student of Hugh of Saint Victor. Robert probably had been a colleague of Andrew and Richard and may have been one of Becket's own teachers during Thomas's brief stay in Paris.[120] Presumably at Becket's urging, Robert was one of two poverty-stricken English *magistri* recalled from Paris by Henry II and elevated to bishoprics. Archbishop Becket consecrated Robert as Bishop of Hereford in 1163. But despite Becket's generosity, Robert of Melun joined his brother bishops in repudiating him in 1164.[121]

If Robert of Melun is an example of a Victorine connection that did not hold fast, an obscure figure, John of Saint-Satur, offers an alternative. Saint-Satur was a monastery in the diocese of Bourges which was affiliated with Saint Victor.[122] After Becket fled to France, John wrote to Richard, then prior of Saint Victor, asking for "ten *sous* of Angers" by return messenger. The cash would repay a loan from a friend that had enabled him to leave his monastery and accompany the archbishop in exile. To prove to Richard that he, John, was who he claimed to be, he asked Richard to recall their recent conversation concerning 'Master Andrew' of Wigmore, a mutual acquaintance.[123] John of Saint-Satur constitutes a living link among Becket, Herbert (the archbishop's closest associate in exile), and the Victorine 'network' throughout England, Île-de-France, and Champagne.

The resources of that network were deployed in 1167 in an attempt to reclaim the allegiance of Robert of Melun. At the suggestion of John of Salisbury, Becket solicited the intervention of the leaders of the Abbey of Saint Victor to help shape opinion in England. Its abbot, Ernis, and

---

de Saint-Victor de Paris," *L'abbaye parisienne de Saint-Victor au Moyen Age* (Paris: Brepols, 1991), 38–44.

[119] His opponents were bound by similar, in some cases identical, ties. Witness Robert of Melun.

[120] David Knowles, *The Episcopal Colleagues of Thomas Becket*, 29; Barlow, 20, 35.

[121] Barlow, 45.

[122] Jean Châtillon, "Thomas Becket et les Victorins," 89–90.

[123] Châtillon, "Thomas Becket et les Victorins," 90. See also Beryl Smalley, "Andrew of St. Victor: A Twelfth-Century Christian Hebraist?" *RTAM* 10 (1938): 358–373.

its prior, Richard, sent a letter (probably drafted by John) to Robert,
now Bishop of Hereford. They reminded their former colleague that
as a master in the Paris schools he had upheld the liberties of the
church and railed against bishops corrupted by worldly prestige. Had
Robert himself succumbed to the king's blandishments and forgotten
his own wisdom? They begged him to recall his own teachings, to
detach himself from the king, from Gilbert Foliot the Bishop of London,
and all others who sought to harm Becket.[124]

The intellectual and political influence of the Victorines extended
beyond the sphere of their daughter houses and well beyond France's
royal demesne. As noted earlier, Richard of Saint Victor corresponded
with Abbot Simon of Saint Albans, a Benedictine house with a superb
library. Simon had sought a complete set of Hugh of Saint Victor's
works from Paris.[125] Simon was also responsible for accumulating a
collection of glossed books of the Bible which resemble in physical
design those of Herbert's version of the *Magna Glosatura*.[126] He solicited
from John of Salisbury a complete set of John's political writings, also.[127]
Simon was anxious to collect the best of current theological scholarship,
in volumes that exhibited the latest advances in design and finding-
aids.[128] Becket's warmest welcome when he returned from France in
November of 1170 came from Abbot Simon, whose hospitality he enjoyed before his final journey to Canterbury.[129]

Another link connected Herbert and the Becket circle to French
intellectuals: their supporters in Champagne. During their exile, Becket
and his men relied heavily on the political intervention and material
succor of William of Sens and his brother Henry, Count of Champagne. William of the White Hands, as he was known, was the youngest
of the four sons of Theobald le Grand, fourth Count of Blois and sec-

---

[124] PL 196:1226A–C.

[125] PL 196:1228D–1229A.

[126] Rodney M. Thomson, *Manuscripts from St. Albans Abbey, 1066–1235*, vol. 1 (Oxford:
D.S. Brewer for the University of Tasmania, 1985), 53–55.

[127] Rodney M. Thomson, "What is the *Entheticus?*" *The World of John of Salisbury*, ed.
Michael Wilks (Oxford: Basil Blackwell, 1984. Ecclesiastical History Society), 287–301.
On pages 296–297, Thomson discusses a Saint Albans MS that includes *Policraticus* and
Metalogicon.

[128] On Simon's eagerness for the latest and best, see Thomson, *Manuscripts from St.
Albans Abbey*, 51, 55. For a discussion of book technology generally, see Rouse and Rouse,
"*Statim Invenire* …;" for Herbert's role specifically see Rouse and Rouse, *ibid.*, 208–209,
220 and Mary Carruthers, *The Book of Memory*, 216.

[129] Barlow, 230.

ond Count of Champagne. On his mother's side, Theobald was the grandson of William the Conqueror; his brother, Stephen of Blois, had been king of England.[130] Both Henry of Champagne and his brother, Theobald, fifth count of Blois, married daughters of Louis VII. Their sister, Adele of Champagne, was Louis's third wife and mother of Philip Augustus (Philip II). William's family claimed descent from Charlemagne and rivaled only France's royal house of Capet in prestige and power. William, like his brother Henry, was a patron of literary men. Also like Henry, his patronage derived not only from his leisure interests but also from necessity: "Education was ... part of the equipment of a man who took a position of great power seriously."[131] As archbishop first of Chartres (in 1165, when he was thirty) then of Sens (from 1168), posts which he held simultaneously until 1176 when he became archbishop of Rheims, William was a pivotal figure in European politics, secular and ecclesiastical. Not only was he Becket's host in exile, but from 1162 through 1165 the papal curia of Alexander III had resided in the diocese of Sens. William, as archbishop and as France's papal legate, was involved in most of the major political events and theological debates of his time. He required the services of skilled lawyers, diplomats, and theologians, as well as poets and rhetoricians to cater to his staff's sophisticated literary tastes.[132] He employed distinguished canonists such as Stephen of Tournai and Lombard of Piacenza; he patronized the most accomplished Latin poet of the twelfth century, Walter of Châtillon. That milestone among theological texts, Peter Comestor's *Historia scholastica*, was dedicated to him, as was Herbert's edition of Peter Lombard's Scripture commentaries.[133] After Becket's death in December 1170, Herbert of Bosham wrote the letter describing the murder which circulated under William's name—addressed to Pope Alexander III.[134] Based on John of Salisbury's famous nearly-eyewitness account, Herbert's version detailed the events surrounding the assassination and went a step further (as Herbert was wont to do): it named the murderers and implicated the bishops of London, York and Salis-

---

[130] Stephen's reign, 1135–1154, was a chaotic period of civil war brought to an end by the accession of Henry II.

[131] Benton, "The Court of Champagne as a Literary Center," 585.

[132] Benton, 591.

[133] John R. Williams, "William of the White Hands and the Men of Letters," *Anniversary Essays in Mediaeval History*, ed. C.H. Taylor (Freeport, NY: Books for Libraries Press, repr. 1969), 365–387.

[134] Printed in *Mats.* 7, 429–433.

bury in the crime. Vigorous in his defense of Becket during the archbishop's life, William denounced his murderers with equal vehemence.

The Becket conflict was only one of Archbishop William's concerns, however. When the canons of Saint Victor clashed openly with
their autocratic abbot Ernis in 1170, William was called in to mediate
between him and the irate canons, Richard of Saint Victor included.
William and the pope were forced to intervene against William's brother Henry when the latter tried to have his collegiate 'chapel,' the ca-
thedral-sized Saint Etienne in Troyes, exempted from episcopal rents.[135]
William intervened with another brother, Theobald of Blois, on behalf
of the survivors of a massacre of Jews in that city.[136] His role in the discussion of Peter Lombard's alleged heterodoxy has been noted already.
Finally, we shall see that he was also pressed into service to review theological works by Ralf Niger, an Englishman on the periphery of the
Becket circle who shared some of Herbert's interests in Hebrew language studies.[137]

The web of connections among the Victorines, the *Champenois*, and
the Becket circle can now be expanded to include the Cistercians. Their
abbey at Pontigny, Becket's refuge, had been founded by William of
Sens's father, Theobald IV of Champagne. Becket's household in England had included John of Salisbury, the quintessential twelfth-century
humanist, who had once been the fortunate bearer of a letter of introduction from Bernard of Clairvaux. With Bernard's backing, the young
scholar secured an appointment in the chancery of Theobald, Archbishop of Canterbury (Becket's predecessor and former employer). The
Victorines and the Cistercians, moreover, were allies of long standing.

The Cistercians, like the Victorines, were the products and advocates of ecclesiastical reform that favored a strong papacy, supported by
an episcopacy independent from secular meddling.[138] Throughout the

---

[135] Elizabeth Carson Pastan, "Fit for a Count: The Twelfth-Century Stained Glass
Panels from Troyes," *Speculum* 64 (1989): 366.
[136] Robert Chazan, "The Blois Incident of 1171: A Study in Jewish Intercommunal
Organization," *Proceedings of the American Academy for Jewish Research* 36 (1968): 13–31.
[137] This connection is discussed in detail below.
[138] A further link was forged between Clairvaux and Saint Victor in 1127. Stephen,
Bishop of Paris, attempted to reform the cathedral chapter of Notre Dame by intro-
ducing Victorine canons into its ranks. The existing chapter resisted, supported by the
king. The Cistercians interceded on the bishop's behalf but the conflict escalated: in
1133, the prior of Saint Victor was murdered by members of the cathedral archdeacon's
household. The bishop fled from Paris and was sheltered at Clairvaux. Together with
Bernard, he pleaded for the pope's intervention. Martha Newman, *The Boundaries of*

second half of the twelfth century, nevertheless, the Cistercians played an active role in secular affairs. Some, as in Bernard's case, achieved influence through preaching and their charismatic personalities. Many others, such as Peter of Arras or Baldwin of Forde, moved from the cloister to a bishop's throne, administering the ecclesiastical and secular affairs of their dioceses with equal zeal. Finally, connections to the outside world and the Cistercians were further cemented by men who retired to the order from more active professions in the church. William of Champeaux is merely one example of this last type: first a schoolman, then co-founder of Saint Victor, later a bishop, and finally (on his deathbed) a Cistercian.[139]

Thomas Becket and his circle had long-standing connections with the Cistercians, dating from Becket's promotion to Canterbury. Abbot Maurice of Yorkshire's Rievaulx abbey offered congratulations to the new archbishop as soon as he heard of Becket's appointment. At the same time he urged Becket to "reform the ills of the English Church, especially those caused by secular oppression."[140] But the English Cistercians subsequently proved lukewarm in their support. Maurice's successor, Aelred, appears to have been more sympathetic to the king than to Becket.[141] Even in France, where Becket was received in Cistercian houses almost from the moment he landed, the order's support for the archbishop was mixed. Within what might be called the rank and file of the Cistercians, Becket was acclaimed. Gilbert, the abbot of Clairvaux, and Cîteaux's abbot, Geoffrey of Auxerre, nevertheless joined their English counterparts in exercising detachment from Becket and the high feelings swirling around his cause. On the one hand, the Cistercians had a tradition of supporting the pope against pretenders to his throne; Bernard of Clairvaux had staunchly opposed the papal schism of 1130–1138. The current pope, Alexander III, supported Becket; it was natural for the Cistercians who honored their most famous son's mem-

---

Charity: Cistercian Culture and Ecclesiastical Reform 1098–1180 (Stanford: Stanford University Press, 1996), 146–147.

[139] Another scholar turned Cistercian was Alain of Lille (d. 1203). The traffic continued in the opposite direction, including two of the abbots of Pontigny with whom Becket spent nearly two years. Guichard became Archbishop of Lyons and Guerin was later raised to the see of Bourges.

[140] Barlow, 74–75.

[141] Adriaan H. Bredero, "Thomas Becket et la Canonisation de Saint Bernard," *Thomas Becket: actes du colloque international de Sédières, 19–24 août 1973*, ed. Raymonde Foreville (Paris: CNRS & Beauchesne, 1975), 56. See also Walter Daniel, *Life of Ailred of Riveaulx*, trans. F.M. Powicke (London: Thomas Nelson, 1950), xlix–li.

ory to align themselves similarly. On the other hand, some of Cîteaux's next generation of leaders resisted an overt show of support for Becket on the grounds that they risked alienating not only Henry II but Frederick Barbarossa as well. The 'primitive ideals' of the order clashed with mid-century *Realpolitik*.[142]

In a recent study, Martha Newman suggests that the Cistercians' equivocation in the Becket case does not constitute a rejection of their earlier ideals. On the contrary, she argues the Cistercians were confronted by a new era in ecclesiastical polity. Cistercians used to be able to accomplish change or mediation through personal intervention (especially by charismatic leaders like Bernard or Aelred). But by the mid-twelfth century, the world around them was less susceptible to their variety of moral suasion. Newman suggests that as part of the shift from 'orality to textuality,' the politics and discourse of personal influence gave way to canon law. She notes that the Cistercian response to the Becket conflict in particular indicates this shift.[143] Newman comments:

> When the Cistercians were confronted with a dispute that remained focused on juridical issues, the disjuncture between their vision of a Christian society united by consensus and good character and the emerging view of a society bound by law caught the monks in conflicts that they could neither resolve nor explain.[144]

If the machinery of impersonal administration had displaced personal affiliations and moral suasion, then Becket, like the White Monks, may have been out of his element. Stephen Jaeger, in his study *The Envy of Angels*, cites Herbert's *Vita Sancti Thomae* extensively to support his thesis that education in a moral philosophy that espoused the qualities of *benignitas* and *venustas*—virtues associated with gracious living and 'good character,' acquired by imitating men who embodied them—was under

---

[142] Raymonde Foreville notes that Victorine support for Thomas Becket and his *familia* in exile, exemplified by Richard of Saint Victor, was unstinting both morally and materially. By contrast, she notes the 'mixed' nature of the Cistercian response when faced with Henry II's threats. The rapid growth enjoyed by the Cistercians in Angevin territories made them vulnerable to the king's anger. They had more to lose by taking a strong stand with Becket than did the Victorines whose network of affiliated houses was far smaller. "Liminaire," *Thomas Becket: Actes du Colloque International de Sédières, 19–24 Août 1973*, ed. Raymonde Foreville (Paris: CNRS & Beauchesne, 1975), x.

[143] Martha Newman, *The Boundaries of Charity: Cistercian Culture and Ecclesiastical Reform 1098–1180* (Stanford: Stanford University Press, 1996). See especially her discussion on 201ff.

[144] Ibid., 209.

threat in Becket's lifetime.[145] Similarly, Beryl Smalley suggested that Becket and Herbert lacked the appropriate 'modern' skills to mount an effective counterattack against the king and his lawyers. As Smalley noted, after Becket's flight to France, the king impounded all his property and that of his supporters. Becket and his circle had nothing to rely upon but propaganda "and all the arguments that theology and rhetoric had to offer."[146] Herbert's aptitudes were those of "the literary culture of twelfth-century humanism," not the specialist skills of a canon lawyer.[147]

Allied by common values and, perhaps, discomfort induced by the changing world around them, Herbert and the Cistercians shared another concern. The renewed interest in the Hebrew text of the Old Testament in the twelfth century has been associated by Beryl Smalley and others with the rise of the Cistercian order. M.-D. Chenu commented that renaissances in general and the twelfth-century renaissance in particular are marked by a return to sources, not out of antiquarian interest, but rather out of the desire to use the originary texts of a tradition as a basis for new developments.[148] The Cistercians' interest in retrieving a pure observance of the Rule of Benedict led to a desire to achieve a pure, or at least stable, text of Scripture. This initiative seems to have originated with Cîteaux's third abbot, Stephen Harding, at the turn of

---

[145] *Benignitas* and *venustas* consisted of benevolence, urbanity, cultivation and refinement of manners. They constituted the staples of the *cultus virtutum* central to the pedagogy of the tenth and eleventh centuries. Close imitation of an individual was crucial to the *cultus*. According to Jaeger, new forms of corporate schooling emerged in the twelfth century which emphasized the acquisition of administrative skills over *imitatio* and drove the *cultus* from the schools to courtly society. Stephen Jaeger, *The Envy of Angels*, 292–329.

[146] Smalley, *Becket Conflict*, 38.

[147] Smalley, "A Commentary on the *Hebraica* by Herbert of Bosham," *RTAM* 18:65. Thomas had had some training in canon law while attached to Archbishop Theobald's household. Also, Herbert recalls that he (Herbert) "sat at the feet" of Lombard of Piacenza, one of the great canonists of the age, while Lombard instructed Becket at Pontigny (*Vita*, 7.2). Thus neither man was a complete stranger to 'modern' developments. The record of Becket's campaign against Henry II suggests that all the players deployed canon law and propaganda with equal zeal. See now Duggan's *Thomas Becket*, 14–15.

[148] "The bringing to light once more of the ancient materials is by no means a sufficient cause or the characterizing mark of such an advance of culture; it is an effect incidental to a hunger of spirit. It is within the spirit that the joyous rebirth takes place; the sources just discovered had perhaps been long accessible but had long remained unproductive for want of some spirit to breathe upon the waters." M.-D. Chenu, "Nature and Man: The Renaissance of the Twelfth Century," *Nature, Man, and Society in the Twelfth Century*, trans. Jerome Taylor and Lester K. Little (Toronto: Medieval Academy Reprints for Teaching, 1997), 4. See also "Tradition and Progress" in the same volume, 310–330.

the twelfth century. When trying to provide the new foundation with
an accurate text of Scripture, Harding discovered that existing Latin
translations varied widely from one another. He became convinced that
some versions of Scripture had been corrupted by inaccurate accretions. To confirm his suspicions, he invited Jews from Northern French
communities to consult with him at Cîteaux. Based on those consultations, he decided that anything not included in the Hebrew text must
be a corruption of the Scriptures; he expunged these accretions from
the version of the Bible he promulgated for the Order. It seemed logical
to the Cistercians not to try to restore Jerome's Vulgate text *per se*, but
simply to consult the Hebrew text of the Bible as a guide to correction.[149] Surely, they assumed, they would reach the same end as Jerome.

A later Cistercian, Nicolas Maniacoria (d. 1145?), engaged in an
extensive set of projects to correct the biblical text.[150] Nicolas was a
monk at one of Clairvaux's daughter houses in Italy, Saint Anastasius
of Tre Fontane. He produced a *Suffraganeus bibliothecae*, corrections to the
Latin text of the whole Hebrew Bible, which included a corrected copy
of the Hebraica psalter.[151] Nicolas's corrections to the Gallican psalter
make up his *Libellus de corruptione et correptione psalmorum et aliarum quarundam scripturarum*, edited by Vittorio Peri.[152] In Nicolas's preface to his
correction of the Hebraica, he acknowledges Jerome as his example.[153]
Having discovered discrepancies in the various Greek translations of
the psalms made from the Hebrew, Jerome returned to the Hebrew
sources and consulted with learned Jews. Nicolas announces that he
has chosen to emulate this method. Just as Jerome 'corrected' the

---

[149] See the discussion of both Stephen Harding and Nicolas Maniacoria in Smalley, *SBMA*, 79–81.

[150] A. Wilmart, "Nicolas Manjacoria, Cistercien à Trois-Fontaines," *Révue Bénédictine* 33 (1921): 136–143.

[151] Some of the surviving portions of the *Suffraganeus bibliothecae* have been edited and published, but not the psalter. See J. Martin, *Introduction à la critique générale de l'Ancien Testament* 1:cii–cvii (Paris: Maisonneuve, 1887) and H. Denifle, "Die Handschriften der Bibel-Correctorien des 13. Jahrhunderts," *Archiv für Literatur und Kirchengeschichte des Mittelalters* 4 (1888): 270–276; 475 seq., cited in Wilmart. A separate corrected version of the Romanum psalter has also been attributed to Nicolas. In this version, changes to the Latin text which were made after consultation with the Hebrew are marked with the Hebrew letter *aleph*, discussed by Robert Weber, "Deux Préfaces au Psautier Dues à Nicolas Maniacoria," *Révue Bénédictine* 63 (1953): 3–17. Regarding the use of *aleph*, see page 8.

[152] Vittorio Peri, "Correctores immo corruptores: Un Saggio di Critica Testuale nella Roma del XII Secolo," *Italia Medievale e Umanistica* 20 (1977): 19–125.

[153] This preface is one of the two edited and published by Robert Weber.

psalter according to the Hebrew text, now Nicolas corrects the corrector, for he has found upon consulting 'a most learned Jew' in Rome that Jerome's translation sometimes errs or has been corrupted by scribes.[154] This encounter has inspired him to learn Hebrew himself.[155] Nicolas's *Libellus* of corrections to the Gallican psalter survives in a late twelfth-century copy from Clairvaux. In its preface Nicolas addresses a recipient who had asked him to correct the recipient's psalter according to that used by the Cistercians.[156]

David N. Bell recently endeavored to explode the 'myth' of Hebrew scholarship among Cistercians, downplaying the significance of Harding and Maniacoria. He contends that Maniacoria was probably a Cistercian only at the end of his life; that neither his nor Harding's work materially affected later Cistericans—Bernard of Clairvaux used the Vulgate, not Harding's Bible; and finally, that no other Cistercian hebraist emerged until the seventeenth century.[157] While he may be correct on the first two points, the evidence, especially that offered by Peri's more recent work on Maniacoria, suggests he may be wrong about the third.[158] The further evidence of Herbert of Bosham's highly productive sojourn among the Cistericians at Ourscamp suggests that the Cisterians were at least sympathetic to advanced textual studies. The activities of Ralf Niger, an Anglo-Norman roughly contemporary with Herbert, also indicate that some of the White Monks retained an interest, and possibly expertise, in Hebrew scholarship.[159]

---

[154] "Huius denique ego discordancia reperiens exemplaria, hebraicum nichilominus dissertorem assumpsi et quicquid ille, singulorum subtillisimus indagator, verius approbat diligenter studui exarare." Weber, 10:8–11

[155] "Nam et ego illud forsitan non haberem, nisi quidam Hebraeus, mecum disputans et paene singula quae ei opponebam de psalmis aliter habere se asserens, hoc de Monte Cassino allatum esse penes quendam presbyterum indicasset. Tunc primum ad Hebraeae linquae scientiam aspiravi." V. Peri, 91, lines 2–5.

[156] "Volens psalterium tuum, sicut petieras, abba Dominice, ad examplar nostrum, id est Cisterciensis Ordinis, emendare, amplius hoc quam tuum deprehendi corruptum." Peri, 88; lines 3–5.

[157] See his "*Agrestis et infatua interpretatio*: The Background and Purpose of John of Forde's Condemnation of Jewish Exegesis," *A Gathering of Friends: The Learning and Spirituality of John of Forde*, eds. Hilary Costello and Christopher Holdsworth, Cistercian Studies Series 161 (Kalamazoo, MI: Cistercian Publications, 1996), 135.

[158] Bell seems to be unaware of Peri's work on Maniacoria. Bell argues that far from being sympathetic to the study of Hebrew, early thirteenth-century Cistercians mistrusted literal exegesis of Scripture on the part of their fellow-Christians. He cites John of Forde, who condemned it as "judaizing"; 148–149.

[159] Whether they were interested in Hebrew study for its own sake or not, the Cistercians did maintain remarkably well-equipped libraries which a hebraist like Her-

Ralf Niger was on the periphery of the Becket circle. He corresponded with John of Salisbury.[160] Niger was an Englishman who appears to have studied in Paris in the 1160s. He was sympathetic to
Becket's cause. Ralf's hostility to Henry II led him to side with Henry's
sons when they rebelled against their father. He seems to have spent the
last years of his life in exile in France. Niger wrote commentaries on the
historical books of the Hebrew Bible, some devotional texts celebrating
the Virgin Mary (which led some seventeenth-century editors mistakenly to believe he was a Cistercian), and a revision of Jerome's *Liber
Interpretationis Hebraicorum Nominum (LIHN)*. He also wrote two chronicles of contemporary history, notable chiefly for his disparagement
of Henry II. The text which concerns us here, however, is his version of Jerome's book on the interpretation of Hebrew names. It is an
improved and expanded edition of that reference guide, which Niger
tells us he prepared with the help of a convert from Judaism. He states
in the prologue that he entitled his version *Philippicus* as a tribute to
his interlocutor, Philip. With Philip's help he has corrected versions of
the *LIHN* which were in circulation at the time and provided additional etymologies to those furnished by Jerome.[161] But at the end of his
prologue, addressed to an unknown recipient, he pronounces himself
dissatisfied with the work: with so many variations, it is hard to tell if
he has captured all the true meanings of the Hebrew names. With this

---

bert found useful. The Abbey of Pontigny was one such library. The paradoxical tension in Cistercian intellectual commitments is beginning to enjoy much well-deserved
study. See e.g. Constance Brittain Bouchard, "The Cistercians and the *Glossa Ordinaria*,"
Catholic Historical Review 86 (2000): 183 ff.

[160] John's Letters 181–182, probably dating from 1166, addressed Ralf as *Magister*.
Letters of John of Salisbury, 2:198–209.

[161] Modern commentators G.B. Flahiff and Avrom Saltman have discussed the chronology of Niger's career, his allusion to Hebrew sources, and his attitude toward
the Hebrew language. But neither Flahiff nor Saltman discussed Niger's mention of
Brother Ralf of Clairvaux, although both consulted the Lincoln manuscript of the
Philippicus, the unique version of this work. I am pursuing leads provided by M. Laurent
Veyssiere who has studied the prosopography of Clairvaux in the hope of identifying
frater Radulfus. G.B. Flahiff, "Ralph Niger: An Introduction to his Life and Works,"
Mediaeval Studies [Toronto] 2 (1940): 104–136. Avrom Saltman, "Supplemental Notes on
Ralph Niger," *Bar-Ilan Studies in History*, ed. Pinhas Artzi (Ramat Gan [Israel]: Bar-Ilan
University Press, 1978), 103–113. Saltman notes (110–111) that in his commentary on
Chronicles, Niger criticizes Jewish blindness which he attributes to Hebrew morphol-
ogy, in part. Since vowels are a language's "spirit," Ralf argues that a language with-
out them is incomplete. Niger's view is an interesting counter-witness to the Christian
notion of Hebrew as the *mater linguarum*, discussed in Chapter 3.

modest disclaimer, however, he offers his work to his patron, with the further assurance that it has been 'scrutinized' by his friend, a brother Ralf of Clairvaux.[162]

In Ralf Niger we have an intriguing parallel to Herbert of Bosham: an Anglo-Norman educated in theology at Paris, a biblical exegete with pronounced political views, an enthusiast for the Cistercian way of life, and a satellite in the orbit of William of Sens, Chartres, and Rheims.[163] To a certain extent, Ralf parallels Herbert's failures, too: like Herbert, his career ended in obscurity. On one hand, it could be argued that men trained as Herbert and Ralf were, as generalists in the liberal arts and theology, were outmoded by the end of the twelfth century. They lost out to specialists in law, numeracy, and bureaucracy—the clerics who built the "persecuting society," as R.I. Moore has argued.[164] By this reckoning, Herbert and Ralf had indeed outlived their usefulness. On the other hand, this chapter has indicated the far-flung public that bought what Herbert, Ralf and other scholars had to sell. Not only did their products—Herbert's psalms commentary, Ralf's revised dictionary—intrigue their rich and powerful patrons, but as has been demonstrated here, patrons and scholars inhabited a shared culture that esteemed wide learning. Their theological interests were likewise

---

[162] The passage reads as follows: "In summa vero profiteor vix aut nunquam de nominum interpretationibus variis occasionibus veritati satisfieri posse. Veruntamen suggero ubi karissime pater et domine quatinus apud equivocum meum fratrem Rad[ulfus] de valle clara qui in claris vallibus sacram scripturam et maxime conscriptiones meas quod ad interpretationes diligentius scrutatus est quod in his non inveneris requirere cureus." Lincoln MS 15, folio 59v. Perhaps *cureus* is a variation on or abbreviation of *correctus*. The word may also be *tureus*, the adjectival form of *tus* or *thus*, which is frankincense, in which case Ralf may be referring to the practices of anointing offerings described in Leviticus, chs. 2 and 6.

[163] According to Flahiff's chronology, Niger was in Paris in the 1160s, in England from the 1170s until the early 1180s, and back in France in the late 1180s until at least 1192. In 1191 the pope, Alexander III, commissioned two bishops, Guy of Sens and William of Rheims (formerly of Sens and Chartres) to serve as censors for Niger's theological works. Flahiff noted: "The choice of the archbishops of Sens and Rheims as censors points to the conclusion that within their ecclesiastical provinces lay the scene of Niger's life and literary activity during the years since he had left the service of young king Henry. ... [T]he role played by William of the White Hands, as friend and host to Becket and his supporters in the different dioceses of central France over which he had ruled, would easily explain Ralph's preference for this region." Flahiff, 110.

[164] And thereby launch centuries of anti-Jewish propaganda, a thesis whose overbroad outlines has been challenged in recent works. See R.I. Moore, *The Formation of a Persecuting Society* (Oxford: Blackwell, 1987) and responses thereto in J.C. Laursen and Cary J. Nederman's *Beyond the Persecuting Society* (Philadelphia: University of Pennsylvania Press, 1998). See the further discussion in Chapters 4 and 5, below.

remarkably uniform: while neither the Cistercians nor the Victorines stopped only at interpreting the 'letter' of Scripture—members of both orders produced volumes of spiritual exegesis in this period—both groups valued sophisticated textual criticism. Each in its way extolled the ideal of the apostolic man, the *vir apostolicus* also celebrated in Herbert's *Life* of Becket, and the model exponent of the new evangelical awakening of the twelfth-century.[165] In all these circles, ecclesiastical and secular, the knowledge of Hebrew and some level of interest in contemporary Judaism was also valued as a mark of accomplishment. In the thirteenth century, these achievements would pass into the hands of specialists. But Herbert of Bosham's example, reinforced by that of Ralf Niger, demonstrates that Christian hebraism was a significant feature of twelfth-century intellectual and professional life.

---

[165] M.-D. Chenu, "The Evangelical Awakening," *Nature, Man, and Society in the Twelfth Century* (Toronto: Medieval Academy Reprints for Teaching, 1997), trans. Jerome Taylor and Lester K. Little, 239–269, and R.W. Southern, *The Making of the Middle Ages* (New Haven: Yale University Press, 1974), 219–257, and Giles Constable, *The Reformation of the Twelfth Century* (Cambridge: Cambridge University Press, 1996).

CHAPTER TWO

HERBERT OF BOSHAM'S
PSALTERIUM CUM COMMENTO

The manuscript identified simply as a *Psalterium cum commento*[1] and housed at the Chapter Library of the Cathedral of Saint Paul in London is a unique entity. It is, in fact, Herbert of Bosham's attempt to do something no other Christian exegete had ever done.[2] He wrote a running commentary on the literal sense of the last Psalter translated by Jerome (ca. 345–420), the Hebraica. His undertaking was unique for two reasons. First, almost from its inception, Christian commentary has focused on the spiritual or allegorical interpretation of the psalms; furthermore, the text expounded by Christian exegetes from the early fifth century onwards was almost always the so-called Gallican version—never the Hebraica.[3] Herbert was intimately acquainted with the Christian tradition of psalms commentary but deliberately chose to pursue an original approach to the genre. Even Hugh and Andrew of Saint Victor, his likely teachers who also studied the literal and historical meanings of Scripture, never attempted literal commentaries on the

---

[1] Saint Paul's MS 2, catalogued in N.R. Ker, *Medieval Manuscripts in British Libraries I: London* (Oxford: Clarendon, 1969), 241.

[2] "To restrict oneself to the literal sense, of the Psalter particularly, was a strange procedure. I know of no other such attempt in the twelfth century." Beryl Smalley, "A Commentary on the *Hebraica* by Herbert of Bosham," *RTAM* 18:35.

[3] This version, known as the Gallican for the place of its initial popularity, was used in the liturgies of northern Europe after the sixth century and became widely accepted during the reign of Charlemagne in the ninth. It was Jerome's second corrected translation of the psalter, based on the Septuagint, which he completed after he had moved to Bethlehem and had obtained access to Origen's Hexapla at Caesarea. An earlier version of the psalms, the Romanum, was believed to be Jerome's work (he had made one attempt at correcting the psalter while living in Rome). It is likely not the work of Jerome. See Donatien de Bruyne, "Le problème du psautier romain," *Revue Bénédictine* 42 (1930): 101–126. Churches in Italy used the Romanum until the fifteenth century. Also, the Anglo-Saxon church retained the liturgical use of the Romanum and abandoned it only after the Norman Conquest introduced the Gallican psalter. For an overview of the history and use of the various versions, see Victor Leroquais, *Les psautiers manuscrits latins des bibliothèques publiques de France*, 2 vols. (Macon: Protat Frères, 1940–1941), 1:xxiv–xl.

psalms.[4] Herbert's work is directly related to that of the Victorines and others who pursued the 'Hebrew truth' (*hebraica veritas*), yet it broke new ground: in text, sources, and method.[5]

The progenitor of Latin exegetes' search for the Hebrew truth was Jerome, who in turn was indebted to the Greek exegete Origen. Beryl Smalley, whose brilliant studies of the Victorines and Herbert remain foundational, articulated succinctly why Christians pursued this line of inquiry: "A desire to study the text of the Old Testament would always lead scholars to compare the Latin with the Hebrew. The study of Hebrew would always lead to contact with the Jews."[6] Christian exegetes' contact with Jews almost always provoked conflict in some form, whether external or, more rarely, internal in the form of Christian self-questioning. The motives for such contact were themselves mixed and were not confined to scholarly pursuit of historical data. Jerome asserted that he translated this version of the psalms directly from the Hebrew in order to silence Jewish critics who derided Christian versions of the text as inaccurate.[7] The Hebraica version of the psalter, while not used in the liturgy, was widely consulted by Christian scholars.

Nevertheless, when Christian interpreters commented on the Book of Psalms, the Gallican was their usual text.[8] This is not say that the text was fixed with permanence or consistency: the many Latin versions used in various regions' liturgies (the Old Latin, or *Vetus Latina*; the Romanum, and the Gallican) ensured a certain degree of tex-

---

[4] A brief set of comments on the psalms attributed to Hugh is devoted to spiritual exegesis; his text is the Gallican version. *Adnotationes elucidatoriae in quosdam psalmos david*, PL 177:589–634.

[5] This phrase was used repeatedly by Jerome in his commentaries on the Hebrew Bible and in his letters discussing his works. For an early example, see his *Commentary on Ecclesiastes*, the first biblical book he claimed to translate directly from the Hebrew and his first biblical commentary, written in 389 CE; *Corpus Christianorum Series Latina* [hereafter, CCSL] 72, 319: 190. Aryeh Grabois notes Stephen Harding's revival of the term in his "The *Hebraica Veritas* and Jewish-Christian Intellectual Relations in the Twelfth Century," *Speculum* 50: 613–634.

[6] Smalley, *The Study of the Bible in the Middle Ages* (Notre Dame: University of Notre Dame Press, 1978), xvi. [hereafter, *SBMA*].

[7] See the preface to the psalter *iuxta hebraicum* in *Biblia Sacra Vulgata*, 768–769, lines 23–35.

[8] Augustine's *Ennarationes in Psalmos* used the Old Latin text (the one which Jerome sought to correct); but evidence suggests that by 415 Augustine, too, had begun to consult Jerome's Gallican version. Marie-Josèphe Rondeau, *Les Commentaires Patristiques du Psautier (IIIe–Ve siècles)*, 2 vols. (Rome: Pontifical Institute of Oriental Studies, 1982), 1:168.

tual instability—or cross-pollination—from the time of Jerome forward. Two major endeavors to establish an authoritative version of the Gallican psalter arose in the ensuing centuries: the first during the Carolingian period, undertaken by Alcuin and Theodulf, and the second beginning in the twelfth century. The history of this second, twelfth-century, period is more fractured than the first: the impulse for correction and stabilization was felt on several fronts, both monastic and scholastic. The 'Paris Bible,' which included the Gallican version and which was produced in the early thirteenth century, was the eventual fruit of a century's wide-ranging scholarship and *ressourcement*.

That the psalms in translation were, like ancient Gaul, divided in three parts seemed to trouble no one in the medieval church, at least on the level of *meaning*. Discrepancies were irksome only in practice.[9] Commentators on the psalms rejoiced in their options. An obscurity in one translation could be remedied by consulting another; moreover, exegetes could display their erudition by producing contrasts with other versions (*aliae litterae*) and resolving apparent conflicts, or simply commenting on each in their turn. Augustine (354–430) had articulated a rationale for the multiplicity of translations in *City of God* and consciously or not his program was widely emulated. The multiplicity was providential; it provided for greater possibilities for congruity between a given body of readers and their version of the sacred text; the various translations were examples of how divine speech was accommodated to human limitations.[10] Thus, while the Hebraica text was neither prayed nor chanted, it was consulted by exegetes and sometimes by the laity.

The evidence for this last claim is provided by the presence of double and triple Latin psalters which circulated in the West from at least

---

[9] One noted commentator viewed with dismay the proliferation of uncorrected psalters used in the liturgy. Peter Abelard wrote to Heloise on the subject of contemporary hymnody and psalmody: "We still do not know for certain who was the author of the translation of the Psalter which our own French Church uses. If we want to reach a decision on the basis of the words of the variant translations, we shall still be a long way from a universally accepted interpretation and, in my opinion, this will carry no weight of authority. Customary practice has so long prevailed that although we have St. Jerome's corrected text for the rest of the Scriptures, the translation of the Psalter, which we use so much, is of doubtful authority." *The Letters of Abelard and Heloise*, trans. Betty Radice (London: Penguin, 1974), 33. The Latin text appears as the preface to Abelard's collection of hymns written for Heloise and her community at the Paraclete; it is published in PL 178: 1771–1774 and in Victor Cousin, *Petri Abaelardi opera* (Paris: Durand, 1849), Vol. I: 296–298.

[10] See Chapter 3 for an extended discussion of Augustine's hermeneutics and their twelfth-century legacy.

the Carolingian period.[11] These were often *éditions de luxe* created for
wealthy laypeople[12]—although some may have been commissioned by
laypeople for the benefit of monasteries.[13] These books placed two or
three versions of the psalms before the reader, usually the Gallican and
Hebraica but frequently the Romanum, too. To what end? Individual
study? Reassurance that all of the Holy Word was present? A useful
guide to orient people whose familiar liturgy had been transformed
recently by royal edict?[14] All of these were possible explanations. It is
difficult to know how these volumes were used outside of a scholar's
study. Suffice it to say that duplex and triplex psalters were deemed
necessary and useful enough to generate dozens of copies by the twelfth
century.[15]

However well-known the Hebraica text might have been, Herbert
chose a version of the psalter that was not encumbered by a tradition
of textual criticism or commentary. Even Jerome did not comment on
this version in any sustained fashion.[16] He had discussed the Hebraica

---

[11] The Codex Amiatinus (Florence, Bibl. Laur., MS Amiatinus 1) was written at
Jarrow before 718 and contains the Gallican and Hebraica texts. Dominique Markey
asserts that where double psalters are found, they always contain the Gallican and
Hebraica; triple psalters add the Romanum text. See "The Anglo-Norman Version,"
Eadwine Psalter: Text, Image and Monastic Culture in Twelfth-Century Canterbury, eds. Margaret
Gibson, T.A. Heslop, and Richard W. Pfaff (London: Modern Humanities Research
Association in conjunction with Pennsylvania State University Press, 1992), 139–140.

[12] Both Leroquais, *Les psautiers manuscrits latins des bibliothèques publiques de France*, vi–
vii, and Margaret T. Gibson, "The Place of the *Glossa ordinaria* in Medieval Exegesis,"
Ad Litteram: Authoritative Texts and Their Medieval Readers, eds. Mark D. Jordan and Kent
Emery, Jr. (Notre Dame, IN: University of Notre Dame Press, 1992), 7–8, comment on a
catalogue of books owned by Everard of Friuli, a ninth-century layman whose holdings
included a double psalter, together with two other psalters, one written in gold. The
double psalter is now in the Vatican library, Bibl. Apostolica Reg. lat. 11. Other ninth-
century Hebraica psalters survive in the Bibliothèque Nationale in Paris; some of these
are preserved in double psalters. See J.M. Harden, *Psalterium Iuxta Hebraeos Hieronymi*
(London: S.P.C.K., 1922), ix–xvi and H. de Sainte-Marie, *Sancti Hieronymi Psalterium Iuxta
Hebraeos: Édition critique*, Collectanea Biblica Latina XI (Rome: Libreria Vaticana, 1954),
vi–x, for lists of other manuscripts from the ninth through the twelfth centuries.

[13] Christopher De Hamel, *Glossed Books of the Bible and the Origins of the Paris Book Trade*
(Dover, NH: Biblio, 1984), 10–11.

[14] Such may have been the case with the Romanum version of the psalms preserved
in the *Eadwine Psalter* which is accompanied by an Anglo-Saxon gloss; see Patrick P.
O'Neill, "The English Version," *Eadwine Psalter*, 135–138.

[15] In his catalogue of psalter manuscripts in France's public library, Leroquais counted seven double or triple psalters; *Les psautiers manuscrits latins …*, xlvii–xlviii. See also
Harden and Sainte-Marie, note 11 above.

[16] Whether Jerome can even be said to have commented on the Gallican psalter is
uncertain. The *Commentarioli in Psalmos* is probably authentically 'hieronymian.' But the

only indirectly, usually in letters he wrote to inquirers anxious to reconcile discrepancies they had encountered in his translations.[17] While
Herbert's choice was obscure, it was explicable nevertheless in terms of
the desire to establish a firm footing for biblical interpretation, articulated definitively by Hugh of Saint Victor in the first half of the twelfth
century:

> The foundation is in the earth and it does not always have smoothly
> fitted stones. The superstructure rises above the earth, and it demands
> a smoothly proportioned construction. Even so the Divine Page, in its
> literal sense, contains many things which seem both to be opposed to
> each other and, sometimes, to impart something which smacks of the
> absurd or the impossible. … The foundation which is under the earth we
> have said stands for history, and the superstructure which is built upon it
> we have said suggests allegory.[18]

Textual study secured the foundation's foundations, so to speak. In
Hugh's well-known scheme, one studied first the letter of the text
(what the word *is*, its *littera*), then its sense (the *sensus*, what the word
means), then its deeper, contextual meaning (its *sententiae*).[19] Thus, an

---

Tractatus super Psalmos attributed to him by Morin, his editor in the *Corpus Christianorum
Series Latina*, is now assumed to have been Origen's, translated by Jerome into Latin.
The question of authorship remains unsettled; for the sake of convenience they both
will be referred to here as Jerome's. See Marie-Josèphe Rondeau, *Les Commentaires
Patristiques du Psautier*, 1: 154–161.

[17] See especially his Ep. 106, "Ad Sunniam et Fretelam." Saint Jérôme, *Lettres*, 8 vols.,
trans. and ed. Jérôme LaBourt (Paris: Société d'Édition "Les Belles Lettres," 1955), 5:
104–144.

[18] Hugh of Saint Victor, *Didascalicon* 6.4, trans. Jerome Taylor (New York: Columbia
University Press), 140–141. The Latin reads: "Fundamentum in terra est, nec semper
politos habet lapides. Fabrica super terram, et aequalem quaerit structuram. Sic divina pagina multa secundum naturalem sensum continet, quae et sibi repugnare viden-
tur, et nonnunquam absurditatis aut impossibilitatis aliquid afferre. Spiritualis autem
intelligentia nullam admittit repugnantiam, in qua diversa multa, adversa nulla esse
possunt. Quod etiam primam seriem lapidum super fundamentum collocandorum ad
protensam lineam disponi vides; quibus scilicet totum opus reliquum innititur et coap-
tatur, significatione non caret. Nam hoc quasi aliud quoddam fundamentum est, et
totius fabricae basis. Hoc fundamentum et portat superposita, et a priori fundamento
portatur. Primo fundamento insident omnia, sed non omni modo coaptantur. Huic et
insidunt et coaptantur reliqua. Primum fabricam portat, et est sub fabrica. Hoc portat
fabricam, et non est solum sub fabrica sed in fabrica. Quod sub terra est fundamentum figurare diximus historiam, fabricam quae superaedificatur allegoriam insinuare."
Didascalicon de studio legendi, ed. Charles H. Buttimer (Washington: Catholic University
Press, 1939), 118–119. Unless otherwise noted, all subsequent page numbers refer to
Taylor's translation.

[19] *Didascalicon* 6.8–11, 147–151.

exegete would be concerned with establishing the best possible basis for
study, which in the case of the Old Testament might entail a return
to the Hebrew truth. Again, Jerome was the model and guide for
this endeavor. He had argued that the truth of Scripture had been
diluted by inaccurate (or willfully inexact) translations.[20] The translator or exegete who wished to understand the Bible must return to its
undiluted, unpolluted source, *ad fontem*. In the case of the Old Testament, that fount was the Hebrew Bible. Likewise, the discernment of
truth entailed a study of the 'mother of languages,' Hebrew.[21]

In her initial study of Herbert's psalms commentary, Beryl Smalley noted verbal parallels between Herbert's letter dedicating the commentary to his benefactor Bishop Peter of Arras, and Andrew of Saint
Victor's preface to his commentaries on the Prophets. Based on this
evidence, she deduced that Herbert might have been Andrew's student at Saint Victor. The parallels are not precise; passages from Herbert's letter echo Andrew's prologue as a student might paraphrase a
well-known, much-pondered magisterial text.[22] Not surprisingly, many
of the parallel passages convey each man's sense of the uniqueness of
his work and his anticipation of criticism: "Were I writing anything
new, important or enviable," Andrew proclaims, "I should have reason in these bad days to fear ... But I do not strive to din my work
in fastidious ears, deaf to almost everything save the past: 'No one is
obliged to take my gift.'"[23] Similarly, Herbert anticipates rejection by
fastidious enemies of new things. But for him as for Andrew, the work
itself sufficed; he asks only Peter of Arras's acceptance and good will.[24]

---

[20] For his theory that the seventy translators were forced to dissemble for fear of
scandalizing Ptolemy II, see Jerome's "Preface to the Book of Hebrew Questions,"
Hebraicae Quaestiones in Libro Geneseos CCSL 72, 2:16–27.

[21] He wrote to Marcella in 384, "Haec nos de intimo Hebraeorum fonte libavimus,
non opinionum rivulos persequentes, neque errorum quibus totus mundus expletus
est varietate perterriti, sed cupientes et scire et docere quae vera sunt." Ep. 28.5. On
Hebrew as the mother of languages, see his *Commentary on Sophonias*: "ut nosse possimus
linguam Hebraicam omnium linguarum esse matricem, quod non est hujus temporis
disserere ..." PL 25:1384B.

[22] See Smalley, *RTAM* 18:43–45 for the parallels and Smalley's analysis.

[23] Smalley, *SBMA*, 123.

[24] "Quod si forte nova hec nostra super editionem novam vestrorum aures fasti-
dierint inter quam ad sola preter vetera surdescentes, sufficit michi, pater, sufficit michi;
solum sufficiat tibi seu quoquomodo acceptetur, aut ut nece tibi defectus in culpa
erit nec voluntas, ut saltem bone voluntatis meritum sit paruisse et voluisse prodesse."
RTAM 18:32.

Both Andrew and Herbert erected another line of defense against accusations of unwarranted novelty in their work by affirming Jerome as their example. Andrew claimed to follow in Jerome's footsteps, albeit unevenly, when commenting on the prophets.[25] For Herbert, Jerome was the "modern alumnus of the synagogue"[26] (to distinguish him from Paul, whom Herbert describes as the "alumnus of the synagogue"). Like Jerome, they described themselves as toilers in an unglamorous field, but unlike Jerome neither Herbert nor Andrew aspired to advance beyond the study of the literal sense to the thinner air and dizzying heights of spiritual interpretation.[27]

In his letter to Peter of Arras, Herbert characterized his project as a crude and lowly undertaking, the project of a "beast from the reeds" (a play on *calamus*, the reed with which he would have inscribed a wax tablet while drafting his words, as well as a self-disparaging characterization derived from Ps. 67[68]:31):

> May the Lord not judge me, since with my pen, though poor and slight yet given me by Him, I have taken up His words—indeed timidly and even rashly—to be explained or even corrected; may I not be rebuked like the beast of the reeds! To this end may you help me with your prayers, father, especially with the new edition of the psalter translated into the Latin language by father Jerome from the Hebrew truth, untouched by the learned until these days, to which I have put my hand now though it be beyond the strength of my understanding.[28]

Jerome himself promoted the Hebraica psalter's closeness to the Hebrew sources: what could be more basic, more foundational, than a

---

[25] Prologue to Andrew's commentary on Isaiah, printed by Smalley in *SBMA*, 379:5–10.

[26] Prologue to the Psalms Commentary, printed by Raphael Loewe in "Herbert of Bosham's Commentary on Jerome's Hebrew Psalter," *Biblica* 34 (1953): 72:72–74.

[27] In Herbert's case, Smalley links this reluctance to his worldliness. Hugh of Saint Victor, among others, had taught that the cultivation of virtue was a prerequisite to penetrating the mysteries of Scripture's spiritual sense. Herbert's awareness of his own intellectual vanity may have contributed to his reticence on that front. But she also notes that "something more than mere humility must have been needed to impel him to undertake so great a labour. His commentary is a work of minute and loving scholarship." That "something more," an indefatigable dedication to scholarship, links him yet again to Andrew. Smalley, *RTAM* 18:35–36.

[28] "Utinam non me iudicet Dominus, quia verba ipsius cum calamo meo, paupere licet et tenui, prout ab ipso Domino datum, timide quidem, utinam non temere, explananda susceperim, utinam non sicut bestia calami increpanda; ad quod tuis me, pater, orationibus iuves, maxime cum ad psalterii editionem novam a patre Ieronimo sermone latino ab hebraica veritate translatam, et usque ad hos dies a doctoribus intactam, supra sensus mei vires manum iam apposuerim." Smalley, *RTAM* 18:32.

return to the mother of languages? Thus Herbert has put his hand
to the grubby work of commenting on the psalter translated from the
Hebrew truth, to lay the foundation for a solid structure of spiritual
interpretation. It suffices for him to "cleave to the earth" (*terre hereo*),
investigating the lowest sense, that of the 'letter':

> I struggle not towards the lofty, spiritual understanding of the senses, but
> just as with the creeping animals upon the ground, the ground to which
> I cleave, describing in detail only the lowest sense of the letter of the
> psalms, upon which the solid building of understanding may be raised
> by the spiritual architect, as upon a foundation. At the present time it
> is enough for me to put the coarser things in the foundation; may I be
> adequate to this.[29]

In these passages from the letter prefixed to his commentary, Herbert
emphasizes the utilitarian coarseness of his task by comparing himself
to animals: the beast of the reeds, the grazing herd. What seems like
self-deprecation is, however, a veiled claim for mastery. Herbert is
carrying the battle directly to the door of anyone who would disparage
his activities, anyone who would suggest that he is wasting his time on
useless novelties.

Recall that Herbert devoted part of his exile in France to a painstaking collation of Peter Lombard's commentary on the psalms, its patristic sources, and the Gallican and Hebraica texts.[30] This editorial activity
did not exhaust his interest in the psalms, however; having mounted a
glittering defense of the Lombard's scholarship, he still felt compelled
to pursue his own project. The modesty *topoi* invoked above are in fact
part of a vigorous self-defense. Herbert compares himself to "a beast
among the reeds" (for whose destruction the psalmist prays). In Peter
Lombard's commentary on Psalm 67:31, Peter says the beast represents
heretics who distort the words of Scripture or who are blown about

---

[29] Ibid. "… non ad arduam spiritualem sensuum intelligentiam nitor, sed velud cum
animalibus gressibilibus super terram, terre hereo, solum littere psalmorum sensum
infimum prosequens; super quem, velud primum positum fundamentum, deinceps a
spirituali architecto intelligentie structura solida erigatur. Michi inpresentiarum sufficit
in fundamento ponere grossiora; et utinam ad hoc sufficerem."

[30] See Chapter 1. Peter Lombard's psalms commentary together with his commentary on the Pauline epistles became known as the Great Gloss (*Magna Glosatura*). It was
an epitome of Latin Christian spiritual and allegorical exegesis of the psalms inasmuch
as it treated the psalter itself as an epitome of all Christian doctrine. Lombard, like
Hilary of Poitiers, Augustine, Jerome, and Cassiodorus, regarded David as a prophet
whose psalms foretell the coming of Christ, as well as a program of conversion to
Christian life. See the *Praefatio* to the Lombard's commentary at PL 191:55ff as well as
the discussion below.

by winds of perverted teaching. He further compares them to women, light and unstable, who will be dominated by equally erring "bulls," who seek to subvert true teaching:

> *Rebuke the wild beasts of the reed, the congregation of the bulls among the cows of the people, who seek to exclude those who are tried with silver. Rebuke the wild beasts of the reed*, that is, the heretics who are called wild beasts, because they do harm by not understanding. I say *wild beasts of the reed*, or the reeds, either because with the reed or pen they pervert the Scriptures, or because they are the trivial and unsteady; or because there are among them those who are moved by every wind of doctrine (Eph. 4:14). Therefore *rebuke*, because *the congregation of the bulls*, that is, the untamed neck of the arrogant heretics, is among *the cows of the peoples*, that is, among them who are very easily led astray and inconstant, such as silly women. Thus says the Apostle: "For of such are they who make their way into houses and captivate silly women ..." 2 Tim. 3).[31]

Herbert would have known Lombard's teaching on this verse (few would have known it so well) but he opted to compare himself to the beast of the reeds throughout his letter to Peter of Arras. In similar fashion, his comparison of his work to that of grazing animals recalls another unflattering comparison, attributable to Jerome's *Tractatus in Psalmos*.

In a discussion of Psalm 95[96]: 2, Jerome compares Jews and Christians to unclean and clean animals. Following Leviticus 11:3, he notes that clean animals have cloven feet and ruminate. According to Jerome,

> The Jew is single-hoofed, for he believes in only one Testament and does not ruminate. Indeed, he reads merely the letter and does not reflect on it; he looks for no deeper meaning than the literal message of the word. The man of the Church, however, is cloven-footed and ruminates; he believes in both Testaments and often ponders deeply over both, and whatever lies buried in the letter, he brings forth in the spirit.[32]

---

[31] "*Increpa feras arundinis, congregatio taurorum in vaccis populorum, ut excludant eos qui probati sunt argento. Increpa feras arundinis*, id est haereticos qui dicuntur ferae, quia non intelligendo nocent. Feras dico arundinis, vel calami, quia Scripturas pervertunt, quae calamo fiunt: vel quia sunt leves et instabiles; vel quia sunt inter eos qui moventur omni vento doctrinae (Ephes. IV). Ideo increpa, quia congregatio taurorum, id est superborum indomitae cervicis haereticorum, est in vaccis populorum, id est inter eos qui sunt seductibiles et leves, velut mulierculae. Unde Apostolus: Ex his sunt qui penetrant domos, et captivas ducunt mulierculas (II Tim. III)." PL 191:617B

[32] Homily 23, *Homilies of St. Jerome*, vol. 1, trans. Marie Ligouri Ewald, *Fathers of The Church*, vol. 48 (Washington: Catholic University Press, 1964), 186. "Iudaeus unam ungulam habet: in unum enim tantum credit testamentum, et non ruminat. Legit enim tantummodo litteram, et nihil considerat, nihil quaerit intrinsecus. Ecclesiasticus vero

As we have seen, Herbert modestly eschewed the realms of spiritual interpretation but makes no apologies whatsoever for his lack of rumination. He has preempted whatever flings or insults might be tossed at him and twisted them skillfully in his favor. He revered Peter Lombard enough to help salvage the late bishop's reputation with a work requiring enormous dedication and commitment, but he declined to retrace the Lombard's steps.[33] Likewise, Jerome is Herbert's model and mentor, as he was for so many twelfth-century devotees of the literal sense, yet Herbert deviated from his example.[34]

As Chapter 7 will demonstrate in detail, Herbert's chief departure from the hieronymian tradition of exegesis is manifested by his decision not to use Jerome's etymologies of the Hebrew words or proper names in psalm titles. The differences between the texts of the Gallican

---

ungulas findit et ruminat, hoc est, in utroque credit testamento, et in utroque testamento saepe requirit; et quodcumque latet in littera, in spiritu profert." CCSL 78:152.

[33] Smalley notes that Peter Lombard was not likely to have inspired Herbert's interest in the Hebraica nor in literal exegesis; *RTAM* 18:41–42. Marcia Colish has suggested that Peter's psalms commentary demonstrates that he had an interest in textual variants and in the Hebrew language, but the evidence she adduces is derived from the edition of the Lombard's psalter commentary published by Migne in the *Patrologia Latina*, Volume 191. This edition includes materials interpolated into Lombard's text by its sixteenth-century editor, as Ignatius Brady noted in his discussion of the *Magna Glosatura*. Colish claims, for example, that Peter compares his interpretation of one passage to that of the *Glossa Ordinaria* (by name) and in another instance had had recourse to the LXX. Both of these are among the editorial interpolations noted by Brady, as can be demonstrated by consulting Herbert's version of the *Magna Glosatura* in manuscript. Colish, *Peter Lombard*, 1:170–188; Peter Lombard, *Sententiae in IV libris distinctae*, ed. Ignatius C. Brady (Grottaferrata: Collegii S. Bonaventurae ad Claras Aquas, 1971–1981), 1: 51.

[34] See Chapter 3. Jerome's seemingly paradoxical interest in the 'letter' of Scripture as well as his fascination with allegory is well-attested and owes much to his close study of Origen's commentaries. One connection that is less well-known, perhaps, is Jerome's association of the literal sense, and 'history,' with the foundation of Scripture study. His panegyric to his late patroness Paula recalled her thorough study of all the levels of scriptural meaning in language that foreshadowed that of Hugh: "The holy Scriptures she knew by heart, and said of the history contained in them that it was the foundation of the truth; but, though she loved even this, she still preferred to seek for the underlying spiritual meaning and made this the keystone of the spiritual building raised within her soul," Letter 108 to Eustochium, trans. W.H. Fremantle, NPNF, 2nd Series, vol. 6, 209. "Scripturas sanctas tenebat memoriter; et cum amaret historiam, et hoc veritatis diceret fundamentum; magis tamen sequebatur intelligentiam spiritualem: et hoc culmine aedificationem animae protegebat." Ep. 108:26, Saint Jérôme, *Lettres*, trans. and ed. Jérôme LaBourt (Paris: Société d'Édition "Les Belles Lettres," 1955), 5: 194–195.

and Hebraica psalters, although many, are not often differences in substance. Jerome's last translation is a refinement of his earlier efforts.
The most startling and readily discernible differences are in the *tituli psalmorum*. For Jerome, the new version of the titles provided fresh
fodder for allegorical interpretations, based on allusions he deduced
from their etymologies. In the prologue to his psalter commentary, Herbert disagrees with this approach, arguing that Jerome has substituted
interpretations for translations. Christian interpreters, Herbert alleges,
have 'fled' from the literal sense to the spiritual sense, especially when
they interpret the *tituli*.[35] One hears an echo here perhaps of Hugh of
Saint Victor's warning to fledgling exegetes: "I [do not] think that you
will be able to become perfectly sensitive to allegory unless you have
first become grounded in history. Do not look down upon these least
things."[36]

Herbert did not systematically announce his intentions *pace* Jerome
in his prologue to the psalms commentary. His program emerges in
piecemeal fashion. From his statements there we are able to deduce
that his principal interest is the recovery of information intrinsic to
the history of the psalms. He claimed that this information had been
occluded by generations of Christian interpreters. His authoritative
sources for data are *nonnulli litteratores hebreorum*. Thus he opens his
prologue with a discussion of the book's Hebrew title, *cepher tillim* (for
sefer tehillim), explaining that it means a book of hymns or praises written
in metrical Hebrew. The *litteratores* have asserted that ten different types
of hymns are included among the psalms and that they can be grouped
according to their Hebrew names which appear in the titles—or which
would appear, if they had not been 'interpreted out' of the Latin.
Herbert proceeds to adduce a long list of Hebrew explanatory terms
and notes present in the psalms' titles but effaced by Latin translations
cum interpretations.

Herbert's next topic in the prologue is the controversy over the
authorship of the psalms and whether the book is one or many. Contrary to the majority view, represented in his own time by Peter Lombard, Herbert maintains that there were multiple authors of the psalms
as is indicated by the proper names in the *tituli*. Jerome had made this
assertion; more to the point, Herbert notes that this is a point to which

---

[35] This passage is discussed at length in Chapter 6.
[36] *Didascalicon* 6.3, 136.

"omnis hebreorum scola constanter asserit."[37] Still, Herbert reports the opinions of Augustine and Cassiodorus who both had asserted that all the psalms were 'of David.' He declines to pass ultimate judgment on this dispute: *lector videat.* But he concedes that the Book of Psalms has been transmitted under David's name and authority and thus the whole might be regarded as 'davidical' irrespective of the authorship of individual psalms.[38] He then remarks on the differences in the division and numeration of the psalms between the Latin and Hebrew versions, noting that these disparities, like the others he has recorded, have been dealt with adequately already: "super ipso ab ecclesiasticis diligenter satis expositus." He modestly asserts that his method will consist of only "annotating" those small aspects of the psalms, translated from the "pure fount of Hebrew truth," that vary from explanations offered elsewhere by the ecclesiastical teachers.[39] The commentary features a complete text of the Hebraica psalter, interspersed with Herbert's 'annotations,' which are frequently copious. Where he feels that the *ecclesiastici* have done their work satisfactorily, he does not comment on a passage, remarking "ab ecclesiasticis expositus patet," or simply "Patet." In those cases when he reports more extensively on an orthodox interpretation, Peter Lombard's comprehensive commentary on the psalms seems to have served as his source for ecclesiastical opinions.

The Lombard himself had fleshed out the commentary of Anselm of Laon (d. 1117), which seems to have been in the form of a highly condensed interlinear and marginal gloss.[40] Like Gilbert of Poitiers (d. 1154) in the immediately preceding generation of scholars, Peter Lombard wanted to impose a shape and consistency on Anselm's annotations, which themselves were probably only lecture notes. Perhaps Anselm lectured on selected psalms as it suited him, rather than trying to com-

---

[37] Loewe, "Herbert of Bosham's Commentary on Jerome's Hebrew Psalter," *Biblica* 34 (1953): 72.

[38] Loewe, "Herbert of Bosham's Commentary ...," *Biblica* 34 (1953): 75.

[39] "Unde et hunc pertransimus nisi quod solum quedam psalmi puncta annotabimus, que aliter quam sunt in edicione alia, ab ecclesiasticis doctoribus explanata; a puro hebraice veritatis fonte translata sunt." Loewe, "Herbert of Bosham's Commentary ...," *Biblica* 34 (1953): 77.

[40] Herbert reports that Peter Lombard tried to explicate the brief and obscure glosses of his master Anselm. See Chapter 1 and the prologue to the *Magna Glosatura* reprinted in H.H. Glunz, *A History of the Vulgate in England* (Cambridge: Cambridge University Press, 1933), 342 ff.

municate a sense of the whole book.[41] Imposing intellectual order on the psalter was a difficult task; Christian exegetes acknowledged that the book as they knew it could not possibly be arranged in its original form. Its internal chaos was explained by the Babylonian exile. The sacred texts of Israel had been destroyed during the conquest of Jerusalem; Ezra reconstructed them from memory. The scattered leaves of the psalter had been arranged in an artificial order by the community's 'wise men.' This would explain why the psalm which recounts the death of Absalom (Psalm 3) occurs before Psalm 50[51] which records David's repentance for his adultery with Bathsheba.[42]

The history of Christian psalms exegesis is in many ways a history that records the rationalization of problems posed by the psalms texts, beginning with the fundamental questions of authorship, order, historical time and place, but all devolving ultimately on the question of how the psalms should be read as prophecies of that son of David, Jesus Christ. Christian attempts at abstracting meaning—historical or allegorical—from the psalms relied on theories which imposed order, however artificial, on the book. The creation of a rational order or grouping for the various kinds of psalms disclosed their meaning more fully, and vice versa. Once an author had distilled a synthesis of meaning from the psalms, he could then propose how they might be grouped. Not surprisingly, this grouping often took a Trinitarian turn. Hilary of Poitiers, Augustine, and Cassiodorus all posited that the psalms should be considered in groups of three, dedicated to penitence, judgment and mercy, and praise.[43] David was understood to speak in the

---

[41] Anselm of Laon's commentary on the psalms has sometimes been conflated with the *Glossa Ordinaria*. The two texts were probably closely related but by no means identical. See Smalley, "Gilbert Universalis, Bishop of London (1128–1134), and the Problem of the *Glossa Ordinaria*," *RTAM* 8 (1936): 24–60 and Theresa Gross-Diaz, *The Psalms Commentary of Gilbert of Poitiers: From* Lectio Divina *to the Lecture Room* (Leiden: Brill, 1996), 122–131.

[42] Hilary of Poitiers, in a commentary which probably owed much to Origen, attributed the psalter's re-construction to Ezra; *Instructio Psalmorum*, 8, *Tractatus super Psalmos*, CSEL 22. Jerome also promulgated this theory in his preface to the Hebraica; Peter Lombard repeats this explanation in the *Praefatio* to his psalms commentary, PL 191: 59D.

[43] This is the scheme proposed by Augustine and echoed by Cassiodorus and Lombard. See Augustine, *Enn. in Ps.* 150.2, *Ennarationes in Psalmos*, CCSL 40. Hilary asserted that the psalms conformed to the progress of salvation and an individual's moral reform. Three groups of fifty spoke in succession of liberation from sin, reformation of life, and glorification in conformity with Christ; *Instructio Psalmorum*, 9.

voices of three main 'characters' in the psalter, typically Christ in his humanity, in his divinity, and in union with his Church.[44]

In the twelfth century, the impulse for rationalizing the psalms received its most elaborate expression in the commentary by Gilbert of Poitiers, which included a carefully organized system of cross-references designed to guide the reader through the psalms on the basis of their thematic relationships (which owed much to Cassiodorus). The earliest versions of Gilbert's commentary did not include the full text of the psalter, but its author apparently soon realized that readers would lose the thread of his densely interconnected arguments. As a guard against confusion, Gilbert adapted a form of page design used for presenting secular texts and glosses, wherein the full text of the psalter was accompanied in a parallel column with the corresponding passages from his running commentary (a format referred to as *cum textu*).[45] The physical mode of organization in Peter Lombard's commentary was not so elaborate, but like Gilbert he tried to show how the psalter works programmatically, as it were. The Lombard's prologue to his commentary lays out his theological and didactic goals, which stress individual moral reform. Then each psalm is introduced with an *accessus*, a device borrowed from the grammatical instruction current in the liberal arts courses and designed to orient readers to an author's material, intention, and method of treating his material (*modus tractandi*).[46] In this fashion, the reader is guided through individual psalms and reminded periodically of Lombard's overall vision. The earliest version of this commentary (which Lombard worked on in the 1130s but did not allow to be copied until close to his death in 1160), features two columns of text. It is a continuous commentary: the psalms are set out in full, but verse by verse with comments interspersed. This simple format is the one which Herbert adopted for his *Psalterium cum commento*.

Herbert's psalter commentary has not been edited. It exists in a single manuscript copy, probably not the autograph, in the library of Saint

---

[44] Cassiodorus, "Praefatio," Ch. 13, *Expositio Psalmorum*, CCSL 97:15–17; *Explanations of the Psalms*, vols. 1–3, trans. P. Walsh (New York: Paulist, 1990), 1:34–35.

[45] Theresa Gross-Diaz, *The Psalms Commentary of Gilbert of Poitiers*, 25–27; 43–45.

[46] PL 191:57Dff. See also the discussion of *accessus* in Gross-Diaz, 66–96; also R.W. Hunt, "The Introductions to the '*Artes*' in the Twelfth Century," *Studia Mediaevalia in honorem Raymondi Josephi Martini* (Bruges: De Tempel, 1948), and A.J. Minnis and A.B. Scott, *Medieval Literary Theory and Criticism c. 1100–c. 1375* (Oxford: Oxford University Press, 1991), 12–36.

Paul's Cathedral, London. Until now, the only scholars who have published the results of a study of the manuscript are Smalley and Raphael
Loewe.[47] In 1999, the late Leonard E. Boyle, O.P. examined a photo-
copy of the manuscript and suggested that it was most likely English
in origin and probably dated from the early thirteenth century.[48] This
opinion diverges from the assessments of both Smalley and N.R. Ker
that the manuscript might be the work of a twelfth-century French
copyist. The manuscript was examined by Richard Gameson recently,
who judged that it was produced in France sometime in the period
from 1220 until 1240, but most likely no later than 1220 and not much
before that time. The date of production suggested by Gameson makes
it more likely that the manuscript may have been commissioned by
the man who donated the work to the library of Saint Paul's in 1245,
identified by a later inscription as "Henrici de Cornhell." As Smalley noted, Henry of Cornhill was chancellor and later dean of Saint
Paul's: "He has the title of master, but we do not know where he studied."[49] In Gameson's opinion, the surviving version of the work was
produced professionally, and relatively economically, by a scribe who
was most likely provided with an exemplar. Such circumstances of production suggest that the manuscript was copied in or around Paris.
The manuscript shows sign of heavy use: some of its pages are worn
or blackened, indicating that it may have been unbound for reading
and study. Despite these indications of close study, however, the work
is free from later annotations, suggesting that its owner was not necessarily engaged in a study of Herbert's text for itself, but possibly used
it as a reference for some other work of commentary or translation.[50]
As a highly specialized, even *outré*, work that ignores familiar Christian
traditions of psalms exegesis, Herbert's commentary would likely have
been copied for someone whose library was already well-stocked with
standard texts, but whose interests extended to Hebrew language and
Jewish exegetical literature. It is possible, therefore, that in the gener-

---

[47] For a full description of the manuscript, see Smalley, "A Commentary on the
Hebraica by Herbert of Bosham," *RTAM* 18:29; N.R. Ker, *Medieval Manuscripts in British
Libraries I: London* (Oxford: Clarendon, 1969), 241.

[48] Private communication, n.d.

[49] Smalley, "A Commentary on the *Hebraica*," 30.

[50] I am grateful to Richard Gameson for his willingness to examine the manuscript
with me, in the company of Eva De Visscher, on April 6, 2004 at Saint Paul's Cathedral
Library, London.

ation after his death, Herbert's commentary joined a growing archive of Christian works produced for and by Christian scholars anxious to master Hebrew.[51]

In his description of the manuscript, Ker noted its similarity to glossed psalters, meaning that the entire text of the psalter (not just abbreviated lemmata) was given in the course of the running commentary. But unlike a glossed psalter, Herbert's commentary does not set out the text of the psalms in one column with the commentary in a parallel column (i.e., *cum textu*). The text and commentary are run together in a continuous exposition and the comments are often too long to be classed as glosses (comments on certain verses sometimes run 2 to 3 columns). In format, the *Psalterium cum commento* is also distinct from Herbert's edition of the psalms commentary of Peter Lombard as well as from either the continuous or *cum textu* formats favored by copyists of Gilbert of Poitiers' popular commentary on the psalms.

The commentary is written on parchment in double columns on 161 leaves. The text of psalms is written out, verse by verse, in large characters followed by the commentary in a smaller hand. There are occasional interlinear glosses to the psalm verses, usually giving alternate translations for individual words in the text. The manuscript was trimmed to fit its current binding; some valuable marginal comments in the same hand as the body text have been damaged or lost. These marginalia, in Smalley and Ker's judgments, are in the same hand as the body of the manuscript, or in a hand closely contemporary with that of the principal scribe.[52] In most cases they refer to scriptural citations. Marks in the commentary text where Scripture is quoted direct the reader to the citations in the margins. According to Smalley, these conform to a late twelfth-century system of capitulation.[53]

---

[51] The phenomenon of a growing scholarly 'industry,' which made use of and ultimately displaced works in Hebrew produced by Jews, will be discussed in subsequent chapters. Also, Judith Olszowy-Schlanger's examination of thirteenth-century Hebrew psalters of English provenance glossed in Latin has led her to suggest that their Christian owners annotated those works, perhaps in consultation with Jews or with other texts. Possibly Herbert's commentary was deployed in this fashion, by such a user. See "The Knowledge and Practice of Hebrew Grammar among Christian Scholars in Pre-expulsion England: The Evidence of 'Bilingual' Hebrew-Latin Manuscripts," *Hebrew Scholarship and the Medieval World*, ed. Nicholas de Lange (Cambridge: Cambridge University Press, 2001), 107–128.

[52] Gameson has opined that the main text, catch words, and marginalia are all in the same hand.

[53] Smalley, *RTAM* 18:30–31.

Among the marginalia reported by Smalley are two references to the Jewish scholar, Rabbi Solomon ben Isaac of Troyes (known by his acronym, Rashi; d. 1105). Identified in the text simply as *litterator*, the mark over that word is keyed to a marginal note, "Salomon."[54] In a second instance, Herbert refers to a source for Jewish exegesis of Psalm 71[72]:18. In the text, the source is referred to as *interpres*; in the margin, this interpreter is named as *litterator Salomon*.[55] Another marginal note, at Ps. 67[68]:14, identifies the tenth-century Spanish grammarian Dunash ibn Labrat as the source of a comment Herbert quotes from Rashi (who had named Dunash *ad loc.*).[56] Finally, a marginal note at Psalm 5 identifies another of Rashi's sources as *menaem*, referring to Menahem ibn Saruq, whom Rashi frequently names in his psalms commentary and to whom Herbert refers by name in the body of the commentary on several other occasions.[57]

In general, whenever Herbert refers to *litterator* or even *litteratores*, he means Rashi, and the source upon which he relies most heavily is Rashi's own commentary on the psalms.[58] On some occasions he seems to be interpolating additional Jewish exegetical material derived from the *Midrash on Psalms*; this also is sometimes attributed to *litteratores*. Occasionally, however, Herbert distinguishes the midrashic material by claiming its source is *tillim* (the work's Hebrew title is *Midrash Tehillim*). The general identity of the *litteratores* is made known early in the commentary: he informs us that they are *litteratores hebreorum*. Herbert introduces material from Rashi as he would any authoritative source; he writes *secundum litteratorem* as readily as he would write *secundum ecclesiasticum*. He is far less likely to refer (as Andrew of Saint Victor did) simply to *hebrei*, as in *hebrei tradunt* or *hebrei dicunt*. But even less rarely does Herbert make personal references to his Jewish sources. In one instance he refers to *perloquacem meam* and twice to *litterator meus*.[59]

---

[54] At Ps. 23[24]:1; fol. 26v.

[55] At Ps. 71[72]:18; fol. 82r.

[56] fol. 71r.

[57] Neither Smalley nor Loewe noted this reference; it appears on fol. 6v.

[58] See the extended discussion in Chapter 5.

[59] He refers to *litterator meus* at Ps. 23[24]:1 and also at Ps. 67[68]:14: "Sunt qui legunt hic; *plume columbe deargentatae*. Et quantum ad sensum; satis pro indifferenti est. Sed litterator meus dicebat verbum hebreum hic positum magis significare pennarum summitates quas pinnulas dicimus; quam plumas." Fol. 72[ra]. For further discussion, see Chapter 5.

Herbert's use of the term *litterator* to name his Jewish sources, spoken or written, seems to be unusual.[60] The word itself may tell us something about his approach to this material. In antiquity, a *litterator* was simply an instructor in grammar. One who knew how to read Latin was *litteratus*, or lettered, as a result of having been instructed by a *litterator*.[61] Such an instructor would provide more than basic literacy, however. According to the educational program outlined (or better, extolled) by John of Salisbury, the study of grammar provided the basis for acquiring all the other liberal arts. John studied grammar with Bernard of Chartres, who ensured that his students emulated the Latin masters of the gold and silver ages, memorizing their works and imitating their styles in prose and verse.[62] A thorough study of grammar, John proclaimed (quoting Quintilian), laid the 'firm foundation' for all literate endeavor.[63]

The parallels between John's appreciation for the importance of grammar to Hugh of Saint Victor's didactic and exegetical program which emphasized history are striking. Grammar is to the liberal arts what *historia* is to the understanding of Scripture: an indispensable tool for the discernment of right order and true meaning. Hugh himself alluded to the parallel when he wrote "The man who looks down [on the study of biblical history] slips little by little. If, in the beginning, you had looked down on learning the alphabet, now you would not even find your names listed with those of the grammar students."[64] In

---

[60] A slightly later Christian commentator, Alexander Neckam, refers to his debates with *litteratores hebreorum*; Richard W. Hunt, *The Schools and the Cloister*, ed. Margaret T. Gibson (Oxford: Clarendon Press, 1984), 109. Bernard of Clairvaux speaks of "the lettered Jews" as a group to be avoided in a polemic against the Parisian schools. Whether he is talking about actual Jews or Christians is unclear. Smalley, *SBMA* 173, quoting Ep. 106, *Sancti Bernardi opera* ed. J. Leclercq and H.M. Rochais (Rome: Editiones Cistercienses, 1974), vol. 7, 265–267.

[61] Secondary examples given in Lewis & Short suggest the two terms were distinguished by some grammarians; Aulus Gellius opposed a *litterator* to a *litteratus*: the first was a "smatterer," the latter a man of real learning. Bruno S. James's translation of Bernard of Clairvaux's letters reflects this distaste, perhaps; he translates Bernard's *litteratoribus Iudaeis* of Ep. 106 as "for Jewish hacks." *Letters of St. Bernard of Clairvaux* (Chicago: Regnery, 1953), 155. But in DuCange, *litterator* is a term of approval, applied to a wise or prudent person, a definition derived from the works of John of Salisbury.

[62] *Metalogicon* 1.24, trans. Daniel McGarry (Berkeley: University of California Press, 1962), pp. 67–71. The *Metalogicon* was completed in 1159 and sent by John with his *Policraticus* to Thomas Becket, then royal chancellor. Soon thereafter both John and Herbert joined Becket's archiepiscopal household. Subsequent citations are to page numbers in McGarry's translation.

[63] *Metalogicon*, 1.24–25, 71–72.

[64] *Didascalicon* 6.3, 136.

their didactic works both John of Salisbury and Hugh of Saint Victor complained of scholars who shirked fundamental elements of study in their rush to become 'philosophers,' or worse, well-paid masters and careerists.[65] One would imagine that their esteem for the foundation extended to those who provided instruction in grammar and its allied disciplines.[66] We have no reason to think that Herbert of Bosham was anything but sympathetic to Hugh and John's views of contemporary education and scholarship.[67] Herbert did not leave any ruminations on pedagogy or scholarship but he did leave the voluminous evidence of his own painstaking and largely unrewarded work, ranging from his edition of the Lombard's exegetical texts, his biography of Becket (three times longer than any other version) and his ground-breaking psalms commentary. Moreover, he was deeply influenced by Hugh of Saint Victor's educational philosophy and was a close associate of John of Salisbury's. It seems likely that Herbert's application of the term *litteratores* to Rashi and other Jewish exegetes denotes approval and esteem.[68]

Referring to Rashi *et al.* as *litteratores* might also convey Herbert's recognition of colleagues with a shared task. Studies of the pedagogical activities of medieval Jews suggest another reason why Herbert applied the term *litterator* to Rashi. Perhaps it served as a Latin equivalent for the Hebrew *qara* (plural: *poterim*), which designated people who offered basic instruction in reading Scripture at a level just above that of elementary literacy. Alternatively, perhaps it captures the sense of *pashtanim*, those Jewish exegetes of Herbert's generation who, inspired by Rashi, studied Scripture's 'plain meaning' (*peshuto shel miqra*).[69] Many

---

[65] *Didascalicon* 6.3, 136 and 5.10, 134; *Metalogicon* 1.4, 17–20.

[66] John wrote "… [A]nyone who spurns grammar, is not only not a 'teacher of letters' (*litterator*), but does not even deserve to be called 'lettered' (*litteratus*)." *Metalogicon* 1.24, 71.

[67] John is listed in Herbert's catalogue of Thomas's *eruditi* second only to the canonist Lombard of Piacenza: "Post hunc Joannes dictus cognomento de Saresberia natione Anglus; qui ex re nomen habens per Dei gratiam duos sibi in capite sponsae oculos coaptarat, sermone sapientiae et sermone scientiae abunde sibi dato, per spiritum. Hic cum neomartyre nostro in tentationibus ipsius strenue et viriliter ad finem usque permansit." *Vita*, 7.3, *Mats.* 3, 524.

[68] See Eva DeVisscher's discussion of the shifting application of the term *litterator* in Herbert's commentary, applied mainly to Rashi but on occasion also denoting other Jewish authorities. "The Jewish-Christian Dialogue in Twelfth-Century Western Europe: Herbert of Bosham's *Commentary on the Psalms*." (Ph.D. thesis, University of Leeds, 2003), Ch. 2 *passim*.

[69] On the *poterim* and *pashtanim*, see Menahem Banitt, "Les Poterim," *Révue des études*

Jewish exegetes of the period pursued a renewed interest in the plain meaning of Scripture. While Rashi was the most notable exponent of this school, successors to his approach included his grandson, R. Samuel ben Meir (Rashbam), R. Joseph Bekhor Shor, and (indirectly, insofar as he was Spanish, not French), Abraham ibn Ezra. These exegetes, like some of their Christian contemporaries, evinced new interest in linguistic and philological techniques as methods for solving textual cruces; they were concerned with the 'natural' and historical context of biblical texts and so explored the character of the biblical authors with fresh insights (using techniques adopted from the trivium, particularly the *accessus ad auctores* literature). Finally, the Jewish exegetes were concerned with developing interpretations of the biblical text that relied less on atomized allegory derived from etymology. Instead, they considered the biblical narrative in context, i.e., what was the entire book of Jonah about, as opposed to the meaning of a single verse?[70] Thus, when Herbert or the Victorines consulted the Jews, they discovered a group of exegetes whose interests were remarkably similar to their own.[71]

The similarity of interests emerged from partially parallel circumstances. Both communities were affected to some extent by the revival of liberal arts study and its attendant apparatus of text-critical tools (grammar and dialectic particularly). Christians encountered this revival in the schools of Northern Europe while Jews were more likely to develop such interests in Spain, where contact with Islam and its translations of Greek works had occurred. The similarity was also due in part to polemical concerns which engulfed either side. The Jews had been long been condemned by Christian polemicists as 'slaves' to the literal meaning of Scripture, unable to see the predictions of Christ disclosed in the Old Testament. Yet when Christians encountered Jewish allegorical exegesis, they often condemned it as 'fabulous' (in the sense of 'myth-making'). So the Jewish exegetes of the twelfth century endeavored to instruct their own community in the plain meaning of Scripture—which, among other things, contested Christological allegoresis—while preserving a sense of the fuller meaning which might

---

juives 125 (1966): 21–33 and Ephraim Kanarfogel, *Jewish Education and Society in the High Middle Ages* (Detroit: Wayne State University Press, 1993), 80–85.

[70] Michael A. Signer, "*Peshat, Sensus Litteralis*, and Sequential Narrative," *Frank Talmage Memorial Volume*, ed. Barry Walfish, 2 vols. (Haifa: University of Haifa Press, 1993), 1:203–216.

[71] Smalley, *SBMA*, 149–172.

apply to the future of Israel. For their part, Christians like Andrew and Hugh tried to show that even without allegory the text of the Hebrew Bible might still testify, however indirectly, to the Christian truth. Subsequent chapters will demonstrate Herbert's singular awareness of this tension between Jews and Christians and examine his remarkable attempts to reconcile that tension.

CHAPTER THREE

HERBERT OF BOSHAM'S
PSALTERIUM CUM COMMENTO

In 1938, Beryl Smalley published an article entitled "Andrew of St. Victor, Abbot of Wigmore: A Twelfth Century Hebraist."[1] In it, she identified an apparent discontinuity in the development of Christian biblical exegesis. At the beginning of the twelfth century, Christian interpreters emphasized the allegorical interpretation of Scripture's 'higher' senses, but by the end of the century these exegetes had yielded their dominance to the "biblical-moral school" of Stephen Langton, Peter Comestor, and Peter the Chanter.[2] These Parisian scholars were notable for their increased interest in Scripture's literal meaning, and the application of scriptural exegesis to the social and political problems of their day.[3] Smalley was intrigued by the emergence, seemingly *sui generis*, of the later exegetes. Her study of Stephen Langton's biblical commentaries, however, led her to a possible transitional figure: Andrew of Saint Victor (d. 1175), whose literal interpretations Langton cited frequently and approvingly.[4]

From Smalley's essay on Andrew emerged her full-length study of the shift in the nature and contours of medieval Christian exegesis, *The Study of the Bible in the Middle Ages* (1940). Her book's central thesis is that a vein of minority practice had subsisted in Christian exegesis from the time of Jerome (ca. 345–420), which devoted itself to the scientific study of the scriptural text, in contrast to the predominant practice of allegorical interpretation. By "scientific" she meant that some exegetes in the Latin West had followed Jerome's example of basing interpretation of the scriptural text on a close study of the text in its original languages, Greek and Hebrew.[5] In the case of the latter, Christian exegetes nec-

---

[1] *RTAM* 10 (1938): 358–373.

[2] The term 'biblical moral school' was coined by Martin Grabmann, *Geschichte der Scholastische Method* 2 (Freiburg: Herdersche Verlagshandlung, 1911), 476 ff.

[3] See John W. Baldwin, *Masters, Princes, and Merchants: The Social Views of Peter the Chanter and his Circle*, 2 vols. (Princeton: Princeton University Press, 1970), 1:88–116.

[4] Smalley, "Andrew of St Victor, Abbot of Wigmore ..." 358–359.

[5] She describes Origen as the founder of "the scientific study of the literal," and

essarily had had recourse to Hebrew speakers. Jerome asserted that he had studied Hebrew with the help of a Palestinian Jew (in the dead of night and as a means of subduing the unruly flesh, he tells us).[6] Later exegetes who followed his example studied, or claimed to study, Hebrew language and exegesis with their Jewish contemporaries. Smalley maintained that in the twelfth century, social and intellectual conditions prevailed that made scholarly discussions with Jews possible on a hitherto unheard-of scale.

Jerome's accomplishments are the standard against which other Christian hebraists have been measured. Beryl Smalley compared Andrew of Saint Victor's endeavors to Jerome's; so too did Raphael Loewe in estimating Herbert of Bosham's achievements.[7] Yet both Andrew and Herbert, while careful to acknowledge their debt to Jerome, had occasion to distinguish themselves from his example. An inquiry into the origins and meaning of the term 'hebraism' will serve as a preamble to exploring its twelfth-century applications in context.

Jerome's interest in Hebrew had centered around securing a correct text of the Hebrew Bible as the basis for an accurate Latin translation. He was persuaded that the Latin translation derived from the Septuagintal Greek version was flawed. He adduced two grounds for this belief. First, Jerome determined that the Septuagint varied from the Hebrew text available to him. Second, he maintained that variations between texts present in the Hebrew original and those quoted in the Greek New Testament proved that the translators of the Septuagint had imperfectly conveyed the truth of Scripture, perhaps deliberately. Crucial to Jerome's position was his belief that the Hebrew text of Scripture as he encountered it was identical to the text that the Septuagintal translators had used in the second century BCE. Thus he assumed that any variation between the Hebrew text he consulted and the Greek translation widely circulated (and translated into Latin) was the fault of

---

notes that "medieval scholarship will reflect Origen's method, attitude and limitations. The Jew will be consulted on linguistic and historical problems." *SBMA*, 12–13. The third-century Greek theologian established the legitimacy of Christian study of the Hebrew text of Scripture and its variant translations; Jerome modeled himself on Origen and, according to Smalley, "went further;" op. cit., 21.

[6] Ep. 125.10; *Saint Jérôme Lettres*, Tome VI, trans. and ed. Jérôme Labourt (Paris: Societé d'édition "Les Belles Lettres," 1951), 248.

[7] Raphael Loewe, "Herbert of Bosham's Commentary on Jerome's Hebrew Psalter," *Biblica* 34 (1953):44.

the translators, not the result of changes in the Hebrew that might have occurred in the intervening centuries. As William McKane noted:

> … for Jerome, the textual complications of the Greek versions seemed to disappear in the presence of the Hebrew Bible, the *Hebraica veritas*. If he had known more, he would have seen matters differently. The Hebrew text, which he knew, had no rivals, because in the first century A.D. all of them had been suppressed. The explanation of the differences between the Hebrew Bible known to Origen and Jerome and the pre-Hexaplaric Septuagint is, in important respects, that the Greek translators had before them a Hebrew text different from the one which had ousted all rivals … Hence there is a flaw in Jerome's *Hebraica veritas*, because it contains the wrong assumption that the Hebrew text, which he knew, was the only one that had ever obtained and that by virtue of this utter stability it gave access to the "Hebrew truth."[8]

While he consulted Jewish exegetical traditions and occasionally included them in his Scripture commentaries, Jerome's hebraism was chiefly a linguistic or lexical interest. He studied the Hebrew Bible and translated it into Latin in order to provide the best possible basis for Christian exegesis, so that the fullest range of Hebrew prophecies might be shown to have been fulfilled in Jesus Christ.[9] Jerome was less interested in the Jews as Jews than he was in their witness to the truths expressed in the Hebrew language.

By contrast, the Victorines Hugh and Andrew, and especially Herbert of Bosham, were intrigued by the Jews as a source of historical information valuable in its own right. The two canons of Saint Victor and Herbert can be classified as "cultural" hebraists.[10] None was concerned solely or even primarily with the correction of the text of Scripture, although a tradition of *correctores* inspired by Jerome's work surfaced periodically from the fourth century until their own day. These scholars turned their attention instead to a study of Jewish culture, particularly Hebrew traditions of exegesis, to clarify not just the biblical

---

[8] William McKane, *Selected Christian Hebraists* (Cambridge: Cambridge University Press, 1989), 39.

[9] Sarah Kamin, "The Theological Significance of the *Hebraica Veritas* in Jerome's Thought," *Sha'arei Talmon*, ed. M. Fishbane et al. (Winona Lake, IN: Eisenbrauns, 1992) 247–248.

[10] For the distinction between "lexical" and "cultural" hebraists, especially as it applied in the twelfth century, see Michael A. Signer, "Polemics and Exegesis: The Varieties of Twelfth Century Christian Hebraism," *Hebraica Veritas? Christian Hebraists and the Study of Judaism in Early Modern Europe*, ed. Allison Coudert (Philadelphia: University of Pennsylvania Press, 2004), 21–32.

text but the 'world of the text.'[11] McKane comments, "[Andrew's] interest in the literal sense is not simply a narrow grammatical precision, but rather an engaging human interest in the world of the Old Testament, its times, places, circumstances and people."[12]

As the subsequent discussion will demonstrate, Andrew's and Herbert's interests in 'times and places' reflected the theological preoccupations of their teacher Hugh, acclaimed as "another Augustine."[13] Given the widespread assumption that Augustine and Jerome differed sharply on matters relating to biblical interpretation, it seems paradoxical that the Victorines, canons regular living under a monastic rule attributed to Augustine, nevertheless claimed Jerome's example as the warrant for their study of Hebrew language and exegesis. It is desirable, therefore, to offer an overview of these two fourth-century figures and their attitudes toward the 'mother of languages.' After a review of the correspondence between Jerome and Augustine on these topics and a discussion of Augustine's position on the role of Hebrew language, history, and prophecy enunciated in *City of God*, this chapter addresses the efflorescence of hebraism in the twelfth century. Contacts with Judaism that facilitated the study of Hebrew in that century also played a significant role in the emerging concerns of Christian theology and religious practice. In the chapters that follow, these contacts and their consequences will be examined in general and then with specific reference to the career of Herbert of Bosham.

Because Augustine initially opposed Jerome's new biblical translations, the two Fathers have traditionally been regarded as proponents of

---

[11] The term is widely used, notably by Paul Ricoeur. See his "Philosophical and Theological Hermeneutics: Ideology, Utopia and Faith," *Protocol of the Seventeenth Colloquy* [November 4, 1975], ed. W. Wuellner (Berkeley: Center for Hermeneutical Studies in Hellenistic and Modern Culture at the Graduate Theological Union and the University of California, 1976), 24–26.

[12] McKane, 3–4.

[13] One of Hugh's didactic works is a guide to biblical times and places, known as the *Chronicon* or *De tribus maximis circumstantiis gestorum*. The work is unedited and unpublished; excepts were printed by W.M. Green in "Hugo of St.-Victor: *De tribus maximis circumstantiis gestorum*," *Speculum* 18 (1943): 488–492. Hugh's status was proclaimed by various authors extracted in the *Veterum aliquot scriptorum de Hugone Victorino testimonia*, including Johannes Trithemius, the fifteenth-century author of *De scriptoribus ecclesiastici*, who wrote: "Hugo, presbyter et monachus S. Victoris Parisiensis, ordinis canonicorum regularium Augustini, et abbas ut ferunt ibidem, natione Saxo, vir in divinis Scripturis eruditissimus, et in saeculari philosophia nulli priscorum inferior, qui velut alter Augustinus doctor celeberrimus suo tempore est habitus, ingenio subtilis, et ornatus eloquio, nec minus conversatione quam eruditione venerandus." PL 175: 166D.

antithetical techniques of biblical interpretation.[14] Augustine is viewed as uninterested in the study of the Hebrew language and exegesis, while Jerome is esteemed as the first Latin champion of the necessity of learning Hebrew as propaedeutic to the study of Scripture's literal sense. The dichotomy between the two is often oversimplified. While there is some tension between their early positions, Augustine's sophisticated theology of history articulated in *City of God* enabled that tension to be exploited creatively. Hugh of Saint Victor and Herbert of Bosham, student of the Victorines, achieved just such a creative synthesis.

Beginning in the mid-390s, Augustine and Jerome embarked on a correspondence which distinguished their positions on several issues dealing with scriptural interpretation, particularly the status of the Septuagint and its Latin translations, and the interpretation of the second chapter of Paul's Letter to the Galatians. Their correspondence and related works on these topics have contributed to a perception that the two men varied greatly on the relative importance of the Hebrew text of Scripture. Their views on the Hebrew Bible's importance did not vary as much as did their purpose and methods for interpreting the text.

Born *circa* 345, Jerome was educated at Rome as a *grammaticus* in the school of Aelius Donatus. In the 370s, he and some friends (including Rufinus, who would become his bitter enemy during the Origenist controversy) attempted an ascetical retirement at Trier. Apparently finding life in the West insufficiently arduous, Jerome traveled east to Syria, first to Antioch and subsequently to the desert at Chalcis. In the desert he ruined his digestion, had bad dreams regarding his classical education, and endeavored to subdue his flesh using the harsh discipline of learning Hebrew from an apostate Jew. Jerome left the desert in the early 380s for Antioch. He attached himself to the entourage of Symmachus, bishop of that city. Subsequently, Symmachus and Jerome travelled to Constantinople. It is there that Jerome first encountered the *Tetrapla*.[15] This version of Origen's famous *Hexapla* was reduced (as the name implies) to four columns of text: Origen's corrected Greek text of the Septuagint, and the three Greek translations from the Hebrew made

---

[14] McKane makes this point; a recent reiteration of this view appears in Bernice M. Kaczynski, "Edition, Translation and Exegesis: The Carolingians and the Bible," *The Gentle Voices of Teachers: Aspects of Learning in the Carolingian Age*, ed. Richard E. Sullivan (Columbus: Ohio State University Press, 1995), 173–174.

[15] H.F.D. Sparks, "Jerome as Biblical Scholar," *Cambridge History of the Bible* I, eds. P.R. Ackroyd and C.F. Evans (Cambridge: Cambridge University Press, 1970), 510–541.

by the translators Aquila, Symmachus, and Theodotion. Adam Kamesar has suggested that Jerome's encounter with the variant translations, coupled with his growing knowledge of Hebrew, sparked his discontent with the Latin translations of the Septuagint then in circulation. From this early point in his career, Jerome began to believe that the only reliable text of Scripture would be a version derived directly from the Hebrew originals and the best Greek texts of the New Testament.[16]

Jerome traveled with Symmachus to Rome in the mid-380s. The bishop of Rome, Damasus, commissioned Jerome's first project in biblical emendation: a revised Latin translation of the Greek New Testament. Soon after, he began a revision of the Septuagint text of the Old Testament, comparing it to that of Aquila and with "the rolls of the synagogue" as he tells his companion in scholarship, the Roman matron Marcella.[17] In the same letter, Jerome advanced a highly significant reason for his comparative study, one which would recur in many later attempts to defend his activities. Jerome announced that he had been investigating the Hebrew text in order to discover whether the Jews "in their hatred of Christ" had suppressed data in their Scriptures which attested to the truth of Christian revelation. He averred that they have but the precise target of his accusation—whether Aquila, or the Septuagint, or the 'rolls' he consulted in the Roman synagogue—is not clear.[18]

Jerome's knack for making enemies induced him to leave Rome after Damasus' death *circa* 388–389. He departed for the Holy Land with his patroness Paula and her daughter Eustochium. Together they settled in Bethlehem, founding a pair of monasteries for women and men. Jerome's Hebrew studies picked up pace; the years 389–392 were a period of "furious literary activity."[19] Jerome launched his career in the world of international scholarship, as it were, with the publication of

---

[16] Adam Kamesar, *Jerome, Greek Scholarship, and the Hebrew Bible* (Oxford: Clarendon Press, 1993).

[17] Jerome, Ep. 32; CSEL 54.

[18] The accusation of textual corruption had been leveled by Christian exegetes against the *recentiores* (Symmachus, Aquila, Theodotion) as a means of preserving the authenticity of the Septuagint, but Jerome seems to have been the first exegete to raise the question of whether the Septuagint itself might have been corrupted. See William Adler, "Jews as falsifiers: Charges of tendentious emendation in Jewish-Christian polemic," *Translation of Scripture*, ed. David M. Goldenberg (Philadelphia: Jewish Quarterly Review Supplement, 1990), 1–27.

[19] J.N.D. Kelly, *Jerome: His Life, Writings, and Controversies* (NY: Harper and Row, 1975), 141. Proximity to Hebrew speakers doubtless contributed to this increased activity.

three works: *Liber Interpretationis Hebraicorum Nominum* and *De Locis* (guides to Hebrew etymology and onomasty, mainly translations from Greek works), and his *Liber Quaestionum Hebraicarum in Genesim* (Book of Hebrew Questions in Genesis), which he proclaimed as entirely unique.[20] Following quickly after these didactic works were his commentary on Ecclesiastes, whose lemmata he claimed to have translated directly from the Hebrew; his translations from the books of Samuel and Kings; and, in 392, his translation of the psalter *iuxta hebraica*.

Why did Jerome abandon his self-appointed task of correcting the Latin translations of the Septuagint? Why did he begin translating Scripture into Latin from the Hebrew? Jerome had early on mistrusted the many Latin translations made from the variant versions of the Septuagint then in circulation. But even with access to the Septuagint text which he considered authoritative—Origen's *Hexapla* housed at Caesarea—Jerome stopped revising the Latin translations. There seem to have been two reasons for this. First, as early as his Roman period, Jerome suspected that the Hebrew text might contain some fuller disclosure of Christian truths than were accessible in translation. Second, as he tells us in the Preface to his translation of the Pentateuch, he came to believe that the legend of the seventy Jewish translators was nonsense. True enough, Ptolemy II had commissioned the translation in the second century BCE, but all the accretions to the legend—that the seventy had been separated into individual cells and nonetheless achieved seventy exactly identical translations from Hebrew to Greek— were implausible.[21] The seventy, he asserted, were no more "inspired" than any translator: translation was merely a task. But as long as it was only a task, he argued, should it not be done by a Christian? For what the seventy perceived only dimly as prophecy, Christians had experienced in history. He insisted that the seventy translators' ability to render the Hebrew adequately, fully, had been impaired by their failure to experience the revelation of Christ. Christians, therefore, had a pri-

---

[20] Kamesar supports him in this claim. Also, Mark Vessey has made the attractive suggestion that Jerome was actually positioning himself as the Latin Origen: the man who would make Scripture studies respectable in the eyes of the Roman elite by demonstrating the arcana associated with Hebrew language study. See Vessey's "Conference and Confession: Literary Pragmatics in Augustine's '*Apologia contra Hieronymum*'," *Journal of Early Christian Studies* 1:175–213.

[21] The legend of the seventy translators originated with the pseudepigraphical "Letter of Aristeas." For a critical edition of the text and a discussion of its origins and applications, see *Aristeas to Philocrates*, ed. and trans. Moses Hadas (New York: Ktav, repr.1973).

mary claim on the text of the Hebrew Bible, whose fullest truth for
Jerome was inevitably a Christian truth.

An aspect of Jerome's education is significant in this process: Jerome
has been acclaimed as "Donatus' greatest pupil."[22] As such, he was
an exponent *par excellence* of the school of Latin grammarians which
derived its impulses mainly from Stoicism. For Stoics, human instanti-
ations of the divinely ordered meta-language (Logos) had 'fallen' from
their complete identity with that Logos; nevertheless, these instantia-
tions (the *lexis* of human speech) could be purged of their accretions
and divergences from the truth through the study of etymology, which
is the search for the true *logos*.[23] Jerome was true to his training, then,
when he sought to turn back the rivulets of faulty translations toward
the 'fount' of Hebrew truth. Hebrew, he proclaimed, was the mother
of all languages.[24] Return to its source and you have returned to God.
Returning to the Hebrew, then, was as close to God as one might get in
this lifetime.[25]

Despite his preoccupation with lexicography, however, Jerome's exegesis was a two-track system. He discussed the letter of Scripture where
and when textual problems or *cruces* presented themselves, along with
allegorical interpretations which brought the letter, sometimes by very
ingenious means, into alignment with an orientation that understood all
of Scripture as being somehow predictive of Christ. Much of Jerome's
exegesis was abstracted from the works of Origen which Jerome translated into Latin.[26] He had learned from Origen that the Old and New
Testament were in concord. In an early letter, Jerome wrote, "For whatever we read in the Old Testament, that we also find in the Gospel;
and what was gathered together in the Gospel, that is drawn forth

---

[22] Louis Holtz, "A l'école de Donat, de Saint Augustin à Bede," *Latomus* 36 (1977):
522–538.

[23] Martin Irvine, *The Making of Textual Culture: Grammatica and Literary Theory, 350–1100*
(Cambridge: Cambridge University Press, 1994), 20–88.

[24] See the discussion and relevant citations in Chapter 2.

[25] In his defense of his translation projects in *Contra Rufinum* 2.24, Jerome maintained
his loyalty to the Septuagint: he had preached on it daily, prayed with it daily, and
his commentaries make use of it—whenever the text provided him with an even more
christological translation than his own could provide. The spiritual authority of the
Septuagint, to his mind, was by no means vitiated by a return to its "fount." CCSL 79,
60–61.

[26] Jerome's interest in the 'letter' was modeled on Origen, too, as Dennis Brown
notes in *Vir Trilinguis: A Study in the Biblical Exegesis of Saint Jerome* (Kampen: Kok Pharos,
1992),173.

from the authority of the Old Testament: nothing is discordant, nothing diverse."[27] He also learned from Origen that allegoresis supplied the harmony between the two testaments when the letter was seemingly incoherent or discordant.[28] Jerome's two interests, Hebrew language and allegoresis, were married in his onomastical and etymological works. In them he deployed Christianizing etymologies as tools for securing an encyclopedic basis for Christian interpretations: Hebrew place and personal names were pressed into service for demonstrating the complete concordance of the Old and New Testaments.[29] For Jerome, Hebrew was the fountain of Truth; that Truth was Christ; in the end, all Hebrew words could be proven to exhibit the unity of this Truth.

Lexical hebraism, in Jerome's case, describes more than his linguistic competence. The term also captures the nature of his interests. In fact, although Andrew of Saint Victor and others claimed to follow 'unequally' in Jerome's footsteps, twelfth-century hebraism evinced a greater interest in the Jews *qua* Jews than did Jerome's.[30] Both as a transmitter of Origen's works and in his own right, Jerome opened the door to hebraism. It fell to emulators of Augustine to widen the aperture of Christian interest in the history and culture of biblical Israel.

In Augustine (354–430), we encounter a person who had—in Peter Brown's memorable phrase—transcended his education, a thoroughly grammatical and rhetorical education.[31] His treatise on Christian teaching and scriptural interpretation, *De doctrina christiana*, demonstrates Augustine's capacity for self-transcendence. In it, he eschews any notion that etymology will lead to a definitive truth about Scripture. In the first book of *De doctrina christiana*, Augustine argues against positing any univocal interpretations of Scripture. Some charismatics, he cautions,

---

[27] Ep. 18.7.4, trans. Charles Christopher Mierow, *The Letters of St. Jerome* I, Ancient Christian Writers 33 (Westminster, MD: Newman Press, 1963), 87. One hears echoes here of Origen's tenth *Homily on Genesis*: "You see that everywhere the mysteries are in agreement. You see the patterns of the New and Old Testament to be harmonious," *Homilies on Genesis and Exodus*, trans. Ronald E. Heine, Fathers of the Church, vol. 71 (Washington, D.C.: Catholic University of America Press, 1982), 167.

[28] See Henri de Lubac, *Medieval Exegesis I: The Four Senses of Scripture*, trans. Mark Sebanc, Grand Rapids, MI: Eerdmans, 1998), 225–267.

[29] A fuller discussion of Jerome's etymological exegesis appears in Chapter 7.

[30] Andrew invokes this modesty *topos* in the prologue to his commentary on Isaiah; see *SBMA* 123–124.

[31] *Augustine of Hippo* (Berkeley: University of California Press, 1969), 264.

think they have the gift for discerning its true meaning, but the rest of
us are far better served by study and mutual enlightenment. For Augustine, the work of interpretation begins in the Christian community, not
in an individual, and it has as its goal building up the community in the
love of God and the love of neighbor.[32]

Part of building that love is to distinguish how to love rightly—and
what to love. Augustine devotes Books Two and Three of *De doctrina
christiana* to developing rules for discerning meaning. First he describes
the differences between things (*res*), which are real in themselves (a condition which pertains in its absolute sense only to God), and signs (*signa*),
which point to things. The process of interpreting Scripture is a process
of distinguishing things from those signs which may represent or direct
us to things but which are not real in themselves. By learning the difference between things and signs, we learn that we may only rejoice in
God (who alone is real and worthy of love), while referring everything
else that we love and use to its Creator, loving it for God's sake.[33] These
distinctions are crucial, he notes, because even the divinely given signs
of Scripture are mediated through human language and therefore only
partial reflections of the Truth which they communicate.[34] Truth, he
seems to suggest, becomes apparent when an interpreting community
gathers around the multivocal text of Scripture and are transformed by
it in love: "Whoever finds a lesson [in Scripture] useful to the building
of charity, even though he has not said what the author may be shown
to have intended in that place, has not been deceived, nor is he lying in
any way."[35]

From *De doctrina christiana* one learns that Augustine believes that the
possibility of multiple interpretations arising from Scripture is a good
thing, providential in fact. Also, at this point in his career, he endorsed
the authority of the Septuagint and its Latin translations, unlike Jerome.
Three reasons emerge from his discussions in *De doctrina christiana*. First,
he held that the miraculous stories concerning its origins *might* be true.
Even if they were not true, he believed that any translation that was
the product of group consensus must be superior to one achieved by an
individual working alone. Finally, he believed that the Septuagint might

---

[32] *De doctrina christiana* [hereafter, *DDC*], CCSL 32; *On Christian Doctrine*, trans. D.W.
Robertson, Jr. (New York: MacMillan, 1958), 1.35.39–31.36.41.
[33] *DDC* 1.2.2–1.5.5.
[34] *DDC* 2.5.6–2.6.7
[35] *DDC* 1.36.40; Robertson's translation. See also Smalley, *SBMA*, 23.

have been providentially destined for the conversion of the Gentiles all along.[36]

At about the time that Augustine was working on the first three books of *De doctrina christiana*, he became aware of Jerome's translation projects. He received a copy of Jerome's commentary on Paul's Letter to the Galatians and also learned that Jerome was translating the Old Testament directly from the Hebrew. He wrote to Jerome in 394–395 to dispute the older man's interpretation of Galatians and to ask him to stop translating from the Hebrew.[37] Regarding the Septuagint, Augustine wrote that he could not understand why Jerome thought he could find something in the Hebrew that the seventy had not. Surely the translation of the many was preferable to that of one; could Jerome not content himself with amending the Septuagint and making an authoritative Latin translation from it?[38] In his second letter, Augustine amplified his objections. A new Latin translation from the Hebrew would divide the church: the Greek-speaking churches would be using a different text. Besides, if a dispute arose concerning the translation, who— besides Jerome—was knowledgeable enough to adjudicate among the Latin, Greek, and Hebrew texts?[39]

Jerome finally responded to Augustine in 404.[40] He ridiculed Augustine's lack of training in the requisite tools of interpretation. He defended his translation project on the grounds we have encountered before: the Jews had corrupted the various texts of Scripture in their Greek translations, therefore Christians must get to the (Christian) truths of the original language. This response seems to have changed Augustine's mind. His reply to Jerome acknowledged the validity of Jerome's project.[41] Despite this concession, however, Augustine prodded Jerome to clarify his position by posing a few additional questions: these Jews

---

[36] *DDC* 2.15.22

[37] Augustine's initial letter seems to have gone astray. Eventually he wrote again, reiterating his objections. Augustine, Ep. 28; reiterated in Ep. 71, in 403. CSEL 34.

[38] Ep. 28.

[39] Augustine cited the real-life scandal caused in nearby Oea (later Tripoli) when Jerome's new version of the Book of Jonah was read in church. The people were confused, then outraged, to discover that Jerome had translated the name for the bush in Jonah 4:6 as "ivy" rather than the accustomed "gourd." Taking their translation to some local Jews, the Jews affirmed that the Septuagint was correct and Jerome wrong. Even allowing for the Jews' trouble-making propensities, Augustine says, we have to beware of scandalizing the faithful. Ep. 71.

[40] Jerome, Ep. 112.

[41] Augustine, Ep. 82, dating from 404.

who corrupted Scripture—which Jews did Jerome mean? Surely not
the seventy, Augustine says, because what interest would they have,
before Christ, in expunging references to him? Augustine argues, therefore, that differences between the Septuagint and translation from the
Hebrew must be the result of scribal error or mistranslation, not delib-
erate falsehood.[42]

Ruminations over his correspondence with Jerome bore fruit in Augustine's *City of God*.[43] In Book 15, Augustine takes up the history of the
two cities, heavenly and earthly, beginning with the earthly city founded
by Cain. The key to understanding prophecies concerning the cities, he
asserts, is found in Galatians 4:21–5:1.[44] There we learn that Scripture
sometimes speaks in allegories that make sense only to the "children of
grace" who are born spiritual and free.[45] Earlier, in the third book of *De
doctrina christiana*, he had argued that the Jews were in "spiritual slavery"
because they did not know which ambiguous signs to interpret literally
and which figuratively. But what has happened to his hermeneutic
from that work—that a valid interpretation builds up love? In *City
of God*, his concerns over the role of divine grace in relationship to
human endeavor appear to have amended his hermeneutics. Perfect

---

[42] Ep. 82; Augustine also asks a brilliant question: how could an exegete distinguish
his dogmatic concerns from his translation choices? Surely the one must be in the
back of his head while he considered the other (i.e., there could be no pure, literal
translation, unaffected by one's ideology, as it were). To my knowledge, Jerome never
answered this question.

[43] In her edition of the letters, Carolinne White has suggested that Jerome raised
for Augustine the issues of the Bible's textual transmission, which enabled Augustine
to reflect more seriously upon the question of what makes a text "authoritative."
The Correspondence (394–419) between Jerome and Augustine of Hippo (Lewiston, NY: Edwin
Mellen Press, 1990), 40. Similarly, Anne-Marie la Bonnadière speculated that Augustine
wrote chapters 11 through 16 of *City of God* under the influence of his debate with
Jerome, an influence which prompted Augustine to reflect on the meaning of the
Hebrew Bible in the context of Christian salvation history. "Augustin a-t-il utilisé la
'Vulgate' de Jérôme?" *St Augustin et la Bible*, ed. A.-M. La Bonnardière, *La Collection Bible
de Tous les Temps 3, (*Paris: Beauchesne, 1986), 303–312.

[44] Paul's text reads in part, "Tell me, you who desire to be under law, do you not
hear the law? For it is written that Abraham had two sons, one by a slave and one by a
free woman. But the son of the slave was born according to the flesh, the son of the free
woman through promise. Now this is an allegory: these women are two covenants. One
is from Mount Sinai, bearing children for slavery; she is Hagar. Now Hagar is Mount
Sinai in Arabia; she corresponds to the present Jerusalem, for she is in slavery with her
children. But the Jerusalem above is free, and she is our mother. ... Now we, brethren,
like Isaac, are children of promise."

[45] *De civitate Dei*, CCSL 48 [hereafter, *DCD*] 15.2–3; English translation by Henry
Bettenson (London: Penguin, 1984), 597–599.

love among the faithful is a more attenuated prospect. The building-up of love, he now recognizes, requires human freedom to be reoriented by grace. Thus he argues that only the people of the spiritual Jerusalem, freed by grace through their belief in Christ, will be further graced with respite from the internecine strife of the earthly city. It follows that only they will be able to build a community of love, a fit community for interpretation.

Augustine also addressed the problem of competing versions of Scripture. In a startling *volte-face*, Augustine disdains those people who are so wedded to the Septuagint that they cannot admit that the scribes or translators might have erred. He argues instead that a return to the original language, Hebrew, is the only way to determine the historical veracity of the text. Augustine again rejects the idea that the Jews deliberately falsified their own Scriptures, either in the original language or in the Septuagintal translation. He asserts:

> ... I should certainly not be justified in doubting that when some difference occurs between the two versions, where it is impossible for both to be a true record of historical fact, then greater reliance should be placed on the original language from which a version was made by translators into another tongue.[46]

In Book 15 Augustine seems to be developing a case for the *prima facie* historical truth of the Hebrew text. This history is significant, according to Augustine, because the historically achieved events of Israel's life with God have prophetic significance for Christians. On the one hand, he warns against reading historical narratives in the Old Testament in a reductive way, as solely historical. Likewise, he resists the tendency of some interpreters to abstract only allegorical meanings from Israel's history. History, Augustine argues, has intrinsic value and yet that value is not exhausted by its literal sense.[47] There is a third way between

---

[46] *DCD* 15.13, trans. Henry Bettenson, 618. CCSL 48, 472: 89–93: "... recte fieri nullo modo dubitauerim, ut, cum diversum aliquid in utrisque codicibus inuenitur, quando quidem ad fidem rerum gestarum utrumque esse non potest uerum, ei linguae potius credatur, unde est in aliam per interpretes facta translatio."

[47] Writing on the Flood in Bk. 15:27, he argues: "... no one, however stubborn, will venture to imagine that this narrative was written without an ulterior purpose; it could not plausibly be said that the events, though historical, have no symbolic meaning, or that the account is not factual, but merely symbolical, or that the symbolism has nothing to do with the Church. No; we must believe that the writing of this historical record had a wise purpose, that the events are historical, that they have a symbolic meaning, and that this meaning gives a prophetic picture of the Church." Bettenson, 648. The Latin text reads: "Non autem ad praefigurandam ecclesiam pertinere tam mul-

history for its own sake and history as a foundation for allegoresis. The third way consists in the events of Israel's history which have been fulfilled but only superficially; true fulfillment of the 'prophecy of events' rested with Christ. According to Augustine, the history of Israel in all its dimensions was thus especially significant for Christians.

In Book 17 of *City of God*, Augustine systematically examines the history of Israel "from the time of the prophets," that is, from the time of the Babylonian captivity up until the coming of Christ. He culls from that narrative examples of historical events (*res gestae*) which Christians can and should understand as prophecy. He reiterates his argument from Book 15: it is incorrect to read historical accounts in Scripture as mere history; likewise, it is wrong to discount their historical content entirely in favor of allegorical interpretation. Some historical events can be left as history, some can be read as historically fulfilled but still prophetic for the "spiritual Jerusalem." But how are we to know which is which? Augustine asserts that biblical prophecy is multivalent: some prophecies refer partly to the physical descendants of the patriarchs; some to Abraham's spiritual descendants; yet others apply to both: "literally to the bondmaid, symbolically (*figurate*) to the free woman."[48] Thus, events that worked themselves out in Israel's history, achieving a literal fulfillment, may yet hold significance for Christians. These descendants of Sarah's son Isaac who are "spiritual and free" are capable of discerning Christian reality in the foreshadowings of biblical

---

tiplicia rerum signa gestarum, nisi fuerit contentiosus, nemo permittitur opinari. Iam enim gentes ita ecclesiam repleuerunt, mundique et inmundi, donec certum ueniatur ad finem, ita eius unitatis quadam compagine continentur, ut ex hoc uno manifestissimo etiam de ceteris, quae obscurius aliquanto dicta sunt et difficilius agnosci queunt, dubitare fas non sit. Quae cum ita sint, [si] nec inaniter ista esse conscripta putare quisquam uel durus audebit, nec nihil significare cum gesta sint, nec sola dicta esse significatiua non facta, nec aliena esse ab ecclesia significanda probabiliter dici potest; sed magis credendum est et sapienter esse memoriae litterisque mandata, et gesta esse, et significare aliquid, et ipsum aliquid ad praefigurandam ecclesiam pertinere." CCSL 48, 497:102–116.

[48] *DCD*, 17.3; Bettenson, 713–714. CCSL, 48, 553: "Quocirca sicut oracula illa diuina ad Abraham Isaac et Iacob et quaecumque alia signa uel dicta prophetica in sacris litteris praecedentibus facta sunt, ita etiam ceterae ab isto regum tempore prophetiae partim pertinent ad gentem carnis Abrahae, partim uero ad illud semen eius, in quo benedicuntur omnes gentes coheredes Christi per testamentum nouum ad possidendam uitam aeternam regnumque caelorum; partim ergo ad ancillam, quae in seruitutem generat, id est terrenam Hierusalem, quae seruit cum filiis suis, partim uero ad liberam ciuitatem Dei, id est ueram Hierusalem aeternam in caelis, cuius filii homines secundum Deum uiuentes peregrinantur in terris; sed sunt in eis quaedam, quae ad utramque pertinere intelleguntur, ad ancillam proprie, ad liberam figurate."

Israel's history. The church, he writes, is able to recognize itself prefigured in biblical history.

In some cases, prophecies that seem to have been fulfilled within biblical Israel's history may yet be only shadows of a deeper fulfillment. Augustine uses the prophecies told to David concerning his son Solomon as an example: whatever good that might be said of Solomon is said *more truly* of Christ. In the case of Solomon, Scripture "prophesied by historical events." Solomon's deficiencies—his idolatry, for example—are cited as proof that prophetic fulfillment was only partial. In the very incompleteness of the historical event, the eventual completion is hinted at:

> The prophecy contained in the event, not the prophecy expressed in the words, was concerned directly with the old covenant; but it had a figurative application to the new. ... No one who looks at these prophecies *with the eye of faith* [emphasis added] could fail to see that they have been fulfilled.[49]

For Augustine, the prophecies derived from the Hebrew truth remained multivocal and multivalent. Any number of meanings might be derived from the text by the faithful, who are freed by God's grace; the multiplicity itself is providential. The capacity for full understanding of the text was foreclosed to its bearers, however: the Jews in their spiritual slavery could not discern the fullest revelations of prophecy. Still, Augustine argues in *City of God*, as he did elsewhere, that the Jews occupy a privileged place in a Christian view of history. In Book Three of *De doctrina christiana*, he asserts that although the Jews cannot discern the correct meaning of scriptural allegory (because they are blind to the allegories' true Referent) they are still closer to God than the pagans:

> But this servitude among the Jewish people was very different from that of the others, since they were subjected to temporal things in such a way that the One God was served in these things. And although they took signs of spiritual things for the things themselves, not knowing what they referred to, yet they acted as a matter of course that through this servitude they were pleasing the One God whom they did not see.[50]

---

[49] *DCD*, 17.5, Bettenson 724–725. CCSL 48, 563: "... ac per hoc in ea quoque re gesta eadem mutatio quae per Christum Iesum futura fuerat adumbrata est, et ad uetus testamentum proprie, figurate uero pertinebat ad nouum prophetia facti etiam ipsa, non uerbi, id scilicet facto significans, quod uerbo ad Heli sacerdotem dictum est per prophetam. ... Quis autem nunc fideli oculo haec intuens non uideat esse completa?"

[50] Augustine, *DDC* 3.6.10–17.11; *On Christian Doctrine*, trans. D.W. Robertson, Jr. (New York: MacMillan, 1958).

Augustine maintains that the Jews were "very close to being spiritual," a difference from the pagans that had deep significance for him.
When disputing with Jerome over the disagreement recounted in Galatians 2 between Paul and Peter on the observance of Jewish ritual law,
Augustine had asserted the differences that elevated the Jews above the
pagans: they worship the one God (however partially) and they observe
rituals that prefigure Christian sacraments. Augustine grants pride of
place to the Jews. In response, Jerome attacks his "Ebionite" views.
Augustine is little better than a judaizing heretic, Jerome charges, if he
does not admit that a fundamental gulf exists between Christians and
everyone else, Jews included. The gulf that yawns for Jerome is bridged
in part for Augustine by his ability and desire to read history simultaneously as significant in itself, as allegory, and as a record of promises
extended by God over time. Some have been fulfilled, some still await
their fullest expression.

At the same time, Augustine did not relinquish the Septuagint. As
he had in his correspondence with Jerome, he suggests that its variation
from the Hebrew may in fact be providentially ordered. God may have
spoken to the Israelites in one fashion in the original Hebrew. Then the
message was amended in the Septuagint to be more congruous with the
calling of the Gentiles. Each version has a unique place in the history
of salvation; both work together for good.[51]

For Augustine, the history of biblical Israel (its *res gestae*) and its texts
have salvific significance for Christians. The multivocality of the texts
is likewise providential.[52] Inspiration is not fixed in language, by his
account, but transfuses the text, irradiates it. Inspiration occurs in the
encounter between the text and the reader who is—together with a
community of faithful interpreters—transformed in love by it. Such
a community can examine the signs of biblical Israel's history and
distinguish between the prophecies in events and the prophecies in
words, gauging which have been fulfilled. Jerome, on the other hand,
locates truth more concretely in language; his fixity of purpose against
all comers reflects his fixation on that truth.

Following Paul's argument in the eleventh chapter of his Letter to
the Romans, Augustine had maintained that the disbelief of the Jews

---

[51] *DCD* 18.43.
[52] Recall *De doctrina christiana* 3 and his assertion that multiple interpretations are
graciously bestowed by God.

in the face of Christian revelation was a matter of God's mysterious providence. Paul's teaching was interpreted to mean that the eventual universal triumph of Christianity among the nations of the world was contingent for a time on the disbelief of the Jews. They were, as Paul said, "touched with partial blindness until the fullness of the nations should come in." In the fullness of God's time, this blindness would be lifted and "all Israel shall be saved" (Romans 11:25–26). In an attempt to make sense of God's mysterious judgment of God's chosen people, Augustine posited that the Jews must serve a pedagogic purpose for Christians.[53] In the time that will have elapsed from the coming of Christ to the eventual consummation of the world, the Jews' role in the economy of salvation is to prepare the way. "They carry our books," Augustine wrote in his sermon on Psalm 57 [Vulgate 56]; the dispersion of the Jews from Israel after the Bar Kochba revolt in c. 130 CE had ensured that those books would be carried throughout the world. The Jews' books contained the biblical prophecies that foretold Jesus' advent, death, and resurrection. Encounters with diaspora Judaism prepared the nations of the world (*gentes*) for the Gospel truths.[54] For Augustine and his successors in this train of thought, the Jews bore witness in another, equally important fashion. The misery of their alienation from the land of their ancestors, and their sufferings and deprivations in exile all testified to their loss of privilege. The Jews forfeited their status as God's chosen people when they rejected Jesus. The promise had passed from Israel according to the flesh to Israel according to the spirit, argued Augustine. Their exile was part of God's punishment for their disbelief.[55] For if they were still the elect, how else could their condition be explained?[56] Yet, according to Augustine, God's mysterious providence extended to preserving the lives of the

---

[53] Paula Fredriksen has suggested that Augustine's meditations on the mysteries of God's hidden judgments stemmed in part from his reflections on the fate of the Jews. How could God have willed the blindness of God's chosen people? For that matter, how could God will the suffering of any innocent soul? Fredricksen has argued that the Jews' historical situation played a prominent role in Augustine's theodicy. See her "*Excaecati occulta iustitia Dei*: Augustine on the Jews and Judaism," *Journal of Early Christian Studies* 3 (1995): 299–324.

[54] *Ennarationes in Psalmos*, 56[57].9: "dispersi sunt per omnes gentes … ut libros nostros portent;" CCSL 39, 699.

[55] *Enn. in Psalmos*, 56[57].13–14.

[56] See now Lisa A. Unterseher, "The Mark of Cain and the Jews: Augustine's Theology of the Jews." *Augustinian Studies* 33 (2002): 99–121.

Jews so that they might help in the Christian conversion of the world—
a process that would issue in their own conversion at the end of days.[57]

So that this process would continue for as long as was necessary
for conversion of the *gentes*, Augustine cautioned that the Jews, though
despised, should not be injured or killed. Preaching on "Slay them
not," (*Ne occideris eos*), a text from Psalm 58[59]:11, Augustine articulated the teaching which would provide the foundation for Christian
treatment of the Jews for the next seven centuries:

> Behold, the Jews are enemies, about whom this psalm seems to indicate
> that they keep the Law, and therefore it says of them, "Slay them not,
> unless sometime they forget thy law," so that the nation of Jews might
> remain, and by it remaining the multitude of Christians might increase.[58]

A crucial aspect of Augustine's position, as Jeremy Cohen has maintained, was his belief that the Jews *qua* Jews remained as they were
in the Hebrew Bible. Augustine argued that the people of the Old
Covenant had chosen to ignore the New Promise; they were "stationary
in useless antiquity."[59] Far from venerating the Jews for their allegiance
to the *mos maiorum*, Augustine argued that their beliefs and practices
were useful only as signs whose deeper meaning was fully intelligible
only in the light of Christ: "And in truth so they are; they hold the
law, hold the Prophets; read all things, sing all things: the light of the
Prophets therein they see not, which is Christ Jesus."[60] Still, as signs, the
Jews could provide useful data on the events of biblical Israel's history,
whose prophetic significance the Church could apply to itself. As bearers of the biblical books that prophesied Christ's coming, the Jews also
carried the evidence that contradicted their own traditions, according
to Christian exegesis:

> A Jew carries the book that is the foundation of faith for a Christian.
> Jews act as book-bearers for us, like the slaves who are condemned to
> walk behind their masters carrying their books, so that while the slaves
> sink under the weight, the masters make great strides through reading.

---

[57] On the eventual conversion of the Jews, called just before the Day of Judgment by
the prophet Elijah, see Augustine, *DCD*, 20.29–30.

[58] *Enn. in Ps.* 58[59].2.2; CCSL 39, 746.

[59] Augustine, *Tractatus adversus Iudaeos*, 6.8, PL 42:51–64; trans. Marie Liguori Ewald,
Treatises on Marriage and Other Works, ed. Roy J. DeFerrari, Fathers of the Church,
vol. 15 (Washington: Catholic University Press, 1955), 400. Jeremy Cohen, "Scholarship
and Intolerance in the Medieval Academy: The Study and Evaluation of Judaism in
European Christendom," *American Historical Review* 91 (1986): 595.

[60] *Enn. in Ps.* 58[59], CCSL 39, 746.

Such is the shameful position to which the Jews have been reduced, and the prophecy uttered so long ago has been fulfilled: "those who trampled on me he has consigned to disgrace." What a disgrace it is for them, brothers and sisters, that they can read this verse like blind people looking into their own mirror![61]

Augustine's teaching was reiterated and elaborated by Pope Gregory the Great (ca. 540–604).[62] It became the dominant Christian rationale for the continued disbelief—and existence—of Jews in their midst. That rationale rested on three crucial presuppositions. The first, established by Augustine's theory of history, accorded a privileged place for the Jews in connection to Christianity; the Jews were better than pagans, close to being spiritual, and the history of their experience of God—up until the time of Jesus—was formative, predictive, and instructive for Christians. Next, diaspora Judaism's experience of misery and obloquy was likewise significant; according to Augustine, the Jews' material conditions (loss of their kingdom and homeland, their exile and poverty) testified to their rejection by God—albeit a rejection that would be overcome at the end of days. Divine rejection of the Jews further demonstrated divine election of *verus Israel*, the Christians. Finally, as Christianity's "book-bearers," the Jews were in possession of a body of knowledge which, from a Christian perspective, they demonstrably did not understand: the biblical prophecies may have been the Jews' natural resources, but their effective exploitation lay in Christian hands. Ultimately that exploitation would entail the masterful deployment of both lexical and cultural expertise, but the acquisition of expertise would also bring some Christians into close contact with Jews. Such contact, as will be seen, had the potential to unsettle the presuppositions of the Augustinian 'witness of the Jews.'

In the meantime, the study of Hebrew initiated by Jerome was taken up by later generations of Christian exegetes who claimed his intellectual pedigree and who echoed his purposes. The ninth-century Carolingian project of correcting the biblical text was undertaken in part because discrepancies were perceived among the multiple copies of the Scriptures then available. How best to remedy this situation? By return-

---

[61] Sermon on Psalm 57:4, "Those who trampled on me he has consigned to disgrace." Augustine, *Expositions on the Psalms*, vol. 3, trans. Maria Boulding O.S.B. (Hyde Park, NY: New City Press, 2001).

[62] Jeremy Cohen, *Living Letters of the Law* (Berkeley: University of California Press, 1999), 73 ff.

ing to the fount of the Hebrew text, as had Jerome. So Carolingian correctors consulted with contemporary Jews in order to achieve a standard text of the Old Testament.[63] Directed by Charlemagne to establish
a reliable biblical text, Alcuin (*ca.* 740–804) had pursued a conservative
approach to scriptural correction, chiefly by reconciling multiple versions of the available texts of the Vulgate. The tactics of Theodulf (750–
821), bishop of Orleans, were more radical: he reconciled multiple versions of the Vulgate against the Hebrew text then available, apparently
with the help of an apostate Jew. This unnamed 'hebraist,' as Avrom
Saltman called him, rendered a literal Latin translation of the Hebrew
text in tandem with a corrected version of Jerome's more "literary"
Vulgate.[64] Saltman and others have also argued that the Carolingian
era sparked a new interest in the historical books of the Hebrew Bible.
Charlemagne, acclaimed by his courtiers as a new David, adopted a
dynastic ideology supported by the study of the books of Samuel, Kings,
and Chronicles.[65] Saltman suggests that the author of a literal commentary on Samuel and Kings may have been the same hebraist who consulted with Theodulf. Christians needed data to supply the lacunae in
their own commentaries on the historical books; they turned (as Jerome
had before them) to the Jews for raw material.

The commentaries by Theodulf's anonymous hebraist were incorporated by Hrabanus Maurus (d. 856), a student of Alcuin and an
exegetical encyclopedist, into his exegetical works. In the twelfth century, by then attributed to Jerome, they found their way into the *Glossa
Ordinaria*. Theodulf's unknown hebraist, very likely a Jew, had become
assimilated to the identity of Christianity's premier hebraist. Nevertheless, until the thirteenth century, the needs associated with two scholarly

---

[63] The correctors of the Latin texts of Scripture were generally motivated by the
realization that conflicting versions of the texts existed. They eliminated discrepancies
by using Jerome's method: collating the Latin text to the Hebrew. Like Jerome (and as
Gilbert Dahan has noted), the *correctores* assumed that the Hebrew text was immutable
and made no allowance for the possibility of multiple or conflicting *Hebrew* textual traditions. The assumptions underlying these textual practices parallel or even encapsulate
Christianity's theological assumptions regarding Judaism in this period: it was "useless
in stationary antiquity," to use Augustine's phrase. See Dahan's discussion in "Juifs et
Chrétiens en Occident Médiéval: La Rencontre autour de la Bible (XIIe–XIVe Siècles)," *Revue de Synthèse* 4:1 (1989): 6–7.

[64] Pseudo-Jerome, *Quaestiones on the Book of Samuel*, ed. Avrom Saltman (Leiden:
E.J. Brill, 1975), 6.

[65] See Saltman, *Quaestiones on the Book of Samuel*, 1–29; Contreni, "Carolingian Biblical
Studies."

projects drove Christians to consult Jews: correcting the biblical text and fleshing-out their understanding of the Bible's historical narratives. The Jews were regarded as reliable on both counts because Christians assumed that their biblical texts had remained stable since the time of the Septuagint.[66]

In the early twelfth century, Stephen Harding, one of the Cistercian movement's founding fathers, once again evinced a concern for the integrity of the biblical text. As noted in Chapter 1, Harding summoned Jews to Cîteaux and with their assistance edited the Cistercians' version of the Bible. By mid-century, other Christian scholars espoused the task of textual emendation but with a polemical twist learned from Jerome. In the preface to his final translation of the psalter, the *Psalterium iuxta hebraicum,* Jerome had asserted that he made this translation to confute the Jews who, when confronted with Christian claims that the psalms prophesied Christ, replied, "It stands not so in the Hebrew."[67] He sought to overcome such objections by confronting the Jews with the Hebrew truth (*hebraica veritas*). The Jews would then be convicted out of their own mouths, as it were.[68] Similar disputes and a similar agenda fostered the development of twelfth-century Christian hebraism. Increased contact with Jews led to theological discussions, some amicable, some not. Christians encountered a Jewish defense against Christological interpretations of the Hebrew Bible that Christians derived either from translation, etymology, or allegoresis. The Jews insisted that the Christians' Latin text varied from the Hebrew original. In response, Christian scholars attempted to demonstrate that their readings, particularly of the Hebrew prophets, were conclusive and derived from authoritative, correct texts.[69]

In contrast to modern scholars who have emphasized their differences, medieval exegetes emphasized the concordance between Augustine's and Jerome's approaches to interpretation. Hrabanus Maurus asserted that any apparent discord between the Fathers was the fault

---

[66] Recourse to the Jews for textual studies was 'canonized' in Gratian's *Decretum*, Dist. XI, cap. 6, ca. 1140.

[67] "Praefatio," *Liber Psalmorum iuxta Hebraicum translatus, Biblia Sacra iuxta Vulgatam versionem.*

[68] Ibid.

[69] Of course, allegorical interpretations based on whatever version of the text was handy had always maintained the superiority of the Christian claim to scriptural truths. This interest in an accurate text as a basis for more compelling exegesis is the 'scientific' move noted by Smalley.

of the reader.[70] Certainly for as long as allegorical exegesis dominated Christianity's approach to biblical interpretation, the views and methods of Jerome and Augustine were readily assimilable. During the twelfth-century revival of interest in the literal sense, the fourth-century masters offered complementary approaches. Augustine's sweeping vision of salvation history provided an overarching framework which ensured the legitimacy and necessity of both Jerome's lexical hebraism and his christological allegoresis. Viewed in this light, lexical and cultural hebraisms, particularly as practiced by the Victorines, were mutually reinforcing strategies of Christian appropriation of Old Testament texts. The pedagogical program espoused by Hugh of Saint Victor, which elaborated a comprehensive curriculum of the branches of human knowledge as a pathway for the development of virtue, provided the template for including all manner of data about the Jews, Judaism, and Jewish exegesis into an encyclopedia—or archive—of Christian knowledge.

Hugh's genius combined the products of grammatical and historical study in an exegetical framework that made better sense of the increased Jewish presence than his predecessors had done. It allowed for greater contact with the Jews, an increased (although still carefully circumscribed) role for the historical experience of Jews after Jesus' birth, and potential for a more nuanced understanding of Jewish techniques of biblical exegesis. Paradoxically, such increased knowledge also imperiled twelfth-century Christianity's effective management of its 'Jewish question', leaving some pioneers in Hebrew study vulnerable to the accusation of judaizing.

---

[70] John J. Contreni, "Carolingian Biblical Studies," *Carolingian Essays*, ed. Ute-Renate Blumenthal (Washington: CUA Press, 1983), 71–98.

CHAPTER FOUR

COLONIZING THE
TERRITORY OF SCRIPTURE

In a foundational article published in 1953, Raphael Loewe summarized the three-fold purpose of twelfth-century Christian hebraism: the establishment of an accurate translation of the Hebrew Bible into Latin for Christian use; the refutation of Jewish objections to or criticisms of the Latin text; and the development of an authoritative text on which persuasive claims for Christianity's eclipse of Judaism could be based.[1] In the absence of any ability to speak or read Hebrew independently (and in the absence of the pedagogical tools such as grammars and dictionaries that might have provided such independence), Christians necessarily had recourse to Jews even as they formulated their supersessionist positions. Their claims were manifested in two bodies of literature: biblical exegesis and interreligious polemic. The line between these two genres is by no means firm: until the late twelfth century, Christian polemic against Judaism was essentially grounded in exegesis and disputes over the correct interpretation of Scripture. Still, many modern studies of relations between Jews and Christians in this period tend to separate exegetical works from polemical literature. The authors of these studies have relied on an essentially artificial distinction between Christian exegetes who commented on the biblical texts (but who often directly engaged the claims of their rivals in religion) and polemicists whose works explicitly took the form of disputations or tractates against the Jews (but whose truth claims were usually grounded in exegesis).

This chapter argues that exegesis, as a Christian appropriation of the biblical text, was clearly polemical. To describe some twelfth-century exegetes' interests as 'scientific' understates exegesis's function as a tool to delimit the reality of Jewish presence in Northern European culture, used even by those exegetes who made contact with Jewish scholars. The Bible can be compared to a disputed territory rich with resources

---

[1] Raphael Loewe, "The Medieval Christian Hebraists of England I: Herbert of Bosham and Earlier Scholars," *Transactions of the Jewish Historical Society of England* 17 (1953): 232–233.

which the dominant culture sought to exploit—a metaphorical colony. By no means did Jews concede the sacred terrain of Scripture to Christians; they did not cease to 'talk back' to Christian culture. Indeed, in Jewish exegesis of the disputed textual territory, we encounter their forthright rejection of Christian claims.[2] Still, Christians in the twelfth century relied upon Jewish interlocutors as later European anthropologists would rely on native informants. Lacking the tools for independent, direct access to the Hebrew text, Christians who studied Hebrew and Jewish exegesis placed themselves on the boundary between the two cultures.[3] As Christians, they also inhabited a world in which the lines between literary genres was not so fixed as modern taxonomy suggests.[4] What follows is an effort to retrieve the ambiguous status of Christian hebraists by relying on Michel Foucault's theory of 'discursive formations' that operate beyond the categories of text, *oeuvre*, and genre.[5] According to Foucault's formulation in *The Archaeology of Knowledge*, discursive formations that come to be regarded as authoritative impose order and regularity on a set of statements.[6] Authority derives from what Foucault further calls the "archive," which constitutes the "system of [the statement's] enunciability [and] functioning."[7]

---

[2] Two articles by Erwin I.J. Rosenthal are especially instructive on this point: "Medieval Jewish Exegesis: Its Character and Significance," *Journal of Semitic Studies* 9:2 (1964): 265–281 and "Anti-Christian Polemic in Medieval Bible Commentaries," *Journal of Jewish Studies* 11 (1960): 115–135.

[3] Daniel Boyarin, in an article on Justin Martyr, argues that the boundary between the two communities is the locus of formation for both Jewish and Christian 'orthodoxy.' "Justin Martyr Invents Judaism," *Church History* 70:3 (2001): 427–462.

[4] Roger Ray, in an essay on medieval conceptions of history and historiography, makes an analogous point: modern definitions of genre categories often obscure unities and distinctions within medieval works. See his "Medieval Historiography through the Twelfth Century: Problems and Progress of Research," *Viator* 5 (1974): 33–59.

[5] See *The Archaeology of Knowledge* [hereafter, *AK*], trans. A.M. Sheridan Smith (New York: Pantheon, 1972), especially "Introduction" and Chapter Two, "Discursive Formations."

[6] A "statement," for Foucault, is neither a linguistic nor a material entity, neither a sentence nor a material object, but is "a function of existence that properly belongs to signs and on the basis of which one may then decide, through analysis or intuition, whether or not they 'make sense,' according to what rule they follow one another or are juxtaposed, of what they are the sign, and what sort of act is carried out by their formulation (oral or written)." *AK*, 86–87.

[7] *AK*, 129. For any given discourse in any given circumstance, an archive exists but cannot be fully identified or described, since we live within it. It provides the background that supports the apparent truth or reality of our statements. Foucault notes, "We are now dealing with a complex volume, in which heterogeneous regions are differentiated or deployed … Instead of seeing on the great mythical book of

Groups of statements, or discourse, collectively constitute knowledge—an inevitable concomitant of power, in Foucault's view. As knowledge is accumulated and codified in the archive, it functions as a regulatory system that decides what can and cannot be said in a given discipline. Studying the medieval encounter of Jews and Christians through the lens of a particular genre may create a narrative whose unity is predicated on a false distinction (for example, "*this* is polemic, but *that* is exegesis"). In the process, a larger field of discourse which includes both polemic and exegesis is obscured. Dividing the Christian discourse on Jews and Judaism into genre categories prevents us from seeing the broader, sometimes contradictory, power dynamics of that encounter.[8]

Some scholars of the medieval encounter between Jews and Christians, notably Aryeh Grabois in an often-cited article, have suggested that comparable scholarly concerns about interpreting the biblical text fostered, however briefly, an irenic partnership between Christians and Jews.[9] Grabois contrasted these comparatively genial scholarly discussions with the propensity of the "masses" of Christian faithful to act violently against the Jews. Other scholars, in particular Amos Funkenstein and Jeremy Cohen, have tried to establish the contribution that Christian intellectual elites made to the growth of 'popular' anti-Judaism in the late twelfth and early thirteenth centuries.[10] The seeming disjunction between these two schools of thought arises in part from the evidence they deploy. There is a tendency to emphasize the study of either

---

history, lines of words that translate in visible characters thoughts that were formed in some other time and place, we have in the density of discursive practices, systems that establish statements as events (with their own conditions and domain of appearance) and things (with their own possibility and field of use). They are all these systems of statements (whether events or things) that I propose to call *archive*." *AK*, 128, emphasis in the original.

[8] Foucault argued that the overdetermined unity of history can be supplanted or transgressed by analyzing "disqualified" discourse which resists coherence and fragments the formation of authoritative statements. He called the recovery of alternative, disruptive discourse "archaeology."

[9] Aryeh Grabois, "The *Hebraica Veritas* and Jewish-Christian Intellectual Relations in the Twelfth Century," *Speculum* 50 (1975): 613–634; and to a lesser degree Gilbert Dahan; see his "Juifs et Chrétiens en Occident Médiéval: La Rencontre autour de la Bible (XIIe–XIVe Siècles)," *Revue de Synthèse* 4:1 (1989): 3–31.

[10] Amos Funkenstein, "Basic Types of Christian Anti-Jewish Polemic in the later Middle Ages," *Viator* 2:373–382 and "Changes in Christian Anti-Jewish Polemics in the Twelfth Century," *Perceptions of Jewish History* (Berkeley: University of California Press, 1993); Jeremy Cohen, *The Friars and the Jews* (Ithaca: Cornell University Press, 1982) and now his *Living Letters of the Law: The Idea of the Jew in the Medieval Christianity* (Berkeley: University of California Press, 1999).

exegesis or polemical literature almost to the exclusion of the other.[11] Even Gilbert Dahan in his study *Les intellectuels chrétiens et les Juifs au Moyen Âge*, which records and discusses virtually all the major works in either genre, tends to discuss them as simply as genres, rather than as manifestations integral to a spectrum of Christian attitudes towards Judaism.[12] Students of exegesis such as Grabois and Beryl Smalley, or students of polemic like Funkenstein and Cohen, try to account for the growth of either positive or negative relations between Jews and Christians in their respective genres, in isolation. They adduce a trail or pattern in a textual genre which supports a model of amelioration or deterioration in medieval relations between the two groups. But isolating the genres of exegesis and polemic from one another yields a deficient or even false sense of development—whether good or bad—in medieval Christian attitudes toward the Jews. Exegesis and polemic must be considered together, and over time, in order to grasp the complexity and variability of relations between the two groups.

To the degree that not many medieval Christian exegetes also wrote polemical tracts, or *vice-versa*, a segregated approach to these genres may be justified. Yet it fails to take account of the wider contexts affecting the development of both categories of literature, and the fact that exegetes might have read polemic, and polemicists read exegesis; or that these authors might have been active in the same *milieux* at the same time. Their world views and attitudes towards contemporary Judaism would have been formed by many factors, not just the history of a particular genre of literature. Exegesis, moreover, encoded polemic, since a crucial issue for Christians and Jews in the period was the establishment of authoritative interpretations of the text of Scripture.[13] So while some Christians consulted Jews in order to establish the correct biblical text, or to perfect their grasp on the history of biblical Israel, inevitably they were drawn into disputes over the Jews' interpretations of their shared Scripture. The aggravations and opportunities attendant upon a close, even collaborative, discussion of biblical texts and

---

[11] A noteworthy exception to this trend was David E. Timmer's study of polemic in the exegesis of Rupert of Deutz, "Biblical Exegesis and the Jewish-Christian Controversy in the Early Twelfth Century," *Church History* 58 (1989): 309–321.

[12] Gilbert Dahan, *Les intellectuels chrétiens et les Juifs au Moyen Âge* (Paris: Cerf, 1991).

[13] Michael A. Signer, "The *Glossa Ordinaria* and the Transmission of Medieval Anti-Judaism," *A Distinct Voice: Medieval Studies in Honor of Leonard E. Boyle, O.P.*, ed. Jacqueline Brown and William P. Stoneman (Notre Dame: University of Notre Dame Press, 1998), 591–605.

interpretations between Jews and Christians came to the fore in the mid-twelfth century among the Victorines and their student, Herbert of Bosham.

Contacts with Jews in this period had engendered fresh interest in the scriptural text as a historical narrative, which in turn led some exegetes (chiefly the Victorines) to reappraise the role of Judaism in the economy of salvation.[14] This reappraisal was the product of an Augustinian-inspired view of history, which read some of the events in the life of ancient Israel as shadows of still greater events to be worked by God in history for the benefit of humanity's redemption. But some of the principal students of Christian anti-Jewish polemic have argued that in this same period contact with the Jews actually undermined the basis for Augustine's teaching of toleration for the Jews. These conflicting arguments can be partially reconciled, since renewed interest in the history of biblical Israel attenuated and complicated a traditional Christian view of Jews as 'witnesses' to Christian truth. Christian exegetes who pursued interests in the literal, historical sense of Scripture contributed to these complications, a factor which is obscured by the isolated study of Christian anti-Jewish polemics.

Various theories have been formulated to explain an apparent increase in Christian unease with regard to Jews in the twelfth century, notably Jeremy Cohen's analysis of the Augustinian model of Jewish witness and the factors leading to its erosion by the thirteenth century.[15]

---

[14] Jeremy Cohen, in "Scholarship and Intolerance in the Medieval Academy," suggested that medieval Christians first experienced a revived interest in the Old Testament and only subsequently turned to contemporary Jews as sources of information. There is some evidence for this in the ecclesial models spawned by Gregorian Reform, as noted (with some dismay) by Marie Dominique Chenu in his study of the Old Testament's use in twelfth-century theology in *Nature, Man and Society in the Twelfth Century* (Toronto: Medieval Academy Reprints for Teaching, 1997), 146–161; but see also John Van Engen's illuminating discussion of the function of Christian exegesis of Leviticus in "Ralph of Flaix: The Book of Leviticus Interpreted as Christian Community," *Jews and Christians in Twelfth Century Europe* (Notre Dame: University of Notre Dame Press, 2001), 150–170, in which he argues for the "reality of human contact" as a factor which contributed to renewed Christian interest in the Hebrew Scriptures. Similarly, Michael Signer has argued that Christians were motivated by contact with Jewish culture to study the Hebrew Scriptures: "Part of the social reality of Christian thinkers in France from the late eleventh century was the appearance of a vibrant Jewish community." "The *Glossa Ordinaria* and the Transmission of Medieval Anti-Judaism," *A Distinct Voice: Medieval Studies in Honor of Leonard E. Boyle, O.P.*, eds. Jacqueline Brown and William P. Stoneman (Notre Dame: University of Notre Dame Press, 1998), 592.

[15] As discussed in Jeremy Cohen, *The Friars and the Jews* and *Living Letters of the Law*, cited in full above.

In response to Cohen's formulation, I argue that the hermeneutical principles of the school of Saint Victor, whose revived, even intensified, interest in Augustine's theology of history presumably made possible a positive appreciation of biblical Judaism by some Christian exegetes, may also have contributed to the violently negative attacks of Christian polemicists. Victorine exegesis, in other words, acted as a tributary to the stream of polemic. In the twelfth century, the Christian clerics who contributed to each body of literature were buffeted by various challenges to the presuppositions undergirding the Augustinian doctrine of Jewish witness.[16] Together—not separated by artificial genre lines—they formulated responses to those challenges. I argue that twelfth-century Christian responses to Judaism, positive and negative, emanated from this apex or common central point: If God acts in history, and as a result humans should take the study of historical events seriously, then how are we to respond to the aporias of history which defy intelligibility? Further, twelfth-century Christian responses to Judaism, positive and negative, are found in a range of discursive practices that addressed the challenges raised by just those questions. By definition, those practices included suppression and displacement of some possible answers.[17] Analyzing the relationship between the genres of polemic and exegesis, unconstrained by an attempt to provide a global model of either "amelioration" or "deterioration," will illustrate Christianity's difficulties in accepting the aporias that confronted it in the twelfth century: the flourishing of Jews, and Jewish moral and intellectual worth. When history is taken seriously as progressive, and when the evidence of contemporary events is considered salient to charting historical development, then a system that had depended on a kind of stasis (one that bracketed Jews as 'living history' exhibits) crumbles and a new system needs to be articulated.

The presence of a minority population who remained largely unassimilable because of their dissenting religious beliefs was a source of discomfort to the Christians of the Latin West. This discomfort has been characterized variously by scholars in recent decades as anxiety over the changing nature of the commercial and social environment and the unease that Christians felt in response to the application of tools of rational inquiry to their own theological formulations.[18] Schol-

---

[16] For a brief sketch of the presuppositions, see the preceding chapter.

[17] *AK*, 26–27.

[18] Lester K. Little, *Religious Poverty and the Profit Economy in Medieval Europe* (Ithaca,

ars such as Lester K. Little have argued that Christians believed, correctly or not, that Jews were more at ease in medieval European society as it underwent the "Commercial Revolution." As a consequence, Jews became the scapegoats for and targets of Christian fears and anxieties, particularly those related to the rise of urban cultures and a cash economy. In his landmark study, *Religious Poverty and the Profit Economy in Medieval Europe*, Little contended:

> Christians attacked in the Jews those things about themselves that they found inadmissable and they therefore projected on to the Jews. Guilt led to hostility, and hostility to violence, which led to a need for rationalizing the violence, and this rationalization led to a deeper hostility and still more violence, and so the fateful cycle turned. Joined to this guilt that was felt by some was a more simple anxiety about the disorders and uncertainties of urban life and about the behaviour of those increasingly separate, marginal people, the Jews; anxiety itself, quite apart from guilt, can breed hostility. And simpler still was the anger of those who felt oppressed by moneylenders.[19]

Similarly, Gavin Langmuir, R.I. Moore and Anna Sapir Abulafia have argued that the intellectual revivals of the eleventh and twelfth centuries raised questions for Christians about the central tenets of their faith: Why did God become human? How is the Eucharist Christ's true body and blood? What is the nature and proof of Jesus's Messiahship?[20] Some Christians were aware that Jews asked the same questions. This awareness led to an assimilation of questions and questioners: to ask such questions was, in effect, to 'judaize.'[21] Anxiety stemming from

---

NY: Cornell University Press, 1978); Gavin Langmuir, *History, Religion and Anti-Semitism* (Berkeley: University of California Press, 1990); Anna Sapir Abulafia, *Christians and Jews in the Twelfth-Century Renaissance* (London: Routledge, 1995).

[19] Little, *Religious Poverty and the Profit Economy in Medieval Europe*, 56.

[20] See the studies collected in Gavin I. Langmuir, *Toward a Definition of Antisemitism* (Berkeley: University of California Press,1990); R.I. Moore, *The Creation of a Persecuting Society* (Oxford: Oxford University Press, 1987); Anna Sapir Abulafia, *Christians and Jews in the Twelfth-Century Renaissance* (London: Routledge, 1995).

[21] The kinds of behavior that might be labeled judaizing varied in this period. Jan Ziolkowski indicates the accusation's scope in "Put in No-Man's-Land: Guibert of Nogent's Accusations against a Judaizing and Jew-Supporting Christian," *Jews and Christians in Twelfth-Century Europe*, eds. Michael A. Signer and John Van Engen. (Notre Dame: University of Notre Dame Press, 2001), 110–122. Ziolkowski focuses on social or ritual behavior, but the accusation was also applied to exegetes. The Cistercian John of Forde condemned literal exegesis as "judaizing," for instance; see David N. Bell, "*Agrestis et infatua interpretatio*: The Background and Purpose of John of Forde's Condemnation of Jewish Exegesis," *A Gathering of Friends: The Learning and Spirituality of John of*

Christian self-doubt was projected onto the people who had always
doubted: the unfaithful or imperfectly faithful Jews.

Following the work of Gavin Langmuir and Amos Funkenstein,
Anna Sapir Abulafia has demonstrated that one Christian response to
questions arising from the application of rational inquiry to religious
issues was to assert that to be "reasonable" (to possess the capacity
for reason) was synonymous with the capacity to accept the truth of
Christian faith. Abulafia traces both the ambivalence and the ambigu-
ity surrounding the notion of "reason" in the twelfth century.[22] For some
Christians, notably Peter Abelard, reason was closely linked with the
use of grammatical tools for linguistic analysis, and the use of dialectic to reconcile competing authorities. But Abulafia points persuasively
to another possible definition: reason as it was envisioned by the Stoics, understood as an intuitive ability to grasp the truth. This definition
would ultimately result, she suggests, in a pernicious conclusion: if the
truth was understood preeminently to consist in Christian revelation,
then anyone who rejected that revelation was irrational. If reason is the
hallmark of human nature, rejecters of Christ were less than human,
bestial even. Abulafia has argued that this logic, evinced most tellingly
in the diatribe of Peter the Venerable, *On the inveterate stubbornness of the
Jews* (1147),[23] led to deteriorating relations between Christians and Jews
in the twelfth century. These conditions set the stage for the widespread
violence, extortion, and expulsions that the Jews endured at Christian
hands in the thirteenth century.

There were more nuanced appropriations of *ratio* made by Christians in this period. Anselm of Canterbury, for instance, concluded
that Christian faith could not be proved by reason alone.[24] Consent
to Christian truth must be preceded by the gift of faith in grace and
only subsequently can Christian revelation be perceived in accord with
reason.[25] If the starting point of one's argument is not shared by oth-

---

Forde, eds. Hilary Costello and Christopher Holdsworth, Cistercian Studies Series 161
(Kalamazoo, MI: Cistercian Publications, 1996).

[22] Anna Sapir Abulafia, *Christians and Jews in the Twelfth-Century Renaissance*; see especially Part 1.

[23] *Adversus Iudeorum inveteratam duritiem*, ed. Yvonne Friedman, CCCM 58.

[24] A position which Abulafia and Amos Funkenstein have noted; Abulafia, "Christians Disputing Disbelief: St. Anselm, Gilbert Crispin and Pseudo-Anselm," *Religionge-
spräche im Mittelalter*, ed. Bernard Lewis and Friedrich Niewöhner, Wolfenbüttler Mittelalter-Studien 4 (Wiesbaden, Germany, 1992), 131–148; Funkenstein, "Basic Types of
Christian Anti-Jewish Polemics in the Later Middle Ages," *Viator* 2 (1971): 373–382.

[25] By demonstrating why "by reason and necessity" God became human, the end

ers, however, they will never assent to the outcome. Anselm, Abulafia suggests, perceived that Christian polemics against the Jews would not persuade them. Thus Abulafia contends that the arguments advanced in Anselm's *Cur Deus Homo* were not directed at Jews or Muslims (as *infideles*) but rather to Christians who believed in Christ yet had difficulty accepting the necessity for the Incarnation.[26] She acknowledges, however, that Christian theologians were aware that the doubts expressed in their communities were similar to those expressed by Jews, with whom they had increasing contact.[27]

As attractive as Abulafia's thesis is, it does not take into account many of the events, both social and intellectual, of the later twelfth century.[28] Little and Langmuir, on the other hand, provide explanatory theories of historical events that depend heavily on psychological theory (especially the Freudian concept of projection) and which attempt to offer globally applicable explanations for the deterioration in relations between Christians and Jews.[29] More recent scholarship, such as

---

result of Anselm's proof confirmed the veracity of scriptural revelation. His interlocutor Boso affirms: "... I think whatever is contained in the New and Old Testaments has been proved by the solution of the one question we have put forward. For you prove that God was necessarily made Man ... by reason alone. And the God-Man himself establishes the New Testament and proves the truth of the Old. Therefore, just as we must confess his own truthfulness, so no one can refuse to confess the truthfulness of everything that is contained in them both." *Why God Became Man* 2:22, trans. Eugene R. Fairweather, *A Scholastic Miscellany: Anselm to Ockham* (New York: Macmillan, 1956), 183.

[26] Abulafia, "Christians Disputing Disbelief," 131–135, *pace* R.W. Southern, *Saint Anselm: A Portrait in a Landscape* (Cambridge: Cambridge University Press, 1990), 197–202.

[27] Jeremy Cohen disagrees with Abulafia's analysis of the *Cur Deus Homo*, contending instead that the Jews may well have been Anselm's imagined disputants. See *Living Letters of the Law*, 175–179.

[28] In a 1996 essay, Abulafia acknowledged that her area of specialization is the period from 1100 through 1150; "Twelfth-Century Renaissance Theology and the Jews," *From Witness to Witchcraft: Jews and Judaism in Medieval Christian Thought*, ed. Jeremy Cohen (Wiesbaden: Harrassowitz, 1996), 127. This acknowledgement did not prevent her from arguing that Peter the Venerable's tract, by construing the Jews as bestial, constituted the intellectual basis for anti-Jewish violence in the years that follow. More recently she has turned her attention to Christian authors in the latter part of the twelfth century, as in "Twelfth-Century Christian Expectations of Jewish Conversion: A Case Study of Peter of Blois," *Aschkenas: Zeitschrift für Geschichte und Kultur der Juden* 8 (1998): 45–70.

[29] In Langmuir's case, his taxonomy of Christian doubt (explained under various rubrics, such as "rational," "non-rational," and "irrational," is built from local, not global, examples and is susceptible to refinement. For the development of the taxonomy, see *History, Religion and Anti-Semitism* (Berkeley: University of California Press, 1990).

that of David Nirenberg, has challenged these theories on the basis of
local examples and has eschewed the development and application of
global explanations.[30] Nirenberg has suggested that the global theories
of Little, Langmuir, R.I. Moore and others have been motivated by
a present need to structure the past intelligibly—specifically, a need
to understand the Shoah in terms of European history.[31] A historical
account of medieval anti-Judaism thus oriented

> means that events are read less within their local contexts than according
> to a teleology leading, more or less explicitly, to the Holocaust. Similarly,
> instead of emphasizing local or even individual opinions about minori-
> ties, they focus on collective images, representations, and stereotypes of
> the "other." The actions of groups or individuals are ignored in favor of
> structures of thought that are believed to govern those actions.[32]

In contrast to the "teleological narratives" constructed by other medieval historians, Nirenberg frames his investigations more narrowly,
focusing chiefly on southern France and northern Spain in the early
fourteenth century. He has concluded that global theories of the subconscious life of medieval Christians are not sustained by close readings of encounters between Jews and Christians in specific social, political, and religious contexts.[33] He emphasizes instead the extent to which
local communities or individuals made use of "inherited discourse[s]
about minorities" to achieve complex ends. Violence against Jews, in

---

[30] He also rejects the notion of "irrationality" as an explanation for Christian
[mis]behavior. *Communities of Violence* (Princeton, NJ: Princeton University Press, 1996).

[31] Langmuir describes his work as being a direct response to the Shoah; see "Introduction," *Toward a Definition of Anti-Semitism* (Berkeley: University of California Press,
1990).

[32] In addition to challenging the teleological narratives of earlier medievalists, Nirenberg also rejects various "structuralist" approaches to "the historiography of persecution," such as an emphasis on the formation of a persecuting discourse considered
without regard to the "actions of groups or individuals." Nirenberg, *Communities of Violence*, 5.

[33] Kathleen Biddick contests the validity of Nirenberg's approach. In an essay on the
impact of Edward Said's *Orientalism*, she argues that Nirenberg's and other medievalists'
"... chief metahistorical claim (not always announced) relies on their devotion to local
context as a way of exiting from the discursive problems of representation posed by
Orientalism." Of Nirenberg specifically she writes: "Nirenberg uses the 'local' as the
vehicle with which to transpose the study of inter- and intra-religious violence from
the irrational to the rational register. His move, however, cannot reconceptualize the
problem of anti-Semitism *and* Orientalism, since their fabrications from the twelfth
century have relied precisely on who got to draw and redraw the line between what
counts as rational and what counts as irrational." "Coming out of Exile: Dante on the
Orient[alism] Express," *American Historical Review* (October 2000): 1239–1240.

his view, was not necessarily the irrational action of mobs conditioned by subconsciously imbibed "structures of thought" but rather the outgrowth of strategic decisions to use that discourse to achieve political or economic gain.[34] In sum, Nirenberg argues that when assessing the outbreak of violence against Jews and other despised medieval minorities, "context matters."[35]

Nirenberg deals with a different time period and region than those discussed in this book; similarly, he deals with different phenomena, chiefly the social, political, and economic underpinnings of violent outbreaks against Jews and others. But his central point is instructive in a twelfth-century context: "... any inherited [persecuting] discourse about minorities acquired force only when people chose to find it meaningful and useful, and was closely shaped by these choices. Briefly, discourse and agency gain meaning only in relation to each other."[36] This chapter will demonstrate that Herbert of Bosham's example further undermines the notion of monolithic persecuting discourse against the Jews. The discourses which did arise, furthermore, can be more plausibly ascribed to a complex of forces, rather than to a teleological narrative imposed by latter-day historians. The *ways* in which Christians experienced ambivalence as a result of their contacts with Jews were doubtless as many and varied as the contacts themselves.[37] Well into the latter part of the twelfth century, some cordial contact between Jews and Christians at all levels of society was possible—even if its likelihood was diminishing.[38] Still, Nirenberg's findings refine but do not

---

[34] "The more we restore to those outbreaks of violence their own particularities, the less easy it is to assimilate them to our own concerns, as homogeneity and teleology are replaced by difference and contingency." Nirenberg, 7.

[35] Nirenberg, 51.

[36] Nirenberg, 6. His emphasis on the relationship of discourse and human agency recalls Gabrielle Spiegel's formulation of "the social logic of the text," made in response to postmodernism and the "linguistic turn" in historical studies. See "History, Historicism, and the Social Logic of the Text," *Speculum* 65 (1990): 59–86.

[37] The function of ambivalence in Christians' encounters with Jews is discussed below.

[38] Robin Mundill makes this point: "Early in the thirteenth century, lay and clerical entrepreneurs who gained land by paying off Jewish debts clearly did not have troubled consciences about dealing with Jews. On the other hand the debtors who lost their land were certainly troubled. Their indebtedness and loss caused resentment and fuelled hatred for the Jew and possibly even for their new landlord. However, there must also have been a group of debtors of whom little is known, who managed to repay their debts and who might well have actually gained from transacting business with Jewish financiers. Thus, there were many Christians who were directly or indirectly involved with Jewish finance and who naturally had varying attitudes towards the Jews." Robin

negate the foundational insights of Little, Langmuir, and others. The continuing presence of Jews in Western Europe's cities and towns was an ongoing witness against the presuppositions of Christian universalism. And, ironically, after Jews were expelled from Europe in the thirteenth through the fifteenth centuries, they remained as literary tropes or *figurae* to whom Christian anxieties were attached. The enduring function of the "virtual Jew" suggests that "persecuting discourse" has a life of its own, independent of actual contact with Jews.[39]

A final explanatory theory of particular relevance to theological discussions, and whose global application is more readily tested in exegetical and polemical works, is advanced by Jeremy Cohen in *The Friars and the Jews* (1982) and since refined a later book, *Living Letters of the Law* (1999). Cohen endeavors to explain how and why the basis of Christian toleration of Jews in the Latin West, promulgated by Augustine and made church policy by Pope Gregory the Great (ca. 540–604), eroded in the thirteenth century. A crucial aspect of Augustine's position, Cohen maintains, was his belief that the Jews *qua* Jews remained as they were in the Hebrew Bible. Augustine argued that the people of the Old Covenant had chosen to ignore the New Promise; they were "stationary in useless antiquity." But their very nature as static representatives of biblical Israel rendered the Jews useful to medieval Christians eager to understand the Old Testament. As enactors of 'living history,' the Jews performed a useful explanatory function. Cohen argues that this rationale was sorely tested in the twelfth century by a series of changes. In the course of a general trend of increasing population and prosperity which encouraged the growth of urban centers, more Christians came into contact with Jews in cities and towns, an event which had theological as well as social consequences.

The social and intellectual developments that spurred twelfth-century Christians to articulate their faith in new paradigms have been charted by Richard Southern, Beryl Smalley, M.-D. Chenu, and others. Recapitulating these scholars' views, Cohen has observed:

R. Mundill, *England's Jewish Solution: Experiment and Expulsion, 1262–1290* (Cambridge: Cambridge University Press, 1998), 45. See also Herbert's reports of his contact with his interlocutor, discussed in Chapter 5.

[39] Sylvia Tomasch argues in her essay, "Postcolonial Chaucer and the Virtual Jew" that England's expulsion of Jews in 1290 and the lingering, literary, "virtual" Jew helps to facilitate "unremitting replay of perpetual Jewish crimes by containing Jews in an eternal, orientalized present," 248. *The Postcolonial Middle Ages*, ed. Jeffrey Jerome Cohen (New York: Palgrave, 2000), 243–260.

Those who cultivated Christian spirituality no longer confined themselves to the monastery but turned directly to the natural world, seeking
to understand it, to rationalize it, and to incorporate all of its facets into
the totality of Christian life. The rebellion against patristic methodology,
the insistence on a more scientific explication of texts, the demand that
religious ideas bespeak the *realia* of history—all these contributed to a
renewed interest in and the greater influence of Jewish books in twelfth-
century Christendom.[40]

Having turned outward, twelfth-century Christians' perspectives were
considerably altered by encounters with non-believers who did not
share their view of the principles that organized the world around
them. One vehicle for discovery was the ever-increasing recovery of
texts from classical antiquity, which testified to the existence of pagan
learning whose tenets, especially in the disciplines of the *artes*, challenged Christians to attain greater intellectual sophistication. Another
vehicle was the encounter with Islam, facilitated by the Moslem hegemony in most of Iberia. The encounter with Jews, especially in the
developing cities of northern Europe, represented a particularly pressing challenge.

Cohen has identified another aspect of twelfth-century changes in
Christian self-perception and perception of others.[41] Increased interaction between Christians and Jews in the commercial realm, as well as in
the world of biblical studies, yielded disquieting information for Christians. They discovered that the Jews had not stood still; they were not
identical to biblical Israel. Rather, the Jews were discovered to have a
battery of postbiblical literature—Mishnah, Talmud, *midrashim, tosafot*—
with which they lived out the commandments of the Torah, interpreted
Scripture, and sustained their communities of faith in exile.[42]

From the writings of Petrus Alfonsi, a Jewish apostate who converted
to Christianity in Spain around 1100, Christians could learn about the
postbiblical Jewish literature that sustained the Jews in their 'disbelief.'[43]

---

[40] Jeremy Cohen, "Scholarship and Intolerance in the Medieval Academy: The
Study and Evaluation of Judaism in European Christendom," *American Historical Review*
91 (1986): 596.

[41] Cohen's examination of this process began in *The Friars and the Jews* (Ithaca:
Cornell University Press, 1982), continues in his essay "Scholarship and Intolerance
…" and receives a sustained treatment in *Living Letters of the Law* (Berkeley: University of
California Press, 1999).

[42] Jacob Katz, *Exclusiveness and Tolerance: Studies in Jewish-Gentile Relations in Medieval
and Modern Times* (West Orange, N.J.: Behrman House, 1961).

[43] John Tolan, *Petrus Alfonsi and his Medieval Readers* (Gainesville: University Press of

As such, the Talmud was regarded as an impediment to the Jews'
eventual conversion. The Talmud was also criticized for occasional
statements deemed blasphemous by Christians. Cohen argues that the
discovery that the Jews clung to more than the Torah disrupted the
traditional Augustinian economy. Now the Jews could not only be
deemed blind or ignorant, but stubborn as well: they preferred the
texts of their perverse traditions, Christians claimed, to the open and
clear testimonies of Scripture. This stubbornness could be blamed on
the Jews themselves and not on God's mysterious providence. Peter the
Venerable's tractate against the Jews articulated this view; it relied on
Petrus Alfonsi's *Dialogi contra Iudaeos* for its data on the Talmud.

Amos Funkenstein, whose foundational article stimulated the study
of genres of medieval Christian polemic against Judaism, argued that
Peter the Venerable thereby launched a downward spiral in Christianity's regard for Judaism in the mid-twelfth century.[44] Funkenstein and
others have based their contention on two aspects of Peter's teaching.[45] The first is his condemnation of Jewish postbiblical literature,
which laid the groundwork for later Christian accusations that the Jews
were 'heretics' who had deserted Scripture in favor of their own writings. The second aspect, accented especially by Anna Sapir Abulafia,
is Peter's insistence that possessing faith in Christian teaching is equivalent to possessing reason—a position that renders all unbelievers as
irrational and less than human. Advocates of Peter the Venerable's pivotal role have argued that from around 1150 onward, the noose of intolerance tightened around the necks of Jews in Christian Europe. Peter's
position has been viewed as having led more or less directly to the
condemnations and burnings of the Talmud in Paris in 1240 and in
Barcelona in 1263, to the branding of Jews as unfit citizens of a Christian state, and to their expulsion from England in 1290 and repeated
expulsions from portions of France beginning in 1189.

By contrast, Cohen argues Peter the Venerable cannot be regarded
as the beginning of the end of Christian toleration of Judaism in the
medieval West.[46] Cohen judges that the Christian encounter with Jew-

---

Florida, 1993) provides a discussion of Alfonsi's theological and scientific works and an
analysis of the distribution of manuscripts.

[44] Amos Funkenstein, "Basic Types of Christian Anti-Jewish Polemic in the Later
Middle Ages," *Viator* 2:373–382. See now his *Perceptions of Jewish History* (Berkeley:
University of California Press, 1993), 173–201.

[45] For example, Anna Sapir Abulafia.

[46] *Living Letters of the Law*, 261–265. Gavin Langmuir also notes that Peter the Vener-

ish postbiblical traditions led to an eventual rejection of Augustine's position that the Jews should enjoy at least some measure of tolerance in the West. Peter the Venerable, in Cohen's assessment, represents a symptomatic response to a cluster of issues that complicated twelfth-century Christian apprehensions of (and about) Judaism. The problem with Funkenstein's thesis regarding Peter as a cause of increased Christian hostility toward Jews is that, as Cohen has pointed out, Peter's treatise against the Jews was not widely distributed.[47] While the text from which he drew most of his knowledge of the Talmud, the *Dialogi contra Iudaeos* of Petrus Alfonsi, enjoyed wide circulation (seventy-nine copies of the manuscript are extant), other Christian scholars in the twelfth century seem not to have made the same sort of use of it—or the use they made of it did not lead to a mass movement that condemned Jewish postbiblical literature. Furthermore, despite the lack of evidence for Funkenstein's assertion that Peter the Venerable's tract engendered hostility against the Jews, present-day scholars of the polemics that arose from the Jewish and Christian encounter in the twelfth century tend to pass over in silence the polemical treatises of the second half of that century. Did those treatises, like Peter's, condemn the Jews as bestial? No evidence has been advanced to show that they have; in other words, there is no demonstrable textual history to support Peter's influence. In the absence of a textual genealogy, Funkenstein causally linked the invective of Peter the Venerable's tract to events on the popular front, such as the blood libels which began to arise in England and northern Europe starting around 1140 or the violence associated with the second Crusade.[48]

The debate over Peter the Venerable's influence once again raises questions regarding the applicability of a global or general explanation for Christian hostility toward Jews. Rather than linking Peter's text causally to events of "popular" violence against the Jews, the text and

---

able's actual influence was comparatively minor; Langmuir's discussion of Peter focuses on how he reacted to challenges to his triumphalist view of Christianity; "Peter the Venerable: Defense Against Doubts," *Toward a Definition of Anti-Semitism* (Berkeley: University of California Press, 1990), 197–208.

[47] Yvonne Friedman, who edited Peter's diatribe for the *Corpus Christianorum*, noted that only four manuscript copies of the work survive, indicating the book's limited circulation; "Introduction," *Adversus Iudeorum inveteratam duritiem*, CCCM 58, xxviii.

[48] Gavin Langmuir similarly relates Peter's "irrational hatred" of the Jews to subsequent outbreaks of "indisputably irrational fantasies about Jews" in "Peter the Venerable: Defense against Doubts," *Toward a Definition of Anti-Semitism*, 197–208.

the events can be better described as related elements in the same discursive field which tried to uphold Christian dominance even as it managed Christian anxieties prompted by vexing challenges. Jews, too, participated in that discursive field through their own exegetical works, polemics, and attempts at political interventions. Long before Peter's mid-century encounter with the Talmud, the Jews of northern Europe had been terrorized by Christian armies of the First Crusade in 1096. The first accusation of ritual murder was made against the Jews of Norwich in 1144. In other words, physical violence against the Jews began well before the supposed intellectual basis for intolerance was fully in place. Indeed, Bernard of Clairvaux tried to stem the tide of attacks on Jews in France and the Rhineland in the early months of the Second Crusade (1147) by using the traditional Augustinian argument in favor of their preservation.[49] By contrast, the First Crusaders' massacres of Jews in the cities along the Rhine suggests tolerance may have owed little to the residual effects of Augustine's unofficial edict.[50] In Cohen's revised and expanded study of the reception of the Augustinian doctrine of witness and its eventual rejection, he emphasizes the "graduality" of its displacement:

> All of these developments had the potential for "hollowing out" [Anna Sapir Abulafia's term] the Augustinian doctrine of Jewish witness, with its fundamental maxim of "Slay them not." Yet these seeds planted at the beginning of the twelfth century, at times haphazardly and unwittingly, germinated and bore fruit slowly. One cannot overemphasize the graduality of this process. While some seemed to move farther away from Augustinian teaching, others appeared to reaffirm it quite strenuously. But the rising and sharpening interest in the Jew proved irreversible, especially as contact between Christendom and the non-Christian world increased.[51]

---

[49] Cohen, *Living Letters of the Law*. See also Yvonne Friedman, "An Anatomy of Anti-Semitism: Peter the Venerable's Letter to Louis VII, King of France (1146)," *Bar-Ilan Studies in History*, ed. Pinhas Artzi (Ramat-Gan [Israel]: Bar-Ilan University Press, 1978), 87–102.

[50] Cohen argues, however, that, "One surely ought not to behold in the crusaders' [of 1096] anti-Jewish violence a conscious repudiation of the Augustinian doctrine of Jewish witness or a reversal in medieval Jewish policy that marked the 'beginning of the end' for the Jews of the Middle Ages," on the grounds that Jews in northern Europe in the twelfth and thirteenth centuries flourished and prospered together with the general population. He argues instead that the Crusaders' attacks "awakened Christian society to the anomaly of the Jews' position: enemies / killers of Christ whose lives and errant religion God had protected for the greater good of Christendom." *Living Letters of the Law*, 151.

[51] Cohen, *Living Letters of the Law*, 217–218.

Jeremy Cohen's emphasis on the gradual nature of changes that affected the status of Jews of medieval Europe usefully refines other, more schematized accounts derived from Christian polemical literature. He amply illustrates the complexity of the position of 'the Jew' as a token in Christian theology and self-understanding. As a 'tool to think with,' Cohen's "hermeneutical Jew," constructed by Christian polemics, served multiple purposes—sometimes positive but more consistently negative. By examining Christian writers of the early and medieval periods, Cohen also demonstrates that attitudes toward Judaism must be accounted for, at least in part, in terms of a theologian's overall *oeuvre*. Cohen notes:

> With his roots at the very core of its received doctrine and its worldview, medieval Christianity's hermeneutically crafted Jew could assume a variety of appearances; relative measures of harshness and moderation in these representations fluctuated widely over time; not even in the works of an individual theologian can one always expect to find a perfect logic and consistency.[52]

In its latest iteration, Cohen's account of the role of Judaism constructed by medieval Christianity is elegantly articulated. He demonstrates convincingly that charting the evolution, and devolution, of Augustine's doctrine of Jewish witness provides a critical measure of "prevailing Christian constructions of Jews" at given times and places.[53] But even his careful analysis has until recently been limited to a familiar canon of Christian anti-Jewish polemic. In *Living Letters of the Law*, he examined neither exegetical material in general, nor polemical works from the second half of the twelfth century. Cohen's account of the lacunae, elisions, and seeming contradictions in the Christian narrative of Judaism could, in consultation with these materials, be argued with even greater precision. In fact, in an recent essay examining Honorius Augustodunesis' commentary on the Song of Songs, Cohen himself has demonstrated that Christian exegetical works sometimes defy Christianity's "conventional wisdom" on the status of Jews and Judaism. He concludes:

> For all of its scholastic detachment and imaginative allegorical symbolism, Honorius's *Expositio* on the Song of Songs belongs to the real world of interaction between medieval Christians and Jews—a world whose nuances, complexities, and ambivalences militate against the neat gener-

---

[52] Cohen, *Living Letters of the Law*, 392.
[53] Cohen, *Living Letters of the Law*, 16.

alizations of the retrospective historian, a world whose vitality demands our appreciation measure for measure, text by text, image by image.[54]

By focusing on polemical literature, Funkenstein and Cohen, and their critics and adherents, have largely disregarded the exegetical literature of the period. In so doing, they have overlooked a key source for elaborating the narrative of medieval Jewish-Christian relations. Whether Christian or Jewish, twelfth-century biblical commentaries are saturated with assertions of truth-claims established by authority, reason, or both. Similarly, exegesis was a major constituent of interreligious polemic in the twelfth century which centered on the production, analysis, or refutation of scriptural *testimonia*. Overlooking the history of Jews' and Christians' "encounter around the Bible," as Gilbert Dahan called it, constitutes a major lacuna in any global narrative of the wider encounter between people of the two faiths.[55] The history of exegesis further complicates the attempt to construct a global narrative of Christians' reactions to Judaism—indeed, it may point the way to a new narrative. The exegetes and the polemicists may not have been identical; they seem not to have been for the most part.[56] But they lived in the same small world, united by interest, education, and personal ties. Elucidating the motives and *modi operandi* of twelfth-century exegetes, especially those interested in the "literal" meaning of the scriptural text and in the Hebrew language, may temper the perception of a Christian world where genres of literature (exegesis, polemic) and their authors can be clearly separated into distinct camps. In his volume *Les intellectuels chrétiens et les Juifs au Moyen Âge*, Gilbert Dahan has delineated the scope of the problem facing contemporary historians of the medieval encounter:

> One will not be surprised to see our course connected around these two axes: encounter and confrontation. The result of this survey will aspire to gauge in its entirety the reflection of the intellectuals: we will ask whether

---

[54] Jeremy Cohen, "*Synogoga conversa*: Honorius Augustodunesis, the Song of Songs, and Christianity's 'Eschatological Jew,'" *Speculum* 79 (2004): 309–340; 340.

[55] Gilbert Dahan, "Juifs et Chrétiens en Occident Médiéval: La Rencontre autour de la Bible (XIIe–XIVe Siècles)," *Revue de Synthèse* 4:1 (1989): 3–31.

[56] Rupert of Deutz and Peter Abelard are two exceptions to this rule. But even Abelard's disputation among a Jew, a Christian, and a Philosopher was not widely circulated (three manuscripts, according to Tolan, 98–99). It is not clear why—besides Abelard's fame—that that treatise rates much importance as an indicia of Christian attitudes, e.g., the importance accorded it in Jeremy Cohen's *Living Letters of the Law*.

they had had an awareness of this apparent contradiction, whether they were able to resolve it, and what place this question occupied among them.[57]

While modern scholarly study of medieval Christian hebraism and its exponents has tended to emphasize the possibilities for irenic encounter between Christians and Jews, the texts produced by Herbert of Bosham and the Victorines Hugh and Andrew testify to the complex nature of the contradiction cited by Dahan. Some of the same intellectuals who encountered Jews around the Bible also engaged in confrontation with their interlocutors. Sometimes that confrontation spilled over into self-questioning, or into conflict within the Christian intellectual community.[58] The varying aspects of this confrontation raise questions: how could a laudable interest in the Hebrew language and Jewish exegesis, the better to establish the witness of the Jews to Christian truth, be distinguished from heretical judaizing? Why did such contradictory responses arise within the same community and sometimes within the same person?

One way to capture the complex responses of Christian exegetes who oscillated between the axes of encounter and confrontation would be categorize them with Jeremy Cohen's "renaissance men and their dreams." Writing in reference to Peter Abelard, Hermannus *quondam Judaeus*, and Alan of Lille, Cohen argues: "Twelfth-century Christendom produced countless visions of personal religious fulfillment and the most expeditious route for achieving it; these too contributed to

---

[57] "On ne sera pas surpris de voir notre demarche s'articuler autour de ces deux axes: la rencontre, l'affrontement. L'aboutissement de cet examen visera à jauger dans son ensemble la réflexion des intellectuels: nous nous demanderons s'ils ont eu conscience de cette apparente contradiction, comment ils ont pu la résoudre et quelle place occupe chez eux cette question." *Les intellectuels chrétiens et les Juifs au Moyen Âge*, (Paris: Cerf, 1990), 13. At the end of his monumental study, Dahan admits that this contradiction remains largely unresolved. He describes the attitudes of Christian theologians toward Jews as "bi-polar," noting, "On ne sera pas surpris non plus que chez certains—voire chez la plupart—des penseurs, cette bipolarité ait abouti à une vue en quelque sorte schizophrénique des juifs: au juif quotidien et réel, avec qui l'on discute volontiers de Bible ou de science, se superpose ce que nous avons appelé le 'juif théologique,' un juif irréel, en qui viennent se mêler, s'additioner divers stéréotypes—nés d'abord de la réflexion des théologiens." 585.

[58] In the first case, Herbert himself may be the best example, as will be shown. In the second case, the controversy among the Victorines which resulted in Richard's *De Emmanuele* is the epitome. John of Forde is another example (see David N. Bell, "*Agrestis et infatua interpretatio*: The Background and Purpose of John of Forde's Condemnation of Jewish Exegesis"), as is Walter of Saint Victor's *Four Labyrinths of France* (*Contra quattuor labyrinthos franciae*), excerpts of which are printed in PL 199.

the evolving Christian idea of the Jew."[59] Cohen links Abelard, Herman, and Alan because each "dreamed" his way to a new perspective on Judaism; he unites them around the theme of religious exploration sanctioned by subconscious speculation and dreaming.[60] If personal religious fulfillment is a valid category within which Christian responses to Judaism can be analyzed, then it could reasonably include the no less personal path espoused by the Victorines, whose works Cohen does not examine in this context. Hugh of Saint Victor's educational program is especially pertinent: humans make progress toward God by restoring God's image within. Alienation from God is the result of lost wisdom; its remedy is the accumulation of knowledge, infused by the gift of God's grace. Mastery of the liberal arts prepares the student-pilgrim for study of Scripture, which in turn leads to the practice of virtue, then contemplation of the divine.[61] Hugh elevated the study of history to a new dignity because the Incarnation had imbued history with a saving purpose. In a seminal article on Hugh of Saint Victor's theology of history, Grover A. Zinn distilled Hugh's perspective:

> Given the actual situation of man's present existence, qualified by the fact of sin and its fruits, it is only through history that man can begin to overcome the temporality, finitude, instability, and death-ward movement of life. As the result of this conviction, Hugh's theology unites in an intimate manner that which is most inward, the renewal of the *imago dei* at the innermost core of the human person, and that which is preeminently outer, namely the succession of deeds done in time (*ordo rerum gestarum*) which comprises the divine "work of restoration."[62]

---

[59] *Living Letters of the Law*, 270.

[60] None of these figures was especially noted for his exegesis and Cohen examines only their ostensibly polemical works. The gap between Herman's autobiographical tale and Alain of Lille's *De fide catholica* is probably about thirty years.

[61] The *locus classicus* for this scheme is Hugh of Saint Victor's *Didascalicon*. Latin edition by C.H. Buttimer, *Hugonis de Sancto Victore Didascalicon de studio legendi* (Washington: Catholic University Press, 1939); English translation by Jerome Taylor, *The Didascalicon of Hugh of St. Victor: A Medieval Guide to the Arts* (New York: Columbia University Press, 1961, repr. 1991). J.W.M. Van Zwieten discusses how Hugh's individual treatises on grammar and geometry can be seen as integral to his overall pedagogical goals in "Scientific and Spiritual Culture in Hugh of St Victor," *Centres of Learning: Learning and Location in Pre-Modern Europe and the Near East* (Leiden: Brill, 1995), 177–186.

[62] Grover A. Zinn, "*Historia fundamentum est*: The role of history in the contemplative life according to Hugh of St. Victor," *Contemporary Reflections on the Medieval Christian Tradition: Essays in Honor of Ray C. Petry*, ed. George H. Shriver (Durham, NC: Duke University Press, 1974),136.

A thorough study of Scripture, grounded in world history, was propaedeutic for fruitful meditation on the nature of God's saving work
done in time, both before and after the birth of Jesus Christ.[63] This
meditation issued in the restoration of the inmost person. Victorine
exegetical works thus were directed to a personal, spiritual end. As
Beryl Smalley remarked in *The Study of the Bible in the Middle Ages*,
"[Hugh's] great service to exegesis was to lay more stress on the literal interpretation *relatively* to the spiritual, and to develop the sources
for it."[64] Hugh extended and nuanced the Augustinian perspective on
Judaism and its role as pedagogue to Christianity. Hugh and his student
Andrew of Saint Victor also followed self-consciously in the footsteps
of Jerome, turning to the Jews among their contemporaries in order
to secure the text of Scripture, from its foundation up, as the basis of
a thoroughly Christian *paideia*. The Victorines united the impulses of
Augustine and Jerome in a unified study of Scripture's literal sense (*littera*) within its narrative context (*historia*). The study of history laid the
foundation for contemplation, because an appreciation for the sacred
text's "first meaning" prepared the student to understanding spiritual
allegories derived from Scripture.[65] Moreover, a grasp of the literal and
figurative teachings of the Bible were the prerequisites to grasping (and
being grasped by) the tropological or moral sense of Scripture, which
would result in a saving transformation of the human person.

As Marie-Dominique Chenu has pointed out, Hugh's aim, in his
didactic as well as his exegetical works, was to supply the data which
would illuminate history as an "articulated continuity," intelligible to
the informed observer and reflective of "the initiatives of God within
the time of mankind."[66] In other words, the Victorines' interest in the

---

[63] Hugh's didactic works included the *Chronicon*, a tabular chronicle of all known
human history which provided the context for scriptural events. Grover Zinn notes
that English interest in the *Chronicon* was strong; Hugh's work was adapted by Ralph
of Diceto in his *Abbreviationes chronicorum*. As Zinn points out, Ralph (d. 1202) was dean
of Saint Paul's, to which the only known copy of Herbert of Bosham's manuscript was
donated in 1254. See Grover A. Zinn, "The Influence of Hugh of St. Victor's *Chronicon*
on the *Abbreviationes chronicorum* by Ralph of Diceto," *Speculum* 52 (1977): 38–61.

[64] *SBMA*, 102. The emphasis is Smalley's.

[65] Hugh also believed that mastery of the literal sense was needed before a student
moved to higher levels of study; in part it acted as a brake on unbridled allegorization.
See *Didascalicon*, 6.3.

[66] Marie-Dominique Chenu, "Theology and the New Awareness of History," *Nature,
Man and Society in the Twelfth Century*, trans. Jerome Taylor and Lester K. Little (Toronto:
Medieval Academy Reprints for Teaching, 1997), 168, on Hugh's emphasis on the *series
narrationis*.

historical narrative of Scripture was not motivated solely by 'scientific' scholarship.[67] Hugh understood the historical sense of Scripture, as had Augustine, as a fundamental part of the economy of salvation. In history's 'prophecy of events,' God's plans for human salvation were worked out, however obscurely. In the interests of clarifying Scripture's historical narrative, Hugh and Andrew both explored unfamiliar territories in their biblical commentaries. They studied the historical books of the Hebrew Bible. Andrew wrote commentaries on the prophets, long-neglected by Christian exegetes. As Grover A. Zinn has demonstrated, Hugh proposed a teleological scheme of history which describes the progress of humanity toward redemption:

> Man must know himself as ignorant, estranged, distracted and divided. Scripture speaks to him of this, and also offers the way of healing and restoration. *History is the new mode of divine presence.* The work of creation, by virtue of which man once beheld his Maker within and perceived his power, wisdom and goodness without, is no longer capable of manifesting the divine presence. A new approach is necessary and it is found in the works of restoration—a series of events in time with historical reality which also, because of their transcendent reference, offer a point of mediation with the divine.[68]

The very belief that God acts in history—acted in the Exodus, acted at the Resurrection, and will act at the end of days—was a feature of what Chenu has called the "evangelical awakening" of the twelfth century. Not only did Christians in this era reawaken to the idealism of the primitive church, they also awakened to a renewed sense of the ultimate purpose, responsibility, and dignity of human actions. For if God acts in history, and humans are also actors therein, then surely our actions—at least those made in response to God's self-offering—matter. Sorting out the layers of history and the scope of human action proper to each was crucial to charting the unfolding eschatological trajectory.[69]

---

[67] See also the discussion of Hugh of Saint Victor by Henri de Lubac, "Hugues de St. Victor," *Exégèse Médiévale* II.1 (Paris: Aubier, 1961), 287–301. For a discussion of the conflicting evaluations of the Victorines taken by de Lubac and Smalley, in particular Smalley's claim that they were scientific exegetes, see Deborah L. Goodwin, "Herbert of Bosham and the Horizons of Twelfth-Century Exegesis," *Traditio* 68 (2003): 133–173.

[68] Grover A. Zinn, "*Historia fundamentum est* ...," 158. Emphasis added.

[69] Writing on the immensely popular "narrative" history of the Bible, Peter Comestor's *Historia Scholastica*, Chenu commented: "[Comestor's] history sanctioned and extended the current usage, in the schools and in preaching, of the historical-literal method of Saint-Victor; it was to become, along with the *Sentences* (but without provoking controversy as Peter Lombard's work had done) one of the basic books of the

Hugh of Saint Victor's educational program and his theory of history typically have been celebrated for their optimistic vision of human redemption, made possible by God's mighty works enacted upon the world's stage.[70] His interest in the Hebrew language and Jewish exegesis similarly has been cast as a positive aspect of his work, deriving from a generously universal view. Hugh's vision makes room for the Jews; like Augustine, he emphasized (as others had not) the unique significance of Jewish history in Christian faith.[71] In his sketch of world history, Hugh displaced a listing of secular rulers in favor of counting down the years through the succession of Jewish High Priests.[72] His monumental *De Sacramentis* argues forcefully for the validity of Jewish rituals as salvific in their day; God has never denied the means of grace to faithful people, and has only increased that means through the Incarnation.[73] Hugh regarded the saving work of Jesus Christ's birth, death, and resurrection as a transhistorical phenomenon. Human history before and after the Incarnation is replete with evidence of God's salvific will for humanity in the form of sacraments appropriate to every age. In his *De Sacramentis*, Hugh adopted the epochal scheme found in Paul's Letter to the Romans and in Augustine's *Enchiridion*, chapter 118. Humans have lived in three conditions: under nature, under law, and under grace. All people, of whatever epoch, who acknowledged the one, true Creator God were united in the household (*familia*) of Christ, soldiers (*milites*) in his war against the Devil.[74] This household, according to Hugh, included pagans from the epoch of natural law, Jews from the age of the writ-

---

century. ... The biblical reform of the Victorines thus lent a scientific support to the evangelical movement. It furnished the elements for a transition from the monastic interpretation of the Bible (in the *collatio*, collection and comparison of texts) to the scriptural theology of the mendicants (in the *lectio*, sytematic explication of the masters)." Chenu, "The Evangelical Awakening," *Nature, Man and Society in the Twelfth Century*, 250.

[70] See especially Richard W. Southern, "Presidential Address: Aspects of the European Tradition of Historical Writing 2: Hugh of St Victor and the Idea of Historical Development," *Transactions of the Royal Historical Society* 21 (1971): 149–179.

[71] On this topic generally, see Rebecca Moore, *Jews and Christians in the Life and Thought of Hugh of St. Victor*, University of South Florida Studies in the History of Judaism, #138 (Atlanta: Scholars Press, 1998).

[72] In his *Chronicon*; see William M. Green, "Hugo of St.-Victor: *De Tribus Maximis Circumstantiis Gestorum*," *Speculum* 18 (1943): 484–493 and Grover A. Zinn, "The Influence of Hugh of St. Victor's *Chronicon* on the *Abbreviationes chronicorum* by Ralph of Diceto," *Speculum* 52 (1977): 38–61.

[73] *De Sacramentis*, 1.8.11; 1.12.1–6.

[74] *De Sacramentis*, Prologue, PL 176:183; 1.8.12, PL 176:312.

ten law, and Christians. Hugh maintained that the sacraments of every epoch were sufficient thereunto—God had never failed to provide the means of restoration to believers. Ancient Israel's ritual practices, therefore, were true sacraments in Hugh's opinion, not shadows as Augustine had held.[75] But with the coming of Christ, the sacraments of the former age were vitiated. The destruction of the Temple in 70 CE testified to the obsolescence of Israel's cult. From that point onward, Hugh relegated Judaism to useless antiquity, as Augustine had before him. The relevance of Israel's history ended with the Temple. In her study of Hugh of Saint Victor and Judaism, Rebecca Moore points to the irony of Hugh's situation: "Hugh's sacramental vision results in a paradox. On the one hand, he turns to living Jews in order to understand the Bible so that he can write a theology of history. On the other, his history excludes the very people who help him, in part, to write his theology."[76]

The paradox identified by Moore suggests that Hugh's theology of history can be seen as more than an element in an individual, interior restoration of the divine image.[77] Rather, his comprehensive educational and theological system can be set beside other twelfth-century intellectual projects that imposed order and structure on various bodies of knowledge, the better to understand, rationalize, and "incorporate all its facets into the totality of Christian life," as Jeremy Cohen has observed.[78] As significant as Hugh's program might have been for an individual, it also created a cohesive master narrative, which served, as

---

[75] *De Sacramentis* 1.11.1–2; see Rebecca Moore's discussion of this point, which notes that the faithful Jews of the Hebrew Bible were, according to Hugh's scheme, proto-Christians; *Jews and Christians*, 121–128. For a helpful comparison of Hugh's views with those of his contemporaries, see Stephen D. Benin, "Jews and Christian History: Hugh of St. Victor, Anselm of Havelberg and William of Auvergne," *From Witness to Witchcraft: Jews and Judaism in Medieval Christian Thought*, ed. Jeremy Cohen (Wiesbaden: Harrassowitz, 1996), 203–219.

[76] Rebecca Moore, *Jews and Christians in the Life and Thought of Hugh of St. Victor*,134.

[77] As Moore notes, in the *De Sacramentis*, Hugh "[relies] on the Bible as a source in Jewish history for the aetiology of current Christian practices. ... [T]his use is an appropriation and a re-interpretation of Jewish tradition, rather than an understanding of Judaism on its own terms." *Jews and Christians*, 133.

[78] Jeremy Cohen, "Scholarship and Intolerance," 596. An objection to the generally benign view of Hugh's historiography, comparable to mine, has been raised by Kathleen Biddick in a trenchant essay, "The ABC of Ptolemy: Mapping the World with the Alphabet," in *Text and Territory: Geographical Imagination in the European Middle Ages*, eds. Sylvia Tomasch and Sealy Gilles (Philadelphia: University of Pennsylvania Press, 1998). See her discussion of Hugh on pages 274–276.

did the monastic historical writing prevalent in this period, to construe reality in terms favorable to the author's community.[79] If history is for Hugh the "integrating structural principle of order" in the "exposition of the truth of the Christian religion," then history necessarily must be Christianized.[80] By extension, "Judaism on its own terms," as Moore has put it, is functionally de-historicized.[81] Hugh's ultimate concern is with God's deeds done in time, not human achievements. The greatest of God's deeds, the one that signals God's purposes most clearly, is the Incarnation. The history of the Jews is significant only to the extent that it plays a role in the unfolding of this event. As Moore has pointed out, progress—in Christian time and history—"nullified" the efficacy of alternatives like Judaism.[82] Hugh's system, articulated in his pedagogical works and in the *De Sacramentis*, is both a sacramental and a scientific appropriation of Judaism.[83] What Beryl Smalley and others have identified as the Victorines' contributions to scientific (understood as presumably neutral, or even positive) knowledge of the Hebrew language and Jewish history formed part of a broad spectrum of medieval discursive practices that, consciously or not, constructed a regulated domain for a group of people and beliefs whose very existence represented a provo-

---

[79] Zinn has argued that "the sense of history which Hugh shows in his writings was characteristic of a particular segment of twelfth-century society: monks and canons," noting both cultural and educational practices. He also cites Richard Southern's contention that monks were concerned with history as a means of glorifying their patrons and "to preserve the records of the monastery, thus securing monastic rights in feudal courts." Zinn, "*Historia fundamentum est*", 143, 144–145. See now Michael T. Clanchy's *From Memory to Written Record* (Oxford: Blackwell, 1993); especially the discussion of monastic forgery on 146–149. As Hans-Werner Goetz commented, "[Eleventh- and twelfth-century] authors not only 'wrote history,' they also used the past with certain aims and purposes (though in many cases it may not be easy to demonstrate these interests convincingly)." "Historical Consciousness and Institutional Concern in European Medieval Historiography (11th and 12th Centuries)," a paper presented at the19th International Congress of Historical Sciences, Oslo 6–13 August 2000; www.oslo2000.uio.no/program/papers/m3a/m3a-goetz.pdf.

[80] The phraseology is Grover Zinn's, from his "*Historia fundamentum est*", 141.

[81] Kathleen Biddick uses the term "detemporalization" to describe this translation; see discussion below, and "The ABC of Ptolemy," 269–270.

[82] Moore, 39–40.

[83] In a provocative and illuminating consideration of Hugh's *Desciptio mappe mundi* and his other pedagogical tools, Kathleen Biddick argues that "What once functioned heuristically in Carolingian biblical pedagogy came to be joined among the Victorines to theological notions of the visible and sacramental—that is, *mappae mundi* could now be deployed as a technology of the visible, not unlike the sacraments themselves, especially the Eucharist." "The ABC of Ptolemy," 275.

cation to Christian dominance.[84] The data of Hebrew etymology, of Jewish history, ethnography, and material culture, gathered by the Victorines and incorporated into their exegetical works and pedagogical tools, were part of an explanatory system that "managed" the Jews—or at least, managed Christian anxiety about their continued, baffling presence. This data-gathering effort accommodated the impact of the Jewish presence and neutralized some of its disquieting effects, to say in effect: "Yes, the Jews are significant, but only to a degree."[85]

Hugh's educational program, as borne out in both his exegetical and theological works, placed new emphasis on historical knowledge as a basis for biblical interpretation, as well as emphasizing fundamentals of grammar as a resource for explicating texts. Describing Andrew of Saint Victor's commentaries as exemplary realizations of Hugh's methods, Frans Van Liere writes:

> Understanding words is the field of grammar. There is nothing surprising, therefore, about Andrew's extensive use of grammar while explaining the Biblical text. After understanding the words, we are prepared for the next step: understanding the facts they denote by knowledge of history and science. Well equipped with a knowledge of the *trivium* (the science of words) and the *quadrivium* and history (both of which comprise the science of things and facts), we can understand the Biblical text, and prepare ourselves for the allegorical interpretation that leads to higher truth.[86]

He further notes, "It is important always to bear in mind that if we study Andrew's commentaries out of the context of the spiritual attitude of St Victor, we gain a false impression about their 'scientific character.'"[87]

The Victorine "spiritual attitude," as articulated in Hugh's *Didasalicon*, emphasized the restoration of the human person through the graced acquisition of knowledge and virtue, culminating in meditation on divine truths. Mastery of the seven liberal arts was propaedeutic to

---

[84] Again, Foucault's concept of the archive is useful here.

[85] Kathleen Biddick has included the Victorine pedagogical program among the processes she describes as "detemporalization," or "the ways in which medieval Christians used technology to translate the corporeal co-presence of Jews among whom they lived into a temporal absence. ... [I]t is essentially a process by which in this case Jews were taken out of time." "The ABC of Ptolemy," 269–270.

[86] Frans Van Liere, "Andrew of St Victor (d. 1175): Scholar between Cloister and School," *Centres of Learning: Learning and Location in Pre-Modern Europe and the Near East* (Leiden: Brill, 1995), 193.

[87] Van Liere, 194.

this larger goal, and the goal itself invested the realm of human learning with seriousness and worth. Luce Giard has argued:

> ... [Il] faudrait plutôt saluer en Hugues de Saint-Victor le premier car-tographe qui ait cherché à rassembler l'agir et le savoir des hommes sur une même carte, pour y dessiner un seul itinéraire, celui qui con-duit l'ame à Dieu, selon un projet de voyage qui hante tout le Moyen Age. Avec le *Didascalicon*, Hugues de Saint-Victor en donne la version intellectuelle; ses textes mystiques, et singulièrement son grand traité *De sacramentis christianae fidei*, en donnent la version interieur.[88]

Giard echoes Richard Southern's argument that Hugh "appears to have been the first to treat the mechanical arts on the same level as the theoretical ones, and to analyze their component parts with equal thor-oughness."[89] But her use of the term "cartographer" is highly sugges-tive: Hugh's system mapped the world of useful, and ultimately trans-formative, knowledge.[90] The goal of acquiring knowledge ran parallel to the goal of the universal history which undergirds the *De Sacramentis*: the restoration of the human person and the restoration of the world in their proper orientation to God. Richard Southern described Hugh's program as both scientific and spiritual:

> Hugh of St Victor's view of history is remarkable for its general upward movement in every department of life. Although he says nothing to contradict Augustine, yet the uniformity of the movement of ascent, the co-operation of man and God in this movement, the single thread which binds the earliest efforts of man to the final result, and the close similarity between the general historical movement and the movement of the individual soul towards God—these features are certainly not Augustinian in inspiration. Their originality lies in giving a historical setting to a view of man which was the driving force behind the scientific movement of the twelfth and thirteenth centuries. ... [Hugh] had wanted to make history a subject capable of systematic study among the other sciences of his day.[91]

---

[88] Luce Giard, "Hugues de Saint-Victor: Cartographe du Savoir," *L'Abbaye Parisienne de Saint-Victor au Moyen Age*, ed. Jean Longère (Paris: Brepols 1991), 269.

[89] R.W. Southern, "Aspects of the European Tradition of Historical Writing: 2. Hugh of St Victor and the Idea of Historical Development," *Transactions of the Royal Historical Society* 21 (1971): 172.

[90] Kathleen Biddick argues that Hugh's literal and figurative cartographies are "links in a chain of graphic translations that dispossessed medieval Jews in different ways." She traces those links from the twelfth to the fifteenth centuries and in the process touches on Hugh's hermeneutical method. "The ABC of Ptolemy," *passim*.

[91] Southern, "Hugh of St Victor and the Idea of Historical Development," *TRHS* 21:172.

Hugh's view of history dignified the tools by which insights into historical events could be gathered.[92] Southern, like Beryl Smalley, captured this movement with the use of the qualifier "scientific"— what better way for the twentieth century to bestow its esteem? More recently, too, Luce Giard hailed Hugh's *carte de savoir* as "modern," owing to the fact that it valorized the "savoirs, théoriques ou pratiques."[93]

Students of medieval historiography have long cautioned against accepting the products of medieval historians as straightforward statements of plain fact.[94] While Hugh was not a historian *per se*—Southern aptly notes, "[Hugh's] historical thoughts came to him not through writing history but through writing theology and biblical commentaries, and through teaching the liberal arts"[95]—and although his interest in history served his theological program, some general observations about principles of medieval historiography will demonstrate that Hugh's approach was no less ideological than it was scientific. In other words, Hugh's emphasis on history led him to extol the *trivium*'s contribution to the scientific investigation of the biblical text and its historical context. But the converse may be true: whether its subject was "universal history," the history of a monastic foundation, or the genealogy of a noble house, rhetorical practices taught by the liberal arts reinvigorated historical writing in the twelfth century.[96] As Roger Ray, Nancy Partner, John Ward and others have demonstrated, history-writing in the twelfth century was a growth industry focused on explanation and persuasion.[97] Ward wrote: "The twelfth century was an unusual period

---

[92] Roger Ray has noted that grammatical skill-building exercises had their benefits for history-writing, too. "Medieval Historiography through the Twelfth Century: Problems and Progress of Research," *Viator* 5 (1974): 51–52.

[93] Giard, 269.

[94] See Roger Ray on Bede and his modern commentators; "Medieval Historiography …," 43–46.

[95] Southern, "Hugh of St Victor and the Idea of Historical Development," *TRHS* 21:164.

[96] See Roger Ray, "Medieval Historiography …," 33–59.

[97] In addition to works already cited, see Nancy F. Partner, *Serious Entertainment: The Writing of History in Twelfth-Century England* (Chicago: University of Chicago Press, 1977) and Janet Coleman, *Ancient and Medieval Memories: Studies in the Reconstruction of the Past* (Cambridge: Cambridge University Press, 1991). An important overview of medieval historiography is Peter Classen's "*Res Gestae*, Universal History, Apocalypse: Visions of Past and Future," *Renaissance and Renewal*, eds. Robert L. Benson and Giles Constable with Carol D. Lanham (Toronto: Medieval Academy Reprints for Teaching, 1991), 387–417.

in that persons of exceptional literary ability found the 'web' of events (they use the word *tela*) sufficiently challenging to devote more scarce time, ink, and parchment to it than at any previous time in western history."[98] Arguably, a significant challenge that confronted twelfth-century historians was the increasingly visible presence of Jews in their midst, a presence which did not always confirm the presuppositions of Augustine's doctrine of Jewish witness.[99] In an essay that argues a case parallel to my point, Valerie Flint suggested that

> ... some kinds of medieval historical writing, especially the world chronicle, may have been undertaken less for themselves than as responses to a particular demand. This demand was generated in its turn by a particular kind of enquiry; enquiry legitimate, even desirable; but enquiry of a type which, if left to itself, could constitute a threat to the basis of Christian society.[100]

Flint discussed the threat posed by astrology and magic; the vexing question for twelfth-century "scientists"[101] was which *kind* of knowledge about the stars and their movement was legitimate and useful—and which kind engendered dangerous occultism and a fatalism noxious to the Christian view of historical development? A parallel question can be posed with regard to Christian study of Hebrew language (itself linked to the occult[102]) and Jewish exegesis: How much was healthy? How much was dangerous? By deploying the resources of the liberal arts in the scientific study of history, Hugh of Saint Victor helped to create the conditions that made the twelfth century's 'Jewish question' manageable. For a time, the web created by his theology of history was elastic enough to enable contact with the Jews, and the accumulation of increased knowledge about the Jews. It preserved a delicate

---

[98] John O. Ward, "Some Principles of Rhetorical Historiography in the Twelfth Century," *Classical Rhetoric and Medieval Historiography*, Studies in Medieval Culture 19 (Kalamazoo, 1985), 103.

[99] See Chapter 3 for a discussion of these presuppositions.

[100] Valerie Flint, "World History in the Twelfth Century; the 'Imago Mundi' of Honorius Augustodunensis," *The Writing of History in the Middle Ages: Essays Presented to Richard William Southern*, eds. R.H.C. Davis and J.M. Wallace-Hadrill (Oxford: Clarendon Press, 1981), 238.

[101] Including Hugh of Saint Victor, as Flint notes; "World History in the Twelfth Century," 236.

[102] Joshua Trachtenberg reports, "... the tradition of Hebrew of the sorcerer's tongue was enough to identify both the language and the sorcerer as Jewish." *The Devil and the Jews* (New Haven: Yale University Press, 1943), 63.

counterpoise (to use Flint's felicitous term) between the Augustinian doctrine of witness and the influx of new data that contradicted that doctrine.

By believing that God tells us something in historical events, humans must confront (if not account for) the aporias of history: the things that defy understanding. For Augustine, such an aporia was God's apparent rejection of the Jews, the chosen people. Paula Fredricksen has argued that this aporia formed the central problem of Augustine's theology of history, and forced him to resort to the formula of the "mysterious hiddenness of God's judgement" to explain this and other sufferings by the innocent.[103] Christians also had to account for realities that defied theological schematization. If the Jews, presumably abandoned by God, prospered in the twelfth century, how could their anomalous good fortune be explained?[104] Ambivalence of this kind has been linked by modern scholars both to the rise of intellectual anti-Judaism and to popular violence against the Jews. As Amos Funkenstein has observed, the more medieval Christians knew about Jews and Judaism, the more hostile they became.[105] Christian exegetes who explored the historical background and literal meaning of Scripture with the help of Jewish interlocutors came face-to-face with the fact that the Augustinian precept that the Jews were 'stationary' was false. Also, by virtue of their research and contributions to wider knowledge of contemporary Judaism, Christian scholars alerted others to that unsettling discrepancy. The recognition that historical development entails change, and not all of it bad, led to the erosion of a theology of history based on stasis.[106]

Hugh of Saint Victor's younger colleagues, Andrew of Saint Victor and Herbert of Bosham, were among the twelfth century's most assiduous gatherers of data from Jewish sources. As pioneers, they were vulnerable to suspicion and outright attack. To a degree, Hugh's

---

[103] "*Excaecati occulta iustitia Dei*: Augustine on the Jews and Judaism," *Journal of Early Christian Studies* 3 (1995): 299–324.

[104] Robert Chazan, *Medieval Jewry in Northern France* (Baltimore: Johns Hopkins University Press, 1973), alludes to this kind of questioning by Christians as a "practical" matter, but it was a theological problem too. To Christians, the Jews' condition of poverty and impotence was a mark of God's rejection; what could their prosperity mean?

[105] Amos Funkenstein, *Perceptions of Jewish History* (Berkeley: University of California Press, 1993), 173–201.

[106] Roger Ray has noted that medieval writers used the structure of the *temporum series* to undergird "a theological idea of development and change." "Medieval Historiography," 38.

hermeneutic of the literal sense provided a rationale for their endeavors. In Hugh's transhistorical scheme, all people were or could be "Hebrews:" that is, all people are on a journey from a literal to a spiritual realm.[107] Successful journeys yield growth in virtue and wisdom, and end (with God's help) in contemplation. Provided the study of the literal sense is anchored by this wider purpose, it increases the base of human knowledge from which one ascends closer to the divine. The study of the literal sense for its own sake, to the seeming exclusion of this spiritual goal, was suspect: to be only literal-minded and not to aspire to an understanding of Scripture's spiritual sense was to judaize. In other contexts in this period, 'judaizing' described various activities: to adopt the customs or practices of Jews, to exhibit sympathy for Jews, to lend money, or simply (in a sermon by Bernard of Clairvaux) to live in a city. But in the context of Victorine hermeneutics, judaizing seems to have been a pejorative term applied to a reading practice that fell short of Hugh's goals. It was an accusation made against Andrew of Saint Victor by his near-contemporary, Richard.

Andrew of Saint Victor announced in his commentaries that he would confine himself to the literal meaning, being unworthy to pursue deeper truths. His commentaries, he asserts, are modest affairs—simply the tissue of other men's comments. The term "other men" seems to have referred nearly as often to Jewish exegetes as to Christians. His commentaries demonstrate that Andrew consciously emulated Jerome's interest in the Hebrew language, as well as his interest in Hebrew traditions.[108] Although Andrew invoked Jerome's example, he did not pursue it slavishly. Like his Jewish contemporaries, he was

---

[107] In a sermon on Ecclesiastes, Hugh suggested that a "Hebrew" was someone who was moving from a carnal to a spiritual condition, based on his etymology of the word *Hebraeus*: "Hebraeus transiens interpretatur. Hebraeus ergo factus est iste ad contemplandam sapientiam. Et erat quidem ipse etiam prius Hebraeus secundum carnem, sed hebraeus non fuit secundum veritatem, donec transire coepit ad contemplandam sapientiam. Quemadmodum Judaeus secundum carnem dicitur, et Judaeus secundum veritatem, ita alius Hebraeus est secundum carnem, et alius Hebraeus secundum veritatem. Qui autem in manifesto secundum carnem Judaeus est et qui in manifesto secundum carnem Hebraeus est, non vere Judaeus est, et non vero Hebraeus. Sed qui in occulto secundum spiritum Judaeus est, et secundum spiritum Hebraeus est, vere Judaeus est et vere Hebraeus. Nam multi transeunt secundum carnem, et non transeunt secundum veritatem; quia non transeunt ut perveniant ad veritatem." *In Salomonis Ecclesiasten Homiliae XIX*, "Homilia X: De reliquis vanitatibus usque in eum locum: 'Stultus in tenebris ambulat.'" PL 175: 174A–174C.

[108] Andrew of Saint Victor, Prologue to Isaiah, "venerabilem itaque Ieronimum, licet impari pede sequentes ...," printed in Smalley, *SBMA*, 379:5–6.

more interested in the contextual analysis of biblical narrative than in
Jerome's more "atomized" approach to biblical verses[109]—Jerome was
prepared to interpret any word or verse Christologically if the occasion
warranted. Andrew located his exegesis within the historical context of
the whole biblical book under discussion, as opposed to projecting it
into the larger Christian narrative pattern assumed by most Christian
exegetes.[110] Also, he corrected Jerome's translation when necessary, substituting the data he had gleaned from his Jewish interlocutors (which
occasionally were incorrect, while Jerome's had been right). Andrew
discusses the meaning of Hebrew words that lay behind obscurities in
the Latin translations, and provides Jewish interpretations even for such
traditionally Christological passages as Isaiah 7:14. Andrew's willingness to leave unchallenged the Jewish translation of *almah* as "young
girl" (not "virgin") in that passage, and to cite the Jewish interpretation that the passage referred only to Isaiah's prophecy about the
reign of Hezekiah scandalized his colleague, Richard of Saint Victor. Richard castigated Andrew's position in his tract *De emmanuele*.[111]
J.W.M. Van Zwieten analyzed that exchange against the backdrop
of Hugh's hermeneutical theory.[112] He concluded that the acceptable
boundaries of Victorine-inspired hebraism could be delimited by the
distinction between *lectio historicus* and *sensus historicus*, distilling both
terms from Hugh's didactic works. The first, *lectio historicus*, refers to
reading for the historical and literal meaning of the text and connotes
"objective" scholarly study. The *sensus historicus*, however, incorporates
the Hugonian notion of the narrative sweep of history in which God
is enacting God's redeeming work. Thus, an exegete who concentrates
on the *lectio historicus*, particularly when consulting Jewish sources, but

---

[109] For a comparison of Andrew with contemporary Jewish exegetical techniques, see
Michael A. Signer, "*Peshat, Sensus Litteralis*, and Sequential Narrative," *Frank Talmage
Memorial Volume*, ed. Barry Wallfisch (Haifa: University of Haifa Press, 1993), 203–216.

[110] This is not to imply that Andrew accepted the testimony of his Jewish sources
uncritically. As Michael A. Signer has pointed out, "Andrew was aware of the boundaries of Jewish explanation which were acceptable. ... Despite the derogatory remarks
by Richard [of Saint Victor] with respect to Andrew's exegesis of the Emmanuel passage in Isaiah 7:14, Andrew knew and affirmed that Jewish messianic hopes were fool-
ish." "*De doctrina christiana* and the Exegesis of Andrew of St. Victor," *Reading and Wisdom:
The* De doctrina christiana *of Augustine in the Middle Ages*, ed. Edward D. English (Notre
Dame: University of Notre Dame Press, 1995), 92.

[111] PL 196:601–666. Richard refers to *judaizantes nostri* in Chapters 2 and 4 of Book
One at cols. 607C and 609B.

[112] J.W.M. Van Zwieten, "Jewish Exegesis within Christian Bounds," *Bijdragen, tijdschrift voor filosofie en theologie* 48 (1987): 327–335.

neglects to situate that reading under the rubric of the *sensus historicus*, is in danger of judaizing. If by judaizing one means that Andrew was unduly sympathetic to the Jews or blindly accepting of their interpretations of the biblical text, then Richard's charge that his fellow Victorine was a judaizer was unwarranted.[113] But if to judaize means to abandon an interest in the spiritual sense, then Richard may have been justified. Andrew was no more a slave to Jewish exegesis than he was to Jerome's example. Still, Andrew's willingness to accept a Jewish interpretation of a biblical text as its literal sense left the basis of Christian interpretation of the text's higher, spiritual sense deracinated.[114] For Richard, as it would have been for Hugh, this is a symptom of judaizing.

It fell to Herbert of Bosham to maneuver Christian hebraism back under the comparative safety of Augustine's theology of history, in an attempt to navigate between Hebrew language and exegesis and orthodox Christian interpretation. Herbert's course took him beyond the exegetical horizons of his masters Hugh and Andrew, in that he accorded real weight to issues posed by postbiblical Jewish history. He took seriously, as other Christians had not, the messianic and eschatological expectations of his Jewish contemporaries. Because he took both Jewish history and contemporary experience seriously, Herbert was compelled to grapple with the aporias created by the totalizing narrative of Christian salvation history. Herbert might almost be called a witness *for* the Jews, given his proximity to crucial events of the late twelfth century. He was a witness to the sufferings of the Jews, to their counter-claims to Christian hegemony, and to the dissonances awakened in Christians by the events unfolding around them.

---

[113] See Signer, "*De doctrina christiana* and the Exegesis of Andrew of St. Victor," 92–93; Loewe's demurral in "The Medieval Christian Hebraists of England: Herbert of Bosham and Earlier Scholars," *Transactions of the Jewish Historical Society of England* (London, 1953), 239–240 and Andrew's text *ad loc.*

[114] So Smalley argues: "Discussions with Jewish scholars brought up the interpretation of Old Testament prophecy. The Jews had been accused of interpreting Scripture 'according to the letter,' instead of according to the life-giving spirit. Was their interpretation of Old Testament prophecy to be called the 'literal sense' of the prophecy, while the Christological interpretation went under the heading 'spiritual or allegorical'? This division seemed to clash with the received [Christian] teaching that the literal sense was true and basic. It gave too much to the Jews." "The Bible in the Medieval Schools," *Cambridge History of the Bible*, ed. G.W.H. Lampe (Cambridge: Cambridge University Press, 1969), vol. II, 214. For further discussion of this point, see Chapter 5.

CHAPTER FIVE

THE LINGUISTIC AND CULTURAL
HORIZONS OF HERBERT'S HEBRAISM

The previous chapter alluded to the aggravations and opportunities experienced by Christian exegetes, particularly the Victorines, as a consequence of contact and intellectual exchange with their Jewish contemporaries. Herbert of Bosham represents the conjunction of these two experiences in perhaps their most neuralgic form. Intrigued by Jewish exegesis and sympathetic to Jewish eschatological hopes, Herbert recorded doubts about his Christian faith. Moreover, his exegetical endeavors were carried out against a background of events and texts that evince increasingly complex responses to Judaism in the midst of Northern Europe. This chapter begins by placing Herbert and his hebraism in the context of his many-sided social and intellectual *milieux*. This context is especially important as it demonstrates the extent to which the Victorine legacy of relatively positive attitudes regarding Jews and Judaism collided with hostile attitudes embodied in Christian polemical literature. Herbert was uniquely placed at the confluence of these attitudes, and may have witnessed some of the events associated with the deteriorating status of Jews in Northern Europe. Also, a limited prosopography of his intellectual and political associates suggests that these attitudes—whether positive or negative—were never solely the product of contact with Jews, but were conditioned by a complex array of factors.

Herbert's link to the Victorine school of exegetes was proposed by Beryl Smalley when she published the first overview of his psalter commentary's contents in 1951: "The literal sense, consultation with Jews, these point to the biblical school at Saint Victor."[1] Smalley noted however, that since neither Andrew nor Hugh of Saint Victor wrote commentaries on the psalter, the usual method of identifying an intellectual debt by determining direct or indirect reliance on a previous text is foreclosed to scholars seeking to elucidate the connection between Her-

---

[1] Smalley, "A Commentary on the *Hebraica* by Herbert of Bosham," *RTAM* 18:42. See Chapter 1.

bert and the Victorines. Still, there is a similarity in method between Herbert and the Parisian canons, a similarity which aligns Herbert more closely to Hugh of Saint Victor than to Andrew. Although Herbert, like Andrew, is fascinated by philological data gleaned from Jewish sources, Herbert attends to the role played by the Jews in the unfolding of salvation history with a care and consistency that recall Hugh's approach. But he surpasses Hugh, insofar as he recognizes that his Jewish contemporaries have their own conception of salvation history, an eschatology oriented toward their restoration from exile to the land of Israel.[2]

Herbert's apparent sympathies in this regard are all the more remarkable given his *milieux*. While we cannot know for certain the extent of his contacts with Andrew or Hugh of Saint Victor, since in his extant works Herbert did not claim them as his teachers, we do know that he was a student of Peter Lombard. Herbert championed the Lombard's work, particularly his commentaries on the Book of Psalms and the Pauline epistles, even when his former *magister* was subject to intense scrutiny for presumably heterodox opinions.[3] Peter Lombard's psalms commentary is thoroughly in the Christian tradition of psalms exegesis. It relies heavily on the allegorical and spiritual interpretations of Augustine, Jerome, and Cassiodorus. It is, moreover, markedly anti-Jewish in tone, even more so than his patristic exemplars.[4] Despite his pride in his association with Peter, attested in Herbert's remarkably detailed edition of the Lombard's psalter commentary, Herbert did not emulate his psalms exegesis in style or content.

Also, throughout the network of churchmen and intellectuals who formed his circle in England and in France, Herbert would have encountered many authors who turned their contacts with Jews to very different purposes than he did. Christian polemical tracts against the Jews dating from the second half of the twelfth century are largely unstudied; nearly all are unedited.[5] Among them are works by Bartholomew, Bishop of Exeter, an opponent of Becket who nevertheless took

---

[2] This aspect of Herbert's thought is discussed in Chapter 6.

[3] As discussed in Chapter 1.

[4] Examples included in Chapters 6 and 7 indicate some of the major differences between Peter Lombard's approach and Herbert's.

[5] Some of these works are discussed by R.W. Hunt in "The Disputation of Peter of Cornwall against Symon the Jew," *Studies in Medieval History presented to Frederick Maurice Powicke* (Oxford: Clarendon Press, 1948), 143–156. See also Dahan, *Les intellectuels chrétiens et les Juifs* … passim.

John of Salisbury into his household after the archbishop's death.[6] Bartholomew wrote a *Disputatio contra iudeos* which he dedicated to the new Archbishop of Canterbury, Baldwin (formerly the Cistercian abbot of Forde).[7] Baldwin was also the dedicatee of Herbert's *Life* of Thomas Becket. Another close contemporary and likely acquaintance of Herbert produced a similar work, also in dialogue form. Walter of Châtillon's *Tractatus contra iudaeos* might well have been known to Herbert.[8] Walter is remembered today chiefly as the greatest Latin poet of his age. He enjoyed the patronage of Bishop William of Sens, a strong supporter of Becket with whom Herbert corresponded and for whom Herbert wrote at least one letter.[9] It seems highly likely Herbert would have encountered him at some point during his long exile in France. These two dialogues, and a slightly later work by Peter of Cornwall,[10] seem to represent a shift from tractates ostensibly directed at the Jews themselves to intramural dialogues intended to bolster doubting Christians' faith by addressing their most pressing questions.[11]

Christian exegetical and polemical works of the preceding centuries asserted that contrary to Jewish counter-claims, Jesus is the Messiah predicted by the prophecies contained in the Hebrew Bible. These three late twelfth-century disputes are distinct from earlier versions of this age-old argument because they debate whether Jesus was the Messiah *whom the Jews expect*. This change in emphasis indicates that Christians had acknowledged a qualitative difference between the Mes-

---

[6] These former enemies were in fact old friends; Bartholomew, Thomas Becket, and John of Salisbury were all "cadets" in the household of Theobald, the Archbishop of Canterbury whose reign preceded Becket's. See Avrom Saltman, *Theobald, Archbishop of Canterbury*, 165 ff and Barlow, *Thomas Becket*, 31.

[7] For his part, Baldwin wrote a tract condemning his clerics' propensity for doubting the Real Presence in the Eucharist. See Smalley, *BC*, 76 n. 69. On Bartholomew, see R.W. Hunt, "The Disputation of Peter of Cornwall against Symon the Jew," 147–148, Smalley, *SBMA*, 170–171, and Adrian Morey, *Bartholomew of Exeter, Bishop and Canonist* (Cambridge: Cambridge University Press, 1937).

[8] PL 209; Cohen, *Living Letters of the Law*, 273n9; Dahan, *Les intellectuels chrétiens et les Juifs*, 388–389, 435, 498–499.

[9] John R. Williams, "William of the White Hands and the Men of Letters," *Haskins Anniversary Essays in Mediaeval History*, ed. C.H. Taylor (Freeport, NY: Books for Libraries Press, repr. 1969), 374–376.

[10] Peter, a canon of Aldersgate, London, dedicated his *Liber disputationem Petri contra Symonem Iudeum de confutatione Iudeorum* to Stephen Langton, Archbishop of Canterbury. Smalley, following Grabmann, classified Langton with the "biblical-moral school of exegetes," *SBMA*, 196 ff.

[11] Dahan, *Les intellectuels chrétiens et les Juifs*, 419.

siah whom the Jews awaited and the Christian preaching of Jesus as
Messiah. The change further suggests that increased contact with Jews
and with Jewish critiques of Christianity drove Christians to confront
another historical aporia. The Jews believed that the reign of the Messiah would usher in an age of justice and peace. They would be restored
to the land of Israel and with the Messiah pass judgment on the crimes
of the nations. While Christianity had long referred these eschatological
events to the second coming of Christ, medieval Christians appear to
have been stung by the Jewish critique of Christian *mores* in this world,
at the present time.[12] As noted in the preceding chapter, during the age
of the "Evangelical Awakening," Christians became more aware of the
institutional church's deviation from the ideals of its primitive exemplar.[13] In this context, the question of whether Jesus is rightly the Messiah became more painfully vexed. Once, Christians could argue that
the exemplary piety of the few (e.g., monastics) compensated for the
riotous living of the laity.[14] But new standards of personal holiness and
a deeper concern with the likelihood of one's own salvation unsettled
this complacent equilibrium.[15]

Herbert of Bosham was a witness to the resulting unease. In his *Life*
of Becket, he recorded his own doubts about whether Jesus is indeed
the Messiah. If not, will God count as sinful a Christian's belief in Jesus
and his participation in the sacraments?[16] In his distress, he sought out
Becket (whose spiritual counselor Herbert had been). The archbishop
was able to allay his fears with a few words.[17] In its context, the story
reinforces Herbert's portrait of Thomas's sanctity—in the manner of
the Desert Mothers and Fathers, Thomas can 'say the word' that

---

[12] For an example of Jewish criticism, see Joseph Kimhi, *The Book of the Covenant*,
trans. Frank E. Talmage (Toronto: PIMS, 1972), 32–33, 48.

[13] M.-D. Chenu, "The Evangelical Awakening," *Nature, Man and Society in the Twelfth
Century*, 239–269.

[14] As Gilbert Crispin did, in his *Disputatio Iudei et Christiani*, sections 60–61; *The
Works of Gilbert Crispin*, eds. Anna Sapir Abulafia and Gillian R. Evans (London: British
Academy, 1986).

[15] Chenu, "The Evangelical Awakening." See also Giles Constable, *The Reformation
of the Twelfth Century* (Cambridge: Cambridge University Press, 1996), especially 293–295
and 325–328.

[16] The dedicatee of Herbert's *Life* of Becket was Theobald, author of a screed
decrying clerical doubts about the Eucharist. One wonders how Theobald received
this confession.

[17] Herbert, *Vita Sancti Thomae*, 3.13. This encounter seems to have happened before
their exile in France.

will heal his supplicant.[18] While Herbert's purpose might well have been to extol yet another of Thomas's virtues, the story is also highly suggestive. It illustrates how a Christian, in close contact with Jews and Judaism, might be moved to embrace their questions as his own. Subsequent discussion will show how Herbert's reaction against certain triumphalistic expressions of Christianity and his exegesis of the psalms were mutually conditioned. His habitually Victorine view of salvation history was challenged and expanded by considerations of whether Jesus was the Messiah and whether the world was as it should be. His ambivalent experience led him to an unprecedentedly sympathetic decision: based on history and human events, the Jews were right to doubt Christian accounts of the proofs and effects of Jesus' messiahship.

This sense of dissonance was probably heightened by the intermittent explosions of violence against Jews that erupted in France and England in the second half of the century. In 1171, for example, Herbert remained in self-imposed exile in France. His whereabouts in this period are unknown, but it is likely he was in the county of Champagne or in Paris. In either case, he probably would have known about the outbreak of violence in Blois, close to Sens, in which more than thirty Jews were burned by Theobald, count of Blois. Theobald was the brother of Count Henry of Champagne and Archbishop William of Sens and Chartres—both intimates of Becket and Herbert. The Blois incident illuminates the powerful emotions sparked when contact between Jews and Christians was construed (for whatever purpose) as transgression. Theobald of Blois had angered his vassals by allowing a Jewish woman free rein, apparently in moneylending activities.[19] Their resentment found an outlet when spurious reports that a Jew had murdered a Christian youth and disposed of his body in the Loire reached the city.[20] The count executed rough justice on the Jewish community, ordering the immolation of most of its people. Others were imprisoned and held for ransom. The Jewish communities of Northern France, organized by Rabbi Jacob Tam, appealed to Archbishop William of Sens to intervene. The archbishop was asked to carry the ransom to

---

[18] Benedicta Ward, SLG, *The Sayings of the Desert Fathers* (Kalamazoo, MI: Cistercian Publications, 1984), xxii. I am grateful to John Van Engen for suggesting this parallel.

[19] Susan L. Einbinder argues persuasively against alternative readings of the evidence which had suggested that the woman was Theobald's mistress in "Pucellina of Blois: Romantic Myths and Narrative Conventions," *Jewish History* 12 (1998): 29–46.

[20] Robert Chazan, "The Blois Incident of 1171: A Study in Jewish Intercommunal Organization," *Proceedings of the American Academy for Jewish Research* 36 (1968): 14–15.

his brother, in order to secure the release of the few surviving prisoners and the bodies of the dead for burial. As recorded in letters and a Jewish chronicle proximate to the events, this mission was successful. The surviving evidence, none of it from Christian sources, does not provide us with enough information to discern all the undercurrents—political, economic, or social—that conspired to make such an attack on Blois' Jewry possible, although Susan Einbinder has argued that "latent economic resentment" contributed significantly to the outbreak.[21]

The accusation against the Jews that ignited the Blois incident was murder. It had its echoes throughout northern France and the Anglo-Norman kingdom during the second half of the twelfth century. The first accusation that Jews had murdered a Christian child for cultic purposes was launched in Norwich in 1144. After that time, the 'blood libel' of ritual murder was perpetrated at irregular intervals in both countries.[22] Again, as a resident in both France and England throughout this period, Herbert may well have been aware of some of these incidents. He was well-connected to many of the officials who presided at the time of the events. He was also a member, at least tangentially, of the intellectual circles that occupied themselves at the end of the century with reflecting on the social or theological effects of contacts with Judaism.

A more powerful case can be made for the likelihood of Herbert's contact with another significant figure connected to anti-Jewish violence. Herbert's last patron in England was William Longchamp, Bishop of Ely. William was named royal justiciar (a regent, in effect) after Richard I left on the Third Crusade in 1190. In that capacity, William investigated the massacre of the Jews of York, a horrific event which

---

[21] Einbinder, "Pucellina of Blois," 36. Nor is it possible to evaluate with certainty why other Christian rulers refused to act on claims of ritual murder; Robert Chazan notes that Theobald's brother, Henry count of Champagne, rejected Christian claims that a ritual murder had taken place in the town of Épernay, *Medieval Jewry in Northern France*, (Baltimore: Johns Hopkins University Press, 1973), 57.

[22] Robin R. Mundill, *England's Jewish Solution: Experiment and Expulsion, 1262–1290* (Cambridge: Cambridge University Press, 1998), 52, catalogues the instances of twelfth-century blood libels which led to violence against Jews in England: 1144, blood libel in Norwich (little William of Norwich, reported by Thomas of Monmouth); 1168, alleged torture/murder of Harold of Gloucester; 1181, similar allegation at Bury St. Edmunds; 1183, murder of Adam of Bristol; 1192, murder of a French boy employed by a Jewish cobbler. Also, following the coronation of Richard I in 1189, widespread violence swept the country from London to York, culminating in the massacre of York's Jewry in March, 1190.

was the climax of a wave of anti-Jewish violence in England, seemingly ignited by Richard's coronation in September 1189.[23] Unable or unwilling to identify the ringleaders of the crime, William punished York's Christian citizens *en masse* by levying heavy fines on the community. The entire citizenry was held liable for the destruction of York's fortress (where the Jews had taken refuge and which they had set on fire after all hope of rescue had passed), and the revenues lost to the crown as a result. The Christians of York had murdered one of the wealthiest Jewish communities in England; with them had died a substantial source of royal tax revenues.[24] William Longchamp did not last in office for very long after prosecuting the citizens of York. His unpopularity has been attributed to various factors—chiefly his rivalry with his fellow justiciar Hugh de Puiset, Bishop of Durham. But one wonders if his effort, however half-hearted, to do justice in York might have provided a subtext for his more general unpopularity?[25] One of the last surviving documents associated with Herbert of Bosham is a letter from William Longchamp. William refers obliquely to his political difficulties and inquires after the progress of Herbert's *opusculum* on the Hebraica.[26]

Herbert was in a good position to witness a marked increased of hostility to Jews related to an increase in commercial contact and its concomitant perception: some Christians believed that Jews were exerting too much influence in their affairs. Secular and clerical nobles in France and England enjoyed the liquidity that borrowing money from Christian and Jewish lenders had provided. Many such high-ranking borrowers secured their loans with pledges of real property. When the debtors proved unable to discharge their obligations, their creditors sold off the property to the highest bidder—sometimes a Jew, more often

---

[23] R.B. Dobson, "The Jews of Medieval York and the Massacre of March 1190," Borthwick Papers No. 45 (York: St. Anthony's Press, 1974).

[24] Dobson, "The Jews of Medieval York and the Massacre of 1190," 30.

[25] William was already chancellor to King Richard I; he was appointed joint justiciar when the king went on crusade in 1190. Within the year he had ousted the other justiciar, Bishop Hugh of Durham, was appointed papal legate and effectively become the acting head of church and state in England. His administration was very unpopular, and in 1191 a series of disputes led to a rebellion by the king's brother John and England's barons who deposed William from office. See David Balfour, "The Origins of the Longchamp Family," *Medieval Prosopography* 18 (1997):73–92 for details of William's career.

[26] "Et praeterea noveritis quod desiderio intimo desideravimus ut opusculum super psalmos ab Hebraica veritate a Patre Hieronymo translatos vestra discretio complevisset, ut impedimento non esset quidquam ulterius, quin vestra praesentia et optatis colloquiis uteremur …" PL 190: 1474D.

members of the emerging *bourgeoisie* or a bishop eager to aggrandize his holdings at the expense of a debt-encumbered monastery. The transfer of land, traditionally the most prestigious source of wealth, into the hands of people who appeared to be profiting in the new cash economy was a source of considerable irritation.[27] The indebtedness to Jews of monks and clerics (even Thomas Becket was reportedly in debt to a Jewish lender) presumably scandalized the Christian faithful and may have helped feed the spate of anti-Jewish polemic produced at the episcopal level in England from the 1180s to 1200.[28]

In both England and France, the regimes of kings or counts sought to minimize the mistrust attendant upon business contacts between Christians and Jews by instituting bureaucracies which would safeguard the records of their transactions. In 1194, Hubert Walter, Archbishop of Canterbury who was simultaneously justiciar of all England, issued the 'Ordinances of the Jewry.' Some of its stipulations were, no doubt, retroactive and simply formalized existing arrangements, such as ensuring that bonds issued between the two groups would be witnessed, formulated in standard language, registered with a governmental official, and deposited in a community archive, one of the *archae iudaeorum* situated throughout the kingdom.[29] The institution of England's Exchequer of the Jews at the direction of an individual who was simultaneously primate of the English church and a ranking royal official illustrates the powerful confluence of interests that affected Jewish life within the Anglo-Norman realm. Robert Chazan has pointed out parallel developments which emerged in France, both in the royal demesne and in the counties. These French developments were modeled on the highly articulated and efficient Angevin bureaucracy. It is not clear that a comparable confluence of interest between the episcopal hierarchy and the monarchy prevailed in France, although some circumstances are suggestive. When, in 1189, Philip Augustus of France expelled all the Jews from the royal demesne (a comparatively small region, consisting chiefly of Paris and the Ile-de-France), he awarded Paris' largest synagogue,

---

[27] See Mundill, *England's Jewish Solution: Experiment and Expulsion, 1262–1290*, passim. Robert Chazan records instances of similar resentment in northern France.

[28] On Thomas's debt, see William of FitzStephen's *Vita Sancti Thomae*, PL 190:136A. Evidence of the increase in polemic at the episcopal level consists in the tractates against the Jews written by Bartholomew of Exeter, Peter of Cornwall, pseudo-William of Champeaux (addressed to Bishop Alexander of Lincoln), and (possibly) Peter of Blois.

[29] The ordinances were printed by Joseph Jacobs, *The Jews of Angevin England: Documents and Records* (London: David Nutt, 1893), 156–159.

now vacant, to the Bishop of Paris, Maurice of Sully.[30] Maurice was a noted preacher and among French bishops second only to William of Sens in his support for Thomas Becket.[31] On the other hand, that same William, Archbishop of Sens and later of Reims—uncle to King Philip and France's papal legate—appears to have acted on behalf of the Jews of Blois. Also, his brother Henry, Count of Champagne, rejected Christian claims of a ritual murder fomented against some of his Jewish subjects in the 1170s. This seemingly contradictory state of affairs in France recalls Nirenberg's thesis: violence against the Jews was in many ways a local phenomenon, sparked by local events, personalities, and politics. From the pattern of local events it is difficult to theorize a global model that accounts satisfactorily for the state of relations between Jews and Christians at the end of the twelfth century.

Herbert of Bosham had ample opportunity to encounter not only Jews and Judaism, but more especially his Christian cohort's vexed and complicated responses to the challenges and opportunities that contact with Jews provided. Among his contemporaries, several noted scholars produced anti-Jewish tracts, seemingly in the service of an Anglo-Norman episcopate who regarded Jewish influence as deleterious to the faithful. But Herbert, highly regarded as a scholar by men of influence, resisted this avenue for advancement. He, like Bartholomew of Exeter or Peter of Cornwall, might easily have submitted a *Dialogus contra Iudeos* for the delectation of an Archbishop of Canterbury. He did not. Some of the reasons for his refusal have been sketched here; others will be addressed in the course of considering the extent and possible sources of his Hebrew knowledge.

Raphael Loewe, who published the first extensive study on Herbert of Bosham's psalms commentary in 1953, expressed the opinion that Herbert might have been the finest Christian hebraist produced by the Western Church between Jerome in the fourth century and Reuchlin at the end of the fifteenth century.[32] Until recently, no other study of Herbert's work has been attempted since Loewe's essay and transcriptions

---

[30] William Chester Jordan, *The French Monarchy and the Jews* (Philadelphia: University of Pennsylvania Press, 1989), 32.

[31] G.B. Flahiff, C.S.B, "Ralph Niger: An Introduction to his Life and Works," *Medieval Studies* [Toronto] 2 (1940): 110.

[32] Raphael Loewe, "Herbert of Bosham's Commentary on Jerome's Hebrew Psalter," *Biblica* 34:44–77, 159–192, 275–298. Regarding his assessment of Herbert's Hebrew competence, see page 54.

were published.[33] His assessment of Herbert's expertise in Hebrew and rabbinics has been generally accepted. Still, some further evaluation of Herbert's Hebrew knowledge ought to be ventured at this point, particularly since Loewe never dealt explicitly with the mechanisms by which a medieval Christian might have learned Hebrew.

Modern scholars of the Christian study of the Bible in the Middle Ages have agreed with Beryl Smalley's assertion that Christians learned rudiments of the Hebrew language from Jewish interlocutors. They relied on conversations with Jews for whatever knowledge they might have gleaned concerning Jewish exegesis or liturgical practice.[34] Thanks to the force of Loewe's arguments, Herbert is regarded as the lonely exception to this general rule: according to him, Herbert could read and understand both Biblical and rabbinic Hebrew and was well-versed in rabbinic and medieval Jewish exegesis. Loewe builds his case for Herbert's ability to read Biblical and rabbinic Hebrew on four main points. First, he argues from Herbert's corrections to Jerome's translation of the Hebraica psalter that Herbert discriminates among nuances in the Hebrew text at a level suggesting significant expertise in the language. Second, Loewe discerns in Herbert's commentary some data which might have come from the *Targum* (the Aramaic paraphrase) to the *Kethuvim* ('the Writings,' or Hagiographa), the division of Hebrew scripture which includes the psalter. Loewe concurs in scholarly opinion that Rashi did not have access to this *Targum*. Thus, the appearance of targumic material in Herbert's commentary suggests that he did have such access—and indicates that Herbert might have read Aramaic as well as Hebrew. In a related argument, Loewe notes that Herbert credits his *litterator* or *litteratores* with material derived from Jewish sources (either *Midrash on Psalms* or other, unknown sources). Frequently this material is not present in existing editions of Rashi's psalms commentary. The presence of this additional material suggested to Loewe that Herbert was able to use Hebrew texts besides that of Rashi.

---

[33] See now Deborah L. Goodwin, "A Study of Herbert of Bosham's Psalms Commentary (c. 1190)." (Ph.D. diss., University of Notre Dame, 2001) and Eva S. De Visscher, "The Jewish-Christian Dialogue in Twelfth-Century Western Europe: Herbert of Bosham's *Commentary on the Psalms*." (Ph.D. thesis, School of Theology and Religious Studies, the University of Leeds, 2003).

[34] Beryl Smalley, *SBMA*, 155–156; Michael A. Signer, "Introduction," *Andreae de Sancto Victore Opera IV: Expositionem in Ezechielem* (CCCM 53E, 1991), xxi–xxii; F.A. van Liere, "Andrew's Commentary on Samuel and Kings in the Exegetical Tradition," *Andreae de Santo Victore Opera II: Expositio hystorica in librum regum* (CCCM 53A,1995), xxix–xxxvii.

Finally, there is Herbert's use of Rashi's psalms commentary itself. As Beryl Smalley observed fifty years ago, there is Rashi "on almost every page" of Herbert's commentary.[35] When Herbert's Latin text is compared to the edition of Rashi's commentary prepared and translated into English by Mayer I. Gruber,[36] Loewe's assessment is convincing:

> There seems little reason to doubt that Herbert worked from an actual MS of Rashi, and is not dependent upon oral information. The verbal similarity is sometimes so close that, even if he were repeating what he was told, we would have to picture his informant virtually dictating from the copy of Rashi in front of him.[37]

Loewe thus discounts the likelihood that Herbert acted as a stenographer for a Jewish interlocutor. By extension, the improbability of this *scenario* bolsters his argument that Herbert was capable of working directly from a manuscript of Rashi's commentary. But here we must weigh the relative merits of improbabilities: was Herbert more likely to have as much mastery of Hebrew as Loewe claims than he was to rely on close collaboration with an interlocutor? There were precedents for collaboration between Christians and Jews over the text of scripture in this period.

Later in his essay, Loewe himself calls attention to a passage from Herbert's commentary on Psalm 88[89]:52. There, Herbert embedded in his exegesis a description of his methods, and an oblique portrait of his companion in study. The verse in itself is significant; Herbert is discussing the phrase *quibus exprobraverunt vestigia christi tui*, where *christi* translates the Hebrew משיח (*mashiach*) or "anointed:"

> "Those with which they have reproached" is better understood to be about the Messiah himself, as indeed the more skilled Jewish *litteratores*, knowledgeable about their writings, have agreed. Clearly the end of the verse may be interpreted as being about the Messiah. So that the meaning is, "those with which," meaning the reproaches, "they have reproached the footsteps of your Christ," that is, the end of the King Messiah. This is the *litterator's* explanation. And behold the words themselves of the explanation according to my *perloquaceum*, translated from Hebrew into Latin by faith unless I am mistaken. He adds in his explanation of the psalm that passage in Gamaliel, speaking about the Messiah in terms of what is here, which similarly cites the word used at the end of

---

[35] Smalley, *SBMA*, 191.

[36] *Rashi's Commentary on Psalms 1–89 (Books I–III)* (Atlanta: Scholars Press, 1998) [hereafter, Gruber].

[37] Raphael Loewe, "Herbert of Bosham's Commentary on Jerome's Hebrew Psalter (I)," *Biblica* 34 (1953): 60.

the psalm, in the saying about 'the footsteps of your Messiah:' "A cruel
judgment will arise at the footsteps of the Messiah," meaning the end of
the Messiah. Therefore the Jewish *litterator* like the churchman explains
that this is said about the Messiah.[38]

Herbert reports here that he and his interlocutor (*perloquacem meum*)
agree that both Christians and Jews understand that this verse refers
to the Messiah. Apparently, his interlocutor even used the Latin *Christus* to translate משיח (*mashiach*). His Jewish companion also passed on
valuable supporting data: the Mishnah itself alludes to this psalm-verse
when referring to the "catastrophic preludes" which will precede the
Messiah's coming.[39] Loewe also notes that Rashi's exegesis of this verse
mentions the Mishnah, but with less detail than that offered by Herbert. Interestingly, Loewe does not consider the question of whether
this exchange between Herbert and his interlocutor is exceptional or
typical; he simply recounts it. We could regard the episode instead as a
significant illustration of what may have been Herbert's typical working
method.

Herbert is always gratified when he can demonstrate that the *litterator* and the *ecclesiasticus* are in open agreement, especially on the crucial
issue of Jesus's messiahship (which is how he chose to interpret his interlocutor's use of *christus* to translate משיח: not just any anointed one has
been affirmed, but Jesus). This rare point of agreement, attained in conversation with his interlocutor, may be the reason why Herbert recounts
this incident in such detail. Yet he may be describing his usual working methods—critical review of Jerome's translation, close consultation
of Rashi's text—conducted at the elbow of an interlocutor. His Jewish colleague's familiarity with rabbinics enabled him to expand Rashi's
telegraphic references for Herbert's benefit. The *content* of their conver-

---

[38] "… Vel quod dicit; *quibus exprobaverunt* etc. pocius de ipso messia intelligendum;
in quo eciam periciores iudeorum litteratores scriptis suis scio consensisse. Ut videlicet
versiculi istius finis; super messia explanetur. Ut sit sensus, *quibus*, scilicet opprobriis,
exprobraverunt vestigia Christi tui. Id est finem regis messie. Hec est litteratoris explanancio;
et ipsa eciam explanacionis verba secundum quod ab hebreo in latinum perloquacem
meum fide ni fallor translata [est expunged] sunt. Et addit in explanacione sua super
hunc psalmi locum Gamalie, qui de messia loquens istius quod hic in fine psalmi
ponitur similiter verbum ponit, dicens quod in vestigiis messie; iudicium crudele crescat
[*sic*] vestigia messie vocans; messie finem. Igitur litterator iudeus sicut ecclesiasticus;
quod hic dicitur super messia interpretatur." Printed in Loewe, "Herbert of Bosham's
Commentary," 68. Eva De Visscher has corrected Loewe's *perloquacem* with *per loquacem*;
109.

[39] *Mishnah* Sota 9.1; see Loewe, "Herbert of Bosham's Commentary," 68–69.

sation on this occasion might have been extraordinary; but the *method* which the anecdote illustrates may well have been typical. Moreover, this anecdote may also be grounds for supposing that Herbert was not capable of working independently with Hebrew texts.

As Loewe readily acknowledges, any analysis of the relationship of Herbert's commentary to its possible sources is greatly complicated by the fragmented history of Rashi's text and other medieval Hebrew commentaries, lexica, etc.[40] No twelfth-century manuscript of Rashi's psalms commentary survives today.[41] Later manuscripts and early printed editions of Rashi's commentary vary widely from thirteenth-century manuscripts, the earliest versions available to modern editors. Some of the variations are clearly signaled by the later scribes and editors; others simply appear in the text.[42] Raphael Loewe has suggested that Herbert's text of Rashi's commentary may have been a fuller version than those which survive, or may have already begun to accrue additions and interpolations (such as those from the *Targum* to Psalms). Likewise, material once present in Rashi's original version might have been excised by later commentators.[43] It is virtually impossible to establish the state of Rashi's commentary as Herbert might have encountered it. Consequently, it is difficult to establish the degree of Herbert's indebtedness to, or independence from, Rashi or other Hebrew sources. Likewise, Herbert's degree of indebtedness to or independence from oral exchanges with a Jewish interlocutor is very difficult to assert with any degree of certainty.

Despite the difficulties of establishing Herbert's level of competence in Hebrew by comparing his commentary to his likely sources, it will be useful, if no less speculative, to consider how he might have learned Hebrew. Was it possible or even likely that a Christian could achieve competence in both Biblical and rabbinic Hebrew, not to mention Aramaic and even Arabic, as Loewe suggests? What tools, teachers, or opportunities for language instruction existed? What were the vehicles for contact between Jews and Christians that might have provided Her-

---

[40] Loewe, 60–61.

[41] This fragmented history of Rashi's texts is hardly surprising. Rashi's scriptural and Talmudic commentaries were among the books burned in Paris in 1240 after the ecclesiastical trial and condemnation of the Talmud. Gilbert Dahan, "Juifs et Chrétiens en Occident Médiéval: La Rencontre autour de la Bible (XIIe–XIVe Siècles)," *Revue de Synthèse* 4:1 (1989): 3–31; 28.

[42] Gruber, Introduction, 37–42.

[43] Loewe, 60–61.

bert the chance to learn Hebrew from a Jew?[44] These questions will be examined in light of the likely modes of contact between Christians and Jews "autour de la Bible," in Gilbert Dahan's phrase and in general communal life.[45] Seen in this light, Herbert may emerge as more representative than has been previously assumed.[46]

Well before Herbert's time, a few other isolated figures were acclaimed for their knowledge of Hebrew. At the end of the eleventh century, monastic chroniclers in France extolled the linguistic skills of Sigo of Saint Florent (Saumur, in Anjou) and Sigebert of Gembloux (in Namur), respectively. There is always the chance that such *encomia* were the products of wishful thinking. Great learning, evidenced by mastery of several languages, was an estimable quality which any monastic necrology might want to claim for one of its members.[47] Sigo, for example, was purportedly knowledgeable in Hebrew and Greek to such a degree that he corrected his abbey's service books and sets of scriptures.[48] Sigo's fame might have been legitimately bestowed. The

---

[44] One could also ask, how much Hebrew might he have learned from Christian sources (such as Jerome's texts)?

[45] Gilbert Dahan, "Juifs et Chrétiens en Occident Médiéval: La Rencontre autour de la Bible (XIIe–XIVe Siècles)," *Revue de Synthèse* 4:1 (1989): 3–31.

[46] Judith Olszowy-Schlanger recently described a manuscript from the third quarter of the 13th century, Longleat MS 21, that includes a complete glossary of biblical Hebrew. She theorized that the dictionary was the work of one or many Christian scholars, possibly aided by a Jewish informant. The sophistication of the glossary, which consists of 4000 entries and makes reference to an extensive array of Hebrew sources, led Olszowy-Schlanger to suggest that such a work is the product of serious, sustained interest in Hebrew scholarship in England on the part of Christians. "A Thirteenth-Century Glossary of Hebrew, Latin, French, and English Words" (Paper presented at the Fortieth International Congress on Medieval Studies, Western Michigan University, Kalamazoo, MI, May 7, 2005). The manuscript, which also includes a Hebrew psalter glossed in Latin, was discussed briefly by Raphael Loewe in "The Medieval Christian Hebraists of England: the *Superscriptio Lincolniensis*," Hebrew Union College Annual 28 (1957): 205–252.

[47] Inasmuch as Jerome claimed such knowledge for his long-time associates, the Roman matron Paula and her daughter Eustochium, it is not surprising that later generations of male religious would do likewise. See Jerome's Ep. 104. Peter Abelard also exhorted Heloise and her sisters at the Paraclete convent to study Hebrew and Greek, in language borrowed from Jerome in his Ep. 9, "De studio litteratum," PL 178: 325A–336A.

[48] "... et insuper litteras hebraicas et graecas peritissimus legendi et scribendi. Hic bibliothecam nostram, psalterium, missales, textus, epistolas Pauli, actus Apostolorum ad unquem correxit et emendavit ..." *Historia Sancti Florentii Salmurensis*, ed. P. Marchegay and E. Mabille, *Chroniques des églises d'Anjou* (Paris, 1869), 296. Cited in Grabois, "The *Hebraica Veritas* and Jewish-Christian Intellectual Relations in the Twelfth Century," *Speculum*, 50 (1975): 613–634.

province of Anjou was home to several Jewish communities and notable scholars, with whom Sigo perhaps consulted.[49] Gembloux's chronicles recount that Sigebert, who taught at Metz for thirty years, "was very dear to the Jews of the city because he was skillful in distinguishing the Hebrew truth from other editions; and he agreed with what they told him, if it were in accordance with the Hebrew truth."[50] Apparently Sigebert's contacts with the Jewish scholars of Metz were frequent and cordial.[51]

These two examples, each dating from about 1070, are exceptional and isolated. The spectrum of possibilities for Christian hebraism extends and deepens in the twelfth century, however. Christians sought out Jews to help them reconcile the variations among their biblical texts. The next major example is Stephen Harding, third abbot of Cîteaux. Discovering that his abbey's volumes of scripture were riddled with inconsistencies from one volume to the next, he turned to Jewish scholars for help.[52] In a project that yielded the 'Cistercian Bible,' a revision completed around 1109, Stephen and the Jews went through the scriptures together. Based on what he found (and learned in discussions in the vernacular: "lingua Romana inquisivimus"), Stephen either added to or, more typically, excised portions from the Latin text. His reliance on the vernacular suggests that Stephen himself had no facility in Hebrew.

A rigorous project of correcting the biblical text was undertaken by Nicolas Maniacoria at mid-century.[53] Nicolas addressed his efforts chiefly to the psalter, reviewing the three versions of the text (Roma-

---

[49] "La province d'Anjou comprenait plusiers communautés juives assez anciennes. Joseph ben Samuel Tob Élém (Bonfils) qui vivait vers le milieu du XIe siècle, est mentionné avec le titre de rabbin de Limoges et Anjou," Henri Gross, *Gallia Judaica: Dictionnaire Géographique de la France d'après les Sources Rabbiniques* (Amsterdam: Philo Press, 1969 [repr.]), 65–66.

[50] Smalley, *SBMA*, 79; citing Godescalc, *Gesta Abbatum Gemblacensis*, PL 140:641.

[51] Gross, *Gallia Judaica*, 347.

[52] "Unde nos multum de discordia nostrorum librorum, quos ab uno interprete suscepimus, admirantes, Judaeos quosdam in sua Scriptura peritos adivimus, ac diligentissime lingua Romana inquisivimus de omnibus illis Scripturarum locis, in quibus illae partes et versus, quos in praedicto nostro exemplari inveniebamus, et jam in hoc opere nostro inserebamus, quosque in aliis multis historiis Latinis non inveniebamus." PL 166:1375A. Stephen's activities are also noted in Chapter 1.

[53] In her doctoral thesis, Eva De Visscher has argued that Herbert, too, was chiefly interested in the task of establishing a corrected text of the psalter; "The Jewish-Christian Dialogue in Twelfth-Century Western Europe: Herbert of Bosham's *Commentary on the Psalms*." See especially Chapter 2.

num, Gallican, Hebraica) with the help of a Jewish interlocutor in
Italy.[54] He sought out a "most subtle and learned" Jew, who helped
him to reconcile discrepancies in the texts: "Having discovered conflicting exemplars [of the Psalters], I employed a learned Hebrew and I
have taken pains to write down carefully whatever that most discerning
investigator among them approved as the most correct."[55] Nicolas cast
a cold, objective eye on accretions that the Latin text of the Hebrew
Bible had acquired over time. He pointed out that the errors of ignorant scribes led them to misplace the names of Hebrew letters in the
alphabetical psalms; he gives a careful and correct list of the letters in
his *Libellus*.[56] He was no less critical of traditional exegesis. Like Herbert of Bosham after him, Nicolas had little use for the *tituli psalmorum*
of the Gallican psalter, so divorced were they from the *Hebraica veritas*.[57] Nicolas also dismissed various Christian translations (and the theories behind them) for the Hebrew word *selah*, which appears in many
psalms. He reports that a *Hebreus* told him that the word was supplied
by the psalms' authors to make up lacking syllables, so that the verses
would scan properly when sung. He repeats this explanation twice, once
in the preface to his corrected Hebraica psalter and the second time in
the *libellus*.[58]

The mid-twelfth century exegetical projects of the Victorines Hugh
and Andrew were separate from but related to these projects of correction. They seem to have been done with the help of Jewish interlocutors rather than by Christian scholars having independent knowledge
of Hebrew. By mid-century, however, more and more evidence emerges

---

[54] See also the discussion of Maniacoria in Chapter 1.

[55] "Huius denique ego discordancia reperiens exemplaria, hebraicum nichilominus
dissertorem assumpsi et quicquid ille, singulorum subtillisimus indagator, verius approb-
abat diligenter studui exarare." Robert Weber, "Deux Préfaces au Psautier Dues à
Nicolas Maniacoria," *Révue Bénédictine* 63 (1953):10, lines 8–11.

[56] *Libellus de corruptione et correptione psalmorum et aliarum quarundam scripturarum*, edited
by Vittorio Peri in "Correctores immo corruptores: Un Saggio di Critica Testuale nella
Roma del XII Secolo," *Italia Mediovale e Umanistica* 20 (1977): 124–125.

[57] Weber, 10–11.

[58] In the Hebraica preface, he attributes this theory to a Spanish 'Hebrew' who was
learned in many languages: "Hebreus quidam hispanus diversarum linguarum litteris
eruditus, super hoc ait, 'Quociens psalmographus iuxta vocum consonanciam et pedum
distinctionem in versu procedere non valebat, metri defectum verbi huius apposicione
supplebat.'" Weber, 12, lines 15–28. Cf. Peri, 98, lines 19–25. This explanation does not
accord with Abraham ibn Ezra's nor with that of David Kimhi. See David Kimhi (who
refers to ibn Ezra) in *Commento ai Salmi* I: 1–50, trans. Luigi Cattani (Rome: Città Nuova
Editrice, 1991), 92.

that some Christians were learning the Hebrew alphabet sufficiently well to write it.[59] Still others learned to read some Hebrew with enough confidence to claim acquaintance with Hebrew reference works. This is not to say that these Christians could actually read the texts: rather, their smattering of reading knowledge introduced them to the existence of a wider world of Hebrew scholarship that extended beyond the Bible. With their own incipient literacy came a greater appreciation for the tools of biblical commentary and lexical study which their Jewish contemporaries consulted. In a sense, the movement toward an independent literacy in Hebrew (though by no means accomplished yet) may have also implied a concomitant ability to imagine a *paidaea* or curriculum that encompassed certain Hebrew texts. To be able to allude to that corpus of authoritative texts would imbue one's own findings with legitimacy.[60] Put another way, some twelfth-century Christians began to explore the outline and contents of Judaism's 'textual community,' hitherto closed to them due to their inability to read Hebrew.[61] To describe that community was the first step toward reimagining it as a community of their own.[62]

This process can be described in terms analogous to those that some scholars have used to describe the emergence of Christian culture in the Latin West, understood in distinctly *textual* terms, as Martin Irvine

---

[59] Such as the scribe of Odo's *Ysagoge in Theologiam*, ed. Arthur Landgraf in *Écrits Théologiques de l'École d'Abélard* (Louvain: Spicilegium Sacrum Lovaniense #14, 1934), xlvii–xlix. Also, Maurice of Kirkham claimed to have studied Hebrew for three years in his youth; his Hebrew hand was admired by York's Jews (or so he states); see M.R. James, "The Salomites," *Journal of Theological Studies* 35 (1934): 289.

[60] The impulse to legitimate one's work with reference to Hebrew scholarship is nicely illustrated by Ralf Niger, who revised Jerome's *Liber Interpretationis Hebraicorum Nominum* with the help of a Jewish apostate, Philip. Philip guided his consultations of written authorities; Ralf corrected Jerome's interpretations only in cases where all his authorities (written and verbal) concurred: "Neque enim converso meo interpreti credere volui Machuere [sic] vel Aruch astipularentur interpretationi. Sed neque his fidem adhibebam nisi Judei consentirent. Sed neque his tribus assentiebam nisi de veteri testamento vel saltim de Gamalielo suo talis interpretationis significationem ostenderent." *Phillipicus*, fol. 59v; cited in George B. Flahiff, "Ralph Niger: An Introduction to his Life and Works," *Mediaeval Studies* [Toronto] 2 (1940): 122.

[61] To use Brian Stock's coinage; see *The Implications of Literacy* (Princeton: Princeton University Press, 1983), 88–92.

[62] As Jeremy Cohen has argued, Christian recognition of the textual community of post-biblical Judaism generated mounting hostility toward the Jews, especially in the thirteenth century. By that point, the Christian task of "reimagining" a world of Hebrew texts had become instead a project of appropriation—or destruction.

has suggested, building on the work of Brian Stock.[63] Irvine especially has noted how Late Antique pagan culture, mediated by the vehicles of *grammatica* and attendant concepts of *latinitas*, was transformed at the hands of Augustine, Cassiodorus, and Bede. The transformation centered around the establishment of a canon of authoritative texts and a tradition of commentary associated with them, a shift from Vergil to the Bible, in essence. Around the canon, a community developed. One enters a textual community through the process of appropriating the texts and their history of interpretation. Medievalists such as Stock and R.I. Moore have argued that the relationship of a community to its authoritative texts could become attenuated—although no less authoritative for that reason. Not everyone in a medieval textual community was actively literate in its traditions, yet even those who could not read the central texts accorded authority to them. Moore has argued that adherents of some such communities possessed 'passive literacy,' which might consist only in their notional assent to the authority of a certain body of writings.[64] The authority ascribed to the communally accepted canon by the actively literate—those people actively engaged in mediating the texts to others through teaching, preaching, and contributing to the commentary tradition—was enough to encompass others within its ambit.

So likewise twelfth-century Christian hebraists, whether inexpertly or passively literate in Hebrew and Jewish exegesis, might have existed on the margins of the Jewish textual community. Christian hebraists like Herbert of Bosham were necessarily within the ambit of the Jewish community, the only source of an authoritative textual tradition. By the last quarter of the twelfth century and into the first quarter of the thirteenth, a cadre of Christian scholars had emerged which claimed acquaintance with the *libri Gamalielis* (a euphemism for the Talmud and rabbinic literature[65]), and with the lexica of Menahem ben Saruq, Dunash ibn Labrat, and R. Nathan ben Yehiel of Rome. Some of these Christians also claim to have studied Hebrew themselves. This, too, is

---

[63] Brian Stock, *The Implications of Literacy*; Martin Irvine, *The Making of Textual Culture: Grammatica and Literary Theory, 350–1100* (Cambridge: Cambridge University Press, 1994), 3–38.

[64] R.I. Moore, "Literacy and the Making of Heresy," *Heresy and Literacy, 1000–1530* (Cambridge: Cambridge University Press, 1994).

[65] On the possible referents for this term, see Frans Van Liere, "Twelfth-Century Christian Scholars and the Attribution of the Talmud," *Medieval Perspectives* 17:2 (2002), 93–104.

a change: Hebrew knowledge had been claimed *for* an individual (perhaps only to establish his scholarly reputation). Now, individual scholars actively affirmed their mastery of Hebrew. The goal may be the same: literacy in Hebrew and Greek were perhaps 'rhetorical flourishes' used by scholars to inflate their reputations.[66] As we have previously indicated, this group of Hebrew scholars was almost entirely English or Anglo-Norman: Odo, the author of the *Ysagoge in Theologiam*; Maurice of Kirkham, an Augustinian prior from Yorkshire; Ralf Niger, a satellite of the Becket circle; Herbert of Bosham, and Alexander Neckam, a Paris-trained theologian turned canon. All these scholars necessarily sought their higher training in France and were already multi-lingual (in Latin and French, if not also Anglo-Saxon). They had had to make their own ways in a highly competitive academic world. They were all secular clergy rather than monks (urban, mobile, and thus easily able to make contact with Jews). Their activities as literate men in the Anglo-Norman world doubtless exposed them to the exchange of Hebrew and Latin documents used by their contemporaries to secure property and cash. All of them attested access to Hebrew scriptures written in Hebrew. In summary, all these men had the means, motive, and opportunity to learn the rudiments of that language—or to claim that they had done so. Their desire to learn might have been supplemented by their desire to parade the latest and best skills, the better to impress potential employers.

Another feature of this cohort's Hebrew knowledge was a professed ability to discriminate among the scholarship of their Jewish peers. As noted above, Stephen Harding sought out Jews learned in their scriptures ("Judaeos quosdam in sua Scriptura peritos adivimus"). Subsequent adventurers in this brave new world would make even stronger claims: Herbert claimed to have consulted *peritiores iudeorum litteratores*.[67] Besides beginning to define the curriculum of Christian hebraism, Herbert and the men of his generation began to differentiate between learned and 'the most learned' Jews. Whether this claim has substance is less significant than the fact that it is made: the claim evinces self-confidence, if not actual mastery.

---

[66] Smalley suggested that Herbert's claim to know Greek would probably dissolve as a "rhetorical flourish;" "A Commentary on the *Hebraica* by Herbert of Bosham," *RTAM* 18 (1951): 41.

[67] As in Psalm 88[89]:52, discussed above. He makes similar claims at Psalm 5:1, 41[42]:1, and 87[88]:11.

Construing the Christian encounter with Judaism in terms of crossing the boundary into the northern European Jewish textual community suggests other techniques to describe the position of Christian
hebraists, drawn from colonial discourse analysis. Although typically
applied to the modern history of European colonialism's tools and
effects, some of its methods have been applied by medievalists, especially in literary studies.[68] Its application to the Christian encounter
with Judaism sparked by biblical scholarship seems especially apt. In
this case, the utility of colonial discourse analysis, or its successor methodology of postcolonial theory, stems from its technique of looking
across genre lines to discern how ideology is embedded in all forms
of literature and hence in the 'knowledge base,' or archive, of a culture.

Edward Said's *Orientalism*, originally published in 1978, is generally
regarded as the seedbed of colonial discourse analysis. Said argued
that the West created 'the Orient' as a discursive entity. That is, while
colonialism clearly functioned on political and economic levels, it also
helped to foster the conditions that created Orientalism, or "the corporate institution for dealing with the Orient—dealing with it by making
statements about it, authorizing views of it, describing it, by teaching it,
settling it, ruling over it."[69] In turn, the Orientalist body of discourse—
"the enormously systematic discipline by which European culture was
able to manage—and even produce—the Orient politically, sociologi-
cally, ideologically, scientifically, and imaginatively"[70] contributed to the
"production of actual forms of colonial administration and subjuga-
tion."[71] Said insisted that the textual Orient created by Western narratives, scholarly and popular, effectively displaced any 'real' encounter
between cultures.[72] Colonial discourse analysis tries to demonstrate how
that displacement is achieved by examining a broad range of literary

---

[68] See the essays collected in *The Postcolonial Middle Ages*, ed. Jeffrey Jerome Cohen
(NY: Palgrave, 2000), which illustrate, in some cases provocatively, the range of uses to
which the methodology can be put.

[69] Edward W. Said, *Orientalism* (New York: Pantheon, 1978), 3.

[70] Said, 3.

[71] Robert J.C. Young, *Colonial Desire: Hybridity in Theory, Culture, and Race* (NY: Routledge, 1995), 160.

[72] Said, 5–6; see also 20–21: "… the written statement is a presence to the reader
by virtue of its having excluded, displaced, made supererogatory any such *real thing* as
'the Orient.'… [T]hat Orientalism makes sense at all depends more on the West than
on the Orient, and this sense is directly indebted to various Western techniques of
representation that make the Orient visible, clear, 'there' in discourses about it."

genres.[73] Subsequent practitioners, such as Homi Bhabha and Gaya-tri Spivak, have focused on the dynamics of displacement and sought to bring the voices of the 'other' Orient to the surface. I am bracket-ing, for now, discussion of the critiques of these authors.[74] One criticism that is germane, however, is that in his formulation of the dynamics of Orientalism, Edward Said overlooked Judaism, both in the terms of its status as an 'Orientalized' form of knowledge developed by Christians as well as the role of European Jewish scholars in the study of Mid-dle Eastern languages and cultures.[75] Indeed, as some medievalists have argued, the Jews were the subject of internal colonization in medieval Europe. As such, they were subjected to the material forms of exploita-tion common to colonialism, as well as to being recreated in textual or discursive forms that displaced their lived reality.[76]

Also pertinent to this discussion is the work of Homi Bhabha, who extends Said's analysis of the strategic location of Orientalist authors and the strategic formation of the Orientalist archive,[77] in an attempt to overcome binary oppositions of colonizer/colonized, powerful/power-less, black/white. Bhabha's formulation also restores some degree of agency to subject peoples: they are not merely passive ciphers in the colonist's imagination, but shape the colonial encounter through vari-ous kinds of tacit or open resistance.[78] The encounter is neither one-

---

[73] Said writes, "[Orientalism] is rather a *distribution* of geopolitical awareness into aesthetic, scholarly, economic, sociological, historical and philological texts ... it *is*, rather than expresses, a certain *will* or *intention* to understand, in some cases to control, manipulate, even to incorporate, what is a manifestly different (or alternative and novel) world; it is, above all, a discourse that is by no means in direct corresponding relationship with political power in the raw, but rather is produced and exists in an uneven exchange with various kinds of power. ... Indeed, my real argument is that Orientalism is—and does not simply represent—a considerable dimension of modern political-intellectual culture, and as such has less to do with the Orient than it does with 'our' world." *Orientalism*, 12; emphasis in the original.

[74] See the thorough discussion in Bart Moore-Gilbert's *Postcolonial Theory* (London: Verso, 1997).

[75] As discussed in Susannah Heschel's "Revolt of the Colonized: Abraham Geiger's *Wissenschaft des Judentums* as a Challenge to Christian Hegemony in the Academy," *New German Critique* 77 (1999), 61–85.

[76] Sylvia Tomasch elegantly outlines the complexities of understanding the condition of Jews (in her case, the Jews of thirteenth century England) in terms of colonialism in her essay "Postcolonial Chaucer and the Virtual Jew," *The Postcolonial Middle Ages*, ed. Jeffrey Jerome Cohen (NY: Palgrave, 2000). See especially pages 249–252.

[77] *Orientalism*, 20.

[78] For a thorough discussion of the range and limitations of Bhabha's approach, particularly as it concerns agency and political resistance, see Moore-Gilbert, 130–151.

sided nor top-down but played out on the borders (or interstices) of cross-cultural contact:

> [Bhabha] has shown how colonial discourse of whatever kind operated not only as an instrumental construction of knowledge but also according to the ambivalent protocols of fantasy and desire. Ambivalence is a key word for Bhabha, which he takes from psychoanalysis where it was first developed to describe a continual fluctuation between wanting one thing and its opposite (also "simultaneous attraction toward and repulsion from an object, person, or action.")[79]

According to Bhabha, being torn between the object of desire which is simultaneously a source of repulsion results in the creation of a 'stereotype' of the Other which is necessarily unstable. Contrary to the commonplace notion of a stereotype as a fixed, reductive caricature,[80] Bhabha argues that a stereotype generated by the colonial experience is infused with positive and negative qualities, either of which can be accentuated according to the circumstances and requirements of the person (or culture) that generates the stereotype.[81] The shifting valence of the stereotype, reconstructed in response to changing conditions, helps to explain the ambiguous representations of Jews that we encounter in the twelfth century especially—a period when European Christians were confronted with experiences that challenged existing explanatory models for the perdurance of Judaism.

Bhabha's application of ambivalence to the colonial situation is closely paralleled by sociologist Zygmunt Bauman's analysis of the status of Jews in Europe.[82] Bauman argues that the history of Christian Europe's

---

[79] Young, 161.

[80] Bhabha argues that colonial discourse constructs the stereotypical colonial subject as "fixed" or static, as "that particular 'fixated' form of the colonial subject which *facilitates* colonial relations, and sets up a discursive form of racial and cultural opposition in terms of which colonial power is exercised." "The Other Question," *The Location of Culture* (London and New York: Routledge, 1994), 78; emphasis in the original. Notwithstanding this reliance on fixity, however, Bhabha's point is that the stereotype is inherently unstable, because it is "a form of knowledge and identification that vacillates between what is always 'in place,' already known, and something that must be anxiously repeated." Op. cit., 66.

[81] This is Moore-Gilbert's summation of the function of stereotypes presented by Bhabha in "The Other Question." In the essay, Bhabha argues "Stereotyping is not the setting up of a false image which becomes the scapegoat of discriminatory practices. It is a much more ambivalent text of projection and introjection, metaphoric and metynomic strategies, displacement, overdetermination, guilt, aggressivity; the masking and splitting of 'official' and phantasmatic knowledges to construct the positionalities and oppositionalities of racist discourse." "The Other Question," 81–82.

[82] "Allosemitism: Premodern, Modern, Postmodern," *Modernity, Culture, and "the Jew"*,

deep ambivalence toward Jews and Judaism negates the simple categories of anti-Semitism or philosemitism. He argues instead for the use
of the term 'allosemitism,' which refers to

> the practice of setting the Jews apart as people radically different from
> all the others … it does not unambiguously determine either hatred or
> love of Jews, but contains the seeds of both, and assures that whichever of
> the two appears, is intense and extreme. The original non-commitment
> (that is, the fact that allosemitism is, perhaps must be, already in place for
> anti- or philosemitism to be conceivable) makes allosemitism a radically
> *ambivalent* attitude.[83]

Christians have been ambivalent about Jews, Bauman argues, in part
because Jews historically embodied ambivalance,[84] "simultaneously attractive and repelling," serving as Christianity's "alter ego, marking the
spatial and temporal boundaries of the Christian civilization." Bauman
contends that ambivalence gives rise to "all ordering concerns": putting
a thing in its place is a response to perceived disorder. Ironically,
however, the act of ordering also creates ambivalence: "all classification
has its leftovers which span the sacrosanct divide between the classes."
Bauman concludes his assessment of premodern allosemitism:

> The Christian Church's struggle with the unassimilable, yet indispens-
> able modality of the Jews bequeathed to later ages two factors crucial to
> the emergence and self-perpetuation of allosemitism. The first, the cast-
> ing of the Jews as the embodiment of ambivalence, that is of dis-order;
> once cast in this mould, Jews could serve as the dumping ground for all
> new varieties of ambivalence which later times were still to produce. And
> the second, the *abstract Jew*, the Jew as a concept located in a different

---

eds. Bryan Cheyette and Laura Marcus (Stanford: Stanford University Press, 1998),
143–156. Sylvia Tomasch's essay, "Postcolonial Chaucer and the Virtual Jew," cited
above, introduced me to Bauman's thesis. Tomasch's study notes that positive and
negative representations of Jews sometimes coexist pictorially or textually in medieval
literary works: "As we have seen in other post/colonial texts, in the *Canterbury Tales* 'the
Jew' is never entirely or solely negative; in certain instances the sign can be understood,
at least superficially, as philo-Semitic." She adopts "allosemitism" as a conceptual tool
that accounts for these ambivalent representations. *The Postcolonial Middle Ages*, 249–
250.

[83] Bauman, 143; emphasis in the original.

[84] Bauman asks rhetorically: "How did the Jews become ambivalence incarnate?
There was from the start, from the times of antiquity, an incongruous, in a way absurd
feature in the Jewish mode of existence which must have made neighbours pause and
wonder: a numerically tiny nation, negligible as a military power, one of the many petty
pawns the ancient empires passed from one to the other …—and yet a nation imbued
with the sense of grandeur, of being chosen, of being the hard centre of the world and
of history …" "Allosemitism," 147.

discourse from the practical knowledge of "empirical" Jews, and hence located at a secure distance from experience and immune to whatever information may be supplied by that experience and whatever emotions may be aroused by daily intercourse.[85]

Herbert of Bosham stands at the threshold of these developments, both spatially and temporally. He was not "located at a secure distance" from practical knowledge of real Jews, but interacted closely with them. His achievements as a hebraist, while perhaps less unique or isolated than has been previously imagined, foreshadow the next generation's work but were distinctly different from it. The thirteenth century witnessed the development of the tools Christians needed to gain expertise in Hebrew without the help of Jews. It would also usher in the age of expulsions that exiled Jews from daily intercourse with their Christian neighbors. The abstract—or stereotypical, hermeneutical, virtual—Jew, a construct vital to Christian thought at least since Augustine, would continue to change, both in terms of its theological utility (as discussed in the preceding chapter), but also culturally. What Bauman calls the toxic waste of order-making would marry the abstract Judaism of the emerging encyclopedic archive of Christianity to the "narrative assault" on Jews, engendered in stereotypes and sustained in the tales of blood libel, host desecration, and well-poisoning—even in those regions of Europe which had been made *Judenrein*.[86] That assault was well-launched in Herbert's time, but he and others still enjoyed—and were vexed by—their status as frontiersmen, collecting new data from which Christianity's authoritative representations of Judaism would be distilled.[87] Close readings of passages from Herbert's psalms commentary demonstrate how attraction, affinity, and ambivalence were played out in the context of his lived encounter with Jews and Judaism. But how did that encounter happen? Where and how did twelfth-century Christians study Hebrew?

---

[85] Bauman, 148.

[86] Bauman, 148. The term "narrative assault" is Miri Rubin's; see her *Gentile Tales: The Narrative Assault on Late Medieval Jews* (New Haven: Yale University Press, 1999).

[87] Edward Said's perspectives on both authority and representation as a mode of extending cultural hegemony are instructive here. On authority he writes, "There is nothing mysterious or natural about authority. It is formed, irradiated, disseminated; it is instrumental, it is persuasive; it has status, it establishes canons of taste and value; it is virtually indistinguishable from certain ideas it dignifies as true, and from traditions, perceptions, and judgments it forms, transmits, reproduces." *Orientalism*, 19–20.

The first formal schools of instruction in 'oriental' languages appear to have been founded by the Order of Preachers only in the first half of the thirteenth century.[88] In the absence of formal instruction, then, a twelfth-century Christian might seek the services of a Jewish apostate. But how many such converts to Christianity were able to read Biblical or rabbinic Hebrew? A larger question is thus raised: what did it mean for a medieval Jew in northern France, for example, to 'know' Hebrew? Would such knowledge be adequate to enable a Jew, apostate or otherwise, to instruct a Christian?

The notion that literacy and numeracy were widespread among medieval Jews has been a long-held, widespread belief among medievalists. Only recently, however, has this question been subjected to measured, objective analysis, chiefly at the hands of Ephraim Kanarfogel and, before him, Bernhard Blumenkranz.[89] Until their work established otherwise, extravagant claims had been made for the extent, complexity, and formality of a Jewish system of education in medieval Europe, ranging from primary schools, to academies, to a virtual university at Rouen, this last posited by Norman Golb.[90] In tandem with the presumption of widespread Jewish literacy and the Jews' concomitant ability to serve emerging forms of 'bureaucratic' government, R.I. Moore has suggested that anti-Jewish sentiments of the late twelfth and early thirteenth centuries were fomented by Christian clerics who sought to maintain a monopoly of skills indispensable to Europe's rulers.[91] Thanks chiefly to Blumenkranz and Kanarfogel, a more nuanced view of the educational facilities that promoted Jewish literacy is emerging. In particular, both scholars have pointed to earlier tendencies to extrapolate from data found in some communities to a general theory regarding the education of all Jews across Europe. The educational opportunities available to Jews in northern France, England, and Germany (*Ashkenaz*) was not uniform, nor was it by any means identical with that of Jews in southern France, Iberia, or the rest of the Mediterranean region (*Sefarad*). Kanarfogel argues persuasively for a decentral-

---

[88] Smalley, *SBMA*, 338–339.

[89] Ephraim Kanarfogel, *Jewish Education and Society in the High Middle Ages* (Detroit: Wayne State University Press, 1993); Bernhard Blumenkranz, "La Synagogue de Rouen," *Art et archéologie des Juifs en France mediévale*, ed. B. Blumenkranz (Toulouse: Privat, 1980), 277–303.

[90] Norman Golb, "Les Écoles Rabbiniques en France au Moyen Age," *Revue de l'histoire des religions* 102 (1985): 243–265.

[91] R.I. Moore, *The Formation of a Persecuting Society* (Oxford: Blackwell, 1992), 135–140.

ized system of Jewish education in *Ashkenaz*. Children were educated at home, or in the homes of more prosperous family friends or relations, by itinerant instructors (*melammedim*). Even when they grew older, Kanarfogel maintains, the education of some students in academies (*yeshivot*) was still an essentially home-based affair. Promising students were taken into the household of an eminent scholar, whose work as a teacher might have been supported financially by the larger community. Kanarfogel demonstrates convincingly, however, that even these *yeshivot* were not communal schools on the order posited by Robert Chazan, for instance, nor was their existence predicated on a formal system of community-funded elementary education.[92]

While the work of Kanarfogel and Blumenkranz may have corrected the perception of the scope and elaborateness of medieval Jewish education in *Ashkenaz*, the supposition that Jews were more likely to be literate and numerate than their Christian contemporaries is still generally accepted. Along the spectrum of "orality" to "textuality," Jews were more dependent on literacy as a mechanism of maintaining religious and social unity, for instance.[93] Living in widely-scattered small communities, they had frequent recourse to experts in *halakhah* who lived at a distance and with whom they communicated in writing. The Jews' difficult task of negotiating the boundaries between ritual practices that maintained their religious unity and distinctiveness and the need to survive in the dominant Christian society would have been impossible, and terrifying, without access to the virtual community created by correspondence and the exchange of *responsa*.[94] Similarly, as Michael Clanchy has pointed out, the use of written documentation to seal business exchanges arose chiefly in the twelfth century as a means for accommodating social dislocation. Old ways of affirming communal ties (and binding contracts) based on visual ritual or shared symbols gave way to documents, especially among people no longer bound by custom or language. Clanchy based his theory on a study of the bureaucracy of the Plantagenets and Angevins in England. The Norman ruling class resorted to extensive record-keeping in order to

---

[92] See Kanarfogel, Chs. 3 and 4.

[93] Brigitte Bedos-Rezak, "The Confrontation of Orality and Textuality: Jewish and Christian Literacy in Eleventh- and Twelfth-Century Northern France," *RASHI 1040–1990: Hommage à Ephraim E. Urbach*, Patrimoines Judaisme, ed. Gabrielle Sed-Rajna (Paris: Cerf, 1993), 545.

[94] Jacob Katz, *Exclusiveness and Tolerance* (W. Orange, NJ: Behrman House, 1983), 24–47.

maintain control over its Anglo-Saxon subjects. While earlier transactions in Anglo-Saxon England had been secured through ritual and preserved in communal memory, Anglo-Norman society was a textual community founded on mutual suspicion.[95] The mutual mistrust that Clanchy documents among contracting parties of Anglo-Saxons and Normans was doubtless heightened between Christians and Jews. To the barriers of custom and language was added the barrier of ultimate allegiance. Thus, business contacts between Jews and Christians were committed to paper early and often. Clanchy noted that England's first public 'archive' was the *archa iudaeorum* at York which held the records, in Hebrew and in Latin, of transactions between that city's business people of both faiths.[96] Although not systematically organized until after 1194, England's *archae* were extant in some form at least by 1190 if not earlier. Christian rioters at York destroyed the records stored in the Minster of that year during the violence that decimated York's Jewish community.[97]

Finally, but by no means least, the singular importance of literacy as a feature of Jewish religious practice should be noted. To read and study the Torah was a meritorious act of devotion and piety, a *mitzvah* or commandment. Every letter of scripture was worthy of study and could disclose riches of insight. Communal worship in the synagogue depended on the presence of at least ten adult males able to read the weekly portions from the unpointed Torah scrolls. Parents were thus enjoined by duty and devotion to educate their children, a religious duty known as *hinnukh*.[98] Children were taught either by their father or by a *melammed* (tutor) to read the Hebrew alphabet and to begin to read the Bible.[99] Christians were apparently aware that Jews were committed to educating their children more extensively than they themselves were. That at least is the conclusion drawn by contemporary scholars from a passage frequently cited in support of the superiority of medieval Jewish

---

[95] M.T. Clanchy, *From Memory to Written Record: England 1066–1307*, 2nd ed. (Cambridge: Blackwell Publishers, 1993); see especially Ch. 2, "The Proliferation of Documents."

[96] Clanchy, 167.

[97] R.B. Dobson, "The Jews of Medieval York and the Massacre of March 1190," Borthwick Papers No. 45 (York: Borthwick Institute of Historical Research, 1974).

[98] Christoph Cluse, "Jewish Elementary Education in Medieval Ashkenaz," *Seriis Intendere: A Collection of Essays Celebrating the Twenty-fifth Anniversary of the Centre for Medieval Studies*, ed. Sharon A. Hanen (Leeds, 1994), 7–14; 7.

[99] Kanarfogel, 31. See also Ivan G. Marcus, *Rituals of Childhood: Jewish Acculturation in Medieval Europe* (New Haven: Yale University Press, 1996).

education. The passage was unearthed by Arthur Landgraf when he edited a collection of commentaries on Paul's epistles by a student of Peter Abelard, and was translated and reproduced by Beryl Smalley in *The Study of the Bible in the Middle Ages*:

> If the Christians educate their sons, they do so not for God, but for gain, in order that the one brother, if he be a clerk, may help his father and mother and his other brothers. ... But the Jews out of zeal for God and love of the law, put as many sons as they have to letters, that each may understand God's law ... A Jew, however poor, if he had ten sons would put the all to letters, not for gain, as the Christians do, but for the understanding of God's law, and not only for his sons, but his daughters.[100]

Since Smalley published this passage, it has been reproduced often by scholars of the medieval Jewish-Christian encounter. Curiously, no one seems to have returned *ad fontes*, either to the context of the comment in Landgraf's edition or to the source named there. The Abelardian commentator is discussing Ephesians 6:4: "And you, fathers, do not provoke your children to anger, but rear them in the discipline and admonition of the Lord." He writes:

> Indeed "rear in the discipline," etc. Hence it is that the Jews are often able to charge us, as the blessed Jerome says in that passage, where is said about Susanna: "For her parents being just, have educated their daughter according to the law of Moses." (Dan 13:3) [The quotation translated by Smalley follows.][101]

In Jerome's commentary on Daniel 13, the relevant portion reads:

> "For her parents being just, have educated their daughter according to the law of Moses" (Dan. 13:3). This testimony must be used for exhorting parents: May they teach not only their sons but their daughters as well, according to the law of God and the divine word.[102]

---

[100] Smalley, *SBMA*, 78.

[101] "Imo 'educate in disciplina,' etc. Hinc est iudei nos multum possunt arguere, sicut beatus Jeronimus dicit super illum locum, ubi de Susanna dicitur: 'Et parentes eius, cum essent iusti, erudierunt filiam suam secundum legem Moysi' [Dan 13:3] ..." The quotation translated by Smalley follows, ending] "... omnes ad litteras mitteret non propter lucrum sicut christiani, sed propter legem Dei intelligendam, et non solum filios, sed et filias ..." Arthur Landgraf, ed. *Commentarius Cantabrigiensis in Epistolas Pauli e Schola Petri Abelardi*, vol. II (Notre Dame, IN: Publications in Medieval Studies, 1939) 433–434.

[102] "*Et parentes eius erant iusti et docuerunt filiam suam iuxta legem Moysi.* Hoc utendum est testimonio ad exhortationem parentum: ut doceant iuxta legem Dei sermonemque divinum non solum filios sed filias suas." *Commentariorum in Danielem Libri III (IV)* CCSL, 75A, 945.

All of the material interpolated by Abelard's student may have reflected contemporary reality but one wonders if in fact, either in the time of Jerome or Abelard, Jewish girls were educated (like Susanna) in the Law of Moses? Did training in God's Law necessarily entail literacy and numeracy, or only oral instruction? Modern scholars affirm that this passage testifies to Christian awareness of Jewish educational practices, and some scholars imply that such awareness was widespread. This is a difficult conclusion to support, however, as this manuscript is unique and seems not to have circulated widely.

Better evidence for Jewish commitment to education is found in Jewish sources, such as R. Joseph Kimhi's polemical work *The Book of the Covenant*. The rabbi's evidence for the wholesomeness of Jewish life, compared to that of Christians, includes a reference to the Jews' willingness to "raise their children, from the youngest to the oldest, in the study of the Torah."[103] Such a comment in a polemical treatise designed to instruct Jews how to respond to Christian critiques suggests that the Jews were well-aware that their attention to their children's upbringing was remarkable. Among the Jews of Northern Europe in the Middle Ages, elementary instruction in Hebrew seems to have been done orally; no grammars or lexica suitable for children (or other beginning students) survive from the eleventh or twelfth centuries. In a series of articles and essays accompanying critical editions, Menahem Banitt has postulated the existence of an Old French translation or paraphrase of the Hebrew Bible, a *Targum* in effect. He has argued that the translation was transmitted orally and was used to teach young children or women how to read and interpret scripture. Fragments of the translation surface in two forms. The first form are the *la'azim*, or vernacular glosses, present in Rashi's biblical and Talmudic commentaries (and in those of the earlier generation of Rhenish scholars). The *la'azim* translate difficult, obscure, or antique words from Biblical Hebrew into contemporary Old French for the benefit of non-specialist readers. Rashi himself drew some of his glosses from the work of teachers he called *poterim*, whom Banitt describes as teachers at the next level of instruction beyond the *melammedim*.[104] He writes:

---

[103] It would be useful to know if the Hebrew here refers to all children or only male children. *The Book of the Covenant*, ed. and trans., Frank E. Talmage (Toronto: Pontifical Institute of Medieval Studies, 1972), 32.

[104] See also the helpful discussion of the various categories of instruction in Kanarfogel, *Jewish Education and Society in the High Middle Ages*, 80–85.

We may also assume that, as was the case in later centuries and in other countries, it was with the translation of the Bible into the vernacular that the children took the second step of their Jewish education, after having learned to read and write. The teachers who taught according to this method are doubtless alluded to by Rashi when he speaks of the *poterim*.[105]

Banitt asserts that traces of the *poterim*'s vernacular translation survive in a second form, that of Hebrew-Old French glossaries from the thirteenth century. The glossaries consist of Hebrew words defined by one or two Old French words, transliterated by Hebrew characters.[106] To use the glossaries, therefore, one would need at least a rudimentary knowledge of the Hebrew alphabet and pronunciation. Banitt has edited and published two glossaries which, he suggests, provide fragmentary evidence for what was once a complete vernacular translation.[107] He argues, "the vernacular gloss does not strictly correspond to the Hebrew word [in the glossary], but shows lexical and syntactical deviations which can only be ascribed to an underlying running translation."[108] No written copy of such a translation survives, however.

The work of the *poterim* relates to the discussion of Jewish literacy and the general prospects for how a Christian might learn Hebrew in several ways. First, we know from Rashi's own testimony that the *poterim* were active in his lifetime if not earlier.[109] Thus, even before the dawn

---

[105] Menahem Banitt, "The *La'azim* of Rashi and of the French Biblical Glossaries," *World History of the Jewish People: The Dark Ages 711–1096*, ed. Cecil Roth (New Brunswick, NJ: Rutgers University Press, 1966), 293. See also *idem*, "Les Poterim," *Revue des Études Juives* 125(1966): 21–33.

[106] Ben Zion Wacholder notes that the use of the Latin alphabet was forbidden by the Talmud, which might explain why the French glosses were written in Hebrew characters. Wacholder, "Cases of Proselytizing in the Tosafist Responsa," *Jewish Quarterly Review* 51(1960): 302–304. Raphael Levy argued that medieval Jews simply did not know how to write in Latin characters but this seems unlikely, given the level of business transactions engaged in by Jews and Christians who exchanged documents written in *both* languages; Levy, "The Use of Hebrew Characters for Writing Old French," *Mélanges de Langue et de Littérature du Moyen Age et de la Renaissance offerts à Jean Frappier* (Geneva: Librairie Droz, 1970), vol. II: 646. Also, there is evidence that by the late twelfth century, some Jews owned Latin manuscripts, either for purposes of study or as objects of valued pawned by Christians; see Wacholder, 302–304.

[107] *Sefer ha-pitronot mi-Bazel (Le glossaire de Bâle)*, ed. and ann. by Menahem Banitt (Jerusalem: Académie nationale des sciences et des lettres d'Israël, 1972); *Le glossaire de Leipzig*, ed. and ann. by Menahem Banitt (Jerusalem: Académie nationale des sciences et des lettres d'Israël, 1995).

[108] Banitt, "The *La'azim* of Rashi," 294.

[109] Rashi occasionally mentions the explanations of the *poterim* in his psalms commentary. See Gruber, 78 n. 3, 312 n. 104, 338 n. 46.

of the twelfth century, Jewish children were being taught the rudiments of their tradition in both Hebrew and in the vernacular languages of *Ashkenaz*. In a sense, Jews in this period were taught how to communicate elements of their religious life in a language that, willy-nilly, they shared with Christians. So a Christian who inquired about Judaism from a contemporary Jew was likely to receive a well-articulated vernacular response. Willing or not, Jews were equipped to talk about their culture through the vehicle of a familiar language.[110] Secondly, the Hebrew-French glosses that appeared in the thirteenth century (and for the most part, early in that century) did not simply materialize out of thin air. Banitt makes this useful analogy: "It is precisely the richness of these glossaries that led to the disappearance of the older ones, in the same way as Rashi's successful commentaries caused his sources to remain uncopied, and therefore to be lost."[111] Quite possibly manuscripts of Hebrew-French glossaries existed in the twelfth century. Moreover, the glossaries relied not only on the definitions provided by the *poterim*, but by the early thirteenth century had expanded to include *la'azim* culled from the commentaries of Rashi, his grandsons R. Samuel ben Meir (Rashbam) and R. Jacob Tam (Rabbenu Tam); R. Joseph Qara, R. Joseph Bekhor Shor, and R. Eliezer of Beaugency—all sources identified in the thirteenth-century manuscript edited by Brandin and Lambert (BN hebr. 302).[112] It is likely, therefore, that a systematic effort had been made to collect an exhaustive biblical dictionary for the use of twelfth-century Jewish readers in northern France, drawn from the best contemporary sources.[113] It would have been possible for a Christian who had learned the rudiments of the Hebrew alphabet and received some tutoring in Hebrew grammar to grasp at least some of the definitions and comparisons offered in the glossaries.[114] Certainly a Christian could have learned much by studying the glossaries with the help of a Jew (or an apostate).

---

[110] A condition described by Signer, "Introduction," CCCM 53E, xxii.

[111] Banitt, "The *La'azim* of Rashi," 294.

[112] Louis Brandin and Mayer Lambert, *Glossaire Hébreu-Français du XIIIe siècle* (Geneva: Slatkine Reprints, 1977).

[113] Brandin and Lambert identified dialects from Champagne, Lorraine, and Burgundy-Comte among the *la'azim* provided in the *Glossaire*.

[114] An encounter on this level between a Christian and a Jewish instructor in Hebrew might address Gilbert Dahan's criticism of Andrew of Saint Victor and other Christian exegetes of the 'plain meaning.' Dahan thinks that Christians repeated haggadic material obatined from Jewish interlocutors and mistakenly assumed it represented the 'plain meaning' or *peshat*. Dahan argues that Christians thus did not obtain the most

Still, all the evidence that accompanies the surviving thirteenth-century glossaries (Banitt has studied six) suggests that they were developed for use within the Jewish community. Whether a Jew would have shared such knowledge with a Christian unless coerced is unlikely, although not impossible. Negative evidence, in the forms of behavior prohibited by some Jews, suggests that some such scholarly interaction did take place. A good source for such negative evidence is the *Sefer Hasidim*, a late-twelfth century document of the pietist movement of Jews in the Rhineland. The book cautions its readers repeatedly against consorting with Christians, against reading or even owning Latin books, against teaching Hebrew to non-Jews, and against the proud, worldly manners of their northern French co-religionists, who delighted in dialectic and in showing off their knowledge. It seems that some northern French Jews might have engaged in some or all of the behaviors disparaged by the *hasidim*.[115]

The prohibition against teaching Hebrew to non-Jews is particularly important for our purposes. The author of the *Sefer Hasidim* forbade it, but whether this prohibition represents actuality or simply a *desideratum* is unclear.[116] What is clear is that by the middle of the twelfth cen-

'scientific' exegesis from the true *savants* (whom he apparently associates with the *pashtanim*, as interpreters of the plain meaning were called). Perhaps, however, Dahan (like Smalley) confused science (*viz.* modern philology) with learning as the medievals understood it. If Andrew and other Christians sought out the "most learned" of the Jews, they may not have been sent to *poterim* or *pashtanim*. They would have been sent to Judaism's most comprehensive scholars, ones who knew the tradition best. It would be ironic if what Dahan and Smalley defined as the most advanced forms of exegesis were in fact viewed by medieval Jews as intermediate or even introductory forms. Gilbert Dahan, "Juifs et Chrétiens en Occident Médiéval: La Rencontre autour de la Bible (XIIe–XIVe Siècles)," *Revue de Synthèse* 4:1 (1989): 3–31; 15.

[115] See the materials from the *Sefer Hasidim* arranged under the headings "L'activité intellectuelle des juifs ..." and "Les Juifs dans la ville et leurs rapports avec leurs voisins," in *Le Guide des Hassidim*, sel. and trans. Édouard Gourévitch (Paris: Cerf, 1988), 253–374. Whether this disparagement had any actual effect is unknown: the radical movement of pietism that engendered the *Sefer Hasidim* was a small, idealistic sect according to Ivan G. Marcus, *Piety and Society: The Jewish Pietists of Medieval Germany* (Leiden: Brill, 1981); see especially Chapter 4, "The Radical Mode of Sectarian Pietism." Ephraim Kanarfogel discusses the negative reaction of the *hasidim* to the talmudic scholars of twelfth-century Northern France, the *tosafot*, in *Jewish Education and Society in the High Middle Ages*, Chapter 6.

[116] Jacob Katz argued that in this prohibition as in others, *Sefer Hasidim* exceeded the rules separating Jews from Christians articulated in *BT Avodah Zara*. Katz, *Exclusiveness and Tolerance*, 92–99. More recently, Martin Lockshin has suggested (based on a comparison of evidence in the works of Andrew of Saint Victor and R. Samuel ben Meir [Rashbam]) that Jews in Northern France did teach some elements of Hebrew

tury, some Christians were beginning to learn the elements of Hebrew, either from Jews or from apostates. Hugh of Saint Victor (d. 1141) and Andrew of Saint Victor (d. 1175) exhibited elementary knowledge of the language in their scriptural commentaries. Book Two of the *Ysagoge in Theologiam*, a mid-century work by the otherwise unknown Odo, was intended by its author to cite key scriptural texts (such as the decalogue and verses from the prophets) in Hebrew, in order to refute Jewish exegesis.[117] Odo proposed to provide the Hebrew text of scripture, the same text transliterated into the Latin alphabet, and then a literal translation of the text into Latin. In his prologue to Book Two of the *Ysagoge*, the author discusses aspects of the Hebrew alphabet as they relate to the letters of the Latin alphabet he has chosen for his transliterations.[118] Odo's tripartite method of presentation breaks down after the first verse given in Hebrew; his scribe apparently gave up the attempt to transliterate Hebrew in Latin characters. But the Hebrew texts are rendered throughout the *Ysagoge* at the places designated by Odo, and were apparently the work of an inexpert Latin scribe.[119]

The existence of a group of psalters, many of them Anglo-Norman in origin, which contain the Hebrew text annotated with a Latin superscription or with a parallel Latin text, suggests that Odo was not alone in his interest in Hebrew nor in having found a scribe able to write Hebrew, expertly or not.[120] One Hebrew-Latin parallel psalter manuscript of English provenance has been dated to the mid-twelfth century. In independent studies of the manuscript, Raphael Loewe, Margaret Gibson, and G.I. Lieftinck have all asserted that the scribe for

---

to Christians, notwithstanding the judgments to the contrary reached by the Tosafists (as the Talmudists of that region and period are known). "Teaching Torah to Gentiles in Jewish Law and History," *Facing In and Facing Out: Relations with Gentiles in the Eyes of Jewish Traditionalists* (Toronto: Centre for Jewish Studies at York University, 2001), 21–22.

[117] Edited by Arthur Landgraf in *Écrits Théologiques de l'École d'Abélard* (Louvain: Spicilegium Sacrum Lovaniense #14, 1934).

[118] Landgraf, 126–129.

[119] Anna Sapir Abulafia, "Jewish Carnality in Twelfth-Century Renaissance Thought," *Christianity and Judaism*, ed. Diana Wood. Studies in Church History, Volume 29 (Oxford: Blackwell for the Ecclesiastical History Society, 1992), 59–75; 65.

[120] See now the study by Judith Olszowy-Schlanger, who suggests that a high level of Christian expertise in Hebrew made the production of these psalters possible; "The Knowledge and Practice of Hebrew Grammar among Christian Scholars in Pre-expulsion England: The Evidence of 'bilingual' Hebrew-Latin Manuscripts," *Hebrew Scholarship and the Medieval World*, ed. Nicholas de Lange (Cambridge: Cambridge University Press, 2001), 107–128. She further argues that this expertise was most likely gained by collaboration between Jewish and Christian scholars and scribes, 113–114.

both portions was trained in the Latin tradition but was also a competent Hebrew scribe.[121] As Gibson pointed out, given the absence of written grammars and the like, one way for a Christian to learn Hebrew
(or, more likely, to reinforce his reading knowledge) would be to study
a familiar text in both languages.[122] In her recent study of Herbert's
commentary, Eva De Visscher has demonstrated striking textual links
between the Scaliger manuscript and Herbert's amendations to the text
of the Hebraica. She argues that these links confirm the existence of a
body of Hebrew-Latin materials which could have been used by Christian students of the Hebrew language in the mid- to late-twelfth century.[123] Like the Hebrew-French glossaries, most of the other bilingual
psalters date from the early thirteenth century. But as with the glossaries, these texts probably mark an efflorescence of ongoing development, not its earliest buds. Also, it is not at all surprising that the earliest of these Hebrew-Latin parallel or interlinear psalters appeared in
England or Northern France. Thanks to the Plantagenet and Angevin
commitment to documentation, the Anglo-Norman realms were probably most likely to foster the development of multilingual scribes. Likely,
too, were the chances that even a casual observer could have examined documents in both Latin and Hebrew, much less a deeply inquis-
itive scholar like Herbert. Such encounters might easily have led to
discussing the rudiments of Hebrew with an interlocutor.[124]

---

[121] MS Scaliger Hebr. 8. Margaret T. Gibson, *The Bible in the Latin West* (Notre
Dame, IN: University of Notre Dame Press, 1993), 66; G.I. Lieftinck, "The 'Psalterium
Hebraycum' from St. Augustine's Canterbury Rediscovered in the Scaliger Bequest at
Leiden," *Transactions of the Cambridge Bibliographical Society* 2:2 (1955): 97–104; Raphael
Loewe, "The Medieval Christian Hebraists of England: The *Superscriptio Lincolniensis*,"
Hebrew Union College Annual 28 (1957): 205–252. See also Beryl Smalley, *SBMA*, 338–355.
Malachi Beit-Arié has raised the possibility, however, that MS Scaliger 8 could have
been written by a Jewish scribe. See his *The Earliest Dated Anglo-Hebrew Manuscript Written
in England (1189 CE)* (London: Valmadonna Trust Library, 1985), 7–9. He notes that the
MS contains among its marginalia a Hebrew prayer for deliverance of a type found in
MSS written by Jews.

[122] Gibson, *The Bible in the Latin West*, 66.

[123] De Visscher, "The Jewish-Christian Dialogue in Twelfth-Century Western Europe: Herbert of Bosham's *Commentary on the Psalms*," 83–91.

[124] Twelfth-century evidence of such a possibility is provided by the *Starrs and Jewish
Charters Preserved in the British Museum*, Vols. 1–3, eds. Israel Abrahams, H.P. Stokes, and
Herbert Loewe (Cambridge: Jewish Historical Society, 1930–1932). As the authors note
in the Introduction to Volume 1, "The Jews from the first must have had their bonds
and their releases in connection with their financial dealings," referring to, among
others, a document dating from 1182 which relates the original terms of a loan and its
subsequent release, in Latin and in Hebrew (xiv). For a transcription of the document,

In conclusion, Jews were more likely to be literate and numerate than their Christian contemporaries. Many were probably trilingual (in Hebrew, the vernacular, and Latin).[125] In all likelihood not every Jew in every community was able (or required) to read rabbinic Hebrew. But as this brief overview suggests, much of the Jewish education for basic literacy and for training in scripture took place in the vernacular. This process apparently created a basic set of vernacular working tools for understanding biblical Hebrew with some references to rabbinics, as well. While these tools were doubtless intended for internal consumption, it is not unthinkable that a sympathetic, curious Christian like Herbert could have gained access to them and to a qualified teacher.[126]

A by-product of the imposition of administrative constraints on business dealings between Jews and Christians might have been an increased knowledge of Hebrew among some Christians. The records in the *archae iudaeorum* were maintained in both Hebrew and Latin. Jewish parties to transactions or to legal cases swore on the Torah scrolls (not the Gospels, obviously). Christians who did business with Jews, including high-ranking clerics, may have had numerous opportunities to learn some rudiments of Hebrew.[127] Another avenue for possible contacts between Christians and Jews might have existed in episcopal households. English bishops had considerable commercial contact with Jews in the twelfth century, either in their episcopal capacities or previously

---

see Volume I: 118–119. The Christian creditor was Richard Malebisse, later a fomenter of violence against the Jews of York in 1190. *Starr* was an English corruption of the Latin *starrum*, in turn derived from the Hebrew *shetar*, meaning a written commercial document. "Introduction," Volume 1:xv.

[125] Such is Clanchy's opinion: *From Memory to Written Record*, 201–202; see also *Medieval English Jews and Royal Officials: Entries of Jewish Interest in the English Memoranda Rolls, 1266–1293*, ed., trans., ann. Zefira Entin Rokéah (Jerusalem: Hebrew University Magnes Press, 2000), xix–xx.

[126] Eva De Visscher also has concluded that Herbert was dependent on help from a Jewish interlocutor and makes the attractive argument that his references to *litterator meus* apply (at least sometimes) to a Jewish colleague; "The Jewish-Christian Dialogue in Twelfth-Century Western Europe: Herbert of Bosham's *Commentary on the Psalms*," Chapter 3 especially. See also Judith Olszowy-Schlanger, "The Knowledge and Practice of Hebrew Grammar among Christian Scholars in Pre-expulsion England ..."

[127] Raphael Loewe made this suggestion in his article, "The Medieval Christian Hebraists of England: Herbert of Bosham and Earlier Scholars," *Transactions of the Jewish Historical Society* (London, 1953), 233. Concerning the *archae iudeorum* he wrote: "There survives a letter addressed, in Hebrew, to William le Breton, Justice of the Jews in 1235. My late father [Herbert Loewe] who edited it, concluded from internal evidence that he was probably expected to be able to read it for himself."

as heads of religious houses or cathedral chapters. It may even have been possible that Jews were accorded some standing within episcopal or abbatial households.[128] The Jew from Mainz with whom Gilbert Crispin conducted his disputation in the 1090s was described as the abbot's *familiaris*. This term connotes a member of a household (especially, as in later English, an episcopal household[129]), which is the most common use made of the term in the many *Vitae* of Thomas Becket.[130] No mention of Jews in the *familia* of Thomas Becket has yet come to light, but it is possible that Herbert of Bosham might have encountered a Jewish "dialogue partner" within his archbishop's household.[131]

It is evident that some Christian scribes were able to write fluently in Hebrew (although not always at the level of a 'professional' Jewish scribe[132]) and were producing books from which Christians might have polished their reading skills, even in the twelfth century. There is even a record of a converse case: a late-twelfth century Christian convert to Judaism used the Latin Vulgate as a crib for studying the Tanakh.[133] Without concurring entirely with Raphael Loewe's initial evaluation

---

[128] I am grateful to Dr. Mark Zier, who made this suggestion in a discussion at the Medieval Congress at Kalamazoo, May 5, 2000.

[129] According to DuCange, *familiaris* connotes a person closely attached to a king or prince (by extension, therefore, to a prince of the Church). See also OED, "familiar" (substantive), attested in 1460 as referring to a member of an episcopal household.

[130] R.B. Dobson speculates that influential clerics, like the Archbishop of York, might have imported learned Jews after the conquest to provide them with scholarly interlocutors in exegesis: "But how far the Jewish scholars known to Maurice of Kirkham were either permanently settled in York or represented the learned fringe of a large Jewish community within the city are very different matters. They are probably best interpreted as exotic members of the large *familia* of a wealthy Anglo-Norman prelate, protected by their position in Archbishop Gerard's household from the harsh realities of urban life ..." "The Jews of Medieval York and the Massacre of March 1190," Borthwick Papers No. 45 (York: Borthwick Institute of Historical Research, 1974), 5. Dobson gives no evidence for this kind of association of Jewish *familiares* in episcopal households—except for an oblique reference to Gilbert Crispin on the grounds of what Dobson claims is his interest in Hebrew scholarship; Dobson did not note that Gilbert identified the Jew of Mainz as a *familiaris*).

[131] One of the charges leveled against Becket at his trial in Northampton was that as chancellor he had failed to repay a debt of fifty marks owed to a Jewish lender and secured by a claim on the royal treasury, a transaction which testifies to Becket's dealings with Jews as chancellor, if not as archbishop. The money had been spent on Becket's triumphant campaign against the French city of Toulouse. Becket had understood the money to be a gift; at his trial, the king was eager to portray his archbishop as an embezzler and thief. See William FitzStephen's account of the trial in his *Life* of Becket, *Mats.* III, 53–54; see also Barlow, 111.

[132] Smalley, *SBMA*, 348–349.

[133] Wacholder, "Proselytizing," 302.

of Herbert's expertise in Hebrew, one can affirm that it was feasible for Herbert to have acquired the rudiments of the language which he claims to have done in his youth.[134] Thus equipped, and with further study and help, he may have had fruitful and enlightening encounters with a sympathetic Jewish interlocutor.[135] Such an interlocutor might have been the aperture through which Herbert advanced both in his understanding of Hebrew and in his appreciation for the situations faced by his Jewish contemporaries. What might have begun as a purely lexical study, fuelled by Herbert's omnivorous curiosity, grew into an intense interest in the religious experiences and expectations of medieval Jews. The Hebrew language, for Herbert, became the key that unlocked a world which few of his fellow-Christians bothered to consider real.

To help in assessing the range of Herbert's knowledge of Hebrew, the appendix collects examples of Herbert's corrections or amendments to the text of the Hebraica psalter. The examples illustrate the nature and range of Herbert's studies. They also indicate his willingness to introduce refinements to Jerome's translation based on his own expertise, and to declare his independence from his authorities, whether Latin or Hebrew. Occasional 'Gallicanisms' creep into the text upon which Herbert comments: these are variants more familiar to Herbert (or his scribe perhaps) from the version of the psalms used in the liturgy. But in most cases, the variations from Jerome's Hebraica text seem to have been introduced by Herbert deliberately.[136] These examples reveal the freedom with which Herbert treated Jerome's authority. He was supremely confident in his reading of the Hebrew psalter, relying on his own authority to introduce a translation which he regarded as more correct or more "consonant" than Jerome's. In the process, he also

---

[134] As he claimed to have done in the dedicatory letter prepended to the psalter commentary; see Smalley, "A Commentary on the *Hebraica* by Herbert of Bosham," *RTAM* 18 (1951): 29–65; 32.

[135] It seems unlikely that Herbert worked with an apostate Jew. If he had, he probably would have identified him as Ralf Niger did in the *Philippicus*, a work named for his interlocutor. By the end of the twelfth century, Herbert had witnessed or heard of the increased violence against the Jews of England and northern France. To divulge the name of his interlocutor might have imperiled them both. His silence on the topic may well be a mark of concern and respect.

[136] See now Eva De Visscher's study for its thorough evaluation of the extent of Herbert's facility in Hebrew, as well as his dependence on (and independence from) both Christian and Hebrew text-critical traditions; "The Jewish-Christian Dialogue in Twelfth-Century Western Europe: Herbert of Bosham's *Commentary on the Psalms*."

refined the meaning of consonance. Earlier Christian exegetes used the term to describe aptness and parallelism between the prophetic *res gestae* of the Hebrew Bible and their fulfillment in the Christian testament. For Herbert, the term had a chiefly technical application and referred to the Latin translation which captures the Hebrew meaning most accurately.

Some of Herbert's amendments were based on interpretations he encountered in Rashi's commentary on the psalms. In other cases, Herbert simply argued that his translation was "more consonant" with the original Hebrew. Herbert thus appeared to make changes independently of Rashi's version of the psalms text. Since there is no surviving twelfth-century version of Rashi's commentary on the psalms, this independence is far more difficult to measure. Perhaps Herbert had access to a fuller version of Rashi, replete with interpolations. Perhaps he did not: perhaps he or his interlocutor used other Hebrew authorities as well, particularly the *Mahbereth*, the dictionary of Hebrew roots compiled by Menahem ben Saruq, a tenth-century Spanish scholar. Herbert mentioned the *Mahbereth* by name, usually when a parallel discussion in Rashi's psalms commentary text had included a reference to Menahem's work. In at least one instance, however, he refers to *menaem* independently.[137] In other cases, Herbert silently introduces variant readings which might have been the result of consulting Menahem's lexicon, or perhaps some other grammatical source-book.[138] Since Herbert did not always choose to follow leads provided by Rashi, we might conclude that he had his own sense of how to translate and explicate the psalms most 'consonantly.'

Taken individually, these excerpts from Herbert's commentary may appear to be the work of a man intent on textual criticism or correction of the most precise or minute kind. Taken in the aggregate, however, and as the final example discussed in the Appendix shows, Herbert's task is demonstrably broader and deeper than mere correction. Herbert's *lexical* precision, whether he attained it personally or with the

---

[137] In a marginal note at Psalm 5, attached to a discussion of Hebrew words in the psalm-titles. The handwriting of the marginalia is very close to that of the main text of the commentary and so seems to be Herbert's work or that of his scribe; fol. 6v.

[138] As noted earlier, a few Hebrew-vernacular glossaries survive from the early thirteenth century, possibly based on the work of the *poterim*, glossators who translated or paraphrased the Hebrew Bible in the vernacular. Rashi (d. 1105) used vernacular glosses in his scriptural and Talmudic commentaries. Andrew of Saint Victor also used vernacular glosses, as did his (and Herbert's) contemporary, R. Samuel ben Meir.

help of a Jewish interlocutor, actually serves to open up a new exegetical horizon, the horizon of *cultural* hebraism.[139] The best translation, in Herbert's view, is a translation which accounts for the cultural context of the Hebrew word or concept under discussion. In some cases, particularly those of the *tituli psalmorum*, this means that the best translation is no translation at all—because translation as practiced by Jerome had wrenched the titles out of their proper historical and cultural context. Also, and more significantly, Herbert's lexical hebraism is the tool by which he marries the exegetical horizons of Christian faith to Jewish eschatological hopes. Through his exceptionally close attention to individual words, their meanings, and their contextual meanings, he unifies seemingly irreconcilable world-views.

---

[139] For the distinctions between lexical and cultural hebraism, see the discussion in Chapter 3.

CHAPTER SIX

HERBERT'S HERMENEUTIC
OF THE LITERAL SENSE

Since Herbert of Bosham was the only Christian exegete in his time to attempt a literal commentary on the psalter, his hermeneutic of the literal sense demands examination. Within the text of the psalms commentary itself, Herbert did not define the 'literal sense' explicitly. As the discussion in earlier chapters has indicated, his working method evidently derived from that of the Victorines. This consisted in commenting on the literal sense by expounding the *littera*, the lexical meaning of a word derived from grammar and etymology, together with whatever that word might have meant to the author in the context of that author's life and times. But words alone do not constitute meaning. Herbert would have learned from Hugh of Saint Victor and his followers that words and their narrative context, set within the larger historical context, were inseparable.[1] The literal sense thus incorporated the sweep of history. Describing the historical sense as it was formulated by Hugh, Grover Zinn wrote, "The historical sense is the narrative structure of the text in historical context, not merely the literal sense of the words."[2]

Without invoking much of Hugh's hermeneutical vocabulary, Herbert adhered to Hugh's principles.[3] He departed from allegorical read-

---

[1] *De Scripturis et scriptoribus sacris praenotatiunculae*, cap.III: "Prima expositio est historica, in qua consideratur prima verborum significatio ad res ipsas de quibus agitur … ut dicatur historia sensus qui primo loco ex significatione verborum habetur ad res." PL175: 12A. See also *Didascalicon* 6.8–11.

[2] Grover Zinn, "History and Interpretation: 'Hebrew Truth,' Judaism, and the Victorine Exegetical Tradition," *Jews and Christians: Exploring the Past, Present and Future*, ed. James H. Charlesworth (NY: Crossroad, 1990), 110. See also Zinn, "Hugh of St. Victor's *De Scripturis et scriptoribus sacris* as an *Accessus* Treatise for the Study of the Bible," *Traditio* 52 (1997): 111–134.

[3] Herbert seldom, if ever, uses Hugh's term *sententia* for "deeper meaning." Also, it should be noted that Hugh never included the psalter in his list of biblical books to be studied historically. In fact, he ranked it next-to-last (just before Song of Songs) among the books which students of the allegorical sense should approach. This suggests that Hugh viewed the psalter as a very difficult and highly allegorical text; *Didascalicon* 6.4.

ings *ab ecclesiasticis* and "followed the letter"—a process which involved locating a psalm's situations and speakers in their historical context. When Herbert interprets a psalm *ad litteram*, he usually repeats exegesis derived from Rashi (R. Solomon ben Isaac, d. 1105), his authority for historical information. These data consist of 'factual statements' (often Rashi's plain meaning or *peshat*) and amplificatory statements which smooth out the lacunae in biblical narratives. This amplificatory material can be identified with *derash* (homiletic explanations), frequently supplied by Rashi from *Midrash Tehillim* and other sources of *aggadic* material. Rashi was Herbert's source for etymological or lexicographical information. Following the principle that Scripture is best explained by Scripture, Rashi often explained unusual terms or perplexing situations in the psalms by referring to another locus in the Hebrew Bible. Herbert frequently records Rashi's explanations and citations.[4] In the process of transcribing or translating Rashi's web of cross-references, Herbert often appears to have 'decoded' their polemical import, as the material discussed below will demonstrate.

Beryl Smalley regarded Herbert more as a continuator of the work of Andrew of Saint Victor than of Hugh. In her view, Andrew was a Christian exegete who restricted himself to explicating the literal sense and who relied on Jews for data concerning the historical narrative of the Hebrew Bible.[5] Like Andrew, Herbert pronounced himself unworthy to study the deeper meanings of Scripture and busied himself with exploring its *fundamentum*.[6] Also like Andrew, Herbert prefers to locate a psalm's context in Israel's history rather than teasing out its eschatological or messianic import. But there were occasions when Herbert

---

[4] Rashi's pattern of citation often reflected the rabbinical hermeneutic of *gezerah shavah* whereby a word used in one biblical context is explained by invoking the word's use in a different context, with the understanding that the reference then incorporates the whole of the secondary context. Thus if Rashi explains a seldom-used Hebrew term in Psalms by invoking its use in Balaam's predictions against Edom in Numbers or Isaiah's prophecies against Idumea, then we can assume that he intends his readers to understand the passage in the psalm as an anti-Edomite (that is, anti-Christian) statement. On *gezerah shavah*, see H.L. Strack and G. Stemberger, *Introduction to Talmud and Midrash*, trans. Markus Bockmuehl (Edinburgh: T. & T. Clark, 1991), 23 and Raphael Loewe, "Herbert of Bosham's Commentary on Jerome's Hebrew Psalter," *Biblica* 34 (1953), 182–183.

[5] Beryl Smalley, "Andrew of St. Victor, Abbot of Wigmore: A Twelfth Century Hebraist," *RTAM* 10 (1938): 358–373 and *SBMA*, 112–172.

[6] See the discussion in Chapter 2 of Herbert's exegetical method as it relates to that of the Victorine educational program promulgated by Hugh and enacted (in varying ways) by Andrew and Richard.

and his *litterator* Rashi both asserted that a psalm's principal message
was not confined to the era of the Davidic monarchy. For Rashi, certain psalms prophesied events associated with the end of days and the
appearance of the Messiah. For Herbert, some psalms prophesied the
coming of Jesus Christ. Since for Herbert such prophecy was now fulfilled in history, the correct literal interpretation of some psalms concerned *rex noster messias*. In this regard, Herbert's approach seems to
mark a departure from Andrew. According to Smalley, Andrew asserted
that the literal interpretation of Hebrew Scripture was what the Jews
said about it. Andrew prescinded from discussing deeper meanings,
especially Christological ones, in his commentaries, unless the discussion were unavoidable.[7]

Smalley argued that Andrew relied on Jewish exegesis as a source
for the sacred text's first, fundamental level of meaning. Andrew's willingness to grant authority to his Jewish sources led to the unintended
consequence of denying Christianity's claims to primacy of interpretation of all senses: literal as well as figurative and spiritual. She noted
that Andrew's contemporaries were discomfited by this attitude:

> Discussions with Jewish scholars brought up the interpretation of Old
> Testament prophecy. The Jews had been accused of interpreting Scrip-
> ture 'according to the letter,' instead of according to the life-giving spirit.
> Was their interpretation of Old Testament prophecy to be called the 'lit-
> eral sense' of the prophecy, while the Christological interpretation went
> under the heading 'spiritual or allegorical'? This division seemed to clash
> with the received [Christian] teaching that the literal sense was true and
> basic. It gave too much to the Jews.[8]

Smalley concluded that Herbert of Bosham tried to apply a more critical and consistent hermeneutic of the literal sense to biblical prophecy.
She argued that he attempted to determine which of the psalms spoke
in their literal sense of Christ and which could be understood solely
in terms of their Old Testament background. In her opinion, Herbert endeavored to differentiate between messianic prophecies intended

---

[7] Smalley, *SBMA* 170–171. Similarly, Loewe suggests that Andrew only critiqued
Jewish exegesis when not to do so would border on heresy; "The Medieval Christian
Hebraists of England: Herbert of Bosham and earlier Scholars," *Transactions of the Jewish
Historical Society of England* 17: 239. But see M. Signer, "Introduction," *Andreas de Sancto
Victore: Expositio in Hiezechielem*, CCCM 53E, xxxii–xxxvii, who adduces evidence of
Andrew's consistent disparagement of Jewish eschatological expectations and messianic
hopes.

[8] "The Bible in the Medieval Schools," *Cambridge History of the Bible* ed. G.W.H.
Lampe (Cambridge: Cambridge University Press, 1969), 2: 214.

by the psalms' authors and those prophecies deduced by Christians expounding the 'spiritual' sense. Smalley suggested that his attempts anticipated the exegetical precept formulated by Thomas Aquinas, that the literal meaning of Scripture includes everything the human author of the text had intended to say:

> Which psalms should Christians take as messianic in the sense that David was expressing a direct foreknowledge of Christ? In such cases his prophecy would belong to the literal meaning. Which psalms referred to Old Testament history only? These would be interpreted as messianic according to the spiritual interpretation. Previous commentators did not feel obliged to face the question, since they saw the whole book as part of Christian revelation ... A commentator on the literal sense would have to tackle the problem head on. ... Herbert showed more clarity and firmness than Andrew in trying to distinguish prophecies which should be interpreted christologically in their literal sense from those which need not be.[9]

Did Herbert have a systematic method which guided his assertions that some psalms were 'literal prophecies' of Christ while others were not? Throughout his commentary, he contrasts the psalms commentaries of the 'ecclesiastics' (Peter Lombard and his patristic sources) with those of the *litteratores*—his Jewish authorities, chiefly Rashi.[10] Smalley maintained that Herbert identified a fair proportion of the psalms as literally messianic.[11] In fact, in most of these cases, Herbert identifies the psalm in question as messianic 'according to the ecclesiastics.' Smalley's assertion, therefore, requires some modification. Throughout his entire commentary, Herbert claims only a subset of the psalms are messianic 'according to the letter.' Yet Rashi did not provide him with grounds for these claims.

Smalley acknowledged that Herbert was unsystematic and occasionally confused in his analyses. One could go further and argue that he did not originate a new approach to the literal exegesis of prophecy. Rather than anticipating Aquinas, Herbert might better be described as an assiduous pupil of a previous generation—that of Hugh of Saint Victor and Rashi. According to Hugh, the literal sense describes the plain narrative of events in history. Herbert concurred. Also, like Rashi, Her-

---

[9] *BC*, 84–85. On his (inchoate) relation to Aquinas, see *RTAM* 18: 63; cf. *SBMA*, 101, on Hugh.

[10] See Chapter 2.

[11] By her count, Herbert identified 10 of the first 25 psalms in the commentary as "messianic" in their literal sense. *SBMA*, 193.

bert set most of the psalms in their context in biblical history, explaining them in terms of ancient Israel's struggles and triumphs. But for Herbert, as for Hugh, the explication of Scripture in its historical context hardly exhausted its possible meanings. As Grover Zinn has shown in his studies of Hugh's *De scripturis et scriptoribus sacris*, the study of history supplied for Hugh the 'middle term' in the process of typological or allegorical identification between Scripture's literal sense and its deeper meaning. The diligent reader did not leap from the 'surface of the letter' directly to spiritualized allegory; rather, she or he needed to understand the historical ground of the letter, the event to which the letter referred, and thus the event's greater significance within the long narrative of salvation history.

> Hugh is attempting to restore the middle term in a relationship which he sees as comprising a three-member set in which the one thing (the word) signifies a second thing (the animal lion), by which the third thing (the person of Christ) is signified. ... Only by first understanding fully what the word, as word, signifies (a person, place, deed, or the like) can a person then advance to the next stage to ascertain the deeper meaning which is signified by the thing that is signified by the word. ... Hugh wants to focus on the need to recover a sense of the reality of 'deeds done in time' as the key foundation for all exegesis and, indeed, all theology. The fact that Scripture deals with the *materia* of history as its main topic, a topic that was perceived as something of a stumbling block in the *Didascalicon*, becomes a primary datum in Hugh's new view of the exegetical task.[12]

One might expect that Herbert, as a reader of Hugh, would have developed a method for interpreting the psalms grounded in typology, through which he constructed correspondences between historical events and events in the future.[13] Herbert does explicate some psalms in terms of Israel's history, and denotes as literal prophecy those events whose greater significance he regarded as Christological. He did not do so consistently, however. While he expounded many of the psalms according to a literal-historical hermeneutic, my study so far suggests

---

[12] Grover A. Zinn, Jr., "The Influence of Augustine's *De doctrina christiana* upon the Writings of Hugh of St. Victor," *Reading and Wisdom: The* De doctrina christiana *in the Middle Ages*, ed. Edward D. English (Notre Dame: University of Notre Dame Press, 1995), 56.

[13] Frances Young makes this useful distinction in her article, "Typology," in St. E. Porter, P. Joyce and D.E. Orton, eds., *Crossing the Boundaries: Essays in Biblical Interpretation in Honour of Michael D. Goulder* (Leiden: E.J. Brill, 1994), 29–48.

that Herbert's decision that a psalm foretold Christ was determined by the weight of tradition rather than by a rigorously applied method.

Two criteria govern Herbert's decision that a psalm is messianic or Christological in its literal sense. The first criterion is the Christian tradition of psalms interpretation. Psalms mentioned either in the New Testament (especially those in the Epistle to the Hebrews and in the Gospels) or with great frequency in the *adversus iudaeos* literature are consistently identified by him as messianic.[14] Besides making a bald assertion that these psalms (e.g. 2, 22, 110) speak in their literal sense of Christ, Herbert gives us no indication of any methodology driving his selection. Instead, Herbert's hermeneutic of the literal sense reflects typically Christian polemical concerns, which lead him to assert that "things that were said obscurely then are now made manifest by completed events."[15] Herbert's literal sense corresponds, as it did for Hugh of Saint Victor, with the plain narrative of events in biblical history, with the implicit understanding that the *relevant* history was the history of salvation.

His second criterion was whether traditional Jewish exegesis, which he encountered in Rashi's psalms commentary and elsewhere, testified to a messianic reading. Rashi's commentary presents an interpretation of the psalms in the context of biblical Israel. But as Sarah Kamin and others have demonstrated, Rashi's exegesis was not confined to expounding only the 'plain meaning of Scripture.'[16] His commentary offers a selection of aggadic material, organized around interrelated themes, and anchored by references to the plain meaning. In particular,

---

[14] In a private communication, Theresa Gross-Diaz alerted me to Nicholas of Lyra's similar practice, which helped me spot the parallel in Herbert. See now her "What's a Good Soldier to Do?: Scholarship and Revelation in the Postills on the Psalms," in *Nicholas of Lyra: The Senses of Scripture*, eds. Philip D.W. Krey and Lesley Smith, Studies in the History of Christian Thought, vol. 90 (Leiden: Brill, 2000), 111–128.

[15] "Quae quidem tunc obscure dicta, nunc re completa manifestata sunt," Ps. 117:1, fol. 135[va]. His statement paraphrases Augustine's Tractate 101 on John's Gospel, chap. 14: "Nunc ergo quod illis tunc obscurum fuit, et mox manifestum est, jam nobis utique manifestum est ..." Likewise, one hears an echo of Hugh of Saint Victor, *Didascalicon* 6.6: "Unde consequens est, ut Novum Testamentum, in quo manifesta praedicatur veritas, in hac lectione Veteri praeponatur, ubi eadem veritas figuris adumbrata occulte praenuntiatur. Eadem utrobique veritas, sed ibi occulta, hic manifesta; ibi promissa, hic exhibita."

[16] Or *peshuto shel miqra*; Sarah Kamin, "Rashi's Exegetical Categorization with Respect to the Distinction between *Peshat* and *Derash*," *Immanuel* 11 (Fall 1980): 16–32. See also Michael A. Signer, "Rashi as Narrator," *Rashi et la culture juive en France du Nord au moyen âge*, eds. G. Nahon and C. Touati (Paris-Louvain: Peeters, 1997), 103–110.

Rashi provides historical and linguistic proofs as grounds for denying Christian claims.[17] He rejected certain messianic interpretations by 'our rabbis,' noting that the Christians have used them to claim that the psalm's meaning is best understood in terms of Jesus Christ.[18]

Thus, when Herbert encountered Rashi's contradiction of rabbinical interpretations that had asserted certain psalms (e.g. Psalm 2, 22, or 110) were messianic, he (Herbert) reacted violently, accusing his *litterator* of blindness, hatred, and "perfidy". From Rashi, Herbert had learned of variant Jewish traditions, some ancient and some modern, concerning the messianic psalms. That Rashi is his authority on the literal sense is clear. Yet Herbert disregarded Rashi's interpretation of the literal meaning of the messianic psalms when that interpretation departed from the preponderance of Christian—or ancient Jewish—tradition. There are occasions, however, when Rashi's interpretation suggested to Herbert some correspondence between the *litterator*'s notion of the Messiah and his own. Rashi's commentary on psalms is not a strictly literal interpretation, nor is its only goal the refutation of Christian claims. The goal of Rashi's commentary is to offer comfort and hope to Israel in exile.[19]

Surprisingly little has been written about the overall message of Rashi's psalms commentary.[20] Esra Shereshevsky has suggested that the commentary was written with knowledge of, and in response to, Christian psalms commentary, specifically that attributed to Jerome.[21] This view was not supported by Sarah Kamin, whose penetrating studies have done much to explicate Rashi's exegetical methods.[22] In a series

---

[17] Michael A. Signer, "King/Messiah: Rashi's Exegesis of Psalm 2," *Prooftexts* 3 (1983): 273–284; see also Mayer I. Gruber, *Rashi's Commentary on Psalms 1–89 (Books I–III)*, 54–55 n. 6, 394 n. 19, 413 n. 43.

[18] Specifically at Psalms 2, 21, 45, 72, and 110 (Hebrew numeration); see Smalley at *RTAM* 18: 57.

[19] On Rashi and other twelfth-century Jewish exegetes who pursued this goal, see Michael A. Signer, "God's Love for Israel: Apologetic and Hermeneutical Strategies in Twelfth-Century Biblical Exegesis," *Jews and Christians in Twelfth-Century Europe*, eds. Michael A. Signer and John Van Engen (Notre Dame: University of Notre Dame Press, 2001), 123–149.

[20] Michael A. Signer, "King/Messiah: Rashi's Exegesis of Psalm 2," *Prooftexts* 3(1983): 273–284.

[21] Esra Shereshevsky, "Rashi's and Christian Interpretations," *Jewish Quarterly Review* 61 (1970–1971): 76–86.

[22] See especially "Affinities Between Jewish and Christian Exegesis in Twelfth-Century Northern France," *Proceedings of the Ninth World Congress of Jewish Studies*, eds. M. Goshen-Gottstein and D. Assaf (Jerusalem: Magnes Press, 1988), 154 n. 49, and "Rashi's

of essays devoted to Rashi's exegetical practices, Michael A. Signer
has argued that Rashi performed a narrative function, structuring his
commentaries in two ways. Firstly, Rashi provided the equivalent of an
accessus to each work (informing the reader how to read the commentary by shaping the reader's encounter with its substance). Secondly,
Rashi selectively used homiletic material (*derash*) while providing a narrative framework based on the scriptural text's plain meaning (*peshuto
shel miqra*). This process created a new narrative through the fusing of
scriptural lemmata with midrashic explication:

> Rashi's commentaries provide a narration of the biblical text which
> structures its meaning in harmony with the rabbinic tradition. This
> correlation of biblical narrative and rabbinic tradition is what makes the
> narrator concept a more wholistic description than the dialectic of *peshat*
> and *derash*.[23]

The narrative thus reconstructed by Rashi is neither univalent (just the
literal sense) nor polyvalent (as midrash appears to be). Rather, the
narrative runs its course through biblical history but, like a river, bears
depths of meaning along with it.

In his psalms commentary, Rashi used both *peshat* and *derash* to lay
out his reinterpretation of the eschatological message of the psalter. The
chief compendium of midrashic commentary on the Book of Psalms
is *Midrash Tehillim (Midrash on Psalms)*; this was probably available to
Rashi in some form. He appears to refer to it when he quotes material "from an aggadic midrash," for instance.[24] The material collected
in *Midrash on Psalms* is powerfully messianic and eschatological in its
orientation; the rabbis are very free with references to the messianic
age and its attendant consequences, both for Jews and for Christians.
Rashi approached this material with some caution, however. A painful
dilemma faced Jewish exegetes of the medieval period. While it is
unlikely that Rashi was writing in response to Jerome's commentary on
psalms, he was nevertheless aware that Christians read many (if not all)
of the psalms as Christological prophecy. Rashi developed strategies to

---

Exegetical Categorization ..." See also A. van der Heide, "Rashi's Biblical Exegesis:
Recent Research and Developments," *Bibliotheca Orientalis* 41 (1984): 292–318 for a useful
review of literature and debate surrounding Rashi's methods.

[23] Signer, "Rashi as Narrator," 106.

[24] *Midrash Tehillim* was a relatively late compilation of rabbinical commentary on
the psalms; one theory suggests that it may not have reached the form now preserved
in printed traditions until the thirteenth century; Strack and Stemberger, *Introduction to
Talmud and Midrash* (Edinburgh: T. & T. Clark, 1991), 350–352.

undermine the messianic reading of biblical passages which Christians had adopted and applied to Jesus Christ. One mechanism for undermining Christological interpretations was to assert that a psalm could be understood according to its literal meaning in its context in biblical Israel's history.[25] At the same time, Rashi needed to explicate texts that supported Jewish eschatological hopes.

Rashi's solution to this paradox was to be selective in his choice of midrashic material. He incorporated material from *Midrash on Psalms* and other sources which coalesced with his endeavor to show that the psalms predict stages of the messianic future: the nations (Gog and Magog) versus Israel; the defeat and punishment of the nations by King Messiah; the nations' payment of tribute to Israel's God and Israel; the judgment of the nations and the institution of the messianic reign.[26] Given that *Midrash on Psalms* is itself polemical and messianic, one needs to distinguish how Rashi limited the scope of his interpretation. He seems to have done so by concentrating on two themes: the assurance of God's future punishment of 'Esau' (Israel's oppressor) and Israel's need to remain faithful despite the trials of exile. Rashi's message is directed to his contemporaries in Northern Europe. By associating the voice of David in the Book of Psalms with the whole of Israel (*Knesset Yisrael*), he both used the psalms as historical evidence and interpreted them as future prophecy. He urged that Israel should not be dismayed by the wealth and power of its enemies.[27] He reminded Israel of God's faithfulness and the certainty that the exile would end.[28] Rashi focused, furthermore, on the perfidy of the Gentiles and the certainty of their eventual punishment (however prosperous 'Esau' or 'Edom' presently seemed).[29] Rashi consistently marshaled the historical testimony of biblical Israel's experiences to support his (and the prophets') predictions for Israel's future deliverance.

While Rashi was careful to divest *midrashim* of their messianic ideas that might have given support to Christian positions, he included much aggadic material that resonated with eschatological overtones. Sometimes aggadic material was included only to be discounted. Using an

---

[25] Michael A. Signer, "King/Messiah: Rashi's Exegesis of Psalm 2," *passim*.
[26] These are themes explicitly stated in Rashi's exegesis of Pss. 26, 45, 46–48; 59, and 68 (Hebrew numeration).
[27] Pss. 16, 22, 25, 31, 36, 37, 40, 49, 59, 62 offer examples (Hebrew numeration).
[28] Pss. 11, 20, 21, 42, 43, 50, 66 (Hebrew numeration).
[29] Pss. 9, 10, 22, 25, 29, 53, 59, 66, 69 (Hebrew numeration).

old trick of forensic rhetoric, Rashi thus introduced evidence for his point. An example, drawn from his exegesis of Psalm 8's title, illustrates this technique:

> *On the Gittith.* A musical instrument that comes from Gath where there were [craftsmen] available to produce it. Our rabbis said that [the title *On the Gittith*] refers to Edom, which in the future will be trod like a winepress [*gath*] in accord with what is stated in the Bible, "I trod out a vintage alone," (Isa. 63:3). However, the content of the psalm does not support that.[30]

Rashi's method of commentary thus deftly weaves scriptural allusions together with *midrashim*. A competent reader, one who shared Rashi's thought-world which unified Scripture and rabbinical literature, would read Rashi and be assured that just as God's past promises to Israel were fulfilled, so too would be the messianic promises.[31]

Herbert was just such a competent reader, insofar as he recognized the allusions to Jewish eschatological expectations embedded in Rashi's text. It is clear that Herbert read Rashi (or had Rashi read to him); more important, he understood the themes underlying Rashi's psalms commentary: to comfort the people of Israel in their current condition of exile, to offer them hope of returning to Israel, and to assure them of their enemies' eventual punishment. He recognized that the Jews of his time still awaited a Messiah who would defeat the erring nations in a great battle, that the Jews expected to be restored from their dispersion to enjoy peace and prosperity in Israel, and that God would dispense justice from Jerusalem.[32] Herbert states that the work of "our King Messiah," as he often called Jesus Christ, had been fulfilled only in part (*ex parte impletum*). He concurred with the Jews' belief that their present

---

[30] Gruber, 72. The bracketed interpolations are his.

[31] "In Rashi's exegetical framework, Scripture and the Rabbis constitute a single world. Therefore, one may derive the meaning of one from the other. His commentaries fuse rabbinic literature and the Hebrew Bible into a seamless text. At the same time, they insist upon discovering the *Peshuto shel Miqra*, bringing out the plain meaning of the biblical text in a narrative order that reduces the number of rabbinic midrashim relevant to a specific passage in Scripture." Michael A. Signer, "How the Bible Has Been Interpreted in Jewish Tradition," *New Interpreter's Bible* (Nashville: Abingdon Press, 1994) vol. 1, 74. For the notion of literary competence, constituted by a reader's knowledge not only of a language but of its literary genres and conventions, see Jonathan Culler, *Structuralist Poetics: Structuralism, Linguistics and the Study of Literature* (Ithaca, New York: Cornell University Press, 1975), 113–130.

[32] Herbert acknowledges especially that the Messiah will fulfill the prophecies of Ezekiel 37–39.

"captivity" in the Latin West was the worst calamity of their history. Most significantly, he agreed that this calamity awaited a messianic deliverer.

Herbert departed from the predominant Christian view that the Jews' suffering in exile was fitting punishment for 'Christ-killers.' He made no claim that the Jews serve as witnesses, in the Augustinian sense, for Christianity's superiority. His interpretation of the psalms stressed instead the provisional nature of Christianity's triumph. For Herbert, Jesus is the Messiah who is still to come, because his work remains incomplete. While he accused the Jews of stubbornness and blindness, he did not ascribe the delay of the *eschaton* to their resistance. On the contrary, he seems to have agreed with Rashi that the conditions for the Messiah's coming have yet to be met.

In a comparable departure from prevailing Christian attitudes, Herbert also revisited the story of Jacob and Esau. The narrative of sibling rivalry had been used by both Christians and Jews to understand their contemporary situations. Each group saw itself as Jacob, the righteous brother, and regarded the other as Esau, the reprobate passed over by God. Christians associated the Jews with the older brother whose rights had been set aside in favor of them, representatives of a younger faith. Rabbinical tradition wove the story of Esau together with the histories and prophecies related to the nations he fathered, known variously in the Bible as Amalek, Edom, or Idumea. They conceded that the Christians, figuratively understood as Esau, presently enjoyed the "fatness of the earth" as prescribed in Genesis 25, but asserted that God would overturn this blessing at the end of days.[33] Insofar as theirs was an eschatological expectation, Jewish speculation on the fate of Esau in relation to that of Israel was connected to discussions of the Messiah. Influenced by Rashi's commentary, which subtly alludes to the Messiah and not so subtly to the present bad behavior and ultimate judgment of Edom, Herbert reversed the traditional Christian understanding of Jacob and Esau. The rest of this chapter considers the nature of the Messiah and the figurative identities of Jacob and Esau as they were worked out in Herbert's commentary in close consultation with Rashi's. First, a discussion of Herbert's commentary on Psalm 44[45], *My heart has uttered a good word*, will make his exegetical method and program

---

[33] Gerson D. Cohen, "Esau as Symbol in Early Medieval Thought," *Jewish Medieval and Renaissance Studies*, ed. Alexander Altman (Cambridge: Harvard University Press, 1967), 19–48.

more concrete. Then an examination of Psalm 79[80] will illustrate his atypical approach to the 'givens' of his own tradition.

Christian tradition since the Epistle to the Hebrews identified Psalm 44[45], a 'royal wedding song,' as a messianic psalm celebrating Christ, God's anointed one, and his union with the Church, his bride. The crucial verse is quoted in the first chapter of Hebrews: "Thou hast loved righteousness and hated iniquity; therefore God, thy God, has anointed thee ..." (Psalm 44[45]:8). Christian apologists since Justin Martyr insisted that this verse demonstrated that Christ was God's anointed, the Messiah whom the Jews await.[34] Moreover, they read this verse as testimony both to the Trinity and to the Incarnation. One God having anointed another was proof that Jesus was God's chosen one both in his divinity and in his humanity.[35]

Not surprisingly, the issue of anointing also loomed large in Rashi's commentary on the psalms. On several occasions he insists that kings and officials generally are anointed; the term need not refer to the Messiah, still less to Christ. In his exegesis of Psalm 44[45] Rashi deflects the association of unction from the Messiah. Instead, Rashi interprets Psalm 44[45] as a hymn of praise to Torah scholars, who like "kings" are wedded to the queen of righteousness, the sacred scrolls. Their learning, he maintains, will help to effect the eventual conversion (and conquest) of the Gentiles (v. 6b). In his commentary, Herbert presents the traditional Christian reading: the psalm celebrates the union of Christ with his Church. But he also presents Rashi's exegesis. The *litterator* is wrong, he alleges, yet he is intrigued by Rashi's interpretation of the spousal imagery; Herbert says repeatedly throughout that he pursues Rashi's 'metaphor.'[36] When Rashi endeavors to neutralize verse 8,

---

[34] Justin Martyr, *The Dialogue with Trypho*, trans. A. Lukyn Williams (London: S.P.C.K., 1930), 63.4; 84.3.

[35] For example, Augustine, *Enn. in Psalmos* 44[45]:17: "'God' then was 'anointed' for us, and sent unto us; and God Himself was man, in order that He might be 'anointed:' but He was man in such a way as to be God still. He was God in such a way as not to disdain to be man. 'Very man and very God;' in nothing deceitful, in nothing false, as being everywhere true, everywhere 'the Truth' itself. God then is man; and it was for this cause that 'God' was 'anointed,' because God was Man, and became 'Christ.'"

[36] It is clear that metaphor inheres in the literal meaning of the text for Herbert. Similarly, Rainer Berndt suggests that metaphor formed part of Andrew's strategy for limiting his engagement with the "deeper meaning." He says that when Andrew discusses the relation between a biblical event/thing [*res*[1]] and its deeper meaning [*res*[2]], he is employing metaphor (though the examples Berndt cites don't use this term) and metaphor is "un procédé de rhetorique exprimant seulement ce que dit la *vox* à laquelle

however, maintaining that "'anointing with oil' can be employed in connection with any expression denoting 'promotion to office,'"[37] Herbert vigorously disagrees. He writes:

> But in the course of pitying this song of love by the blind and miserable synagogue, I am incapable of marveling enough at its hatred. Out of hatred of our King Messiah, it alters and falsifies the evangelical Scripture. Or rather because they do not desire our messiah, but they expect theirs who is still to come, a great and holy king. Why do they not adapt to this very clear Scripture; O obstinate envy, always persecuting the Holy One? They do not wish to give this song of love to our King Messiah but carry it off to theirs.[38]

Herbert caps his case by stating that Paul, the 'alumnus of the synagogue,' clearly (*aperte*) taught that this psalm is messianic when he quoted it in the Epistle to the Hebrews.[39] Despite having accused the Synagogue of blindness and hatred, Herbert continues to lay out Rashi's interpretation of the psalm. Most notably, he follows Rashi's identification of the shift in subjects at verse 10. The psalm no longer speaks of the Torah scholars, but addresses the Congregation of Israel in the character of God's 'daughters.'

Rashi's interpretation of the last half of the psalm contains his message of comfort to diaspora Israel. He reads these verses as metaphors of the relationship that will prevail among God, Israel, and the nations at the end of days. God will 'desire Israel's beauty' and reward her good deeds. Seeing this, the nations—especially Edom (that is, the Gentile nations)—will bring her tribute. Apostates restored to Judaism will be presented to God as an offering (citing Isa. 66:20 in his discussion of

---

[37] Gruber, 214.

[38] Ps. 44:8, fol. 47[vb]: "Verum in hoc amoris cantico excecate et misere synagoge conpaciens; satis nequeo odium admirari. que regis nostri messie odio scripturam quasi evangelicam; vertit sic et intervertit. Aut quia nolunt nostro. suo messie quem adhuc regem magnum et sanctum venturum expectant. hanc tam manifestam scripturam cur non adaptant; O livor pertinax semper sanctum persequens. Messie regi nostro amoris hoc canticum dare nolunt; et suo adimunt."

[39] Ps. 44:8, fol. 47[vb]: "Quod tamen magnus ille synagoge alumpnus quodam inter litteratores legis emulator vehementissimus. ad regem nostrum ecclesie sponsum messiam referendum; aperte docet dicens sic." Also, see now the discussion by Eva De Visscher concerning Herbert's reliance on Paul in "The Jewish-Christian Dialogue in Twelfth-Century Western Europe: Herbert of Bosham's *Commentary on the Psalms*." (Ph.D. Thesis, University of Leeds, 2003), Chapter 4 especially.

il [Andrew] revient toujours; il reste donc au niveau du sens littéral." Rainer Berndt, *André de Saint-Victor (+1175): Exégète et Théologien*, Bibliotheca Victorina II (Paris: Brepols, 1991), 184–185.

verse 14), while all the nations will endeavor to imitate Israel's virtues.
Rashi glosses verse 15 as follows:

> *maidens in her train, her companions*: This means that the people from the
> Gentiles will run after them, in accord with what Scripture states, "They
> will take hold of a Jew's garment ..., saying 'Let us go with you, for we
> have heard God is with you.'" (Zech. 8:23)

Following Rashi, Herbert asserts that in the end of days, the nations
will bring tribute to Israel, as the prophet Ezekiel foretold. Just as Rashi
had, Herbert identifies the maidens of verse 15 with the Gentiles.[40]

Herbert clearly understood the eschatological import of the verse
from Zechariah for the Jews. A final citation from his commentary
on Psalm 87[86], verse 7, will illustrate this point: "I will remember
the proud and Babylon among those who know me; Behold there are
Palestine and Tyre with Ethiopia [saying] 'This one was born here.'"
Again following Rashi, Herbert explains that this verse refers to the
nations who are brought by Israel to the knowledge and worship of
God. Like Rashi, Herbert again cites Isaiah 66:20: "Out of all the
nations they shall bring all your brothers as an offering to the Lord."
Herbert amplifies this statement by citing the verse from Zechariah
which he and Rashi had deployed in Psalm 44[45]: "In those days ...
they will [take hold of the robe of a Jew,] say[ing] 'Let us go with you,
for we have heard that God is with you.'" (Zech. 8:23). Herbert explains
that the psalm verse, understood in light of the prophecies, expresses
the Jews' expectations of the future under the Messiah. Christians, he
writes, see that this verse has been fulfilled *in part* by Christ and the
apostles. He adds that it will be fulfilled completely at the end-time,
when all Israel will be saved (cf. Rom. 11:26).[41]

---

[40] We know from a thirteenth-century Jewish source, the *Sefer Nizzahon*, that the
meaning of Zechariah 8.23 was disputed in Jewish and Christian polemical texts. The
author of the *Sefer Nizzahon* wrote: "[after first discussing Zech. 8:20–22] ... The heretics
explain this is a reference to Jesus, who sat in Jerusalem and whom the nations sought
so that they could follow him in their error. The answer is in the adjoining verse, as it
is written, 'Thus says the Lord of hosts: In those days ten men from all the languages
of the nations shall take hold of the edge of a Jew's garment, saying, We will go with
you, for we have heard that God is with you.' The verse thus testifies that they will
come to the God of the Jews and not of the Christians, that it is referring to our God
in heaven, and it embodies a prophecy concerning the end of days." David Berger,
ed. and trans. *The Jewish-Christian Debate in the High Middle Ages: A Critical Edition of
the* Nizzahon Vetus (Philadelphia: Jewish Publication Society of America, 1979), 125–
126.
[41] Ps. 86[87]:4, fol. 102ra: "... Adeo eciam quod exortantes se invicem et explorantes

Herbert of Bosham encountered in Rashi a Jewish exegete whose orientation was to the future, as well as to Israel's glorious past and often dolorous present. Influenced by Rashi, he redefined some of the commonplaces of Christian exegesis. He allowed Zechariah 8:23 to support both Jewish and Christian eschatological expectations, albeit because he believed that in the 'end of days' the Messiah will be shared by Christians and Jews. Herbert's distinction as an exegete lay in his outlook, not in his method. Like Hugh of Saint Victor, he read the narrative of ancient Israel *concorditer* with the whole scope of salvation history. Therefore, the words of the psalms may refer to events which find their fullest meaning outside Israel's ancient history. What is said historically of David—that he was anointed—can be said still more truly of Jesus Christ. History forms the basis of Herbert's method for construing the literal sense, even as it expands the literal sense beyond the bounds of the past and into the eschatological future.[42] But unlike Hugh, Herbert finds himself compelled by his encounters with Rashi's text to consider the historical experience of contemporary Jews, not only that of ancient Israel.[43] His interpretive horizon included those messianic and eschatological yearnings of diaspora Israel which struck

---

qui sint de israelitis et dominum scientibus; adducent in ierusalem; offerentes eos quasi donum domino. Iuxta quod scriptum est *Et adducent omnes fratres vestros de cunctis donum domino* (Isa. 66:20) Et alibi. *In diebus illis in quibus apprehendent fimbriam viri judei dicentes Ibimus vobiscum. Audivimus enim quod deus vobiscum est* (Zech. 8:23). Judei; istud sub messia suo expectavit futurum. Ecclesiatici vero iam vident per christum et per apostolos ex parte impletum; in fine vero conplendum quando omnis israel salvabitur ..." Romans 11:26 reads "et sic omnis Israhel salvus fieret."

[42] Herbert writes at Ps. 117[118]:29, fol. 136[va–b]: "Quam sit insulsa quam disserta ista quam prosecuti sumus super psalmum istum secundum hebreos exposicio in qua messias tollitur eciam tardo manifestum. Quam vero lapida quam consona. Quam aperta sit si messias interseratur prophecia; psalmi maxime ultima iudicant. Ubi dicit *Lapis quem reprobaverunt* (Ps. 117:22) et cetera. huius profecto lapidis virtutem melius quam phariseus in lege edoctus; piscator simplex sensit et ennarravit dicens *Ad quem accedentes lapidem vivum ab hominibus quidem reprobatum. a deo autem electum et honorificatum.*(1Pt 2.4) Et infra *vobis quasi credentibus honor. Non credentibus autem. Lapis quem reprobaverat edificantes. hic factus est in caput anguli.*(1 Pt. 2.7) Solet queri; si qua tangatur hystoria cum dicitur lapidem quem repro. et cetera. Ego vero notens adinvencionum quorundam nenias scribere. sed pocius velut fabulosa preterire. dico non hiis verbis historiam tangi; sed per hystoriam methaphoricam de messia sic prophetatum esse. Et dicitur hic historice messias lapis; sicut alibi in psalmo populus israel hystorice per methaphoram vinea appellatur ibi. *Vineam de egypto transtulisti.* (Ps. 79 [80]). Et vinea mea domus israel est."

[43] Rebecca Moore, *Jews and Christians in the Life and Thought of Hugh of St Victor* (Atlanta: Scholars Press, 1998), 134; *eadem,* "The Jews in World History according to Hugh of St Victor," *Medieval Encounters* 3(1997):1–19.

him as valid.[44] While he deprecated the Jews' expectation for a human Messiah, a warrior-deliverer, Herbert acknowledged that as long as Israel languished in captivity, Jesus Christ's messianic work could be regarded as only partly fulfilled.

This novel formulation regarding the messiahship of Jesus resulted from Herbert's acceptance of Rashi's critique of Christianity embedded in the latter's psalms commentary, coupled with Herbert's awareness of Rashi's message of comfort to the Jews of Northern Europe. Rashi's psalms commentary, as noted earlier, had a double purpose: Rashi created a narrative from the psalter which highlights the certainty of Israel's redemption as well as the certainty of Edom's punishment. The touchstone for this dual assurance is the tensive symbol of Jacob and Esau. That is, Rashi framed the psalms' messages of comfort to diaspora Israel in terms of the eventual fulfillment of God's promise to Rebekah, affirmed in Isaac's blessing: that Esau the elder son will serve the younger son, Jacob. But Rashi needed to account for why the prophecy had not yet been achieved even as he reaffirmed its promise, attenuated during Israel's longest period of exile.

Throughout his psalms commentary, Rashi identifies the 'wicked' in the psalms simply as 'Esau.' Esau and the nation he engendered, Edom, are understood by Rashi, as they were for the Rabbis, as Israel's paradigmatic enemy throughout its history. More particularly, Esau and Edom represent imperial Rome and, by extension, its successor, Latin Christianity.[45] By the time of Rashi (1030–1105), the Jewish communities of Northern Europe had experienced the horrors of the Rhineland massacres in 1096. Christian crusaders bound for the Holy Land vented their zeal against the infidels nearest at hand and attacked centers of Jewish settlement in Mainz, Speyer, Worms, and Cologne. These physical attacks coupled with ongoing Christian theological polemic against the Jews resulted in veiled (and not so veiled) references to the brutality of Edom making their way into Jewish exegetical works in this period, including Rashi's psalms commentary.[46] The difficulties of the present age were linked by the commentators to the promises of the future: the suffering Jewish people would, if they remained faithful

---

[44] Especially perhaps against the background of recent events like the massacres at Blois and the expulsion of Jews from France's royal domain.

[45] Gerson D. Cohen, "Esau as Symbol in Early Medieval Thought," *passim*.

[46] See E.I.J. Rosenthal's analysis of medieval Jewish exegetes, "Anti-Christian Polemic in Medieval Bible Commentaries," *Journal of Jewish Studies* 11 (1960): 115–135.

to their covenant, be liberated by the Messiah who would usher in a new era of justice, peace, and prosperity—and who would judge the nations, notably the 'sons of Esau.' Rashi's allusions to Esau and Edom in his psalms commentary can be read as polysemous: they refer to incidents in ancient Israel's history or to events in David's life. But their enduring import concerns Israel's situation *now* in exile, oppressed by Esau's offspring, awaiting redemption in the time to come.[47]

Rashi's interpretation of Psalm 79[80] aptly illustrates his reflections on Israel's condition in exile. He organizes his exegesis around the refrain that recurs three times in the Psalm: "Restore us, O God; Let your face shine, that we may be delivered," which appears first in verse 4. The refrain is repeated in verse 8, with an additional divine name: "Restore us, O God of Hosts." Finally, in verse 20, the refrain reads "Restore us, O Lord God of Hosts." Rashi uses the three invocations of the divine name to ground his eschatological interpretation in biblical history. He asserts that the psalmist (in this case Asaph) has foreseen three of Israel's 'troubles' and prays for Israel's deliverance. The three 'troubles' are Israel's captivities at the hands of Babylon, Greece, and Edom. The first captivity is described in vv. 1–4; Rashi emphasizes here the nation's escape from near-annihilation at the time of Mordecai and Esther.[48]

The second 'trouble' is Israel's oppression by the 'Greek kings.' Rashi reads vv. 5–8 as pertaining to this period, but he does not discuss it. The Greeks form part of his demonstration from biblical history that Israel is delivered from oppression, but his focus in this psalm is Edom.

---

[47] Whether Rashi makes overt reference to the Rhineland massacres in his psalms commentary is a disputed question. See Gruber, "Introduction," 5, for references to positions for and against. In addition to the psalms discussed at note 48, see Rashi on Psalm 47:10, where he refers to *kiddush ha-shem*, "sanctification of the name" or martyrdom. Likewise, the theme of scholars willing to give their lives in defense of the Torah, discussed below, might be derived from Rashi's own background as a student in the Rhineland, where later the leaders of the *yeshivot* were murdered. As the "S" chronicler of the destruction of Mainz wrote, "… On that very day the crown of Israel fell. Then the students of Torah fell and the scholars disappeared. The honor of the Torah fell." Robert Chazan, *European Jewry and the First Crusade* (Berkeley: University of California, 1987) 204.

[48] In his exegesis of verse 4, which enjoins God to 'appear' at the head of Ephraim, Benjamin, and Manasseh, Rashi asserts that deliverance is God's gift, granted even to the unworthy through God's mercy and the merits of the patriarchs. Rashi suggests that these three are named as examples of men who, though they were wicked, were granted victories over Israel's enemies. But note, too, that his citations relating to Ephraim and Manasseh also recall past instances of Israel's near-annihilation.

Thus, in the middle of what *should* be the 'Greek section' of the psalm,
Rashi introduces a discussion of Esau. At verse 6, Rashi discusses
the lemma "And you made them drink a third (*shalish*) of tears." He
recounts four interpretations of the term *shalish*. The first he owes to
R. Moses ha-Darshan: 'third' represents the length of the Babylonian
exile. At 70 years, it was a third of the Egyptian exile.[49] Alternatively,
this 'third' could refer to the Greeks as third among Israel's captors
(by a calculation that lumps the Babylonians and Persians together).
From Menahem ibn Saruq came the suggestion that *shalish* means a
'measure' or 'vessel.' Finally, Rashi proffers the interpretation of 'our
rabbis' drawn from *Midrash on Psalms*: *shalish* refers to the three tears
wept by Esau when he realized that Isaac had bestowed the patrimony
on Jacob (Gen. 27:34).[50] Rashi concludes his discussion of verse 6 saying,
"because of [the three tears] [Esau] merited living by his sword as it is
stated in the Bible." Rashi cites Genesis 27:40: "By your sword you
shall live, and you shall serve your brother; but when you break loose
you shall break his yoke from your neck."[51]

This citation of Genesis 27:40 highlights Rashi's emphasis on Esau
and Edom. It explains for him (as in *Midrash on Psalms*) that Esau owes
his temporal wealth and power to his "three cries" because remorse
at the loss of the patrimony merited him a living by his sword. But
Genesis 27:40 is freighted with a second meaning, from *Targum Onkelos*:
Esau cast off Jacob's yoke because Israel transgressed the Torah. The
situation will be reversed when Israel regains righteousness.[52] Rashi
offered his readers philological and historical explanations of *shalish*,
but the interpretation to which he gives pride of place is midrashic—
and conceivably eschatological.[53]

Verses 9–20 of Psalm 79[80] recount Israel's sufferings at the hands
of her third and final enemy: Edom. Israel is the vine plucked from
Egypt (verse 9) whom God had planted in the land of the seven nations.
There she thrived and prospered (vv. 10–12). But the psalmist asks

---

[49] A calculation of the length of the Egyptian exile derived from *Seder Olam* per
Gruber; 379 n. 12.

[50] Rashi parses "a great and bitter cry"—two adjectives and a noun—to yield the
three tears.

[51] Rashi cites only 40b, and read it as "If you will be remorseful ..." rather than
"but when you break loose;" Gruber, 377.

[52] See Rashi at Genesis 27:40 and *Targum Onkelos ad loc*.

[53] Esau's regret at his loss has merited him temporal wealth and power; if God has
so rewarded his three tears, how much more will God do for Israel—this is R. Abin's
assertion in *Midrash on Psalms ad. loc.*, but Rashi does not cite it.

"Why then hast thou broken down its walls, so that all who pass along the way pluck its fruit?" (v. 13) In a sense, Rashi's exegesis of the entire psalm is an attempt to answer the psalmist's *cri de coeur*. Why was the wall breached and the vine ravaged, so that now "a boar from a forest gnaws at it, and the beasts of the field feed on it" (v. 14)? The boar is Edom, of course, identified by Rashi with the fourth beast from Daniel, chapter 7: "It devours, it crushes, and what is left it tramples with its foot." According to Rashi, the boar feeds on the branches of the vine, consumes it, and ultimately burns it. Despite the boar's depradations, however, redemption is in sight. Rashi deconstructs verse 16b as follows:

> *And over the son you have adopted for yourself. Over* Esau, who was dear to his father, who used to call him "my son" (Gen. 27:1, 37), *you have adopted for yourself* the vine, Jacob, in accord with what is stated in the Bible, "You shall serve your brother" (Gen. 27:40).[54]

By breaking up the verse, and reading 'over' in the sense of 'passed over,' Rashi affirms that despite Esau's present enjoyment of worldly power, God adopted Jacob as his first-born, the true Israel. Esau will serve Jacob. The hand of God—a source of opprobrium, not approval—will punish Esau, "the man of your right hand" (v. 18b). Esau's enjoyment of the "fat places of the earth," though ordained by God, will be the limits of his reward.

The commentary's dialectic of oppression and deliverance, suggested at verse 9 by linking the Exodus with the Roman exile, is reiterated in Rashi's conclusion at verse 20. He connects the three exiles with the three pleas for restoration, noting that "each is worded according to the intensity of the exiles, the suffering [borne in each], and the redemption."[55] Rashi implies but does not state that the Roman exile is the worst of Israel's troubles, and that it will be concluded by an act of God equal in magnitude to that of the Exodus.

As the first Christian commentator to attempt a sustained reading of the psalms rooted in biblical history, and who like the Victorines turned to Jewish exegesis for data, Herbert discovered in the psalms commentary of Rashi the historical nuggets prized by his Christian contemporaries. But Rashi's interpretation of the psalms, which reinscribed Jewish messianic expectations long associated with homiletic readings (*derash*) within the 'plain meaning' (*peshuto shel miqra*) of the psalter texts,

---

[54] Gruber, 378.
[55] Gruber, 379.

also prompted Herbert to an unprecedented Christian accommodation
of those expectations.

The text of Psalm 79[80] occasioned in Herbert's commentary—
as it had in Rashi's—a sustained reflection on Israel's condition in
exile. Rashi's summary statement became Herbert's introduction, in
which he explains that the psalm's three sections (indicated by the
three refrains) recount three captivities suffered by Israel. No previous
Christian commentary analyzed the psalm this way. Herbert begins by
seizing Rashi's allusion: he asserts that the last of the three captivities
is the worst, hence the invocation of the divine names multiplies and
intensifies with each refrain. He suggests that the refrains be regarded
as the prayerful 'remedies' for Israel's suffering; the worse the injury,
the more powerful the prayer invoked.[56]

Herbert alleges that two factors increased the gravity of the last trouble: its lengthy duration and the "kinship" (*proximitas*)[57] of the oppressor. Herbert notes that Israel's oppression by Edom began with the
Exodus. The first confrontation experienced by Moses and the people was that with the Amalekites, whom genealogies in Genesis and
Chronicles count among the descendents of Esau.[58] Identifying the

---

[56] Ps. 79[80], titulus, F95[rb]: "Contra has captivitates tres; triplex remedium ponitur.
Et pro modo gravaminis; magis ac magis crescit et cumulatur oracio. Unde et contra
primam captivitatem que gravis factam per azael; orat sic *Deus converte nos*. Ubi apud
hebreos unum solum de dei nominibus ponitur scilicet heloyim. Contra captivitatem
secundam que gravior, facta per antiochum ephiphanen, orat sic *Deus exercituum converte
nos*. Ubi apud hebreos duo dei ponuntur nomina scilicet eloyim et sabaoth. Contra terciam vero captivitatem que ceteris gravior facta per ydumeam, orat in fine psalmi sic
Domine deus excerituum converte nos. Ubi apud hebreos tria dei ponuntur nomina. Scilicet
adonay, eloim, et saboath. Ecce quomodo secundum quantitatem graviminum, gra-
datum crevit; et quasi augmentatum est oracionis remedium." Why Herbert includes
"Hazael" among Israel's worst captivities here is not clear. Rashi comments that the
three 'troubles' hinted at by Asaph in Ps. 79[80] concern the Aramean kings, although
Gruber suggests this attribution was the work of censors substituting Aramea for Edom;
p. 328n23. See also Herbert on the title to Psalm 12, where the four captivities are listed
as "Idumea, Syria, Greece, and *regnum romanorum per vespasianum et titum. Et taceam nunc
egyptios philisteos*." Contrast this with Herbert's discussion of Ps. 41's titulus, where admis-
sion to the list of kingdoms is based on who destroyed or desecrated the Temple: *Tres
israeli captivitates per tria genera super venturas et domus deum desolacionem presignantes scilicet per
regnum babel et iavan et edom*, fol. 43[ra].

[57] *Proximitas* is defined in Lewis & Short as "nearness" but they offer "near relationship" as a tropological meaning derived from Ovid and Quintilian. *A Latin Dictionary*
(Oxford: Clarendon, 1879), 1482.

[58] Gen. 36:12, 16 and 1 Chron. 1:36. The tradition of Shabbat Zakhor remembers
Amalek before Purim. Note above that Rashi mentions Mordecai and Esther in vv.
1–4.

offspring of Esau with the Amalekites provides the source for Herbert's assertion that Israel's long sufferings at Edom's hands has also been aggravated by kinship. This is persecution by a brother. Herbert makes clear the concatenated chain of connections among Amalek-Esau-Edom/Idumea with citations from Numbers, Exodus, and Ezekiel. For instance, he cites Numbers 24:20, Balaam's prediction: "Amalek was the first of the nations, but in the end he shall come to destruction."[59] The full context of this oracle from Num. 24:18–19 is telling: "Edom shall be dispossessed, Seir also, his enemies shall be dispossessed, while Israel does valiantly. By Jacob shall dominion be exercised, and the survivors of cities be destroyed."[60]

The compound nature of Esau's crime—eternal enmity directed towards his brother, manifested in history by Edom's unrelenting persecution of Israel—is a theme from Rashi's psalms commentary regularly reproduced in Herbert's text. Often, as here, Herbert supplies the relevant biblical proof texts, seemingly omitted by Rashi,[61] which predict the downfall of Edom and its future punishment at God's hands.[62] Both commentators, Herbert perhaps even more than Rashi by virtue of the citations he includes, emphasize the perversity of Edom's refusal to abandon its perennial hatred of Israel. This is not hard-heartedness decreed by God but rather maintained willfully by the sons of Esau.[63] But who are the sons of Esau? Does their enmity endure into the present age? As noted above, for Rashi and for the rabbis since the Tal-

---

[59] Herbert on the titulus of Ps. 79[80], fol. 95[ra]: "Unde scriptum est. *Principium gencium; amalech.* (Num. 24:20) hoc est amalech qui de esau; primi inter gentes contra israel fratrem suum insurrexerunt. Sicut scriptum est: *Venit amalech et pugnabat contra israel et post numquam desiit.* (Ex. 17.8) Unde ad ydumeam per prophetam dominus: *Et scies quia ego dominus; eo quod fueris inimicus sempiternus.* (Ezek. 35.4b–5a) Ecce esau israelem persequentis diuturnitas. Nichilominus et proximitas; eo quod super fratrem esau israelem fit persecutus. Unde dominus ad ydumeam: *Et cum sanguinem oderis; Sanguis te persequetur* (Ezek. 35.6b)."

[60] On the messianic traditions associated with this passage, see Raphael Patai, *The Messiah Texts* (Detroit: Wayne State University Press, 1979), 173 and Joseph Klausner, *The Messianic Idea in Israel*, trans. W.F. Stinespring (New York: Macmillan, 1955), 30–32.

[61] Recall that we have no contemporary exemplars of Rashi's commentary and can only conjecture about its contents.

[62] Other examples from Herbert can be found at Pss. 5:7, 68:27, 41, 136:7, 149:9 (Vulgate numeration).

[63] For example, at Ps. 5:7 "*odisti omnes operantes iniquitatem perdes loquentes mendacium virum sanguinum et dolosum abominabitur Dominus. Virum sanguinum et dolosum* generaliter vocat precipue tum esau et semen eius qui fratrem suum israel sine cause ex mero odio persequebatur et frequenter in dolo ipsius sanguinem effundere solet …" (citations from Ezek. 35 follow), fol. 7[vb].

mudic period, the answers are clear: Edom, once identified with pagan
Rome, now represents Christendom.[64] The sons of Esau carry out their
bloody persecutions up to the present age, most recently in violence
committed in the Rhineland during the First Crusade.[65] But did Herbert know of the identification of Esau / Edom with Christianity, and
did he agree with Rashi that Israel still languished in its worst captivity?
His answers to these questions can be discerned by evaluating the rest
of Herbert's commentary on Psalm 79[80], particularly his exegesis of
verses 6, 16, and 18.

Following Rashi, Herbert notes that verses 5 through 8 of the psalm
concern the 'persecution by the kings of Greece,' but he then reproduces most of Rashi's analysis of verse 6. He recounts that 'many of the
Hebrews' say 'third' refers to the Babylonian captivity. He also adopts
Rashi's reading of *shalish* for 'measure' or 'drinking cup.' He notes that
this last definition coordinates with the translation most widely used
by Christians, which rendered the verse "[Will] you give us for our
drink tears in measure?" Herbert also comments that the 'other edition' of the psalter reads *potasti nos in lacrimis in mensura*, conflating in
this rendering the Gallican and Hebraica translations. He is clearly
aware of the close verbal relationship between *shalish* and *calix* for he
goes on to remark: "Ac si diceret; calice potasti nos qui est certa mensura. In quo scriptura intelligere dat: *Quod fidelis deus qui non permittat suos
temptari; supra id quod possunt sustinere* (1 Cor. 10:13)."[66] Rashi relates the
word 'third' to Esau, while "measure" [*mensura*] suggests 1 Corinthians
to Herbert. Rashi works from the deep background of Esau, while Herbert has in mind "Father let this cup pass from me ..." (Mk. 14:36 par.)
and the temptation and suffering motif from 1 Cor. 10. Trading on associations from their respective authorities concerning this psalm, each
exegete selectively appropriated traditional exegesis to suit the context
of his comments. But Herbert omits Rashi's comments on Esau's three
tears. Perhaps it did not appear in the version of Rashi's commentary
consulted by Herbert (and his interlocutor?). Or perhaps he considered
it extraneous. There is one more possibility: Rashi's citation of *shalish*
for 'measure' made it possible for Herbert to align Rashi's interpreta-

---

[64] Gerson D. Cohen, "Esau as Symbol in Early Medieval Thought;" E.I.J. Rosenthal, "Anti-Christian Polemic in Medieval Bible Commentaries," 124.

[65] In his comments on Psalm 47, Rashi alludes to the Rhineland massacres of 1096
stemming from the First Crusade. See also Robert Chazan, *European Jewry and the First
Crusade* (Berkeley: University of California Press, repr. 1996), 148–168.

[66] The quote is in Cassiodorus, *Expositio Psalmorum, ad. loc.*

tion with Herbert's authoritative Christian traditions. Perhaps, having found a pleasing point of coincidence, Herbert simply decided to stop there.[67] He did not ignore, however, the importance accorded to Esau in Rashi's comments.

The portion of the psalm devoted to Israel's troubles with Edom begins for Herbert, as it had for Rashi, at verse 9. He writes:

> Finally, he (the psalmist) comes to that third captivity or rather persecution of Israel, which was worse because more wicked than the others, borne of the fraternal hatred that had been between Jacob and Esau. He speaks of Israel under the metaphor of a vine, saying how that vine was transported from Egypt, and the expelled tribes uprooted like scattered and pernicious seedlings, so that it could be planted in the promised land.[68]

Rashi's exegesis *ad loc.* had mentioned Rome, not Esau and Jacob. On his own initiative, Herbert emphasizes the theme of fraternal hatred and affirms Rashi's reading of the vine as Israel.[69] Acceding to the Jewish tradition regarding this metaphor led Herbert to reject a compelling Christian tradition which reads "vine" here and elsewhere allegorically, appropriatively, as the Christian Church or even as Christ (see John 15:1–5). This is a crucial departure. Affirming that the vine is Israel sets Herbert's course for identifying the vine's destroyers in verse 14. Herbert's exegesis runs counter to profound currents in Christian interpretation. Thus verse 14 testifies to the assaults made on Israel by its enemies:[70]

> Just as Israel was named through the metaphor of the vine, so now the metaphor of *the boar of the forest* names the destroyer of the vine, clearly Esau. He is signified as a beast of the field because he was a hunter

---

[67] Herbert is always heartened when the *litterator* agrees with the *ecclesiasticus*. Raphael Loewe refers to Herbert's "inward glow of satisfaction" on these occasions; "Herbert of Bosham's Commentary ...," *Biblica* 34 (1953): 56.

[68] Ps. 79[80]:9, fol. 96ra: "Ad terciam deinceps que ceteris gravior quia sceleracior erat; israelis captivitatem seu pocius persecucionem; accedit, ex odio fraterna orta que inter iacob et esau fuerat. Et loquitur de israel sub methafora vine, dicens quomodo vinea illa de egypto translata et eiectis gentibus quasi aspersis et perniciosis germinibus extyrpatis; ut terra promissionis plantata fuerit."

[69] Of course, this is an ancient association, perhaps initiated in the psalter. See also *Targum Onkelos* at Gen. 49:10–12.

[70] Herbert renders the verse as: "A boar from a forest uproots or devastates (*effodit vel vastavit*) and all the beasts of the field feed on it." The variant *effodit* is Herbert's. Note that there is a debate in *Midrash on Psalms* about "uprooting" the vine versus pruning it: uprooting would kill Israel; pruning would enhance her growth.

> ... And as surely as such a beast is called a boar, so therefore [Esau] is
> designated because he was feral and unclean ...[71]

Christian tradition, well-known to Herbert, identified the "boar from
the forest" in verse 14 with either Titus or Vespasian, the Roman
rulers responsible for the razing of Jerusalem and the destruction of the
Temple in 70 CE. Although this reading would be apposite to Herbert's
comments, he chose not to include it. Assimilating the metaphor of
the boar to the Romans would have excluded the likelihood that Esau
and his offspring referred to contemporary Christians. Herbert seems
to leave the latter possibility open.

In his exegesis of verse 16, Herbert's departure from established
Christian tradition is even more marked.[72] Just as Christian commentators consistently identified the 'vine' that God had planted with the
Church, so too they identified the son "whom thou hast confirmed to
yourself" with Jesus Christ.[73] Herbert adheres to Rashi, who identified
the son as Esau. While Rashi had made this association briefly, Herbert supplies the all pertinent citations from Genesis 25 and 27 in his
comment on verse 16:

> He prays thus: May the Lord who planted the vine surely not let it be
> moved; that which he planted with his right hand and confirmed to
> himself; over the son that is over Esau whom Isaac his father used to
> call "son" from a certain prerogative of love, as it is written: "And Isaac
> loved Esau ... but Rebecca loved Jacob" (Gen. 25:28). And from this
> prerogative of love Isaac often called Esau "son," as we read: "and he
> called to him Esau his eldest son. And he said to him, 'My son'" (Gen.
> 27:1). And elsewhere, "Are you my son Esau?" And in such fashion. But
> the Lord confirmed to himself over this son his "vine" which he delivered
> from Egypt, surely the sons of Israel, over Esau. As when Rebecca was
> answered by the Lord, "the elder is intended to serve the younger." That
> is, Esau and Jacob.[74]

---

[71] Ps. 79:14, fol. 96[rb]–96[va]: "Sicut per methaforam israel nominavit vineam, ita nunc
per methaforam *aprium silve* nominat vinee dissipatorem, scilicet esau. Quem per *bestiam
silve* significat; quia venator erat. Sicut et supra, *Increpa bestiam calami* (Ps. 67:31). Et per
talem bestiam scilicet aprium ideo designat eum quia ferus et inmundus erat."

[72] His translation is unprecedented: "et *funda quod* plantavit dextera tua et *super filium*
confirmasti tibi" as opposed to Jerome's "et *radicem quam* plantavit dextera tua et *filium
quem* confirmasti tibi." Herbert follows Rashi and clearly intends *super* to mean "over"
as in "passed over."

[73] Cf. Peter Lombard, *In Totum Psalterium Commentarii*, PL 191 and the *Glossa Ordinaria*
ad loc.

[74] Ps. 79:16, fol. 96[va]: "Orat hoc, ut dominus vineam illam fundet ne scilicet moveri
posse[t] quam plantavit dextera eius et quam ipse confirmavit sibi; super filium id est

Herbert's unique interpretation of the psalm continues in verse 18: "let your hand be upon the man of your right hand and upon the son of man whom you have confirmed to yourself." He states that the 'hand of the Lord' wreaks vengeance (*ultio*) upon the man Esau. Herbert argues that the Hebrew phrase 'let your hand' always indicates God's punishment of the wicked. It could never refer to Jesus Christ or to any righteous person. This is another radical departure from his own tradition as, "the man of your right hand … the son of man" is uniformly understood by Christian interpreters to mean Jesus Christ.

Paradoxically, this 'son of man,' the wicked Esau, is confirmed by God. Herbert explains the apparent contradiction of Esau's punishment and reward by citing his father Isaac's words: "Your blessing will be in the fatness of the earth and the dew of heaven" (Gen. 27:39), which he then explicates:

> The Lord then confirmed Esau to himself and strengthened him; as when Israel apostatized from God. It transgressed against God and the law through idolatry and many other acts. And then Esau, although he was inferior before, was confirmed and strengthened by God over Israel because of its sin. Just as his father Isaac had predicted to Esau himself, saying, "And the time will come when you will rise up and cast off his yoke from your neck."[75]

The explanation that Herbert gives here is notable for its nuanced understanding of Gen. 27:40, which may be the consequence of his awareness of Jewish traditions on this topic. Recall that Rashi cited Genesis 27:40 at verse 6, but had not included the explanation that Esau cast off his brother's yoke when Jacob's descendants transgressed the laws of the Torah.[76]

---

super esau quem pater suis ysaac quasi ex amoris queodam privilegio; filium appellare consueverat. Unde scriptum est: *quod ysaac amabat esau et rebecca diligebat iacob*. Et ex hoc amoris privilegio ysaac esau; crebro filium appellasse legitur ut vocavitque esau filium suum maiorem. *Et dixit ei fili mi*. Et infra. *Tu es filius meus esau*; Et in hunc modum. Dominus vero vineam suam quam de egypto transtulit filios scilicet israel; confirmavit sibi super filium scilicet super esau. Quando a domino rebecce responsum est *quod maior minori erat serviturus*; esau scilicet iacob."

[75] Ps. 79:18, fol. 96vb: "Dominus tunc confirmavit sibi esau et roboravit; quando israel a deo apostavit. Et sicut per idolatrium et per multa alia legem deum transgressus est. Et tunc super israel propter peccata sua; esau a domino confirmatus et roboratus est; cum prius esset inferior. Iuxta quod ipsi esau ysaac pater eius predixerat: *Tempusque veniet cum excucias et solvas iugum eius de cervicibus eius* (Gen. 27:40b)."

[76] In his Genesis commentary at 27:40, Rashi similarly states that Esau and his descendants will live to see Jacob and his sons transgress, so it seems Rashi is reproducing *Targum Onkelos* or *Midrash Rabbah: Genesis*, where Rabbi Huna is quoted as saying, "If

Rashi's comments on Esau's three tears—which implied but did not state the prospect of casting off his brother's yoke—seem here to have been amplified by Herbert. He has not inserted Rashi's comments from verse 6 *per se*, but what he understood of them. More significantly, he seems also to have gone beyond Rashi's psalms commentary to other Jewish sources to find a fuller description of Esau's status after receiving his father's blessing: 'strengthened and confirmed' despite the loss of his patrimony.[77]

At the twentieth and final verse of the psalm, "Lord God of hosts …," Herbert concludes with this observation:

> This psalm has been interpreted by the ecclesiastics as about that detestable[78] and final devastation of the vine by Vespasian and Titus; both of whom could be called *boar of the forest*, since having come from the heathens they were beastly and proud. Because this captivity [is] worse than the others, the names of God here are continually increased; here the change (*conversio*) of Israel, dispersed until the twilight of the world, is prayed for.[79]

As noted above, Christian exegetes associated the "boar" of verse 14 with Titus and Vespasian, whose combined rule resulted in the devastation of Jerusalem. But Herbert suggests here that the *whole* psalm had been interpreted by Christians as referring to this event. He over-

---

Jacob is meritorious, thou shalt serve him, if not thou shalt destroy him," while R. Jose b. R. Halfutha explains, "If thou seest Jacob thy brother throw off the yoke of Torah from his neck, then decree his destruction and thou wilt become his master." *Midrash Rabbah: Genesis II*, trans. H. Freedman (London: Soncino, 1939), 67.7, p. 611.

[77] Compare Abraham ibn Ezra and Rashbam on Gen. 27:40, the casting off of the yoke, and their references to "cry" and its analogue at Ps. 55:3. Neither of these exegetes agrees with Rashi's interpretation, but both clarify its philological underpinnings. Ibn Ezra wrote: "… *tarid* ['thou shalt break loose'] is similar to *arid* ('I cry out') in *I cry out* (arid) *in my complaint* (Ps. 54 [55]:3). According to this interpretation the meaning of our clause is: and it shall come to pass when thou shall cry out, then God will pity you." It is not clear how Herbert would have learned about this aspect of the rabbinical thinking on Esau and Jacob. *Ibn Ezra's Commentary on the Pentateuch*, trans. and ann. H. Norman Strickman and Arthur M. Silver (New York: Menorah Publishing, 1988), 268–272. See also Martin I. Lockshin, *Rabbi Samuel ben Meir's Commentary on Genesis: An Annotated Translation* (Lewiston, NY: Edwin Mellen Press, 1989), 159.

[78] A possible meaning for *unica*, although rare. Also, "unparalleled, unique"

[79] Ps. 79:20, fol. 97[ra]: "Psalmus eciam iste secundum quod et ab ecclesiasticis interpretatus est; de unica illa et ultima vinee vastacione que per vespasianum titum facta est; accipitur. Quorum uterque aper silve vocari potest quia de gentilitate venientes feri et superbi erant. Que captivitas quia ceteris gravior; tripliciter hic et semper cum augmento dei nominum; israelis hic oratur conversio; usque ad mundi vesperam differenda."

states the case. His tradition read Psalm 79[80] in terms of Christianity's supersession of Judaism as the true Israel: the Vine is the Church, which experienced through Christ a new Exodus. Despite his singular reading of the psalm, Herbert has seemingly forced a synthesis of his Christian and Jewish authorities. The psalm is about the Jewish people's sufferings, as he learned from Rashi, and their chief tormentors were the Romans, as Christian tradition taught. Are we to conclude that Herbert associates the boar/Edom with Imperial Rome to deflect the same association from being made with the Christianity of his own day?[80] Or did he acknowledge that Israel's sufferings at Edom's hands endured into the present age?

Evidence supporting the latter case can be deduced from his comment at verse 20: "Because this captivity [is] worse than the others, the names of God [increase] in intensity; the change (*conversio*) of Israel, dispersed until the twilight of the world, is prayed for." The "twilight of the world" (*vespera mundi*) is usually named by Christians as the time when the conversion of the Jews to Christianity might be expected. It signifies the 'end of days,' when the mysterious prediction of Romans 11:25 will be resolved: "the fullness of the Gentiles will come in, and so all Israel will be saved."[81]

But Herbert's characterization of the Jews' "conversion" in verse 20 suggests he understood the term differently. The *conversio* or change as he describes it is prayed for *by the Jews*, who are presently experiencing their worst 'captivity.'[82] They pray to be re-gathered from their dispersion. The return from scattered Exile to the land of Israel is a feature

---

[80] See Psalm 12 titulus, fol. 15ra, where Herbert identifies the fourth kingdom as the Rome of Vespasian and Titus. *Ad loc.*, Rashi does not specify the kingdoms' names.

[81] Typically, Christian commentators also cite Psalm 58[59]:15 in this connection: *Convertentur ad vesperam, et famem patientur ut canes; et circuibunt civitatem.* Significantly, Herbert does not discuss the conversion of the Jews at Psalm 58. Rather, he follows Rashi and attributes the events of the psalm to their biblical context in 1 Samuel—the psalm is about David's flight from Saul.

[82] As material from Ps. 41 [42] demonstrates: Herbert argues that the psalm speaks prophetically of Israel's captivities under Babylon, Greece, and "Edom." This data is supplied by Herbert himself, amplifying Rashi. He follows Rashi closely in the latter's analysis of the stag's "cries" mentioned in verse 2. Rashi suggests the deer cries out in her birth pangs. Herbert goes a step further and compares the hind in her birth pangs to Israel's *current* anguish: "Et istud de *cerva sicut* et illud prius de cervo; presenti isrealis captivi comparacioni congruit qui in captivitatibus velut inter paturitionis angustias; quasi cerva mugiens ad dominum clamare non cessabat," fol. 43ra. Herbert probably learned the comparison between Israel and the hind from Rashi, who points out the likeness at Psalm 22:1, "the congregation of Israel is 'like a loving doe;'" Gruber, 126.

of Jewish eschatological expectation. Herbert was clearly aware of this, as a final citation, this time from Psalm 13, will show. He comments on verse 7: "Who will give out of Zion the salvation of Israel? When the Lord will have turned away the captivity of his people, Jacob shall rejoice and Israel shall be glad."

Herbert's comment on this verse is lengthy but worth giving in full:

> [Paul] uses this testimony against the Jews, that he might show them [the] salvation will be from them, for he says "because a partial blindness touches Israel. Until the fullness of the Gentiles should enter and thus all Israel should be saved, as it is written, 'there will come out of Zion the deliverer and he will turn away [impiety] from Jacob.'..." But it can be asked about that captivity of the people, about to be turned away through him who would come out of Zion—that is, through the King, our Messiah—whether the psalm speaks here of actual or spiritual captivity? And it can be said that it speaks of both. Through the Messiah they who are now dispersed and oppressed throughout the world will be led back, as well as [those in] spiritual captivity. When [this will happen] another psalm testifies: "They will return at twilight and shall suffer hunger as dogs." (Ps. 58[59]:7)[83]

Herbert posits two forms of captivity, corporal and spiritual, from which the Messiah will deliver his people. Elsewhere Herbert maintains that liberation applies equally well to Israel's deliverance from exile as to humanity's deliverance from death by the One who rose from the dead.[84] In other words, he seems to hold out the prospect of eschatological deliverance for Jews as well as Christians. The messianic hopes of each are valid—even though, Christian that he is, Herbert maintains Jesus is the Messiah.

The foregoing discussion suggests that Herbert's acceptance of Rashi's commentary as an authoritative text shaped his reflections on rela-

---

[83] Ps. 13:7, fol. 16rb-16va: "Hoc testimonio contra iudeos magister utitur ut ostenderet ipsis ex ipsis salutem fore. Dicit enim *quia cecitas ex parte contigit in israel. donec plenitudo gencium intraret; et sic omnis israel salvus fieret. sicut scriptum est, 'Veniet ex syon qui eripie^{a}t et avertat impietatem a iacob'*(Rom. 11:26≈Isa. 59.20–21). Hoc est quod hic sub interrogacione legitur, quis veniens ex syon id est ex iudeis. *Dabit salutem israel* quasi aliquis scilicet messias. Et tunc *quando dominus* per eum *reduxerit* et cetera. Sed queri potest de qua captivitate populi reducenda per illum qui veniet ex syon, id est per regem nostrum messiam, loquatur hic psalmus an de captivitate actuali an de spirituali. Et potest dici quod de utraque et de actuali sive corporali qua nunc per terras dispersistus et opprimatur ubique; et de spirituali, per messiam reducentur. Quando sicut alibi prophetici psalmus testator: *convertentur ad vesperam et famem patientur ut canes*. Ad quod et magister sicut supra posuimus; hoc psalmi testimonio usus est."

[84] Such as when commenting on Ps. 87[88], fol. 103ra.

tions between Christians and Jews. He seems to have engaged with the eschatological trajectory of Rashi's exegesis; he did not simply mine the 'Hebrew truth' for data about Ancient Israel.[85] Redemption by 'our King Messiah' (as Herbert generally calls Jesus Christ) is a work in progress, awaiting the twilight of the world. His dialogue with Rashi's commentary helped him attain this perspective. How distinctive, however, was Herbert's perspective? Since antiquity, other Christian commentators had posited the eventual salvation of the Jews, basing their argument on the ninth through eleventh chapters of Paul's Epistle to Romans.[86] But the extent and nature of that salvation was variously defined. Twelfth-century exegetes of Romans were similarly divided over the question of whether *all* or only a *remnant* of Israel would be saved, basing their arguments on various interpretations or conflations of Romans 9:27, Romans 11:5, and Romans 11:25–32. Friedrich Lotter has argued that the Cistercians William of Saint Thierry and Bernard of Clairvaux maintained an inclusive view of the Jews' eventual salvation.[87] He suggests that William and Bernard both taught that by the mysterious means of God's providence, at the end of days all Israel would be saved. William's position, expressed in his commentary on Romans, seems fairly unequivocal. His discussion of Romans 11:26 asserts simply that "all Israel will be saved." But his exegesis of Romans 9:25–27 (which Lotter does not consider) seems to suggest that only a remnant of the Jews will be among God's elect, providentially converted to Christianity by the preaching of Elijah.[88]

---

[85] Unlike Christians before and after him, he did not maintain that compared Judaism to Christianity offered a 'realized' eschatology. Cf. Peter Lombard on 79[80]:18: "*Super virum dexterae tuae,* id est filium Virginis. Grande sacramentum hic notatur, et magnum munus Dei ostenditur, quia tandiu salus Israel potuit dubitari, donec Christus venit; sed tunc completa est promissio, ne ultra ab eo discedat Ecclesia, sponso conjuncta." See also Cassiodorus *ad loc.*

[86] See Peter Gorday, *Principles of Patristic Exegesis: Romans 9–11 in Origen, John Chrysostom, and Augustine,* Studies in the Bible and Early Christianity, vol. 4 (New York: Edwin Mellen Press, 1983).

[87] Friedrich Lotter, "The Position of the Jews in Early Cistercian Exegesis and Preaching," *From Witness to Witchcraft: Jews and Judaism in Medieval Christian Thought,* ed. Jeremy Cohen (Wiesbaden: Harrassowitz, 1996), 163–185.

[88] William of Saint Thierry, *Exposition on the Epistle to the Romans,* trans. J.B. Hasbrouck, ed. John D. Anderson, Cistercian Fathers Series no. 27 (Kalamazoo, MI: Cistercian Publications, 1980), 195–196. The belief that Elijah's preaching would convert the Jews to Christianity before the coming of the Antichrist was derived from Malachi 4:5–6, Ecclesiasticus 48:10, and Matthew 17:1; see also Augustine, *City of God,* 20.29–30. The tradition that Elijah and Enoch together would usher in the conversion of the Jews was probably derived from the Latin Tiburtine Sibyl; see Bernard McGinn, *Visions of*

Lotter argues that Bernard affirmed that all Israel would be saved in Sermons 14 and 79 on the Song of Songs. But these assertions regarding Bernard are contradicted in at least one instance by Bernard's own equivocation. At various points within the same sermon, Bernard refers both to the salvation of 'a remnant of Israel' and that of 'all Israel.'[89] In his fourteenth sermon on the Song of Songs, Bernard preached on the themes of Romans 11 but did not affirm that *all* Israel would be saved:

> Blind and quarrelsome, [O Synagogue] you will be abandoned to your error until the whole pagan world that your pride has spurned and your envy obstructed, shall have entered the fold … Yet this will not be total blindness, for the Lord will not entirely reject his people, but will reserve for himself survivors such as the Apostles and the multitude of believers who in heart and mind are one. He will not cast them off forever, a remnant will be saved.[90]

Part of the difficulty for medieval exegetes of Romans lay in the complexity of Paul's own propositions dealing with the mysteries of election and reprobation. In contrast to the position that Lotter attributes to the Cistercians, he notes that Peter Abelard maintained that only the elect of Israel will be saved.[91] Abelard asserted that the expression 'all Israel' applied to the nation of Israel, out of which many—but not all—would be saved. A remnant who heeded the preaching of Enoch and Elijah at the end of days would be converted. Abelard cites Jerome and Isidore of Seville as his authorities.[92]

---

the End: Apocalyptic Traditions in the Middle Ages (New York: Columbia University Press, 1998), 49–50.

[89] In Sermon 79, Bernard proclaimed, "The savior will return to the place from which he had come, so that the remnants of Israel might be saved [*ut reliquiae Israel salvae fiant*] … Let the church hold firmly onto the salvation which the Jews lost; she holds it until the plenitude of the Gentiles may enter in, and thus all Israel may be saved [*sic omnis Israel salvus fiat*]." Quoted by Jeremy Cohen, *Living Letters of the Law: The Idea of the Jew in the Medieval Christianity* (Berkeley: University of California Press, 1999), 233. Latin text interpolated from *Sancti Bernardi opera: Sermones super Cantica Canticorum*, eds. J. Leclercq, C.H. Talbot, and H.M. Rochais, vol. II (Rome: Editiones Cistercienses, 1957), 275.

[90] Sermon 14, Bernard of Clairvaux, *On the Song of Songs* I, trans. Kilian Walsh, OCSO (Spencer, MA: Cistercian Publications, 1971), 98–99. The Latin of the last line reads, "Sed nec repellet in finem, reliquias salvaturus," *Sancti Bernardi opera: Sermones super Cantica Canticorum*, eds. J. Leclercq, C.H. Talbot, and H.M. Rochais, vol. I (Rome: Editiones Cistercienses, 1957), 76–77.

[91] Lotter, 171. On Abelard's attitudes toward Jews and on this issue specifically, see also Michel LeMoine, "Abélard et les Juifs," *Revue des études juives* 153/3–4 (1994): 253–267.

[92] "Et *sic* tandem, id est post eorum introitum, *omnis Israel*, secundum singulas

Herbert of Bosham's teacher, Peter Lombard, echoed Abelard's position. Writing on Romans 11:25, the Lombard argues that the partial blindness suffered by the Jews was the consequence of free will: they chose to resist the divine revelation in Christ. By contrast, those Jews who will be saved through election at the end of days will be saved through God's gracious and mysterious providence. Peter Lombard maintains a distinction between the chosen and the reprobate among Jews and Gentiles; therefore, according to his account, not all Israel will be saved (although he does not conflate Romans 9:27 and 11:25 to conclude, as Bernard apparently did, that only a 'remnant' of Israel would be converted).[93]

Once again, Herbert of Bosham's theological thinking seems to owe very little to the Lombard. Possibly the influence of the Cistercians was more significant to him at this point in his life. The White Monks at Pontigny had been his and Becket's hosts during part of the archbishop's exile. Cistercians at Ourscamp (Arras) seem to have supplied Herbert with a refuge while he completed his psalms commentary.[94] The letter in which Herbert dedicated his commentary to Peter of Arras—once a monk at Pontigny, now a bishop—extolled the Cistercian ethos of *caritas*. Perhaps that ethos contributed to Herbert's irenic

---

videlicet tribus. Unde multi convertentur in fine, praedicatione Enoch et Eliae; non tamen omnes, cum de antichristo Veritas eis dicat, *Alius in nomine suo veniet, illum suscipietis* (Jn. 5:43), ut nec in fine mundi sicut nec in adventu Christi omnes Iudaei convertentur sed solae Domini *reliquiae.*" *Petri Abaelardi Opera Theologica*, I: *Commentaria in Epistolam Pauli ad Romanos*, ed. E.M. Buytaert, CCCM 11 (Turnholt: Brepols, 1966), 265.

[93] Peter Lombard, *In Epistola ad Romanos*, Cap. XI; PL 191:1481B–1495D: "Ecce ostensum est in his verbis praedictis, quare pars Judaeorum excaecata est, scilicet suo vitio, et propter gentes, et pars illuminata, scilicet gratia electionis, et propter patres. Etsi enim quasi de eisdem loquatur, dicendo, inimici et dilecti, quia una gens erat omnium illorum; alii tamen sunt inimici Dei, alii charissimi et dilecti. Sine poenitentia enim. Quasi dicat: Dico quod secundum electionem, et propter patres sunt salvandi, quia non sunt vocati ea vocatione qua multi non praesciti vocantur, qui tamen pereunt, de qua dictum est: *Multi vocati*, etc. (Matth. XXII), sed illa qua vocantur electi, ad quam qui pertinent omnes sunt docibiles Dei, nec potest eorum quisquam dicere, credidi, ut sic vocarer, quia praevenit eum misericordia Dei, qua vocatus est ut crederet. Quae vocatio est sine poenitentia, id est sine mutatione, quia qui audit a Patre venit ad Filium, qui non perdit quidquam de omni dato; quisquis vero perit, non inde fuit: qui inde est, omnino non perit. Propter quod Joannes ait: *A nobis exierunt, sed ex nobis non fuerunt* (I Joan. II). Fuerunt enim de multitudine vocatorum, sed non de paucitate electorum. Si enim fuissent de nobis, mansissent utique nobiscum."

[94] For a discussion of Herbert's interactions with various Cistercian houses, see Goodwin, "A Study of Herbert of Bosham's Psalms Commentary," 33–49 and 56–66.

perspective (towards the Jews, if not towards Becket's opponents).[95] In this connection, the attitude of Adam, abbot of the Cistercian house at Perseigne (d. 1212) and Herbert's near-contemporary, is instructive. Adam declined an invitation from a friend to write an *Adversus Iudaeos* treatise on the occasion of the return of France's Jews from exile in 1198.[96] Adam reiterated the traditional opinion derived from Romans 11 and Augustine: the remedy for Jewish disbelief in Christianity awaited the working-out of God's providence. The desire to confront the Jews, Adam wrote, stemmed not from "the love of the truth but from quarrelsomeness," and only exposed the quarrelsome to censure.[97]

Herbert's position on the salvation of the Jews may have been influenced by some of his Christian counterparts. His distinctive assessment of the provisional nature of Christ's saving work, however, owes much to his encounter with contemporary Jews and Judaism. For despite the potent associations that the text of Psalms 79[80] held for Christians, Herbert's only authority for organizing his exegesis around the Esau—Jacob theme is Rashi. Herbert adopted Rashi's characterization of Esau as Israel's perduring enemy, blinded by jealous, unreasoning rage. Similarly, we have seen that even the age-old Christian association of Psalm 44[45] with Jesus Christ the Bridegroom and the Church his Spouse did not deter Herbert from 'following' the *litterator* and according weight to his interpretation.

Herbert of Bosham's major distinction as an exegete derives from the fact that his version of the history of salvation departs significantly from that of Augustine and Hugh of Saint Victor. While he agreed that the incarnation indisputably illuminated biblical history, Herbert did not follow Hugh's dictum that the rest of history—particularly that of the Jews—was without theological import. While Herbert's exegetical methods were largely derivative from time-honored Christian prece-

---

[95] See the transcription of his dedicatory letter to Peter in Beryl Smalley, "A Commentary on the *Hebraica* by Herbert of Bosham," 31–32.

[96] Philip Augustus of France had expelled the Jews from the royal demesne in 1182 and readmitted them in 1198.

[97] Quoted in Lotter, 182. Note however, that Adam does not express any charitable motivations with regard to the Jews; he goes on to accuse them of obduracy and hardheartedness. If one wastes time arguing with them, furthermore, one risks corrupting the truth itself: "Absit ergo ne incorrupta veritas ad sui defensionem corruptoribus egeat!" Ep. 21, *Ad Amicum*, PL 211: 654A–659C. He, like Bernard of Clairvaux, also uses the Jews chiefly as foils. Both Cistercians complained that some Christians behaved worse than the Jews. See the discussion in Lotter, "The Position of the Jews in Early Cistercian Exegesis and Preaching."

dents, his exegetical *horizon* incorporated human history up to and including his own era. He included within that horizon the experience of his Jewish contemporaries. As a result, his theology of history was future-oriented, animated by the eschatological expectations of both Christians and Jews. Contact with Jews, and with one Jewish exegete in particular, seems to have made Herbert's unique horizon possible. The poignancy of Rashi's arguments, in the context of the people of Israel's contemporary circumstances, prevented Herbert from subsuming the eschatological narrative of the psalms under a totalizing Christian pattern—at least some of the time. The psalter, as interpreted by Rashi, elided and contradicted Herbert's attempts to domesticate the text within a proleptic Christian paradigm of fulfilled promise. Herbert, following Rashi, left the text open to the future, a future belonging to both Christians and Jews.

CHAPTER SEVEN

HERBERT'S EXEGETICAL METHOD:
THE FAITHFUL SYNAGOGUE

Herbert of Bosham, like other Jewish and Christian biblical commentators, was confronted not only with the difficulties presented by the texts of the psalms, but also by their so-called titles. Sometimes cryptic, sometimes straightforward, the *tituli psalmorum* have a long history of interpretation in both traditions. It is easy enough to understand a heading such as "a Psalm of David." But what does one do with titles such as "on the lilies" or "unto the end"? Moreover, names that appear in the titles—Idithun, Asaph, and even Moses, needed explanation— were these authors of the psalms in question? Or were they performers, noted singers and musicians?

In his preface to the commentary, Herbert notes the competing theories current in the Christian tradition regarding the authorship of the psalms. One theory, maintained by Augustine, Cassiodorus, and Herbert's teacher and near-contemporary Peter Lombard, held that David alone was the author of the entire Book of Psalms. The names appearing in the titles were understood to be the names of singers or other notables.[1] The alternative theory, generally attributed to Jerome, argued that the psalms had multiple authors. Herbert follows Jerome on this matter and supports the multiple-authorship theory with data apparently retrieved from rabbinical sources.[2]

Herbert's decision to adopt Jerome's minority report is significant for two reasons. First, having chosen to make a literal commentary on the Hebraica psalter, he also chose to forego the well-established Christian typology which dictated that David, the author of the psalms, was a type of Christ about whom all the psalms are presumed to speak. Because he is commenting on the Hebraica, moreover, Herbert exposits a set of psalm titles which no other Latin Christian exegete had ever

---

[1] A variation of this argument suggested that David might have attributed authorship of certain psalms to other writers. See Jerome's *Tractatus in Psalmos*, CCSL 78, 64.

[2] Fol. 1–1v. See the transcription of the prologue and discussion in Raphael Loewe, "Herbert of Bosham's Commentary on Jerome's Hebrew Psalter," *Biblica* 34:44–77.

discussed systematically—not even Jerome. A large body of material expounding the titles of the Roman and Gallican psalters had been gathered by Herbert's time, and was commonly formulated to present introductions (or *accessūs*) to the psalms. This material constituted a tradition of Christian exegesis that reflected on the psalms as being "of Christ" and his Church, whether prophetically or typologically. Names and phrases in the titles were interpreted in terms of Christian tropes, many derived from Jerome's *Liber Interpretationis Hebraicorum Nominum* and its successors.

The practice of explaining the origin of names derives from the Hebrew Bible itself, particularly Genesis. Place names commemorate significant human encounters with the divine; personal names encode personal qualities, future destinies, or momentous changes enacted in people's lives by God: Esau who is 'red' like his homeland Edom or like his lentil stew; Jacob who is the 'supplanter' but who is renamed Israel, the one who struggles with God. Etymology and etiology were interpretive practices built into the biblical text and elaborated by generations of commentators.[3] Lists of the origins or meanings of names in the Hebrew Bible were in circulation around the time of Philo of Alexandria (20 BCE–50 CE). In Christian tradition, Philo was widely regarded as the originator of these indispensable tools for allegorical interpretation. Lester Grabbe, in a monograph on Philo's use of etymology, suggested that the "pinnacle of achievement was to construct an allegorical interpretation which took into account everything in the text"—numbers, names, and unusual or uncommon words.[4] Etymologies enabled non-Hebrew speakers to weave those mysterious signifiers into a fabric of higher, or deeper, meaning. A version of Philo's list, a Greek work which provided translated etymologies for Hebrew names, was presumably adopted and expanded by Origen in the third century. The man who for a while styled himself as a second Origen translated still another such list into Latin, Jerome (ca. 345–420). In his preface to the *Hebrew Names*, the work most pertinent to our discussion, Jerome wrote:

> Philo, that most erudite man among the Jews, is declared by Origen to have done what I am now doing; he set forth a book of Hebrew

---

[3] I include under the general rubric of etymology the subcategory of onomastics, that is, the interpretation of Hebrew place and personal names.

[4] Lester L. Grabbe, *Etymology in Early Jewish Interpretation: The Hebrew Names in Philo* (Atlanta: Scholars Press, 1988), 46.

names, classing them under their initial letters, and placing the etymology of each at the side. This work I initially proposed to translate into
Latin. ... But I found the copies so discordant to one another ... that I
judged it better to say nothing rather than write what would so justly be
condemned. ... [Having] made progress in the knowledge of Hebrew, I
therefore went through all the books of Scripture ... and in the restoration which I have made of the ancient fabric, I think I have produced
a work which may be found valuable by Greeks as well as Latins. ... I
wished in this also to imitate Origen ... for in this work ... he endeavored as a Christian to supply what Philo, as a Jew, had omitted.[5]

Present in this early work is a principal justification for Jerome's later
translation projects: he was convinced that the fullest truth of Scripture was a Christian truth. Any translation, exegetical tool, or commentary prepared by Jews was, therefore, truncated in its usefulness.
The 'Hebrew truth' so avidly sought by Jerome was a *Christian* truth,
irradiated in the superior light of revelation experienced after Christ.
Jerome espoused the study of Hebrew, the mother of languages, to get
at the truth of Scripture. But he believed that the fundamental meaning of even the Hebrew text disclosed itself in full only after Christ. The
etymologies of Hebrew names provided by Jerome to his Latin audience served as anchors for Christological interpretations of the Hebrew
Bible. They were coordinates on a map whose expanded boundaries
were revealed by the Incarnation.[6]

Discussing Philo, Lester Grabbe notes that onomastical lists made
the mastery of the biblical text possible. 'Canned' etymologies of the
kind used by Philo and his Latin imitators were used not so much in
the service of exegesis, according to Grabbe, but *eisogesis*. That is to
say, Philo—or Jerome—or Peter Lombard—knew what he was looking
for when he turned to the biblical text. His interpretive scope was
already set by an overarching understanding of the passage's meaning.
Etymologies grounded an allegorical interpretation whose outcome was
predetermined. In that sense, etymologies did not tell an exegete, or his
reader, anything new—they chiefly gave shape to, and confirmation
of, the patterns of meaning the exegete already believed existed in the
text.[7] Christian interpreters of the psalms since antiquity believed that
Christ was the key to the psalter. The obscure Hebrew words, names,

---

[5] Jerome, Preface to the Book on Hebrew Names, *Nicene and Post-Nicene Fathers*,
second series, 6:485. See CCSL 72 for the Latin text.
[6] See also the discussion of Jerome's exegetical practices in Chapter 3.
[7] Grabbe, 45.

and place names noted in the psalms and their titles were interpreted with Christ as their key and goal. These etymologies effectively gave Christian interpreters tools to render the text of the Hebrew Bible ever more Christian in meaning. A brief example will suffice. The proper name Korah, as in "the sons of Korah" mentioned in several psalms' titles, acquired the etymology *calvarium* in the *Tractates on the Psalms* attributed to Jerome.[8] Thereafter, Christian exegetes routinely explained that "sons of Korah" referred to Christ: he was the Son who met his fate in the place of crucifixion.

Not surprisingly, the interpretation of Hebrew names—etymologies elaborated into a pattern of Christological exegesis—was "that very favorite device" of medieval Christian exegetes.[9] Or was it? Herbert of Bosham, for one, stood against this trend. On several occasions throughout his commentary he rejects the etymologies used in the Christian tradition. He argues that certain renderings substituted an interpretation for a correct identification. In his preface to the psalms commentary he disparages the practice of relying on etymologies as a source of meaning.[10] He writes:

> Our ecclesiastics, having abandoned the literal sense, flee to a spiritual understanding in the psalms and in various places in the Scriptures, *according to* the interpretation of the Hebrew names. Whence it often happens, in countless places in Scripture but especially in the titles of the psalms, that the interpretation of the name [*nomen*] is found in place of the name.[11]

---

[8] The sons of Korah are mentioned in the titles of Psalms 42, 44–49, 84–85, and 87–88 (Hebrew numeration). On Jerome's etymology, see "De Psalmo LXXXIII," CCSL 78, 95–96.

[9] Beryl Smalley, "Stephen Langton and the Four Senses of Scripture," *Speculum* 6:1 (1931), 62.

[10] Contrast this with Peter Lombard's discussion of the titulus to Ps. 38[39]: "*In finem canticum David pro Idithun.* Legitur in Paralipomenon quod arca Domini reducta a Philisthaeis, David ante eam constituit cantores quatuor millia, et totidem janitores, quibus praefecit filios Core, cantoribus vero praeposuit ducentos octoginta et octo viros, inter quos fuerunt Asaph, Eman, Ethan et Idithun, quorum nomina Esdras frequenter posuit in titulis, tum pro honore mysterii, tum propter nominum interpretationes, per quas subjectorum psalmorum intellectus panduntur, sicut hujus psalmi aperitur sensus." PL 191:389A.

[11] "Ecclesiastici vero nostri omisso sensu litterali; sicut in psalmis ita et per varia scriptura loca, racione interpretacionis hebraicorum nominum ad spiritualem mox intelligenciam avolant. Unde et frequenter accidit per innumera scripturae loca et maxime in psalmorum titulus pro nomine nominis interpretacionem repperiri." Fol. 1ᵛᵃ; printed in Raphael Loewe, "Herbert of Bosham's Commentary on Jerome's Hebrew Psalter (I)," *Biblica* 34 (1953): 71.

The daring of Herbert of Bosham's undertaking should be obvious: he explored the literal meaning of the titles even if that meant rejecting such towering authorities on the 'Hebrew truth' as Jerome. Other Christian exegetes explained the mysteries of the *tituli* by tracing their references to Christ, but Herbert explicated the titles by referring to their historical settings. The source for his historical data is, naturally enough, Hebrew Scripture; his citations are often the same as those used by Rashi in his psalms commentary. He also incorporates non-biblical material apparently gleaned from Rashi's citations of the Talmud or *midrashim*. Moreover, Herbert applies an exegetical principle used by Rashi and practiced by his successors (such as Rashbam): that is, he tries to explain the Hebrew Bible within its own bounds, confining his exegesis to "explaining Scripture by Scripture."[12] But Herbert expands his explanatory canon of Scripture to include the Christian New Testament when—under certain limited circumstances—he follows the trajectory of prophecy beyond the history of Israel.

Although Herbert's stance toward the *tituli psalmorum* was novel, he was not entirely a renegade. His attitude toward the literal sense, and his valuation of the historical significance of people, places, and things, owes much to his predecessors and near-contemporaries at the school of Saint Victor, Hugh and Andrew. Hugh of Saint Victor's pedagogical program emphasized a thorough grounding in historical study. In his didactic works, the *Didascalicon* and *De scripturis et scriptoribus*, Hugh endeavored to quash the over-eager impulses of young exegetes who wanted to 'fly' to the heights of allegory before mastering basic historical data and interpretive skills. Mastery of the 'three circumstances'— people, places, and time—which according to Hugh made up the stuff of history, could not be slighted. Not only would eliding these details entail sloppy scholarship; it would give birth to bad theology. The people and events of the Hebrew Bible rated a particular importance in Hugh's soteriological scheme: they represented milestones in God's project to rehabilitate and restore fallen humanity. Hugh, as much as any earlier Christian exegete, had an overarching pattern into which his interpretations fit, but its authority did not depend on what Beryl Smalley, in another context, called the "probative force" of Hebrew words, derived from their Christianized etymologies.[13] Hugh's authori-

---

[12] This is the principle of *gezerah shavah*, discussed in Chapter 6.
[13] Smalley, "Stephen Langton and the Four Senses of Scripture," *Speculum* 6:1(1931), 73.

tative interpretive framework derived from the narrative pattern of history itself, as God's plan unfolded from creation to redemption. Words, according to Augustine, Hugh, and still later, Thomas Aquinas, were human inventions and thus were only imperfectly able to describe truths. But things, and more especially the things of history, the *res gestae*, possessed a significative power bestowed by God. Thus in Hugh's scheme, and in Herbert's, history trumped etymology as an exegetical tool.

Herbert did not entirely abandon the traditional Christian view that the psalms were 'about' Christ, at least in some ultimate sense. But his version of the Christian tradition was transformed by his contact with Jewish exegesis of the psalms, and by his notion of the literal sense. Herbert's premier authority on exegetical matters was Rashi. I contend that he allocates importance to Rashi's exegesis precisely because Herbert followed an Augustinian-Hugonian model. In this model, the meaning of words is subordinated to the import of events. Who better to describe those events than the Jews who had lived the history? And, insofar as obscure terms in the psalms might require explanations, who better to explain them? Herbert did not cut himself loose from an overarching Christian understanding of the psalter. But that pattern did not impose a necessary, probative value on the words of the psalms. The Hebrew names did not need to be etymologized in order to be significant. Indeed, Herbert's discursive practices, which hewed to a literal meaning according to the dictates of Jewish exegesis, led him to play with the meanings of Hebrew words and names in radical new ways.

A half-century ago, Beryl Smalley suggested that for Herbert, the literal sense includes the scriptural author's use of literary devices such as metaphor.[14] This chapter argues that Herbert's 'fuller' literal sense owes much to his reading of Rashi, whom Herbert recognized as interpreting parts of the psalms metaphorically, even allegorically. For Rashi, as for Herbert, metaphorical multiple meanings freed the text from an explicitly historical anchor, allowing the literal sense to have an extra-historical import. Moreover, Herbert agreed with Rashi that some of the authors of the psalms were prophets, not of Christ alone as

---

[14] My article, "Herbert of Bosham and the Horizons of Twelfth-century Exegesis," *Traditio* 58 (2003): 133–173, addresses Smalley's endeavor to identify and categorize Christian exegetes of the literal sense.

in Christian tradition, but prophets whose foreknowledge was intended for Israel.[15]

A brief look at some of his Christian predecessors' comments on the Asaph psalms (49[50], 73[74], 83[84]) will help to distinguish the unique qualities of Herbert's exegesis. We begin with Jerome, in whose *Liber Interpretationis Hebraicorum Nominum* 'Asaph' is defined twice as 'congregating' (*congregans*) and once as 'gathering' (*conligens* or *colligens*).[16] In the exegetical works on the psalms attributed to Jerome, we are told that Asaph 'means' congregation (*congregatio*) in Latin or synagogue in Greek. Now we have arrived at the heart of the matter, in Christian terms anyway.[17] Pursuing this association, other early Christian exegetes such as Augustine and Cassiodorus attached the epithets 'faithful' or 'unfaithful' to the synagogues that they believed were depicted in the psalms. Thereafter, the psalms associated with the name Asaph were almost universally interpreted as speaking about, or in the person of, that 'faithful synagogue' which accepted Jesus as the Messiah. The examples are too numerous to cite; here is a representative statement from Cassiodorus, commenting on the title of Psalm 49[50]:

> The sense of this name, which is always full of mysteries for the Jews, points to the synagogue, which speaks in this psalm. But here we must understand it as the faithful synagogue of the Lord, which both believed that Christ would come and embraced his coming with exultant antic-

---

[15] Smalley characterized Herbert's attempt to grapple with this problem by comparing his approach to that of his apparent mentor, Andrew of Saint Victor: "... if we compare his interpretation of biblical prophecy with Andrew's we shall see that here, too, he marks an advance. Andrew has simply offered the Jewish explanation as the literal sense. Herbert makes a real attempt to grasp the nettle, to distinguish between passages which might be taken as prophecies of Christ in their literal sense and those which might be left in the Old Testament background. His confusion, where it appears, arises from his idea of the literal exposition." Beryl Smalley, "Herbert of Bosham on the *Hebraica*," *RTAM* 18:63.

[16] CCSL 72, "De psalterio," 48.8; "De Isaia propheta," 49.16; "Interpretationes libri quarti regum" 44.21.

[17] His *Commentiaroli in Psalmos* at Psalm 80 tells us that "Asaph" is interpreted as *congregatio*. CCSL 72, 219.1–2: "Secundus psalmus *pro torcularibus* sub Asaph nomine praenotatur, qui intepretatur congregatio; ut significet ad Deum cuncta referenda." Jerome's *Tractatus* on Psalm 77 states that Asaph was a *chorodidascalis*, as were the sons of Kore and Idithun, *et ceteri ... et iste unus est propheta*— a prophet of Christ. CCSL 78, 64–65. See page 66–67, where he cites the NT to prove that Asaph is a prophet whose prophecy was mistakenly attributed by scribes to Isaiah. Herbert knows this argument and uses it in his Preface. Finally, at Psalm 80, Jerome notes that Asaph is interpreted as "synagogue." CCSL 78, 78.

ipation. In it were numbered the patriarchs, prophets, Nathaniel, and also the apostles and all who believed with pure devotion. [Since in the psalm, the "synagogue" speaks of Christ], the unbelieving Jews are utterly deprived of any excuse, for they do not accept what the very synagogue attests. What then do they worship, if they spurn the words of the synagogue, which they claim to revere?[18]

Cassiodorus adds that the faithful synagogue "now comprises the Christian people" (*in prima sectione fidelis Synagoga loquitur, quae nunc est in populis christianis*).[19] Examples can easily be multiplied demonstrating that Asaph, the faithful synagogue, became a cipher in Christian exegesis of the psalms with resonances in the biblical past, the polemical present, and the eschatological future. It reaches backward to claim the patriarchs and prophets for Christianity, it demonstrates the current eclipse of Judaism by the Church, and it points toward the "end of the law" in Christ.

A citation from Peter Lombard illustrates the views of Herbert's more immediate predecessors. His explanation of the title to Psalm 49[50] echoes that of Cassiodorus:[20]

> For Asaph in Hebrew, the Latin interpretation is "congregation," the Greek is "synagogue," the faithful part which expects Christ is spoken of here, by which the unbelieving Jews are better confounded, and whose voice the Prophet uses here to give more certain testimony concerning the changing of the sacrificial *legalia* into a sacrifice of praise; put as previously, it brought out the change of the same into the sacrifice of the body and blood of the Lord. It also concerns the two advents of Christ, inviting in the first, terrifying in the second. The meaning of the title is this: this psalm is attributed to Asaph, the faithful synagogue, in whose person the prophet speaks.[21]

---

[18] Cassiodorus, *Explanation of the Psalms*, vol. I, trans. P.G. Walsh, Ancient Christian Writers, vol. 51 (New York: Paulist Press, 1990), 479–480; CCSL 97, 440.

[19] CCSL 97, 440.

[20] Not surprisingly, since the Lombard's commentary was a gloss upon that of Anselm of Laon, itself a highly compressed compendium of patristic opinion.

[21] "Asaph enim Hebraice, Latine congregatio, Graece synagoga interpretatur, quae secundum partem fidelem hic loquitur quae Christum exspectavit, per quam magis confutantur increduli Judaei, cujus voce propter certius testimonium utitur hic Propheta agens de mutatione legalium sacrificiorum, in sacrificium laudis, sicut supra egit de mutatione eorumdem in sacrificium corporis et sanguinis Dominici; agit etiam de utroque adventu Christi; per primum blandiens, per secundum terrens. Et est sensus tituli: Psalmus iste attribuitur Asaph, id est synagogae fideli, in cujus persona loquitur hic Propheta." PL191: 0475A.

In Herbert of Bosham's exegesis of Psalm [49]50 one is struck by the absence of any mention of Asaph, even though he does recount certain aspects of the Christian tradition on the psalm common to Cassiodorus and the Lombard. In particular, he avers that the psalm speaks of the transformation of the Temple sacrifices into bloodless sacrifices. Yet he does not nominate a supersessionary 'faithful synagogue' as the vehicle for that transformation. In fact, in none of the psalms associated with the name Asaph does Herbert make the statement, ubiquitous among other Christian commentators, that Asaph denotes the faithful synagogue.

This is not to suggest that Herbert did not comment on 'Asaph,' or that he did not use the term 'faithful synagogue.' He did both, but in ways markedly different from other Christian commentators. Rather than follow any Christian etymology, he adopted the meaning attached to the name Asaph by Jewish exegetes. In Rashi's commentary, Asaph is never explained; we can assume, however, from Rashi's comments that the Asaph of the psalter was a contemporary of David's, the Levite musician mentioned in First and Second Chronicles, and the founder of a dynasty of priestly singers.[22] The songs of Asaph together with those of David were performed when Hezekiah cleansed the Temple. Most significantly for our purposes, Asaph is described as a "seer" in 2 Chron. 29:30.[23] Rashi alludes to Asaph's prophetic abilities in his exegesis of Psalms 73[74] and 79[80]. As we shall see, Herbert adapts Rashi's allusions to suit his purposes.

Herbert's epithets for Asaph include "psalmist" (*psalmista*; Ps. 49[50]), "prophet" (*propheta*), and "psalm-scribe" (*psalmigraphus*; Ps. 73[74]). The historical content of both Rashi's and Herbert's exegesis demands that Asaph be regarded foremost as a prophet, because each exegete contends that these psalms speak of events which happened long after Asaph's lifetime. These events included:

– the miraculous lifting of Sennacherib's siege of Jerusalem during the reign of Hezekiah (Pss. 73, 76);
– the Babylonian captivity (Ps. 79);

---

[22] Herbert's Latin text has been compared to the Hebrew edition of Rashi's commentary prepared and translated into English by Mayer I. Gruber, *Rashi's Commentary on Psalms 1–89 (Books I–III)* (Atlanta: Scholars Press, 1998). The difficulties of establishing a reliable text of Rashi's commentary are discussed in Chapter 4.

[23] References to Asaph's various roles can be found at Neh. 12:46; 2 Chron. 5:12; Ezra 2:41; 2 Chron. 29:30.

- the 'desolating sacrilege' of the Temple by Antiochus Epiphanes
  (Ps. 79) and the subjection of Israel to the latter's abominable laws
  during the Maccabean period (Ps. 77);
- the afflictions suffered after the destruction of the second Temple
  (Pss. 74, 80);
- and an enumeration of the enemies of Israel among whom 'the
  sons of Esau' or Edom—the rabbinical cipher for Christianity—
  figure most prominently (Pss. 75, 82, 83).

Before considering the significance of the fact that both Rashi and Herbert viewed Asaph as a prophet, let us take up the thread of the faithful synagogue. Herbert cut the knot that bound Asaph typologically to
the Christians who succeeded the Jews as God's chosen people. Nevertheless, he used the term 'faithful synagogue' liberally throughout his
psalms commentary. A survey of these references in the commentary
suggests that Herbert labeled as the 'faithful synagogue' that part of
Israel which remained faithful to God's Law during periods of adversity.[24] Herbert took a well-known *Christian* trope, generally understood
by his contemporaries to refer to the Church, but restored the history
of Israel as its frame of reference. Yet he retained the trope. Why?

Herbert attained a nuanced view of the relationship between Christianity and Judaism because he relied on a Jewish commentator on
the psalms who explored Scripture's figurative language and prophecy
in his exegesis, explorations which Herbert adopted in his own literal
interpretations. Herbert relied on Rashi not only for historical data but
also for the scope to pursue certain psalmists' prophetic abilities beyond
the limits of Israel's history and into the era of the New Covenant.
Significantly, Herbert achieved this fuller reading of Rashi using the
tools Rashi provided, not through the simple expedient of a typological reading of figures and events depicted in the psalms. He repeatedly
acknowledges that Rashi has construed a psalm metaphorically (as in
Psalm 44[45], discussed in Chapter 6). He also describes Rashi as having constructed an allegorical reading, applying the technical language

---

[24] His 'faithful synagogue' seems to be a transhistorical phenomenon, a point deduced from comparing the "remnants" spoken of by Second Isaiah, the "good figs"
of Jeremiah, and the Maccabean martyrs who refused to accede the abominations of
Antiochus Epiphanes. Herbert never refers explicitly to such terms from the biblical
record. See the discussion in Chapter 6 on the question of whether all—or some—of
Israel is destined to be saved. On two occasions, he speaks of the "learned ones" of the
faithful synagogue, with whom David consulted regarding his treatment of Idumea (Ps.
44[45]:7, Ps. 59[60] titulus).

of Christian exegesis to his presumably literal source.[25] Finally, at least
once Herbert acknowledges that the *hebreorum litteratores* are capable of
discerning a psalm's spiritual meaning—at Psalm 122:3, which he says
Jews and Christians alike attribute to the celestial Jerusalem.[26] Herbert
was more subtle than his contemporaries in pursuing the ends of Christian theology in that he took the facts attested by Rashi, wove them
together with Rashi's citations of metaphor and prophecy in the psalms,
and formed a web of reference that extended beyond the Hebrew Bible.
In this process he reconciles his Jewish and Christian authorities in
order to establish his ultimately Christian reading of the psalms on
a remarkably innovative basis. He achieves this reconciliation by following Rashi whenever the latter refers to a psalmist's prophecy. Then
Herbert demonstrates how the prophecy applies both to Israel and to
Christianity.

To illustrate Herbert's method at work in his reconstruction of the
faithful synagogue, data from two other sets of psalms will be adduced.
Besides those relating to Asaph, psalms that bear the name Idithun in
their titles (Psalms 38[39], 61[62], 76[77]), and those whose titles include
the term *erudicio* in the Hebraica version (*intellectus* in the Gallican) will
be considered.

Like Asaph, the name Idithun had a traditional etymological interpretation in Christian exegesis. From Jerome's *Interpretation of Hebrew
Names*, Christians learned that Idithun 'meant' *transiliens* or 'leaping
over.' From this interpretation of the name, they derived the notion
(as in Peter Lombard's case, discussing the title to Psalm 76[77]) that
the faithful synagogue (meaning Christians) 'leapt over' the temptations
of this world in order to reach its proper end in Christ.[27] By contrast,
Herbert's exegesis of Psalm 38[39]'s title (*Victori ydithun david*) provides
three explanations of Idithun. One of these explanations accords with
Christian traditions: the belief that Idithun was a prominent choris-
ter or musician.[28] Another suggestion, drawn possibly from Rashi, is

---

[25] One such case is at 73[74]:17; Herbert records that Rashi interprets "darkness"
and "light" as references to Israel's time in exile and redemption therefrom, respectively.

[26] At folio 142[vb].

[27] Peter Lombard on Ps. 76[77] *titulus*: "Psalmus iste attribuitur Asaph, id est fideli
congregationi, quae hic loquitur, et agit pro Idithun, id est de se transiliente in finem,
id est in Christum ultra quem nihil est." PL 191:711C. See also Cassiodorus *ad loc.*

[28] See 1 Chron. 16:41 for an account of Idithun as a singer in the time of David.

that the name refers to a musical instrument.[29] Finally, Herbert suggests that Idithun might refer to the profane laws and mandates imposed upon Israel by its oppressors. Herbert may have learned this interpretation, unknown in earlier Christian exegesis, from Rashi or from the *Midrash on Psalms*. Commenting on Psalm 38[39], Rashi had asserted that Idithun was the name of a person but then mentions an 'aggadic midrash' concerning the word: that it refers to the *haddatot*, the troublesome laws, imposed against Israel.[30]

Commenting on the first verse of Psalm 38[39], "I said, I will guard my ways lest I sin by my tongue; I will silence my mouth, while the wicked is against me," Herbert writes:

> It is the same custom of the faithful in the yoke of captivity or of those who are oppressed in some other way to conceal the words of the law of God from the malice of their unfaithful oppressors and the blindness of their unbelief. Holy things should not be divulged to the unworthy. Especially the hidden things (*archana*) of the faith should be concealed, as it is written elsewhere: 'I have hidden your words in my heart lest I sin against you' (Ps. 118[119]:11) and 'on the willows in the midst of it we have hung up our harps.' And 'how shall we sing the song of the Lord in a strange land?' (Ps. 136[137]:2, 4) And this is what David here in the person of Israel is saying to God.[31]

---

[29] Note that Gruber, *ad loc.*, cites the *Mahbereth Menahem* as Rashi's possible source for this definition.

[30] Herbert appears to expand on his Hebrew sources by citing 1 Macc. 1:46: "And the king sent letters by messengers to Jerusalem and the towns of Judah that they should follow the law of the nations of the earth." Unlike either Rashi or the *Midrash*, Herbert provides a historical context for the time and place in which these "troublesome decrees" were imposed, associating them with the reign of Antiochus Epiphanes. Ps. 38[39] titulus, fol. 39ra: "Ydithun nomen est hic persone unius scilicet victorum vel cantorum qui in cancionibus prefuerant aliis. Unde non solum cantores sed et victores in titulus psalmorum scribuntur quasi aliis precellentes. De quo supra plenius diximus fuerunt tamen qui dicerent ydithun hic instrumenti nomen. Et est secundum hoc sensus talis psalmus david victori in subaudi. Ydithun id est instrumento tali cantandum fuerunt et alii qui traderent per ydithun debere intelligi prophanas leges et mandata ad que observanda israel sepe cogebatur iugo pressus hostili. Sicut scriptum est quod 'rex antiochus libros miserit per manus nunciorum in ierusalem et in omnes civitates iudee ut sequerentur leges gencium terre'(1 Macc. 1:46). Et de huiuscemodi irahelis afflictione; psalmus david victori; pro subaudi ydithun id est pro legibus profanis quibus sepe in afflictione sua premebatur israel. Quod in hoc psalmo et in psalmi titulo prophetice significatur."

[31] "*Dixi custodiam vias meas ne peccem in lingua mea; custodiam os meum silencio. donec est impius contra me*. Idem fidelium in captivitatis iugo seu alio modo oppressorum mos est. Ab infidelibus eorum oppressoribus et incredulitatis malicia obcecatis. eloquia legis dei abscondere. [Sancta] indignis non vulgare et maxime fidei sue archana reticere unde alibi. *In corde meo abscondi eloquia tua ut non peccem tibi* (Ps. 118[119]:11) in corde meo

In this passage, Herbert associates the 'faithful synagogue' with the faithful in captivity who refused to apostatize. He cites Ps. 136[137], a text redolent of the Babylonian captivity, after having alluded in the title to the Greek domination of Israel in the second century BCE. Subsequent illustrations will demonstrate that while the faithful synagogue was a chronologically fluid term for Herbert, he consistently associates it with that part of Israel which refused to abandon its covenant, regardless of the sufferings or penalties imposed on the community. Herbert's apparent refusal to ascribe a specific historical context either to the 'faithful synagogue' or to the afflictions it suffered echoes the open-endedness of the afflictions referred to by Rashi and *Midrash on Psalms*. The references to the unjust laws connoted by the name Idithun, and their association with either Greece or Edom, suggest that Rashi and his predecessors were addressing the afflictions and pressures to apostatize experienced by their own communities. It is difficult to determine how well Herbert himself understood the polemical import of some of these statements. What is most significant in the present discussion is that Herbert clearly identifies the faithful with historical Israel and its sufferings, not with a cadre of proto-Christians.

At Psalm 61[62], Rashi suggests that Idithun is the name of a musical instrument, but again mentions the 'aggadic midrash' that Idithun refers to the *haddatot*, the troublesome decrees. Herbert detects the distinction and explains its consequences. He tells us that if the word is understood to mean an instrument, then we can believe that in this psalm David speaks in his own person, about his own situation. But if we understand Idithun to refer to laws imposed on Israel by enemy nations, then David speaks *in israelis persona*. In the exegesis of the verses that follow, Herbert demonstrates that it is possible to understand the psalm on either basis, although he generally favors the latter (David speaking for Israel suffering in captivity.) His preference is most likely due to the fact that he is following Rashi's exegesis, as he did for most of the psalms, and Rashi's focus throughout is on the corporate experience of Israel in exile and on its eschatological hope to return to the Land.[32]

---

abscondi eloquium tuum ut non peccem tibi Et *super salices in medio eius; suspendimus cytheras nostras*. Et *quodmodo cantabimus canticum domini in terra aliena* (Ps. 136[137]:2,4). Et hoc est ipsum est [*sic*] quod hic david in israelis persona dicens [ad] deum [MS: deus];" Fol. 39[rb].

[32] Herbert comments at v. 1, fol. 62[ra-b]: "In hoc psalmo david prophetice israel afflictiones et maxime captivitates ipsi super venturas significat. Et loquitur in israelis persona. Et sciendum quod captivi sint maxime et incarcerati inter oppressores suos

The last psalm that cites Idithun in its title is the seventy-seventh. Herbert renders the title as *victori super Idithun psalmus Asaph.* Here again he notes that some interpret the name to be that of an instrument, not a man. But there are "many others" (*plerique*) to whom it "seems truer" that Idithun refers to the iniquitous laws imposed upon Israel by its enemies. He concludes that Asaph writes here about the laws forced on Israel like a yoke by its enemies. From this explanation of the title, Herbert deduced a brief *accessus* to the psalm:

> The title, therefore, is like the key to the psalm. It illuminates [*aperit*] the matter and cause, and thus its meaning. Thus the matter of the psalm is Israel's captivity. Its issue is the oppression of wicked laws. But there is hope of salvation [*salutis*], by crying to the Lord. Whence Asaph in the person of the Israelite people, gathered [*constituti*] under Nabugodonosor in the Babylonian captivity says thus … [introducing the first verse].[33]

By adopting Rashi's explanation of the name Idithun, Herbert again rejected Christian traditions that used Jerome's etymology as a tool for detaching the psalms from their historical context. In contrast to his rejection of 'Christianized' etymologies, Herbert readily adopted the etymology suggested by Rashi for Idithun, derived from *haddatot.* The 'troublesome decrees' are those that have confronted Israel throughout its history of captivity and exile.

Given the difficulties inherent in discussing an unfamiliar text, it may be useful to summarize the data assembled so far. This chapter tries to 'triangulate' exegetical concepts used by Herbert, to show how his application of those concepts differs from that of his Christian predecessors. Imagine that the figure or trope 'Asaph' is at the apex of the triangle; at one of the lower corners is 'Idithun.' The two are related along the axis of Herbert's reflection on the nature of the faithful synagogue in its historical concreteness. Bucking the tide of centuries of Christian exegesis, Herbert did not say that Asaph means the faithful synagogue, which in turns means the Church. Rather, he learned

---

et qui potestatem habent super ipsos linguam suam reprimere ut contumeliosa non loquitur vel superbia. Sed quocumque humilia quocumque modestia. Et hoc est quod david dicit in captivi israelis persona."

[33] Fol. 89[va]: "… psalmus iste; asaph est super ydithun id est pro legibus illis ab asaph compositus est; que inimice potestates posuerunt super israel quasi iugum. Titulus itaque quasi psalmi clavis; psalmi materiam et causam et sic intelligenciam aperit. Ut sit psalmi material: israelis captivitatis. Causa; legum iniquarum oppressio. Spes vero salutis ad dominum clamore. Unde asaph in persona israelitici populi sub nabugodonosor in babilonica captivitate constituti sic dicens … "

from his Jewish sources that Asaph, a psalmist and prophet, was able to predict the response of Israel's faithful to the afflictions imposed upon them, including the 'troublesome decrees' (as in Psalm 76[77]). Pursuing the triangle metaphor, we can now add as its final angle the term *erudicio* found in the titles of several psalms. It appears as an epithet describing various authors: *erudicio David, erudicio Asaph, erudicio filii Chore*, et cetera. Again, *erudicio* is a term not found in the Gallican translation; in that version the Hebrew word *maskil* was rendered *intellectus*. It is a small but significant difference in translation: the difference between 'learning' and 'understanding.' Herbert's predecessors nearly always explained the psalmist's *intellectus* as prophetical understanding of Christ's redemptive work.[34]

In early discussions of the terms *erudicio* or *eruditi* in the titles, Herbert limited himself to explanations based on data he gleaned from Rashi. Discussing the title to Psalm 32 Rashi had stated, "[The] Sages said, 'As for every psalm in which it is said, *maskil*, he [David] composed it with the aid of a ghostwriter'."[35] Herbert echoes Rashi. He explains the Latin title, *erudicio David*, with the statement: "The Hebrews say [*hebrei tradunt*] concerning all the psalms in whose titles 'erudition' is prepended, [that they] were related from David through an interpreter (*per interpretem*) and not through himself ..."[36]

When discussing subsequent references to the 'erudition' of the sons of Korah, neither Rashi nor Herbert gave any more information concerning the term, although both eventually asserted that divine inspiration rested upon those authors. At Psalm 44[45], Rashi reported merely that the psalm was written for the sons of Korah by a "ghost writer."[37] Herbert agreed, but only after repeating his definition of *erudicio*. He

---

[34] See Peter Lombard on Ps. 41, for instance: "Et est sensus tituli: *Intellectus hujus psalmi dirigens nos in finem*, id est in Christum, convenit filiis Core, id est crucis quae in Calvaria fuit." PL 191: 415B.

[35] Gruber, 162.

[36] Ps. 31[32], fol. 32[va]: "Erudicio David. Tradunt hebrei quod omnes psalmi in quorum titulis preponitur erudicio; a david per interpretem et non per se ipsum relati sunt; levitis quorum erat cantare eos tempore david in tabernaculo [qui] ante templi fabricam ipse tetenderat. Post vero tempore filii sui salomonis in edificato iam templo."

[37] See Gruber, 212ff. In other cases where psalm-texts mention "learned ones," Rashi suggests that the term refers to the Sanhedrin or even the *bet-midrash*. Herbert renders these allusions to *eruditi* in terms of the "doctors of the law who are, as it were, the soul of the people by whom [the people] are instructed" (Ps. 54[55]:11). Rashi does not mention the *titulus* in his exposition of the psalm; neither does Herbert. But at verse 11, Herbert describes them as the "doctors of the law": *legis doctores qui sunt velud anima populi ab eis erudiendi*.

wrote: "This psalm is the erudition of the sons of Korah, that is, by those who are learned, others are educated. But I say that the psalm was set in order by the sons of Korah."[38] In later psalms, including those in the group attributed to Asaph, Herbert united the theme of a learned person instructing the people with the assertion that divine inspiration had rested on the psalmists who dictated these psalms to a scribe. The combination of learning and inspiration rendered the authors of these psalms particularly gifted, in Herbert's opinion.[39] To illustrate the effects of this coalescence, consider the following examples from Herbert's discussions of Psalms 73[74] and 77[78], both titled *erudicio Asaph*. Concerning Psalm 73[74], Herbert reported that this is the first psalm of lamentation over Jerusalem and of the final "captivity," which occurred under Titus.[40] "Asaph," he wrote, "prophesying the last captivity, thus begins [the psalm] in the person of the faithful synagogue, [saying] 'O God, why have you cast us off unto the end; why is your wrath burning against the sheep of your pasture?'"[41] He did not mention Asaph's erudition in his discussion of the title. Both Rashi and Herbert mentioned Asaph's prophecy, however, at verse 73[74]:9. The verse reads, "We do not see our signs, nor is there prophecy any longer and there is no one among us who knows how long." In his exegesis of the verse, Rashi said that Asaph is prophesying about the period of Israel's exile, which is characterized by a lack of signs of deliverance.[42] Herbert used Rashi's assertion that Asaph speaks prophetically here to provide an expanded, 'Christian' version of that prophecy. Why did he take this step, so common to other Christian exegetes yet so unusual

---

[38] In a brief and uncharacteristic *accessus*-style introduction to the psalm, Herbert writes: "Order. This psalm is the erudition of the sons of Korah, that is, by which they have been instructed, they instruct others. But I say the psalm was set in order by the sons of Korah." The Latin reads: "*victori pro rosis filiorum chore erudicio canticum amoris*. Ordo. Psalmus iste est erudicio filiorum chore id est quo ipsi eruditi alios erudierunt. Psalmus vero dico a filiis chore directus." Fol. 46[ra].

[39] In Herbert's interpretation of the later psalms, Asaph, Eman, and Ethan become "learned" in the same sense that the *intellectus* of the psalmist[s] had been understood by Jerome *et al*. See note 34, above.

[40] Cf. the Lombard *ad loc*.

[41] Titulus to Psalm 73[74], fol. 84[vb]: "*victori eruditionis Asaph vel intellectus. Ut quid* et cetera. Ex dictis patet. Primus lamentacionis et de ultima captivitate per titum facta. Asaph ergo prophetans captivitatem ultimam; in persona fidelis synagoge inchoat sic: *ut quid Deus reppulisti in finem; fumavit furor tuus in gregem pascuae tuae*."

[42] Rashi's comments read: "'signs for us,' which You promised throught Your prophets, 'we have not seen,' and 'we do not see them during the long time we are in Exile. Asaph has prophesied concerning the period of the Exile." Gruber, 341–342.

for him? Perhaps since Rashi had asserted that prophecy is part of the meaning of this verse, Herbert felt free to include a discussion of Christian prophecy within his exegesis of the literal sense. In effect, Rashi had given him permission.[43]

Having been handed the thin end of the wedge, Herbert proceeds to drive it home. He asserts that the 'clear prophecy' of the verse is that the captivity will end after the coming of 'the king, our Messiah.' The 'signs' mentioned in the verse were the Temple sacrifices under the law which had prefigured the Christian sacraments. According to the apostle Paul, the law, the priesthood, and the sacrifices have all been found lacking; likewise the signs and the prophet's ability to interpret them.[44] To support his point, Herbert cites Isaiah's prophecy about the Babylonian exile, when all the "staff and stay and ... the skillful in eloquent speech" were taken away (Isa. 3:1–3). He interpreted this last phrase to mean that those who know how to interpret the law, prophecies, and parables were taken captive. The people ask of the current captivity: "How long, O Lord?" unable as they are to predict its end.

While commenting on Psalm 74:9, Herbert capitalized on Rashi's assertion that Asaph was prophesying about the final exile. He stretched Rashi's point to include his own conviction that the end of the

---

[43] Ps. 73[74]:9, fol. 85[va–b]: "*signa nostra non vidimus non est ultra propheta; et non est nobiscum qui sciat usquequo.* Ecce aperta de ultima post regis nostri messie adventum captivitate propheta. Et vocat signa non ut prius ex divinacionibus coniecturas, sed que erant signa futurorum in lege instituta sacrificia. Et si qua alia per prophetas in tipum futurorum promissa pro quibus omnibus dicit. *Signa nostra non vidimus* scilicet sacrificia, nec alia in tipum futurorum dicta, facta vel promissa. Quod sine sacrificium; nec sacerdos sine quo mane sacerdocium. Nam iuxta quod magister de sacerdocio et lege disputat deficiente sacrificio; necesse est ut deficiat et sacerdocium (Cf. Heb. 7:12). Et ita deficientibus signis; deficit eciam propheta qui israelem captivum consolari et captivitatis finem predicere solet. Et hoc est quod subdit; *non ultra propheta* et etiam *non est nobiscum qui sciat* legem scilicet aut prophetas interpretari. Iuxta quod propheta non tamen de hac prophetans captivitate, plangit ierusalem dicens: *Ecce enim dominator dominus auferet a iuda ierusalem validum et fortem et prudentem eloquii mistici* (Isa. 3:1) id est scientem interpretari legis prophetiarum et parabolarum, *eloquia mistica*. Et hoc ipsum est quod psalmista hic; '*Et non nobiscum qui sciat*.' Et quia ultime captivitatis huius que cura seculi finem terminabitur sicut et seculi finis incertus est, eciam prophetis incognitus subdit propheta hic *usquequo domine* durabit seculi captivitas hec; de hac itaque dierum mistorum captivitate psalmista prophetat hic. De qua et in propheta alio dominus loquens ad sinagogam fidelem quasi sponsam suam predixerat sic: *dies multos expectabis me non fornicaberis et non eris sine viro sed et ego expectabo te. Quia dies multos sedebunt filii israel sine rege sine principe sine sacrificio sine altari sine ephot et sine theraphin* (Hos. 3:3–4)."

[44] Herbert's source is the Epistle to the Hebrews, which he attributed to Paul.

captivity will be signaled by the second coming of Christ. He argued
that Israel's temple worship had been made redundant and that Israel's
prophets had departed from her. None of these points is very striking,
coming from a Christian commentator. But the absence of certain
common Christian themes *is* striking: for instance, Herbert did not say
that Christ, the redeemer of the world, has come and the Jews are too
blind to recognize him. Rather, he seems to regard as legitimate the
Jews' claim that their present life is one of captivity. In Herbert's view,
they can have no release except an eschatological one, given that no
one, apparently, can interpret the "parables and enigmas" for them.

In his discussion of Psalm 78, *Erudicio Asaph; ausculta populus meus legem
meam* (Listen my people to my law), Herbert remarks, "When it says
erudicio, note that in this psalm which is entirely historical, the spirit
is hidden under the veil of the letter. That about which less is said
elsewhere is supplied here … Asaph speaks here in the person of the
Lord, or the Lord through Asaph, to his people Israel." The definition
of *maskil* that Herbert learned from Rashi, that of divine inspiration
resting on a psalmist who dictated his words to a scribe, coupled with
Asaph's biblical identity as a seer, makes plausible Herbert's argument
that a literal interpretation of the text can reveal spiritual content.[45]

Psalm 78 is long; Herbert commented sparingly on it. But at verse
25, he provides us with a concrete example of Asaph's *erudicio*, one that
unites the themes we have examined thus far. The verse reads: "Man
ate the bread of the mighty; he sent them provisions in abundance."
Herbert explains that the bread of the mighty (more familiar to Christians in its Gallican form, "bread of angels") was manna, for which
humans did not labor but which rained down on them from heaven,
gratis. According to Herbert, Asaph's *erudicio* resided in the psalmist's
ability to instruct his people in the meaning of this parable. Asaph's
instruction is unequivocally Christian:

---

[45] The second verse of Psalm 77[78] reads: "I will open my mouth in a parable;
I will utter riddles from ancient times." At this point, Herbert says merely that he
had explained earlier what "parables and enigmas" are. His reference is to an earlier
discussion (at Psalm 48[49]:5), where he defines a parable as that which is clear
to a person of the church (*ecclesiasticus*) but of which a Jew is ignorant. This is a
commonplace of Christian polemic; commentators from Jerome to Peter Lombard
defined parables in these terms. At 48:5, Herbert wrote, "*inclino ad parabulam aurem
meam aperiam in cithara enigma meum.* Parabole sunt cum rerum adducta similitudine quod
de illis dicitur; de aliis intelligitur. Dicens ergo *Inclinabo ad parabolam aurem meam.* Duo
notat et se non ex se parabolice loquuntur. Per quod ostenditur in verbis psalmi huius
moralibus aliquod latere misterium. Quod ecclesiasticus aperit; iudeus nescit." Fol. 51[vb].

And just as the rock was Christ thus also this is the bread of the mighty. Clearly Christ is that bread which came down from heaven. And man ate this bread of the mighty in the desert, just as now the Teacher [Paul] teaches: "all ate the same spiritual food and all drank the same spiritual drink" (1 Cor. 10: 3–4).[46]

As ever when Herbert interjects an explicitly Christological point into his exegesis, his discussion is perhaps more interesting for what he does not say than for what he says. He did not refer to Christ as the "word made flesh" or to the body of Christ as the bread of angels, as did his Christian predecessors. Rather, this passage demonstrates how he limited his Christological reading to situations in the psalms that permitted them. When a psalmist is credited with *erudicio* and is understood by Herbert's Jewish exemplars to have experienced divine inspiration, Herbert does not hesitate to expand on the psalmist's prophetical credentials, or to expand the prophet's horizons beyond the bounds of biblical Israel's history.

Two additional examples will suffice. Psalms 88[89] and 89[90] attribute *erudicio* to two men, Eman and Ethan the Ezraites. Herbert states that Eman dictated Psalm 88 to the sons of Korah. The psalm was transmitted from Korah's sons to the synagogue, just as now it is transmitted from the synagogue to the Church. Eman's *erudicio*, Herbert maintained, consisted in his ability to make clear the mysteries in the psalm, which both the church and the synagogue can understand from its literal meaning. Because Eman was learned, he was able to educate others, first in the synagogue and now in the church. According to Herbert, Psalm 88 encompasses the notion of captivity on two planes: the historical captivity experienced by Israel and the miserable calamity of human captivity to sin.[47] Similarly, the psalmist

---

[46] Ps.77[78]:25 "*panem forcium comedit vir cibaria misit eis in saturitatem. Pane forcium* id est manna. Sed quomodo vocat panem fortium qui pocius ociosorum dici sicut videtur potuisset, ytpote nullo partus labore sed de celis distillans gratis. Sed hic revera est asaph erudicio: parabola et enigma populum suum erudientis et ad misterii inquisicionem provocantis. Et sicut petra erat christus, ita et panis iste forcium; christus est panis scilicet ille que de celo descendit. Et hunc panem forcium comedit vir in deserto. Nam sicut magister docet: *omnes eandem escam spiritualem manducaverunt et eundem potum spiritalem biberunt* (1 Cor. 10:3). Sequitur cibaria scilicet carnes misit eis in saturitatem. Et docet quomodo subdens." Fol. 91[vb]. The verse which Herbert quotes from 1 Corinthians concludes, "for they drank from the spiritual rock which followed them and the rock was Christ."

[47] Titulus, Ps. 87[88], fol. 103[ra–b]: "… Videlicet quod ubicumque in titulis psalmorum ponitur verbum hoc hebreum macethil [for *maskil*]; pro quo nostri transtulerunt *erudicio*. Scias profecto quia psalmi illi non per ipsos qui spiritu sancto mediante sunt

speaks in verse 6 of liberation from death: Herbert maintained that
this liberation applies equally well to Israel's deliverance from exile as
to humanity's deliverance from death by the One who rose from the
dead. Indeed, it was Eman's *erudicio* that enabled him to see these two
realities.[48]

Finally, at Psalm 89, Herbert tells us that the 'faithful synagogue'
speaks here in the person of Ethan the Ezraite. Herbert then outlined
the opposing traditions of interpretation concerning the psalm: 'the
Jew' says the psalm is about Solomon, 'the churchman' (*ecclesiasticus*)
says it is about the Messiah. If it is about Solomon, then the "building-
up of mercy" spoken of in verse 3 refers to the Temple. But according
to Herbert, Ethan in his *erudicio* was also alluding to the time of grace, a
clear prophecy of the coming of Christ. Herbert asserts, moreover, that

psalmorum auctores sed pocius per interlocutores et interpretes qui illis prophetantibus
interfuerunt et scribentes exceperunt, ad aliorum noticiam pervenerint. Qualis est et
psalmis qui mox subsequitur cuius titulus est, *erudicio ethan ezraite*. Ille profecto psalmus
qui ethan prophetante editus est; non per ipsum ethan sed per interpretes qui [inter]
fuerunt cum prophetaret pervenit ad alios. Verisimile; quod per filios chore. Unde quia
proxime eos premiserat eos post non nominat. Ita insinuans quod quorum fuit prius
canticum psalmi eorundem et proximum fuerit. Sed ad presentis psalmi titulum magis
declarandum, revertamur in quo dicitur quod psalmus ille fuerit erudicio eman. Id est
ex hoc psalmo eman fuit eruditus et sapiencior factus; et ex ipso psalmo eciam alii eruditi sunt, primo filii chore, alii scilicet tunc sinagoga nunc vero ecclesia. Et ita ex eo
quod in isto quemadmodum et in plerisque aliorum psalmorum titulis ponitur erudi-
cionis verbum. Ex qua filii chore erudiciores facti sunt et eciam ipse eman cuius tanta
fuit sapiencia erudicior, grande et occultatum psalmi huius manifestum declaratur fore
misterium. Quod utinam cum littera sicut ecclesia et sinagoga intelligeret …"

    [48] Ps. 87[88]:6, fol. 103[vb]: "*inter mortuos liber; sicut interfecti et dormientes in sepulchro
quorum non recordaris amplius et qui a manu tua abscisi sunt*. Liber scilicet a seculo. Sicut
enim mortuo et secula nichil; ita michi et seculo dicit captivis israel; nichil quasi non
reputor inter gentes. De hac vero mortuorum libertate alibi legitur, quod azaria filio
amasie lepra percusso; habitaverit in domo libera. Quia ubi nos habemus in domo
separata; hebreus habet libera. Sita enim fuit domus inter fossas mortuorum. Quod
nos cimiterium; hebrei vocant *bet hachaueroth* quod interpretatur domus fossarum. Bet
enim domus; chaueroth quod nos calvaria dicimus fosse. Unde et dicitur mons calvarie
mons fossarium. Ubi ponebantur corpora dampnatorum non quidem in domo libera;
id est non in cimiterio sepulta qui locus privilegiatus est. Et ideo liber est et qui in ipso.
Unde et bene dicitur domus libera, domus videlicet in tali loco sita. Domus igitur hec
libera; cui nichil et seculo a communi secularium usu et ab omni seculari viris dictione
exempta. Verum in hiis psalmi verbis est erudicio eman ergo ipse eruditus prius alios
postea erudiunt. Nam secundum ecclesiaticum sicut secundum litteratorem iudeum de
israele captivate diximus. Regis nostri messie per hunc psalmum loquentis verba sunt
hec dicens inter mortuos liberum id est inter peccatores liberum se a seculo …"

God's many mercies promised to David and his seed will be fulfilled, because the truth of those promises is unchanging.[49]

A brief synopsis of the argument so far might be helpful. For Herbert, the faithful synagogue was that part of Israel which has remained faithful to its covenants with God, despite the 'troublesome decrees' and pressure to apostatize imposed by the Gentile world. From time to time, the faithful synagogue has been addressed by a 'learned' psalmist, whose *erudicio* encompasses a prophetical foreknowledge of Christ as the deliverer of Israel from its final captivity. Note, however, that this deliverance is yet to come—the full promise of the Incarnation has yet to be fulfilled.

In other, less irenic passages than those presented here, Herbert does castigate the Jews for their blindness and for their rejection of Jesus as the Messiah—although typically only in his exegesis of psalms strongly associated with Christological prophecy.[50] Yet the evidence drawn from the 'Asaph' psalms and those dealing with *erudicio* suggests that he did not view this rejection as final; he seems to have suspended judgment on the Jews until the end-time. Herbert was unusually sensitive to the nuances of Romans 11; like Paul, he understood that the calling of the Gentiles is mysteriously bound up with the fate of the Jews, all of whom in the end will be saved. Guided by Rashi, Herbert of Bosham reconstructed the faithful synagogue on new lines. He retrieved 'Asaph,' a trope that had designated the faithful synagogue of proto-Christians, and refashioned it with reference to Israel's historical situation among the nations. Israel's deliverance from its distress—the pressure to apostatize borne of the 'troublesome decrees,' remembered in the psalter under the figure 'Idithun'—and humankind's deliverance from sin and death will both be accomplished by a Messiah yet to come. The peculiar *erudicio* of some of the psalmists points toward this end. Christian that he was, Herbert lamented that Rashi, his authority of choice, resisted resolutely what he regarded as the plain testimony of the literal sense: "And this is the erudition of Ethan. If only the *litterator* under-

---

[49] Ps. 88[89]:1: "*eruditionis Aethan Ezraitae Misericordias et cetera.* In hoc psalmo in persona sua et tocius fidelis singagoge loquitur propheta ethan qui secundum carnem frater fuit eman. Cuius nomen in precedentis psalmi titulo positum est." v. 3: "... Et nota quod cum dicit seculum misericordia vel quod sempiterna misericordia edificabitur; hic est erudicio ethan et de tempore gratie seu misericordie, perspicua in adventu regis nostri messie prophecia. Et vere promissi tui veritas adimplenda quia promissi tui veritas immobilis est." Fol. 104[vb].

[50] See the extended discussion of this issue in Chapter 5.

stood it ... Then there might be one meaning in the synagogue and in the church!"[51] Working from the instances of metaphor and prophecy noted by Rashi, Herbert finds in the literal meaning of the psalms a vision of God's work in history large enough to include both Christians and Jews. Ironically, even though he insists on a literal reading of the *tituli psalmorum* more precise than that of Jerome, Herbert's *historical* approach to interpretation proves to be open-ended, by virtue of eschewing etymologies that would have fixed the meanings of the titles within an exclusively Christian framework. By reading the *tituli* as precisely as he can in their Jewish context, their levels of meaning float free from traditional Christian interpretations. Granted, Herbert eventually corralled the titles' significations within a Christian theology of history; everything that rises must converge. But he resisted the temptation to subsume Jewish exegesis wholly within a closed Christian system of language and meaning.

Having studied Rashi's text with the help of Jewish interlocutors, Herbert learned that the Jews of Northern Europe were not stationary in useless antiquity, and that they were capable of understanding Scripture's 'higher,' spiritual senses. These were revolutionary insights. Most significant of all, perhaps, is the fact that Herbert did not simply assimilate these insights into an overarching Christian narrative of the end of days. Unlike many of his contemporaries, Herbert seems to have been content to leave in God's hands the mystery that God's chosen people might, at the end of days, consist of both Jews and Christians. Herbert did disparage aspects of Jewish belief. His *mappa mundi*, despite its enlarged borders, includes some ancient landmarks. But he was convinced by the gravity of Israel's suffering in exile and by its faith in God's saving power that the last word spoken in history will not abandon them.[52]

Did Herbert of Bosham put an end to the interpretation of Hebrew names? Hardly. As Mary and Richard Rouse have documented, Jerome's unwieldy guide was reorganized, rationalized, and incorporated into the prefatory material of thirteenth-century Bibles. Ralf Niger,

---

[51] Ps. 88[89]:6, fol. 106rb: "... Et est hic secundum sensum litteralem; erudicio ethan, quam utinam litterator qui locum hunc quasi superioribus psalmi non choerentem in expositum preterit intelligeret. Ut essent in uno sensu synagoga et ecclesia ..."

[52] Rashi's exegesis of the Suffering Servant motif and of the bride in Song of Songs focused on the two figures as epitomizing Israel's sufferings in Exile. Herbert seems to have been aware of these associations (certainly of the latter). See Psalm 87(88) titulus.

Herbert's contemporary, contributed a set of revisions and corrections to the Book of Hebrew Names, formulated in consultation with an apostate Jew.[53] Far from disappearing, this reference work became even more popular and accessible. Nevertheless, Herbert's attitudes may give us the most extreme example of changing attitudes toward etymology and its role in allegorical interpretation. Earlier exegetes, confounded by a lack of data, "fled" to allegory when it seemed the literal meaning was nonsensical. As A.J. Minnis has noted, allegories, particularly those derived from the interpretation of the Hebrew names in the psalter, "explained away" the apparent disunity of the book, its prophecies, and its authors.[54] Most Christian exegetes insisted that the psalter was a unified work by one author which predicted Christ's saving work—but this was a conclusion which could only be reached by finessing historical problems presented by the text.

Herbert openly confronted such historical problems. He tried to solve them by investigating the intentions of the human authors of the psalms, in their respective historical situations. Like Hugh and Andrew of Saint Victor, he was confident that properly instructed exegetes could tease out these data, particularly if they consulted with their Jewish counterparts. Hugh had written, "All Scripture if expounded according to its [literal] meaning, will gain in clarity and present itself to the reader's intelligence more easily."[55] The unity of the psalter subsisted not in an overarching Christian, allegorical narrative, for which the interpretations of Hebrew names "clouded over its seemly beauty with irrelevant comments."[56] Indeed, Herbert seems not to have unified the psalms at all, but treated them as individual historical documents, whose *res gestae narrationis* alone disclosed their divinely intended significance.

For many medieval Christians, etymology remained an illustrative and edifying tool, useful especially in preaching. But its contribution to the project of subjecting the Hebrew Bible to a Christian master narrative was reduced. This is not to say the Christian master narrative was at all undermined by efforts like Herbert's. Indeed, it was so well-

---

[53] The work is Niger's *Phillipicus*, Lincoln Cathedral MS 15.

[54] A.J. Minnis, *Medieval Theory of Authorship*, 2nd ed. (Aldershot: Wildwood House, 1988), 46–48.

[55] Hugh's preface to sermons on Ecclesiastes, PL 175:114C–115A; translated in Smalley, *SBMA*, 100.

[56] Ibid.

established as to be virtually impregnable. Still, the diminution of etymology as an exegetical tool made possible, for Herbert at least, a new
master narrative—focused on the end of days, when both literal and
spiritual truths might be realized.

CONCLUSION

On August 17, 1862, four young men of the Dakota nation attacked and killed a farming family in Meeker County, Minnesota. In the months ahead, attacks and counter-attacks between settlers, militia, and Native Americans escalated until the conflict came to be known as the Dakota War.[1] Between four and eight hundred settlers and an unknown number of Dakota were killed. The outbreak of violence represented the culmination of years of deprivation suffered by the Dakota people following the signing of the treaties of Traverse des Sioux and Mendota in 1851. The treaties had transferred nearly twenty-four million acres of land in the Upper Midwest from the Dakota to the United States government. In the years that followed, thousands of settlers from the east moved to Minnesota and the territories of North and South Dakota. The treaties provided for the resettlement of the indigenous peoples and attempted to induce them to take up farming in place of hunting, trapping, and trading. In exchange for their land, the Dakota were supposed to receive annuities to underwrite their move to agriculture, based on the purchase price of twelve cents an acre. But the money was slow in coming and was often misappropriated by Bureau of Indian Affairs agents; disease, starvation, and rebellion ensued. The Plains peoples resisted the destruction of their way of life, which was accompanied by systematic cheating and corruption by federal agents, local traders, and white settlers, until 1890. Then, at the Battle of Wounded Knee in South Dakota, the 'pacification' of the Plains was complete.

Living in the Minnesota River valley, about a mile from the site where the treaty of Traverse des Sioux was signed, I have been mindful of these events while writing this book. Parallels between the genocide of America's First Nation peoples and the genocide of European Jews

---

[1] A brief, informative, and balanced history of the events of the Dakota War, or Sioux Uprising, is Kenneth Carley's *The Sioux Uprising of 1862*, 2d. ed. (Saint Paul: Minnesota Historical Society, 1976). The Historical Society reissued this volume in 2001 with the title *The Dakota War of 1862*.

are many; the historical record of the events seems charged with horrific inevitability. The efforts by some to intervene, to alter the course
of an apparently preordained destruction, seem sadly feeble. Yet how
many among us would have the courage to stand up to the engine of
conquest and death, fueled by racism, greed, and misplaced religious
fervor?

In the context of this project, I have pondered the particularly vexed
motives and roles of the seemingly innocent 'scientists' who limned the
boundaries between the known and unknown—whether understood in
baldly territorial or broadly cultural terms. Their explorations, often
undertaken in dangerous circumstances and at great personal cost,
provided the data that made expansion possible. Consciously or not,
in other words, they fed the engine of conquest. Here again I see a
parallel between the history of the Minnesota Territory and twelfth-
century Europe. The *Map of the Hydrographical Basin of the Upper Mississippi*, produced by the *emigré* cartographer and naturalist Joseph Nicollet, was one of the outstanding scientific achievements of the early nine-
teenth century. Nicollet made three expeditions throughout the Upper
Midwest between 1836 and 1839; the last, in 1838–1839, surveyed the
entire region between the Mississippi and Missouri Rivers. Nicollet had
trained in France as a mathematician and served as an astronomer
at the Paris Observatory before suffering from political and financial
reverses during the turbulent events of 1830. He was penniless when he
arrived in the United States in 1832 and relied on patronage from other
French immigrants before receiving support from the U.S. Topographi-
cal Engineering Corps.

Nicollet's explorations of the Minnesota region were comprehensive
and precise; his party recorded geological, botanical, meteorological,
and hydrological data, and used the most accurate means then available to map the area's topography.[2] Joel R. Poinsett, then Secretary of
War in President Martin Van Buren's cabinet, advocated that Nicollet's methods be used to map the Rocky Mountains and beyond, to
the Pacific Ocean; "[t]hus Nicollet's explorations and his map were for
the first time publicly linked to the continental policy …"[3] The man

---

[2] My colleague, Robert C. Douglas of the Geography Department at Gustavus
Adolphus College, has confirmed the accuracy of some of Nicollet's calculations using
the Global Positioning System; Tim Krohn, "A Source of Food, Shelter and Life,"
Mankato Free Press, February 7, 2000.

[3] Martha Coleman Bray, *Joseph Nicollet and His Map* (Philadelphia: American Philosophical Society, 1980), 247–248.

himself, however, was frail and ill due to recurring bouts of malaria. He died before the western expedition was launched, and before he could complete his projected three-volume narrative survey which was to accompany his map, issued in 1/600,000 scale in 1842. Still, his methods laid the foundation for the "first map of the entire West that was 'based on correct or approximately correct geographical positions and ... the first to represent western topography in a reasonably accurate manner.'"[4]

Joseph Nicollet was aware that his work fed American imperial ambitions, but he also hoped that his wide-ranging scientific studies would promote enlightened policies of expansion. He despised the craven greed and ignorance of the settlers and their mistreatment of indigenous people, writing in one of his journals:

> Those whom you call children of the forest and whom you found when you took their ground were the *children of God*, more advanced, more moral, more religious than a quarter of your population, more humane, more honest than the hordes of rogues, thieves and assassins who still infect all of the region occupied by the Indians whom you have driven away or annihilated. ... If God renders me worthy, I hope to fill this vacuum in your history.[5]

And his love of the subtle beauty for the prairie, whose hundreds of acres he painstakingly mapped, was profound:

> There is something magical in the variety of impressions one gets from the sight of the prairies. One never wearies of it. ... The fresh breeze that springs up from time to time ... the sweet verdure everywhere, the flowers bedecking it, the blue of the sky, the variations of the atmosphere operating on a grand scale, all these things combine to arouse one, to free one's spirit.[6]

His biographer, Martha Bray, comments that if Nicollet's celebration of the "vast and magnificent" Red River valley had been written for a literary audience, not a government report, the site where he stood might be preserved as a "shrine of beauty." But, she notes, "Nicollet's words were read for non-contemplative reasons and the grasslands were, by their own guileless invitation to man, vulnerable. Today no one can find the place where Nicollet [and his companions] stood; it is lost in the new patterns of modern agriculture."[7]

---

[4] Bray, 270.
[5] Quoted in Bray, 131.
[6] Bray, 239.
[7] Bray 238–239.

As later history shows only too well, the land and its people were entirely vulnerable. Nicollet's monumental project, motivated by scholarly curiosity, devotion to 'pure' science, and a seemingly unadulterated love for the natural world, was ineluctably bound up in westward expansion. It was a classically imperialist, colonialist project, as postcolonial theory would have it: a body of data, carefully accumulated in order to create, preserve, and extend domination, both material and cultural, over precious resources. Nicollet's own motives, opinions, and goals were subsumed, even erased, once his studies became part of the government's archive, understood now in its 'operational,' Foucaldian sense.

It is relatively easy to trace the route that Nicollet's researches took into the archive of American expansion. His was, after all, a government-funded project intended to furnish resources for further exploration and settlement. By contrast, postulating that the archive of Christian hebraism operated purposely to expand Christianity's domain over Judaism is vastly more speculative. It is difficult to argue that the accumulation of knowledge about Jews and Judaism that took place in the mid- to late-twelfth-century was driven by specific and overt goals. It is still more difficult to speculate about the self-consciousness of a figure like Herbert of Bosham. Did he mean to rewrite the Christian theology of history that he learned from Augustine and Hugh? Or did he intend to gather data that might, at some future point and in someone else's hands, provide the means for displacing the Jews as the sources for learning Hebrew? Did he consciously contribute to a new 'cartography' of Christian (and 'Christianizing') knowledge or was he merely a curious surveyor of new territory, intent on the task before him with little thought to its potential effects?

This study has demonstrated that Herbert of Bosham was a Christian exegete who brought his tradition into dialogue with the Judaism of his time through the medium of his literal and historical commentary on the psalms. Primed by the Victorine view of history as a redemptive narrative still open to completion, provoked by his encounter with Rashi, an exegete of the 'plain meaning' also oriented to the future, Herbert was compelled to consider a more inclusive vision of the end of days than earlier Christians had contemplated. His close study of the Hebrew text in its historical context—lexical hebraism, as I have called it here—was Herbert's starting point. It was an aperture opening into another thought-world through which he stepped with remarkable intrepidity. As we have seen, there were limits to his tolerance (to use an

anachronistic term), as there necessarily were for any sincere Christian
who wanted to avoid the accusation of heresy or the label of 'judaizer.'
The most serious question about Herbert's work relates to the nature
of his religious commitments. Where does he stand in the 'genealogy'
of doubting Christians, if indeed such a genealogy can be proposed?[8]
Would Herbert have encountered other Christians who shared his particular views—Christians who were willing to recognize that the messiahship of Christ, the coming of the kingdom of God, was an ongoing
process, working itself out in time not only in relation to Christians
but also to Jews? Would he have encountered other Christians who did
not subsume Jews and Judaism into a conventionally mechanical role
in Christian eschatology (for example, that they existed only so that the
fullness of the Gentiles might enter the Church, and then they—or a
remnant of them—would also be converted)?

It has been suggested that no thoughtful Christian theologian in
the Middle Ages would have argued that human history is redeemed.[9]
Medieval theologians acknowledged that the transformation of sinful
humanity effected by God's grace and mercy in and through the person
of Jesus Christ is not yet complete. The fact that Christians believed
that the conversion of the Jews was itself an eschatological expectation,
not a present-day project, testifies to this awareness of the ongoing
need for redemption.[10] Yet rigorous theological speculation undertaken
in the full awareness of humanity's fallen state and dependence on
grace did not curb the self-assurance of Christian exegetes of the psalms
who were convinced that the promises made to 'Israel' (understood by
them as the Church) were now fulfilled.[11] Some of these same exegetes,

---

[8] Smalley, for instance, compares him with Otloh of Saint Emmeram, an eleventh-
century Benedictine. *BC*, 76.

[9] By Joseph P. Wawrykow in a private communication. In different but related
argument, Anna Sapir Abulafia has suggested that while twelfth-century Christians
were aware that Christianity was not universal, the lack of universality did not produce
doubt as Gavin Langmuir argues. Rather, she suggests, it "served to strengthen the
purpose" of those who sought to bring about a "universal Christendom." *Christians and
Jews in the Twelfth-Century Renaissance* (London: Routledge, 1995), 128–129.

[10] Yosef Hayim Yerushalmi makes this point in response to Rosemary Radford
Ruether's indictment of Christianity's theologically based anti-Judaism. Their respec-
tive essays are included in *Auschwitz: Beginning of a New Era?*, ed. Eva Fleischner (New
York: KTAV, 1977). See Yerushalmi, "Response to Rosemary Radford Ruether," 100.

[11] See the discussion in Chapter 6 concerning Psalm 79[80]:18. Peter Lombard's
exegesis of that verse echoes that of Cassiodorus, who wrote: "There could be some
doubt about the salvation of Israel, but only until the coming of the saving Lord. When
he came, the promise was fulfilled in its entirety; the Church no longer separates from

such as Peter Lombard, were also interpreters of Romans 11, but their careful positions with regard to the eventual salvation of *omnis Israhel* are not always preserved when commenting on the psalms.[12] By contrast, even in the polemically charged genre of psalms interpretation, Herbert eschewed manifestations of Christian triumphalism.

Militating against the thesis that Herbert was rejecting a widespread supersessionist 'realized' eschatology, however, is the fact that his career coincided with the 'Evangelical Awakening,' during which Christians became more self-aware and self-critical.[13] They sought to close the gap between their own lives and the gospel example of Jesus Christ's life. Their identification with the sufferings of Jesus, with his countercultural message of humility and self-abnegation might provide a counter-witness to a historical narrative that emphasizes Christianity's power and dominance in this period. We would need to look for Christians whose choice of this path also entailed a rejection of the Church's perennial anti-Judaism. The evidence of Adam of Perseigne suggests that some Christians chose this path.[14] Against this argument, however, one could adduce the evidence of Dominican and Franciscan contributions to the thirteenth-century movements to controvert, censure, and ultimately convert Jews.[15] Also, one might be able to argue, as does Gavin Langmuir, that the focus on the humanity of Jesus in the twelfth and thirteenth centuries had the effect of diminishing the importance of

---

Him, for she is joined in spiritual love for her Bridegroom." *Explanation of the Psalms*, vol. 2, trans. P.G. Walsh, Ancient Christian Writers no. 52 (New York: Paulist Press, 1991) 290.

[12] In his Romans commentary, Peter Lombard reminds Christians that the Jews were 'reprobated' not for the sake of the Gentiles but because of their own sins. His exegesis of Romans 11:25–32 encapsulates the key themes of Augustine's *City of God*, 20.30: following the preaching of Enoch and Elijah at the end of days, all the Jews will be converted. For his exegesis of Romans 11, see PL 191: 1481B–1495D.

[13] The label is Marie-Dominique Chenu's; see "The Evangelical Awakening," *Nature, Man and Society in the Twelfth Century*, 239–269. For a study of the twelfth century as a period of evangelically inspired reform among monastic communities, see Giles Constable, *The Reformation of the Twelfth Century* (Cambridge: Cambridge University Press, 1996).

[14] See Chapter 6. Noteworthy, perhaps, is the fact that the reform-minded 'new monks' of Cîteaux and its daughter houses were labeled as 'judaizers' by the Benedictines, among others. See Constable, *The Reformation of the Twelfth Century*, 33, 145.

[15] See the studies of Jeremy Cohen cited in Chapter 4. The differing roles of the Dominican and Franciscan friars has recently been articulated by Deanna Klepper. See "Nicholas of Lyra and Franciscan Interest in Hebrew Scholarship," *Nicholas of Lyra: The Senses of Scripture*, eds. Philip D.W. Krey and Lesley Smith, Studies in the History of Christian Thought, v. 90 (Leiden: E.J. Brill, 2000), 289–311.

the Old Testament and with it the toleration (albeit grudging) of Jews in Europe.[16]

In the later twelfth and early thirteenth centuries, Christians in Northern Europe gathered from Jews the tools that they needed to read the Hebrew Bible: we know of Hebrew-vernacular glosses that became the basis for dictionaries. Grammatical texts, written by Jews for Jews (often in Arabic, in Spain), become known by Christians, who also began to write rudimentary grammars of their own. Also in this period, Christians discovered the Talmud, the vast body of biblical commentary and theological reflection that demonstrated that Jews were not "stationary in useless antiquity," but interpreted the Torah in a spiritual way, precisely to keep Judaism alive. As Jeremy Cohen has demonstrated, this last discovery was especially jarring to European Christians. It signaled the development of a fresh reason to reject the Jews: they appeared to have defaulted on their responsibility to be 'living history' for Christians and were thus accused of heresy. The Talmud was put on trial (in 1240 in Paris, later in Barcelona), and burned: the customary punishment for heresy—but not before Christians made copies of it for their own study. Thus the colonized people had been exhaustively studied, their language 'standardized,' their customs docketed, specimens labeled: the work of colonial administration had been done. Not surprisingly, it was precisely in this period, when Hebrew began to be taught at European universities, that Jews were expelled from England, France, and much of Germany.

Herbert of Bosham could not have foreseen these developments; perhaps they would have appalled him. Yet he also evinces disquiet and uncertainty about the role of his fellow pioneers: when does a 'hebraist' become a 'judaizer'? Perhaps his uniquely sympathetic reading of Jewish hopes for the future is simply the culmination of his hebraizing: he reported it as a piece of information to be added to the archive. Or had he passed over the frontier, 'gone native,' even while shielding his own orthodoxy by strategic differentiation? By conceding that the Jews can and do read their own Scriptures spiritually, he advances a wholly new concept. Clearly he lived on a temporal and cultural frontier, in which the settled pattern of Christian theology with regard to Judaism

---

[16] Gavin Langmuir has suggested that the emphasis on Jesus' humanity, especially his sufferings, exacerbated anti-Judaism in the late eleventh and early twelfth centuries. See "Doubt in Christendom," *Toward a Definition of Anti-Semitism* (Berkeley: University of California Press, 1990), 128–129.

was in flux, as his commentary demonstrates. Like Nicollet, he was in some ways a marginal figure, an exile who died in obscurity. Again like Nicollet, Herbert's motives or goals with regard to his project died with him; we can only speculate on the consequences had his work reached a different (or any) audience.

Michel Foucault argued that knowledge and power coalesce in a machine whose operation is as crushing as it is blind. Resistance is futile. Reading the history of the destruction of America's indigenous people or of Europe's Jews certainly reinforces this notion. So does the fact that work like Herbert's or Nicollet's was subsumed into destructive projects seemingly antithetical to those authors' interests and loves. What is more difficult to trace, and yet continues to compel us, is the fact that in circumstances that seem to demand coalescence and uniformity, some voices speak of different routes, alternative journeys, forgotten maps. In the history of Christianity, the institutional church is an easy target, seen by some as the ready ally of all forms of imperialism. Yet here, too, there is an irony. The church's long history also preserves minority voices that rouse the institutional conscience. From time to time, the engine of conquest falters and a half-forgotten vision of a different future is able to emerge. The evidence from Herbert of Bosham's life, career, and works disrupts—and enriches—our notions of the boundaries between medieval Jews and Christians and the horizons that united them, and opens up new prospects. As Yosef Yerushalmi has observed:

> You [Christians] do not have to repudiate everything in the past concerning the Jews. Much of the record is dark. There were also patches of light. There was "reprobation" and there was "preservation" [of the Jews], and each has to be understood in its historical context. It is up to you to choose that with which you will identify.[17]

---

[17] Yerushalmi, "Response ...," 107.

APPENDIX

EXAMPLES OF HERBERT'S HEBREW KNOWLEDGE

The following examples drawn from Herbert's psalms commentary are arranged in three groups.[1] The first group exhibits Herbert's changes to the psalms-text made under Rashi's influence or under the influence of some other authority, named or not. In many of these cases, Herbert justifies his changes on the grounds that they are more consonant with the Hebrew original than Jerome's translation. Occasionally he demonstrates that his more consonant reading can be reconciled with Jerome's. These examples illustrate Herbert's striking independence, however, from either Rashi or Jerome. They also demonstrate his willingness to innovate in order to achieve greater linguistic precision: several of these translations feature twelfth-century Latin neologisms.

The second group of passages illustrates Herbert's treatment of the divine name, and exegetical or etymological data associated with the names of God encountered in the psalms. The various divine names were known to Christian commentators (certainly to Jerome, who discussed them in his letters and commentaries), and their meanings or etymologies were popularized by Isidore of Seville's *Etymologiarum*, Book VII.1.[2] Herbert relates the divine names to rabbinical traditions that linked the names to certain attributes. He then shows how the divine names used in various psalms are consonant with the subject matter of the psalms. Linking his exegesis to the context of Jewish traditions enriches his interpretation and seems to be his warrant for disregarding Christian discussions of divine names and attributes.

The final group of passages focus on Hebrew words used in the titles of the psalms, such as *gittith, ydithun, almuth* or *alamoth*, etc. Jerome

---

[1] *Psalterium cum commento*, St. Paul's MS 2. The commentary is unedited and survives in a single copy, not the autograph, dating from the early 13th century. My transcriptions expand the manuscript's abbreviations but otherwise preserve the original orthography. The MS usually indicates variants by with a interlinear gloss, rendered here as superscript. In the transcribed passages, I have not attempted to regularize punctuation to conform systematically to modern usage.

[2] *Etymologarium sive Originum Libri XX*, ed. W.M. Lindsay (Oxford: Clarendon Press, 1911).

had translated these words in his versions of the psalter. Jerome and subsequent generations of Christian commentators used the Romanum and Gallican versions of the psalms as the bases for allegorical exegesis. Herbert eschews this practice and leaves most of the terms untranslated from the Hebrew (but transliterated into the Latin alphabet). He then endeavors to explain their historical and/or literal meanings, often relying on Hebrew authorities such as Rashi's psalms commentary or *Midrash on Psalms*. The deeper meaning of the *tituli* are thus supplied by a fuller understanding of their historical context, not as mysteries decipherable only through allegory.

In the examples that follow, the lemmata from the Hebraica psalter are given in italics; the parallel lemmata from Herbert's commentary are presented in Roman type, with significant variations in italic. Herbert's commentary follows each lemma. I have approximated his practice of underlining the lemmata under discussion, where and when he does this, by italicizing them. Citations to other scriptural passages are also indicated by italics. Numeration of the psalms and verses follows the *Biblia Sacra Vulgata*, Stuttgart edition.

A. *Herbert's Corrections to the Psalter Text*

1. *Excerpt from Psalm 5:9, fol. 7^{va–b}*

Hebraica: *Domine deduc me in iustitia tua propter insidiatores meos dirige ante faciem meam viam tuam*

Herbert: Domine deduc me in iustitia tua propter *cantatores* meos; dirige ante faciem meam viam tuam

> Vel *domine deduc me in iusticia tua propter inspectores* vel *afflictores.* Verbum enim hebraice sorerai; commune potest esse ad tria hec. Et est idem sensus. Cantores enim vocat hic illos qui quasi in derisum meum cantent. Iuxta quod in psalmo alibi. *Contra me loquebantur qui sedebat in porta. et cantabant bibentes liceram* (Ps. 68:13). Et in propheta: *Factus sum in derisum omni populo meo; canticum eorum tota die.* (Lam. 3:14) Et isti derisores sunt et inspectores, idem enim afflictores. Et dicit hic inspectores israelis; eo quod cotidie expectabant an ipsorum dominus desereret eos et traderet eos in manus eorum.

Herbert's translation of *cantatores* is highly unusual; the Hebrew is שוררי, which he transliterates as *sorerai*. Rashi suggests that this word is derived from a root meaning 'to watch.' Thus the psalmist speaks of his 'watchful foes.' Jerome's translation of *insidiatores* (those who lie in ambush) evokes the same sense, as do Herbert's alternatives of 'observers' (*inspectores*) and 'afflictors.'[3]

Herbert's first choice, however, is 'singers' (*cantatores*). He draws analogies from other biblical passages wherein a good person's enemies sing in derision. The choice seems inexplicable without reference to the Hebrew, in which the root of 'to sing' is שיר (and whose pilel form is שורר). Since Herbert asserts that *soreray* has three meanings, perhaps he had access to a lexicon which gave him this alternative, above and beyond the meanings he could glean from Rashi or from *Midrash on Psalms*.

2. *Excerpt from Psalm 6:8, fol. 8*[rv]

Hebraica: caligavit prae amaritudine oculus meus consumptus sum ab universis hostibus meis

Herbert: *Lanternavit pre ira* oculus meus; *inveteratus est* ab universis hostibus meis.

> Vel *caligavit* et cetera. Quod vero minus usitate ponimus hic lanternavit; ad hebrei verbi hic positi proprietatem exprimendam factum est. Hic enim iuxta hebreum tale ponitur verbum, vero notavit quod hic is cuius oculi caligat visus sic est quasi videat per lucernam igne incluso. Quemadmodum etsi per vitrum intuatur quis. Nec enim in ebreo verbum ponitur hic quo simpliciter solet oculorum caligo designari. Et dicit iste penitens quod prae ira et amaritudine lanternaverit oculus eius. Ira enim et dolor sicut interiorem ita et exteriorem turbant oculum. Vel est hic alia littera scilicet *demolitus [est] oculus meus* que habetur ex libro qui apud hebreos est. Et ab eis mahebereth dicitur quod sonat additio dicit itaque penitens hic oculum suum prae ira et amaritudine demolitum. Demoliri est extra molem facere quod est deicere. Et huius quidem oculi pre amaratudine et ira; quasi extra molem id est extra statum suum sunt facti; prae amaritudine et ira a deo turbati. Unde bene subditur *Inveteratus est* scilicet oculus *ab universis hostibus meis* id est prae ira et angustia que mihi ex persecucione hostium fuit. Ira quippe et angustia sicut iam diximus. Et ut psalmista significat hic oculorum inveteracionem id est defective tanquam ex annorum vetustate inducunt.

In this passage, Herbert corrects Jerome's *caligavit* with a neologism, *lanternavit*, which is derived directly from Rashi's explanation of this

---

[3] Jerome also knew *sorerai* in its transliterated form. In Ep. 106:25, he wrote: " ... apud Hebraeos, *sorerai*, id est, 'hostes mei'." *Saint Jérôme: Lettres*, Jérôme LaBourt, trans. and ed. (Paris: Société d'Édition "Les Belles Lettres," 1955), 5: 115:5–8.

lemma, wherein Rashi had explained that the Hebrew here (עששה [*asesah*]) was a cognate of the noun (עששית [*asasit*]) which means 'lanterne' in Old French. Following Rashi, Herbert explains that the psalmist's eye has been dimmed by weakness or illness, brought on by anger and bitterness and a wave of remorse. Both commentators compare the effect to a glass-enclosed lantern whose panes have been smudged by smoke. The further suggestion made at the end of this extract, that the dimmed perception of the psalmist's eye is comparable to the effects of old age, is also derived from Rashi, *ad loc*.[4]

The notion that the psalmist's eye has been destroyed or damaged (*demolitus est*), which Herbert attributes explicitly to the *Mahbereth* of Menahem ben Saruq, is not cited in Gruber's edition of Rashi's commentary, however.[5] Perhaps this was an interpolation into the text of Rashi used by Herbert, or perhaps this indicates an independent use of the lexicon by Herbert and his interlocutor. The Hebrew here is עתקה (*ot-khah*), a possible meaning for which is to grow old, as Rashi notes.[6]

3. *Excerpt from Psalm 15 [16]:4, fol. 17*[va-b]

Hebraica: *multiplicabuntur idola eorum post tergum sequentium non litabo libamina eorum de sanguine neque adsumam nomina eorum in labiis meis*

Herbert: Multiplicabuntur *dolores* eorum; *ad alienos accelerancium*; non *libabo* libamina eorum de sanguine necque assumam nomina eorum in labiis meis.

> David invitavit israelem ad unius dei cultum dicens dic domino dominus vel deus meus tu. Et ex hoc domino dixit postea david in persona israelis; bona sibi pro venisse sine meritis. Ibi bonum meum non super te. Nunc econtrario docet dolores et mala provenire; illis qui ad deos accelerant alienos id est gentilibus. Et hoc est. *Multiplicabuntur dolores eorum; ad alienos* scilicet deos. *Accelerancium* ac si dicat israel, michi qui unum deum colo gaudium. Sed illis qui plures et ad alienos currant deos;

---

[4] This reading seems to have been adopted in the later glossary (Lambert and Brandin, *Glossaire Hébreu-Français*, 167), where עששה is glossed as *alontérna*.

[5] Gruber notes that many other editions of Rashi do cite *Mahbereth* here, 67. Loewe commented on Herbert's *additio* as a possible translation of *Mahbereth*: "The explanation of *mahbereth* as *additio* is not unsound; the root חבר means fundamentally to *join*, and one of its specialised meanings is to *compose*, in the literary sense." Loewe, "Herbert of Bosham's Commentary ...," 62.

[6] Gruber, 66. Field, in his Latin commentary on the *Hexapla*, similarly renders this as *insenuit*. Frederick Field, *Origenis Hexaplorum* (Hildesheim: Georg Olms, repr. 1964), 2: 93.

dolores. Et dicit David in persona israel *non libabo libamina* eorum scilicet accelerancium ad deos alienos. *De sanquine* id est non faciam libamina de sanquine ad libandum sicut gentiles qui ad alienos accelerant. Solent enim libamina facere de sanguine et sic sacrificare ydolis. Quod hic israel respuit possunt eciam per dolores significare ydola. Ut ibi: *Qui fingis dolorem in precepto* (Ps. 93:20 [Gall.]). Et ibi *qui manducatis panem doloris* (Ps. 126:2 [Gall.]). Idola enim in scriptura variis significanter nominibus, ut nomine doloris nomine mendacii, nomine nichili aliquando nomine vanitatis. Possunt igitur dolorum nomine ydola gencium significari hic. Ac si dicat: multiplicabuntur ydola gencium ad deos alienos currencium. Iuxta quod et in edicione alia, *Multiplicate sunt infirmitates eorum* scilicet ydola. Quibus multiplicatis accelerare non cessabant ad alienos deos currentes ab hiis ad illa. Qualiter et nunc catholici peregere nunc hos sanctorum nunc illos requirunt. Sequitur *necque assumam nomina eorum* scilicet invocationem nominum ydolorum *in labiis* vel super labia mea.

In this verse, Herbert corrects Jerome's *Hebraica* version, which translates *idola* for the Hebrew עצבותם (their sorrows). Rashi also reads 'sorrows' here, which are justly the lot of idolaters.

Herbert reconciles his Jewish and Christian authorities by noting the possibility that 'sorrows' might apply to idolatry. Citing two passages from the Gallican psalter, he acknowledges that idolatry is sometimes identified in Scripture by euphemisms: vanity and lying, for instance. Finally, he addresses the Gallican variant *infirmitates*: idolatry is a weakness or sickness. Even in his own day, he notes, Catholics make pilgrimages to saints' shrines in hopes of cures.

4. *Excerpt from Psalm 15 [16]:5, fol. 17vb*

Hebraica: *Dominus pars hereditatis meae et calicis mei tu possessor sortis meae*

Herbert: Dominus pars *partis* mee et calicis mei; tu *suffultor* sortis mee.

> *Dominus solum pars partis mee et calicis mei* id est dominus pars est quam elegi alii deos alienos. Sed ego te unde alibi pars mea domine. Et non sicut hec pars iacob. Et psalmista hic *Dominus pars partis mee et calicis mei; tu suffultor sortis mee.* Quod est tu es ille qui quasi manum meam suffulciens; posuisti eam super partem bonam. Quale illud de Joseph quod suffulserit manum patris sui ut poneret super capud manasse (Gen 48:17).[7] Ita hic suffulciente domino: partem bonam elegit, sicut scriptum est *Testes hodie*

---

[7] Rashi alludes to this instance by quoting the Hebrew for "lifted up his hand," without citing the incident. But "suffulo/ere" is not the Latin here. Herbert seems to have made this translation himself.

invoco celum et terram; quod proposuerim vobis vitam et bonum. benedictionem et maledictionem. elige ergo vitam (Deut 30:19).[8]

Herbert provides the translation *suffultor* for תומיך. His choice is based on an explanation by Rashi, who suggests *ad loc.* that the word means to uplift or or support. Rashi cites Genesis 48:17, "and he lifted up his father's hand." In the Hebrew, the verbs used in the psalm and Genesis are the same: ויתמך. The Vulgate text at Genesis 48:17 reads "videns autem Ioseph quod posuisset pater suus dextram manum super caput Ephraim …".

Herbert apparently recognizes that the Hebrew used in the psalm and in the Genesis passage are the same, which leads him to select an obscure noun (*suffultor*)[9] to coordinate best with Rashi's reading. In this passage, he makes no effort to reconcile alternative readings from the Hebraica or Gallican texts: he corrects Jerome, based on the parallel Hebrew usages he has learned from Rashi's commentary.[10]

5. *Excerpt from Psalm 35[36]:3, fol. 36ra*

Hebraica: *quia dolose egit adversum eum in oculis suis ut inveniret iniquitatem eius ad odiendum*

Herbert: Quoniam *delinivit* ^{vel palpavit} adversum eius in oculis suis; ut inveniret iniquitatem eius ad odiendum.

Secundum priorem lectionem persequamur. Quasi vere scelus quasi dicendo persuasit impio non timor dei esset ante oculos eius quia deliniendo decepit eum. Ut puta sicut premisimus hic prospera et mala nulla in futuro seu deum presentia non curare. aut tale quid iuxta varios et multiplices temptacionum modos. *Ut inveniret iniquitatem eius ad odiendum.* Quasi vere scelus vel impietas delinivit vel palpavit impium; id est deliniendo decepit. *Ut inveniret iniquitatem* et cetera. Hoc enim invenit et ideo deceptus vel sic: vere scelus dilinivit [*sic*] impium. Et vere deo sic iuste permittente delinicio et decepcio fuit; ut ita *inveniret* scilicet deus. Siqui-

---

[8] The Vulgate reads "vitam et mortem bonum et malum."

[9] Lewis and Short list *suffulcio*, to support, but not the substantive *suffultor*. Souter's *Dictionary of Later Latin*, notes that Rufinus used this term in his *Orig. in Psalmos* 36. hom. 3.8, a work that is missing from Souter's own expanded list of titles. *Suffulcio* as a figurative term for support, dating from 1160, is recorded in R.E. Latham's *Revised Medieval Latin Word List from British Sources* (London: for the British Academy by the Oxford University Press, 1965), 463.

[10] He also follows Rashi in citing Deut. 30.19 to support his reading of *pars* in place of *hereditatem*, and the notion that the hand of one who is supported by God will rest upon (choose) the good.

dem de deo premiserat non timor dei ante oculos eius inveniret tanquam deus in morte impii. *iniquitatem eius* non ad miserandum sed *ad odiendum.* Vel secundum aliam litteram *Quam dolose egit* scilicet scelus et hoc est quod tam diximus *delinivit.* Dolose inquam egit adversus eius scilicet impium. *In oculos suis* ispo scilicet impio ad sceleris suggestionem scienter peccante. Prior vera littera hebreo plus consonat.

Unlike the examples given in the discussion of Psalm 15 above, Rashi does not seem to be Herbert's source for this 'more consonant' reading of *delinivit* or *palpavit*. The Hebrew here is מִי—הֶחֱלִיק. Rashi's comment on this verse distinguished the subject of the preceding verse as Transgression personified, which here 'entices' the wicked person.[11]

Delenio or *delinio* was a twelfth-century word of British coinage, a synonym for *palpare* meaning 'to flatter.'[12] Some modern translators of this difficult Hebrew passage have agreed with this reading: the RSV renders the phrase as "he flatters himself in his own eyes," for instance.[13] In both the Gallican and Hebraica versions, Jerome translated this as *dolose egit*, 'to act deceitfully.'[14] Again, Herbert reconciles his innovation with Jerome, although it seems that he has made a more precise reading, based on his own (or his interlocutor's) grasp of the Hebrew.

6. *Excerpt from Psalm 67:24, fol. 74ᵛᵃ*

Hebraica: *ut calcet pes tuus in sanguine lingua canum tuorum ex inimicis a* temet ipso

Herbert: ut calcet pes tuus in sanguine; lingua canum tuorum ex inimicis a *semet ipso*

> … Unde subdit. *A semet ipso* ab ipso scilicet deo non ab alio. Et dicit hic *a semet ipso* quemadmodum in exceptis actionibus solet dici 'ipse pluit,' 'ipse tonat,' 'ipse choruscat.' Nec est que querat quis ipse de solo quippe

[11] Gruber, 175–176.

[12] R.E. Latham, *Revised Medieval Word-List from British Sources*, 137.

[13] See also *Midrash on Psalms*, trans. William G. Braude, 2 vols., (New Haven: Yale University Press, 1959) [hereafter, *Midrash Pss.*] 1: 416, "For it flattereth him in his eyes …" and Field, *Origenis Hexapla* II, "*Nam blanditur sibi in oculis suis*," ad loc. By contrast, the *Tanakh* (New JPS translation, which notes that the Hebrew meaning is uncertain) reads "because its speech is seductive to him …"

[14] I have found no variants for this form, although the Latin translation of Theodore of Mopsuestia's psalms commentary reads this verse as a reference to Saul's flattering words to David, *blanditiis.* Robert Devreesse, *Le Commentaire de Théodore de Mopsueste sur les Psaumes*, Studi e Testi 93 (Vatican City: Biblioteca Apostolica Vaticana, 1939), 195.

deo intelligitur qui solus in talibus per hoc pronomen significatur sic. In quibus ponit hebreus unum de dei nominibus proprius scilicet 'hv' quod sonat 'ipse' apud nos tanquam si iuxta hebreum dicatur 'hv tonat,' 'hv choruscat' ubi nos 'ipse tonat,' 'ipse choruscat.' Hoc tamen notandum quod cum hic unum sit secundum hebreos de proprii nominibus dei; non nisi deo competit. Cum tamen pronominales dictiones scilicet ille et ipse, apud nos communes sint, sicut deo et aliis. Hic vero in psalmo ubi habemus *a semet ipso*, hebreus habet 'hv.' Tanquam si dicatur apud nos *a semet 'hv'* ex quo iuxta hebrei sermonis proprietatem determinatur; quod dicitur hic *a semet ipso*; ad solum deum referendum. Et quid ipsius solius opus sit; israelis tam victoriosa in sanguine occisorum conversio et ex inimicis reductio.

In this excerpt from a very long comment on Psalm 67:24, Herbert corrects Jerome's translation of a personal pronoun (the Hebraica reads *a temetipso*). He argues that the pronoun refers to God, mentioned in the preceding verse by a name which can only apply to the divinity (*Adonai*), as opposed to the 'you' addressed in this verse by God. He bases his correction on the particle rendered here as '*hv*.' The Hebrew pronoun 'hu' is a third-person singular masculine pronoun: 'he, himself.' Herbert equates it with *ipse*. The manuscript's scribe distinguished between *u* and *v*, however, so it seems possible that Herbert intended the unpointed Hebrew orthography (heh-vav) to be transcribed here, rather spelling out the word phonetically as it were. The word which in Hebrew precedes the pronoun can be read as the preposition מן (*min*) meaning 'from, away from,' etc. Not without reason, then, did Herbert read this as *a semetipso*.[15]

Rashi had divided the last words of verse 24 differently. He read 'hu' as the last syllable of מנהו (*minehu*), which he explicated as 'portion:' "As for the tongue of your dogs, from [the blood of the] enemies its portion." Rashi derived this interpretation with some difficulty from [*man*] in BT *Sukkot* 39b.[16] Contrary to his usual practice, Herbert did not follow Rashi here.[17]

---

[15] It is more difficult to understand Jerome's *a temetipso*; the Hebrew orthography would be quite different.

[16] Gruber, 305.

[17] An interesting comparison is David Kimhi *ad loc*. His exegesis echoes that of Rashi but he interprets *minehu* as two words (as the preposition and pronoun "to him"). Kimhi argues the phrase refers not to God but to the king of Assyria.

7. Excerpt from Psalm 73[74]:3, fol. 85ra–b

Hebraica: *sublimitas pedum tuorum dissipata est usque ad finem omnia mala egit inimicus in sanctuario*

Herbert: Subleva *pavorem tuum ad dissipandum* in finem omnia mala egit inimicus in sanctuario

> Hoc est pavorem tuum qui modo quasi depressus est; dum non timeres. *subleva* id est sine sum leva; desursum perturbaciones super inimicos meos. qui et cui inimici sunt; in mittendo *ad dissipandum* eos in finem id est funditus vel semper. Et supponit mox causam; quia *omnia mala* et cetera. Plerique habent *Sublimitas pedum tuorum dissipata est usque ad finem*. Et vocat pedes domini legis doctores et magistratus vite exemplo et doctrine verbo dictionem in terra quasi circumferentes. Quorum pedum sublimitas erat templum quod pre ceteris in terra venerabantur. Sed prior littera; hebreo plus consonat.

This excerpt illustrates a highly unusual reading on Herbert's part: most sources in either Hebrew or Latin give some form of the term 'feet' or 'steps,' for the Hebrew פְעָמֶיךָ. Herbert insists instead on *pavor*, meaning 'trembling' or 'dread'. Rashi reads the lemma as saying "Lift up your feet for a tumult." But he notes somewhat cryptically that Menahem had treated the noun (pa'am) 'foot,' as a cognate for the verb (p'm), meaning 'to agitate.'[18] Klein's *Etymological Dictionary* supports this alternative, noting that a form of פעם appears as a *hapax legomenon* at Daniel 2:1, meaning 'was agitated, disturbed, troubled.'[19]

Herbert's departure from 'feet' or 'steps' suggests that perhaps he or an interlocutor understood Rashi's very compressed report of Menahem's etymology. Conceivably they may also have had direct access to the *Mahbereth*.[20] Another possible source for Herbert's translation might have been the *poterim*, the Jewish annotators of Scripture who glossed Hebrew terms with Old French (using Hebrew characters to spell the Old French words phonetically). One Hebrew-Old French glossary includes a gloss for this lemma. For פעמיך, the glossary reads *tés trezalemonz*.[21]

---

[18] Gruber, 340 *ad loc.*

[19] Rashi cited Genesis 41:8, "his spirit was agitated" in support of Menahem.

[20] Loewe suggests that Herbert consulted the *Mahbereth* independently of Rashi on occasion. See Loewe, "Herbert of Bosham's Commentary ...," *Biblica* 34 (1953): 62.

[21] Louis Brandin and Mayer Lambert, *Glossaire Hébreu-Français du XIIIe siècle* (Geneva: Slatkine Reprints, 1977), 181. *Trezalemonz* may be derived from *tresaler* whose cognates in Modern French, *tressailement* and *tresaillir*, mean to shudder or tremble.

B. *Herbert's Comments on the Psalter's Use of the Divine Name*

Throughout his commentary, Herbert calls attention to the various divine names used by the psalmists, pointing out particularly apposite uses. Christians had collected information about the names of God from Hebrew sources beginning at least with Jerome (and more likely sooner, with Origen). Jerome's letter to Marcella which discussed the names of God was expanded and anthologized in various forms, most notably by Isidore of Seville in his *Etymologiarum*. Other versions of this letter or lists of divine names circulated in the Carolingian period and in later centuries.[22] Of special interest to Christians was the allegorical significance attached to the various names.

The extant lists of divine names compiled by Latin commentators typically included the data that *Elohim* is the divine name translated as *Deus*. Similarly, *Adonai* was translated by Christians as *Dominus*. Jerome and his imitators distinguished *Adonai* from the tetragrammaton, without seeming to recognize that *Adonai* was used in Hebrew chiefly as a euphemism for the ineffable divine name, the tetragrammaton (יהוה).[23] Jerome's version of the list of names makes this apparent:

> Septimum ADONAI, quem nos Dominum generaliter appellamus. Octavum IA, quod in Deo tantum ponitur: et in ALLELUIA extrema quoque syllaba sonat. Nonum, quod id est, ineffabile putaverunt, quod his litteris scribitur, JOD, HE, VAV, HE. Quod quidam non intelligentes propter elementorum similitudinem, cum in Graecis libris repererint, legere consueverunt.[24]

Confusion about the accurate spelling of the tetragrammaton also reigned amongst medieval Christian commentators. Isidore's version perpetrated some of this confusion; he asserted that the tetragrammaton consisted in יהיה, or "ia ia," as he wrote. Nicolas Maniacoria, the mid-twelfth century corrector of Scripture who consulted contemporary Jews, spelled the name יההו.[25] Herbert himself, on at least one

---

[22] These are usefully digested and compared by Matthias Thiel, "Grundlagen und Gestalt der Hebräischkenntnisse des frühen Mittelalters," *Studi Medievali* 4 (1973): 70 ff.

[23] *Adonai* does appear in the psalter (and elsewhere in the Hebrew Bible) as a divine name, however. Christians were not entirely wrong to list it separately from the tetragrammaton.

[24] Ep. 25, *Saint Jérôme: Lettres*, Jérôme LaBourt, trans. and ed. (Paris: Société d'Édition "Les Belles Lettres," 1949) Tome 2; the text is also available in PL 22:429.

[25] V. Peri, "*Correctores immo corruptores*. Un saggio di critica testuale nella Roma del XII secolo," *Italia Medioevale e Umanistica* 20 (1977): 19–125; 116. Peri's article includes

occasion, says that it is spelled "yod heth vav he," mistaking the second consonant.

By the twelfth century, Christians interested in the etymology and significance of Hebrew names for God had recourse to other, more reliable sources. The *Dialogi* of Petrus Alfonsi was one; he includes (under a discussion of the Trinity) an extended explanation of the reasons why both *Elohim* and *Adonai* are plural names: among other things, this usage confirms the Christian concept of the Trinity.[26] None of the data transmitted by Christians, however, seems to contain the information that Herbert repeats throughout his commentary: that the two most common divine names bespeak distinct attributes of God. God (*Elohim* or *Deus*), is a term that refers to the divine attribute of judgment, while the Lord's name (*Adonai* or יהוה; *Dominus*) connotes mercy. This was well-known to the rabbis; the concept is referred to in *Exodus Rabbah*.[27] Christians discussed these two attributes but the evidence suggests that they did not link them explicitly to the different divine names.[28]

Herbert alludes to this tradition when discussing a psalm-text that refers to either of these divine attributes. When a psalm refers to divine judgment, Herbert notes the aptness of the divine name used elsewhere in the psalm, if indeed the name is *Elohim*. These comments seems to derive from his own reading of the Hebrew; he does not appear to have relied on Rashi for this data.[29]

---

his edition of Nicolas's *Libellus de corruptione e correptione psalmorum et aliarum quarundum scripturaram.*

[26] *Dialogi contra Iudaeos*, PL 157: 606C–613A.

[27] *Midrash Rabbah: Exodus* 3.6, trans. S.M. Lehrman (London: Soncino), 64–65. See also E.E. Urbach, "The Power of the Divine Name," *The Sages: Their Concepts and Beliefs*, trans. Israel Abrahams (Jerusalem: Magnes Press, 1975), 124–134.

[28] For instance, Bernard of Clairvaux discusses divine mercy in contrast to divine judgment in his fourteenth sermon on the Song of Songs, but he does not relate either attribute to specific divine names (nor, in this case, to specific members of the Trinity).

[29] Perhaps, of course, he relies simply on the knowledge that wherever *Deus* appears in the Latin text, he can safely assume that *Elohim* was the corresponding term in Hebrew. I have not found an instance yet where he has corrected the Hebraica text's use of one or another of the Latin equivalents.

1. *Excerpt from Psalm 9:8, fol. 12ra*

Hebraica: *Dominus autem in sempiternum sedebit stabilivit ad iudicandum solium suum*

Herbert: Dominus autem in sempiternum sedebit; stabilivit *ad iudicum* solium suum

> ...Et attendendum quod hic ubi nos habemus dominus in hebreo nomen dei integrum scriptum est. Quod est tetragrammaton id est quatuor litterarum scilicet Ioth heth vau he. Et dico nomen hoc integrum respectu cuiusdam alterius nominis dei quod non est vero velud medietas huius nominis quod est quatuor litterarum. Constat enim illud nomine dimidium; tantum ex duabus litteris istius nominis pleni et integri scilicet Ioth he. Et dicitur ya. Integrum vero domini quod est tetragrammaton cuius illud scilicet ya non nisi medietas est; dicunt hebrei nomen domini ineffabile quod in lamina aurea scriptum est. Et tunc pronunciant illud sic scilicet adonay. ...Restitutum igitur israele et iuxta promissum dominum sicut hic in psalmo dicitur amalech penitus deleto; iustum fuit ut hiis completis consequenter nomen domini velut victoris et iudicis plenum poneretur, quod est tetragramathon pro quo hebreus dicit adonay. Unde et hic ponitur non semiplenum ut dimidium eius quod est ya.
>
> Istud enim dimidium nominis integra scilicet ya alibi positum est; ibi videlicet ubi vire iurando communatur dominus amalechitis quod delens *deleret memoriam eorum de sub celo*. Ubi subditur et dixit *Quia manu sua per sedem ya.*[30] Ubi nos habemus sic dicens *quia manus solius dei* et cetera. Et ita dimidium nominis domini scilicet ya ponitur in comminacione sed integrum ponitur comminacione amalechicis; sedis dominum nomen dimidium ponitur quod est hebraice kez, per duas tam litteras scilicet caph et samech. Verum hic in psalmo postquam certissime prophetata est. Quod est ac si sit iam completa amalechitarum plena delecio nomen sedis domini plenum et integrum ponitur quod est hebraice kizte, per tres litteras scilicet caph et samech, aleph.

Herbert discusses the tetragrammaton for the first time in Psalm 9; as noted above, he (or his scribe) misspells it. Herbert learned from either Rashi's commentary or from *Midrash on Psalms* the theory that

---

[30] Supposedly this is Ex. 17:14–16; the Vulgate text reads: "delebo enim memoriam Amalech sub caelo ... quia manus solii Domini et bellum Dei erit contra Amalech a generatione ..." Cf. TANAKH: "And Moses built an altar and named it Adonai-nissi. He said 'It means, "Hand upon the throne of the Lord!"' The Lord will be at war with Amalek through the ages." The editors of the TANAKH note that the meaning of the Hebrew "kes" is obscure.

'Ya' was a defective version of the Divine Name.[31] By contrast, Jerome and Isidore treated Ia as a separate name, distinct from the tetragrammaton. Jerome wrote while enumerating the names to Marcella: "Octavum IA, quod in Deo tantum ponitur: et in ALLELUIA extrema quoque syllaba sonat. Nonum, quod id est, ineffabile putaverunt, quod his litteris scribitur, JOD, HE, VAV, HE."[32]

In their commentaries on Psalm 9, both Rashi and the authors of *Midrash on Psalms* referred to Exodus 17:16, where both the divine name and the word for 'throne' are truncated, a point which Herbert must explain with reference to the Hebrew, as it is not evident from the Vulgate text: "Ubi nos habemus sic dicens *quia manus solius dei*." The fuller explanation for the truncation is found in the midrash, which seems to have been Herbert's source. In Braude's translation, the relevant passage reads

> The name of God will not be complete and the throne of the Lord will not be whole until the remembrance of Amalek will have perished: Scripture says, "The hand of Amalek is against the thron' of the Lor'" (Ex. 17:16), where one would naturally expect it to say "against the throne of the Lord." But not until the remembrance of Amalek perishes will the throne of the Lord be whole and the name of God complete. Thus it is said "The destructions of the enemy shall come to a perpetual end," (Ps. 9:7), and directly after, follow the words "The Lord is enthroned for ever; He hath prepared His throne for judgment" (Ps. 9:8). Here, behold, the name is complete and the throne is whole.[33]

Herbert concurs in the judgment that the wording of Psalm 9 confirmed the truth of the prophecy embedded in the defective spellings of Exodus 17: "Verum hic in psalmo postquam certissime prophetata est. quod est ac si sit iam completa amalechitarum plena delecio; nomen sedis domini plenum et integrum ponitur."[34]

---

[31] *Midrash Pss.* 1.142 and 2.426n36.

[32] Ep. 25.

[33] *Midrash Pss.* 1:141–142. Rashi's exegesis of Psalm 9 associated the Amalekites with their later contemporaries, the descendants of Esau, meaning "Edom" or Rome. Thus his interpretation carries both polemical and eschatological overtones. See Chapter 5 for further discussion of this topic.

[34] This is not the only time that Herbert talks about "Yah"; see Psalm 67[68]:5, and Loewe's comments on it.

2. *Excerpt from Psalm 44[45]:7, fol. 47*[va–b]

Hebraica: *thronus tuus Deus in saeculum et in aeternum sceptrum aequitatis sceptrum regni tui*

 Herbert: Sedes tua [vel tronus tuus] deus in seculum et in eternam

> Et hunc sicut prius regem; ita et nunc dominum vocant. Pro quo in hebreo scriptum est heloyim. Quod nomen sicut deo deorum ita et dominus aliis commune est. Nomen heloyim apud hebreos sicut nomen dei apud nos. Unde ubi nos habemus *dominus non detrahes* (Ex. 22:28) hebreus habet "heloyim non detrahes." Tale est igitur [hic] secundum litteratorem nomen dei; quale item illud in exodo cum ad moysen dicit dominus, *Ecce constitui te dominum pharaoni* (Ex. 7.1). Et est nomen el apud hebreos singulare eloyim plurale quod sonat iudices vel fortes aut magistri.

3. *Excerpt from Psalm 44[45].8*

Hebraica: *propterea unxit te Deus Deus tuus oleo exultationis* prae participibus tuis

 Herbert: propterea unxit te deus deus tuus oleo exultacionis

> … Sicut hic apud nos bis dei nomen ponitur, ita et apud hebreos supradictum nomen heloyim bis. primum nomen heloyim in [vi] casus vocativi. Quod ex greci sermonis ydiomate manifestum ubi manifeste casus vocativus exprimivi ab aliis casibus per litterature diversitatem distinctus. Litterator vero non vocative sed nominative legitur sic, eloyim eloyim tuus scilicet deus tuus unxit te. Sed more scripture repetit quasi ad confirmacionem vel ex affectu. Et ponitur hic heloyim, ad ipsum creatorem designandum scilicet pro adonay heloyim ergo id est adonay; *unxit te oleo exultacionis*, scilicet gratia spiritu sancti … Litterator itaque nomen eloyim hic quasi equivoce accipit in primo positum commune sit et sicut ad creatorem et ad creaturam pertineat. Secundo vero positum; ad creatorem uno.

In the first excerpt above, Herbert notes the multiple uses to which the term *elohim* might be put. As a plural noun, it referred not only to God (as a plural of majesty, as in Ex. 22) but also bore a secular application. It could refer simply to human 'judges,' as the second excerpt from Exodus, quoted by Rashi *ad loc.*, was intended to show. In Rashi's case, the suggestion that *elohim* referred to Torah scholars (communal 'judges' whose wisdom was at the service of their communities), usefully deflected the common Christian claim that Psalm 44[45] was Christological (e.g., that the name *elohim* referred to Christ's royal kingship).

Similarly, the meaning of verse 8 of the same psalm had been de-
bated by Jews and Christians since late antiquity. Did it refer to the
Anointed One, Jesus Christ, or some future Messiah, still awaited by
the people of Israel? Herbert appears to dispute a reading by Rashi
that asserted God had anointed a human being, given that *elohim* was a
term equivocal in its meaning and applied occasionally to humans (as
in verse 7). But there is no such discussion in Gruber's edition of Rashi's
commentary. In this instance, instead of agreeing with the *litterator*,
Herbert follows a tradition of exegesis that originated with Augustine
and which was echoed by Peter Lombard in his *Magna Glosatura*. This
tradition appealed to the Greek, not the Hebrew, for its authority. As
Augustine wrote

> And observe in what way he expresses himself. "Therefore, God, Thy
> God, hath anointed Thee:" i.e. "God hath anointed Thee, O God."
> "God" is "anointed" by God. For in the Latin it is thought to be the
> same case of the noun repeated: in the Greek however there is a most
> evident distinction; one being the name of the Person addressed; and
> one His who makes the address, saying, "God hath anointed Thee."
> "O God, Thy God hath anointed Thee," just as if He were saying,
> "Therefore hath Thy God, O God, anointed Thee." Take it in that
> sense, understand it in that sense; that such is the sense is most evident in
> the Greek. Who then is the God that is "anointed" by God? Let the Jews
> tell us; these Scriptures are common to us and them.[35]

This seems to be a case where Christian tradition regarding the messianic psalms outweighed Herbert's scrupulous scholarly sense: an appeal to Augustine (particularly as an authority on Greek) is not up to
Herbert's usual standards.[36]

4. *Excerpt from Psalm 49[50]:1*

Hebraica: fortis Deus Dominus locutus est et vocavit terram ab ortu
solis usque ad occasum eius
    Herbert: Fortis *deorum* dominus locutus est; et vocavit terram ab ortu
solis usque as occasum ejus

---

[35] Augustine, *Enn. In Psalmos*, 45:7. Cf. Lombard *ad loc.*: "Et nota quod ait: Unxit te
Deus, cum tamen divinitas ungi non indiguerit; sed hoc dicit, quia homo ille Deus est,
qui secundum quod homo unctus est, secundum quod Deus ungens. Bis ponitur Deus
pro Patre et Filio, et in Graeco aperte alter vocativus est, alter nominativus est."
[36] See Chapter 5 for a more extensive discussion of this issue.

> *Fortis deorum dominus.* Pro quo in hebreo est el eloyim adonay; *locutus est*
> et cetera. El; sonat fortis vel iudex vel deus. Quod ergo dicitur el eloyim
> hoc idem est quod forti forcium vel iudex iudicium vel deus deorum.

Latin Christianity had associated the divine name *El* with strength
(*fortis*) since the time of Jerome, at least. He had based his etymology
on Aquila's Greek rendering from the Hebrew: "Primum Nomen Dei
est EL, quod Septuaginta *Deum*, Aquila, ejus exprimens, id est, *fortem*
interpretatur."[37] But the association with the name *El* with 'judge'
seems to be unique to Herbert and derived from Hebrew sources
or informants.[38] This passage is the first of several in which Herbert
associates the two divine names, *Elohim* (and less commonly, *El*) and
Adonai with the attributes of divine judgment and mercy.[39]

5. *Excerpt from Psalm 55:9–10, fol. 58va*

Hebraica: in Deo laudabo verbum in Domino praedicabo sermonem
   Herbert: In deo laudabo verbum; in domino *laudabo* sermonem

> In hebreo a hoc versiculo ponitur primo eloyim ubi nos deus, post
> adonay, ubi nos dominus, nec sine causa. In hoc enim signatum est quod
> david omni tempore laudabat deum. Sive indicaret ipsum excercendo
> per adversa quod notat nomen eloyim idem sonans quod iudex sive
> parceret consolando per prospera quod notat nomen adonay quod sonat
> dominus. Domini vero proprium est misereri et parcere.

This is Herbert's most explicit statement linking divine names and
attributes. He does not seem to follow Rashi in this or other such
instances, but might have had recourse to *Midrash on Psalms*, which
makes this association *ad loc.*[40] Perhaps Herbert learned this association
from that midrash and proceeded to apply it systematically throughout
his own commentary (as he did in Psalm 49 above, and as he does
subsequently). Or, as suggested above, Herbert could have learned
about this association from other midrashic literature or from a Jewish
interlocutor, to whom the association would have been well-known.[41]

---

[37] Ep. 25.

[38] See also Herbert at Psalm 9:26: "*Nec Deus in omnibus cogitationibus eius.* Id est non
cogitat iudicem. Unde bene in hebreo est hic elohim quod sonat iudicem."

[39] The Hebrew text for Psalm 49[50]:1 includes the tetragrammaton, which Herbert
renders as *Adonay* but which he does not discuss.

[40] *Midrash Pss.* 1: 497–498.

[41] Other examples include Herbert on Ps. 57:12: "*Et dicet homo vere fructus est iusto;
vere est deus iudicans in terra* … Unde et bene hic cum de domini iudicio agitur; ad

6. *Excerpt from Psalm 109[110]:1, fol. 131rb*

Hebraica: *dixit Dominus Domino meo sede a dextris meis donec ponam inimicos tuos scabillum pedum tuorum*

Herbert: Dixit dominus domino meo sede dextris meis donec ponam inimicos scabellum pedum tuorum.

> Et quoniam de christo prout a christo et ab ecclesiasticis diligenter satis expositus est patet, psalmi seriem secundum hebreorum litteratores prosequemur. Ut videat et audiat ecclesia qualiter videns non videat et audiens non audiat nostri temporis sinagoga excecata et surda. Et loquitur in hoc psalmo secundum hebreorum litteratores david de victoria quam habuit abraham adversus reges quatuor. Ut in genesi legitur. Dicit ergo david. Dixit ergo david [*sic*] *Dixit dominus* id est deus *domino meo* id est abrahe quem david dominum suum vocat racione paternitatis quem eciam et filii heth dominum vocaverunt dicentes. *Audi nos domine.* Sunt tamen inter hebreorum litteratores qui dicunt david in persona propria sed sub nomine eliezer servi habrahe loqui hic. Et nota quod primum domini nomen quod hic scribitur, nomen domini est ineffabile scilicet tetragrammaton quod pronunciant adonay. Secundum vero domini nomen quod subsequitur commune est et creatori et creaturis conveniens. Dixit ergo *dominus* scilicet adonay *domino meo* id est christo secundum quod homo; *sede* et cetera hoc secundum ecclesiasticum.

Herbert adheres to the standard Christian position, affirmed since the Epistle to the Hebrews, in his comments on Psalm 109[110]. The psalm is Christological in import. God, the first person of the Trinity, speaks to Christ, the second person, commanding him to sit at his right hand. Herbert reports two Jewish alternative readings. According to the first, the psalm was written by David to commemorate Abraham's victory over the four kings, and David honors Abraham the patriarch with the term *dominus*. The second possibility recorded by Herbert suggests that the psalm was written from the perspective of Abraham's servant Eliezer, who would have addressed the patriarch as 'his lord.'

That Abraham was addressed by God is undoubted: the name used here is יהוה, as Herbert points out, the ineffable name usually pronounced as *Adonai* and translated *Dominus* in Latin. But Herbert claims that the second name, also translated here as *Dominus*, can be applied to humans. As we have already seen, *elohim* was sometimes applied to God, sometimes to humans. But the Hebrew here is not *elohim*, which in

---

designandum cum iusto et impio domini iudicium iustum; nomen iudicis in hebreo ponitur scilicet eloyim; ubi nos deus."

any case would be translated *Deus*. Rather it is אדן: *Adon*, a term occasionally applied to secular kings or lords. Herbert recognizes that the word is not always associated with the deity, but asserts that in this case it refers to Christ in his humanity.[42] Other Christians commentators on Psalm 109[110] make this association automatically, as it were.[43] Herbert, however, pauses over the Jewish alternative interpretations before making the conceptual leap from *Adon* to *Christus*. The hesitation is just long enough to be jarring.

Herbert relied on both Jewish and Christian sources in order to identify the Hebrew versions of the Divine Names used in the psalter. He was aware of traditional rabbinic associations between those names and certain attributes (e.g., justice and mercy). He points out the aptness of these associations even in places where his most probable Hebrew exemplars (Rashi's commentary and *Midrash on Psalms*) do not. He observed, as virtually no Christian exegetes since the third century had done, that the names used in Psalm 109[110]:1 were distinct and that the second (*Adon*) need not apply to the divinity. How did Herbert detect the associations between divine names and their traditional attributes applied by the rabbis? Perhaps he simply relied on a list which cross-referenced the Latin names *dominus* and *deus* with their Hebrew 'equivalents.' In light of his diligent investigations of other Hebrew terms, this seems unlikely. More probably, he had access to a Hebrew-language psalter (perhaps one with a Latin superscription). He may have been able to pick out the divine names in the text, either independently or helped by an interlocutor. His interlocutor was the most likely source of the information regarding the attributes associated with the Divine Names.

---

[42] The relation of *adon-adonai* at Psalm 110 is not discussed in the works on the psalter attributed to Jerome. In the *Commentarioli* attributed to him, this statement appears in a discussion of Psalm 8, however: "*Domine dominus noster*. Prius nomen Domini apud Hebraeos quattor litterarum est, iod, he, vav, he. ... Secundum vero Adonai omnium commune est, quod saepe et in hominibus ponitur." CCSL 72: 191.

[43] David M. Hay notes that the LXX translation differentiated between the ineffable divine name (יהוה) and *Adon*, which they translated as *kyrios* ("lord"). Early Christian interpreters elided this difference and referred to both figures, both understood as divine, as *kyrios*. *Glory at the Right Hand: Psalm 110 in Early Christianity* (Nashville: Abingdon Press, 1973), 21; 47–51. Also, this is a psalm whose christological associations are inescapable; see Chapter 5 on Herbert's hermeneutics for further discussion.

C. *Hebrew Terms Used in the Tituli Psalmorum*

One of the most striking aspects of Herbert's textual criticism of the *Hebraica* psalter was his refusal to adopt Jerome's translations for the obscure Hebrew words that appear in the psalms' titles.[44] Hebrew and Latin exegetes varied widely in their assessment of these terms and their import. While they are now generally assumed to be references to ancient musical instruments, or to ancient hymn-tunes to which the psalms were sung, or some combination of the two, their very obscurity provided a powerful attraction to both Jewish and Christian interpreters.[45] Augustine, for example, was inclined to read the psalm's title as its 'threshold:' from a well-cast figurative interpretation of the title, one could gain entry to the whole meaning of the psalm. Similarly, the rabbis whose *midrashim* are collected in *Midrash on Psalms* could weave webs of intertextual associations between the titles and cognate terms found elsewhere in Scripture or the Talmud.[46]

Herbert, however, eschewed the practice of deriving allegorical or figurative interpretations from the *tituli*'s obscurities. He argued that substituting a translated name for the term at hand was to substitute interpretation for translation, properly understood. Having dealt with Herbert's attitude toward the *tituli* at length elsewhere, my purpose here is to adduce a few examples of his approach to (and knowledge of) the Hebrew language based on evidence from the titles. Examples could be multiplied; only a few are presented here, in the interests of making the demonstration more concise.

---

[44] See the discussion, with examples, in Chapter 7.

[45] Jerome's translations of the titles, particularly in the Gallican version of the psalter, formed the basis for a literature of interpretation in *précis form* which often "travelled" with the psalms (even into the *Douai-Reims* Bible, used by Roman Catholics until the twentieth century. For the history of this literature, see Pierre Salmon, *Les* Tituli Psalmorum *des manuscrits latins* (Paris: Cerf, 1959).

[46] An excellent example of both Augustine's and the rabbis' procedures can be found in their respective commentaries on Psalm 8, where intertextual "changes" appropriate to either tradition are rung upon the term *gittith* (translated by Jerome as *torcular*, winepress).

1. *Example from Psalm 4 titulus, fol. 5ra–b*

Victori in organis psalmus david.

> Sciendum quod ubi nos in psalmorum titulis habemus victori in hebreo
> est lamanscea. Et hoc hebreum verbum iuxta litterarum proprietatem
> que in ipso ponuntur varie vocalatarum potest esse multiorum. Tres
> enim littere sunt hic posite scilicet nun sade heth. Quod enim la pro-
> ponitur; articulus est. Iste vero tres littere simul puncte secundum vari-
> etatem vocalium si ipsis adiungantur; multa significare possunt. Ed ideo
> immo dicimus verbum illud hebreum lamanscea ad multa se habere.
> Potest enim significare finem, fortitudinem, victoriam, vel praepositu-
> ram, seu eciam cancionem. Unde et interpretes verbum hoc in psalmo-
> rum titulis varie transtulerunt. Alii in finem, iuxta quod in edicione alia
> in psalmorum titulis frequenter ponitur in finem. Alii nomen victoris
> posuerunt. Sicut in edicione hac quam pure de hebraice veritatis fonte
> emanasse novimus et nos prout desuper datum suscepimus explanandam
> in psalmorum titulis repperitur verum sive dicatur in finem sicut in alia
> edicione est sive in victoriam; ad idem pertinet. Siquidem finis in psalmo-
> rum titulis pro perfectione est, similiter sive dicatur victori sicut in hac
> edicionem accipitur. Et victoria semper in perfectione est, similiter sive
> dicatur victori sicut in hac edicione est, sive cantori vel praecentori aut
> praeposita; ad quorum utrumque iam sepe dictionem hebreum verbum
> in commune est ut iam diximus idem sensus. Siquidem victoris nomine
> in psalmorum titulis, cantor seu pocius precento vel prepositus intellig-
> itur. Eo quod quasi victor in organis musicorum et cancionibus presit
> aliis. Iuxta quod *dixit david principibus levitarum; ut constituerent de fratribus suis
> cantores in organis musicorum* (1 Chron. 15:16). Et quamadmodum de uno
> precentorum scriptum est *chonenias autem princeps levitarum prophecie preerat et
> ad precinendum melodiam* (1 Chron. 15:22) …

In the Gallican version of the psalter, Jerome had followed the Septuagint which had translated the Hebrew word למנצח as *eis to telos.*
Jerome's Latin was, consequently, *ad finem,* "unto to the end." His later
translation, the Hebraica, features the translation *victori* or *pro victoria*
instead. The reason for his change is indicated in the *Tractatus in Librum
Psalmorum* attributed to him (but more likely the work of Origen, trans-
lated by Jerome or another 'Origenist.')[47] Commenting on the *titulus* to
Psalm 74[75], the *Tractatus*'s author wrote: "*In finem ne corrumpas, psalmus
Asaph cantici.* In hebraeo non habet 'in finem,' sed habet 'victori.' Et
Septuaginta interpretes non valde erraverunt: siquidem victoria per-

---

    [47] For the state of the question of Jerome's authorship, see Marie-Josèphe Rondeau,
Les Commentaires Patristiques du Psautier, 1: 154–161.

fecta est."[48] Clearly Herbert follows his sense here: the psalmist speaks of an end or victory, both of which are understood to have brought about perfection or completion. Latin commentators since Hilary of Poitiers had played with the association of ideas between the psalter's *ad finem* and the echo they heard in Romans 10:4: 'For Christ is the consummation of the law unto justice for everyone who believes' (*finis enim legis Chrisus ad iustitiam omni credenti*). Hence Augustine, in the *Ennarrationes in Psalmos*, frequently relates the 'end' of the psalms with the 'end' of the Law in support of his generally Christological and allegorical exegesis.[49]

In two other works, indisputably Jerome's, he gives a few more clues to the source for his revised translation. Writing to Principia, one of his many female correspondents who shared his interest in biblical philology, he provides a transliteration of Psalm 44[45]'s Hebrew title followed by his Latin translation:

> Quadragesimum quartum psalmum legens in titulo repperi: *in finem pro his qui commutabuntur, filiorum Core intelligentiam, canticum pro dilecto*. In hebraico scriptum est: "lamanasse al sosanim labne core meschil sir ididoth," quod nos latine vertimus: *victori pro liliis filiorum Core, eruditionis canticum amantissimi*. Symmachum more suo manifestius *triumphum pro floribus* interpretatus est.[50]

In Jerome's prologue to his commentary on the Book of Daniel, he contested Porphyry's ridicule of the inclusion of this presumably noncanonical work amongst the Christian Scriptures. Jerome asserted that such blasphemers would be vanquished. Indeed, victory belongs to him by right:

> Si enim cum apprehensi fuerimus ante judices et tribunalia, monet ne cogitemus quid respondere debeamus (Luc., XII): quanto magis contra adversarios blasphemantes, sua potest bella bellare, et in servis suis vincere? Unde et psalmi plurimi illud Hebraicum, quod in titulis ponitur LAMANASSE, pro quo LXX transtulerunt, in finem, magis pro victoria continent. Aquila enim interpretatus est τῶι νικοιωι, hoc est, ei qui praebet victoriam. Symmachus επινικιον, quod proprie triumphum palmamque significat.[51]

---

[48] CCSL 78, 48.
[49] *Enn. in Psalmos* 4.
[50] Ep. 65. Jérôme LaBourt, trans. and ed. *Saint Jérôme: Lettres* (Paris: Société d'Édition "Les Belles Lettres," 1953) 3:143.
[51] PL 25: 492A–C

Herbert is not dependent on Jerome for his transliteration nor for much of the substance of his comments. The twelfth-century hebraist relies chiefly on a discussion of the Hebrew root נצח which he tells us can mean many things, depending on how it is vocalized. While the possible definitions *finis* or *victoria* might have been known to Herbert from Jerome's comments, it is less likely he had a Latin source that could have contributed *fortitudo*, *praepositus*, or *cantor*.[52] Still, these are all valid possibilities for the root נצח and its possible variants. Rashi does not seem to have been Herbert's source (at least not *ad loc.*). Rashi reads למנצח here as 'to the leader,' as does *Midrash on Psalms*.[53]

Whatever his source (perhaps the *Mahbereth*), Herbert effects a reconciliation of his authorities. The author of the *Tractatus* had argued that 'victory' and 'end' both signify completion through Jesus Christ. Similarly but more prosaically, Herbert argues that a choirmaster or precentor is like a victor: "Siquidem victoris nomine in psalmorum titulis, cantor seu pocius precento vel prepositus intelligitur. Eo quod quasi victor; in organis musicorum et cancionibus presit aliis." Despite his confidence in this assessment, Herbert nevertheless retains Jerome's uses of either *victori* or *pro victoria* in the titles throughout the commentary. Sometimes, however, he discusses the directions the psalmists make in the *tituli* to the *precentor* regarding a psalm's text or its instrumental accompaniment. More commonly, Herbert refrains from translating Hebrew words in the *tituli* since to do so violates one of his fundamental hermeneutic practices, that of addressing the psalms-texts in their literal and historical context whenever possible.[54]

---

[52] Cf. Jerome's Ep. 106, to Sunni and Fretela, in which he addressed their questions regarding discrepancies between the Gallican and Hebraica psalter texts, and his reasons for diverging from the Septuagintal authorities. At paragraph 64, while discussing psalm 102[103,] he noted: "'Non in perpetuo irascetur.' Pro quo in Graeco invenisse vos dicitis: 'Non in finem.' Sed verbum Hebraicum 'nese' et 'perpetuum' et 'finis' et 'victoria' pro locorum intelligitur qualitate." Thus Jerome was aware of the root of "lamanaseah" but does not discuss it elsewhere, to my knowledge. *Saint Jérôme: Lettres*, Jérôme LaBourt, trans. and ed. (Paris: Société d'Édition "Les Belles Lettres," 1955) 5: 135.

[53] *Midrash Pss.* 1:70.

[54] See Chapters 6 and 7.

2. *Example from Psalm 5 titulus, fol. 6vb–7ra*

victori pro neiloth psalmus David

Non nulli de antiquioribus hebreorum magistris÷ [Margin: ÷ *ut menaem*] ubicumque in psalmorum titulis ponitur neiloth sive almuth sive getiz sive ydithun instrumentorum genera interpretai sunt. Nehilot vero cum sit instrumenti nomen idem sonat quod adunacio. Similiter cum aliter sit nomen instrumenti tria significare potest scilicet iuventutem, absconditum, aut eciam seculum. Similiter getiz instrumenti nomen; idem sonat quod torcular. Ydithun secundum quosdam nomen instrumenti sonat lex. Et erant psalmi singuli singulis instrumentorum generibus deputati. Ita videlicet ut cantaretur psalmus talis; instrumento tali vel tali. Iuxta quod supra diximus decem esse instrumentorum similiter et canticorum genera ad psalmos pertinencia. Verum in hoc psalmo titulo ponitur neiloth. Et est hic legendum pro instrumento tali cuius nos usum sicut nec aliorum multorum qui veteris legis statueran non habemus. Et est sensus tituli. Psalmus iste david directus est victori id est cantori seu pocius precentori cantandus pro vel super neiloth id est ad vocem illius instrumenti. Vel aliter secundum quod tituli est talis littera victori pro vel super adunacionibus psalmus david. Ita ut non ponatur ipsum hebreum verbum ut supra sed sicut sepe fit pro interpretato interpretacio. Interpretatur enim ut supra iam diximus nehiloth adunatio quasi muscarum pro quo dicunt hebreorum litteratores se in libris gamalielis legere, *nehil sel devorim.* quod est adunacio muscarum scilicet apium÷ [Margin: ÷*(illegible …)xvii me sicut apes*].[55] Et vocat adunationem scilicet inimicorum israel. Et precipue philisteorum contra quos in hoc psalmo oracio est. Et attendum quod epistola quedam que inter gamaliel libris reperitur super psalterii librum in modum commentarioli edita explanavit vim huius hebrei verbi nehiloth pro torrentibus vel hereditatibus. Unde et omnes libri latini habent in huius psalmi titulo pro hereditatibus …

This excerpt from Herbert's exegesis of the fifth psalm's title offers several useful insights into his working methods. First, there is the marginal note to *menaem*, meaning Menahem ben Saruq, author of the *Mahbereth* or lexicon of Hebrew roots. Rashi mentions Menahem by name *ad loc.* Typically Herbert includes Menahem's name when Rashi alludes to this source. Perhaps the marginalia represents a correction made after the fact. Herbert or his scribe correctly identified Menahem's authority with the statement that several of the Hebrew terms that appear in the *tituli* represent the names of musical instruments. Although Herbert

---

[55] The citation seems to be to Psalm 117[118]:12: "circumdederunt me sicut apes et exarserunt sicut ignis in spinis et in nomine Domini quia; ultus sum in eos."

reports this authoritative statement, he, like Rashi, does not accept it as final. He notes that the same Hebrew words (or at least their roots) have other meanings and might be translated differently. Just as *almuth* might have up to three meanings in addition to naming an instrument ("... iuventutem, absconditum, aut eciam seculum"), so too might *neiloth* have multiple meanings. Besides indicating the kind of instrument that the precentor might have used to accompany the singing of this psalm, Herbert argues that *neiloth* might also be translated as *adunatio* (troop, gathering). Still, he cautions against the translation on the grounds he asserts several times throughout the commentary. Simply to translate the Hebrew into Latin is to render an interpretation in place of translation, an offshoot of the allegorical method of exegesis that he elsewhere disparages ("ita ut non ponatur ipsum hebreum verbum ut supra sed sicut sepe fit pro interpretato interpretacio").

That Herbert even discusses the possible translation of *neiloth* in this case is owing to Rashi's influence. In his psalms commentary *ad loc.*, Rashi cites the Talmud (identified by Herbert as *libri gamelielis*) and its usage: *nahil sel deborim*, referring to a swarm of bees. According to Rashi, *neiloth* thus refers to the gathering of Israel's enemies. Herbert either goes further than did Rashi, or has a fuller version of Rashi's commentary at hand, for he identifies the Philistines as the enemies spoken of in this psalm ("Et precipue philisteorum contra quo in hoc psalmo oracio est").[56]

Finally, Herbert identifies two further meanings of *neiloth*, possibly derived from *Midrash on Psalms*. Rashi had cited one; in Gruber's translation his comment reads:

> An aggadic midrash on the Book [of Psalms] interpreted *nehiloth* as a synonym of *nahalah* 'inheritance,' but this is not the meaning of the word. Moreover, the subject matter of the psalm does not refer to inheritance. It is possible to interpret *nehiloth* as a synonym of *gayyasot* 'military troops' as is suggested by the expression *nahil sel deborim* 'swarm of bees.'[57]

Herbert notes the case for 'inheritance,' which appears in various forms in both the Gallican and the Hebraica texts (*omnes libri latini*, as he says). He follows Rashi in dismissing it as an apt translation here, for the reason Rashi states: the text of the psalm has nothing to do with 'inheritance' or related matters. But Herbert had learned still another mean-

---

[56] In Gruber's edition of Rashi's commentary, Rashi quotes the Mishnah (Bava Qama 10.2) silently. See Gruber, 63–64.

[57] Gruber, 63.

ing from *Midrash on Psalms* (which he identified as "epistola quedam que inter gamaliel libris reperitur super psalterii librum in modum commentarioli edita"),[58] that of *torrens*.[59] Scholars 'more learned' in Hebrew, nevertheless, have taught him to use neither *torrens* nor *hereditas* as a translation for *neiloth*, but rather *adunatio*: "Sed ut ab hebreorum peritiorum scriptis didici; non est intellectus huius verbi hic in titulo positi scilicet neiloth; torrens vel hereditas. Sed pocius adunacio."[60] Still, Herbert acknowledges that confusing *nahaloth* (inheritance or torrent) for *neiloth* would be an easy mistake to make. As he notes in his prologue to Psalm 4, confusion can stem from the lack of vowels in the original Hebrew text. Thus he concedes: "potuit facile errare qui transtulit nahaloth transferens pro neiloth."[61]

Finally, it is worth reiterating that Herbert concludes that the psalmist, when speaking of enemies, is alluding to the Philistines. It is not clear how or why he draws this conclusion, except that Herbert attributes this psalm to David, for whom the Philistines were enemies, of course. Rashi does not mention them; nor do sources in the Christian tradition.[62] At verse 2 of Psalm 5, Herbert returns to the issue of the enemies' identity. Imploring that the Lord hear his prayer, the psalmist enjoins divine aid "precipue contra philisteos et ydumeos." With the introduction of Idumea, treated by the Rabbis as a synonym for Edom,

---

[58] Herbert uses this locution (an "epistle in the form of a commentary") several times to describe *Midrash on Psalms* (properly: *Midrash Tehillim*), but he also refers to the same work sometimes as *Tillim*. It is not clear if he recognizes that the two works are the same. In this passage, Rashi does not name the work; he cites "an aggadic midrash" (ומדרש אגדת) without specifying its source. See Gruber, Hebrew section 2–3.

[59] *Midrash Pss.* 1:81, 83; the Rabbis associated *nehiloth* with *nahal*, meaning "river."

[60] The balance of his comments on the titulus reads as follows: "Iuxta quod ut iam diximus in gamaliele habetur nehil sel devorum. Nec esset ut aiunt consequens ut psalmus hic pro hereditatibus inscriberetur, presertim cum nulla in hoc psalmo de hereditate sive hereditatibus vel eciam fiat mentio. Nahaloth vero; idem sonat quod torrens vel hereditas. Quod minime ponitur in presenti psalmi titulo sed pocius neiloth. Et potuit facile errare qui transtulit nahaloth transferens pro neiloth. Et est psalmus iste david directur victori. Ut iam expositum est; est subaudi super vel pro adunacionibus, id est adunaciones scilicet muscarum id est apum id est contra congregacionem inimicorum israel."

[61] See Titulus, Psalm 4 (above): "Iste vero tres littere simul puncte secundum varietatem vocalium si ipsis adiungantur; multa significare possunt."

[62] The Christian tradition did not focus on the historical situation of the psalm. Rather, as represented by Peter Lombard (who drew on Remi of Auxerre, Alcuin, and Augustine), it allegorized the notion of inheritance. Lombard dwelt on the contrast between Abraham's sons Ishmael and Isaac and the parallel contrast between Abraham's successors in faith versus their successors in the flesh. Thus, the psalm testifies to Christianity's position as the *verus Israel*. See PL 191:93C.

Herbert has entered Rashi's realm of associations. Rashi identifies the enemies, the "murderous and deceitful men" of verse 7, with Esau and his descendants. So, too, does Herbert; likewise, the "just man" whom God blesses in verse 13 represents Jacob and his progeny. For Rashi, Psalm 5 is a prayer for the preservation of Israel in its European exile, surrounded by Christians. As Herbert demonstrates throughout the commentary, he is keenly aware of this web of associations and their contemporary significance.[63]

3. *Example from Psalm 6 titulus*

Victori in organis super seminiz psalmus david

> Pro quo interpretes nostri pro octava transtuli erunt pro interpretato interpretacionem ponentes. Quid vero sit victori; ex supra dictis claret. Organa vero vocat nunc non instrumentum aliquod sed notulas psalmi versiculis subscriptas ad quas velud musice psalmus cantari solet voce instrumenti quod hic seminiz dicitur, aliquando precedente aliquando subsequente. Seminiz eius erat ut tradunt hebreorum imitatores litteratores cythare species dicta hebraice seminiz quod sonat octava, a numero octo cordarum nomen accipiens. Et quia ad notem illius instrumenti psalmus iste a levitis cantabatur ponitur in psalmi titulo. *Pro* vel *super seminiz* scilicet super tali instrumento cantatus hoc est ad illius instrumenti vocem sicut et alibi scriptum est; quod mathatias et filii ei *in cytharis* pro vel *super seminiz canebatur* pro quo nos super *octava canebant* (1 Chron. 15.18]

> Pro octava autem quidam putant pro circumcisionem eo forte quod psalmus iste cum circumciderentur filii israel super ipsos inter circumcidentum cantaretur. Que circumcista quia octava fiebat die; nomine octava hic designatur. In hoc autem psalmo loquitur david in sua seu pocius in persona fidelis synagoge pro peccatis suis graviter afflicte, unde et primo secundum formam penitencialium psalmorum.

Compared to his comments on Psalm 5's title, Herbert's handling of Psalm 6's title is straightforward. He reconciles multiple authorities in this passage, beginning with Rashi, who had asserted that a *sheminith*

---

[63] See Chapter 6. In the passage that follows his comment on Psalm 5:7, Herbert cites Ezekiel 35 on the punishment awaiting Edom: "*Virum sanguinum et dolosum* generaliter vocat precipue tam esau et semen eius qui fratrem suum israel sine cause ex mero odio persequebatur et frequenter in dolo ipsius sanguinem effundere solet. Sicut scriptum ÷ est. *Et factum est verbum domini ad me dicens. filii hominis pone faciem tuam adversus montem seyr* (Ezek. 35.1–2). Et infra. *Urbes tuas demolia et tu desertus eris. et scies quia ego dominus; eo quod fueris inimicus sempiternus. et concluseris filios israel in manus gladii in tempore afflictionis eorum* (Ezek. 35:4–5)." Rashi does not cite any of this material *ad loc.* in Gruber's edition.

was an eight-stringed harp. Rashi also cites 1Chron. 15, as Herbert does, although he does not name Mattathias and his sons specifically amongst the priestly musicians listed there.

In the second paragraph, Herbert addresses the term *octava*, Jerome's translation of *sheminith*. Christian tradition associated the notion of the octave with the Last Judgment: as the "Sabbath of Sabbaths," the eighth 'day' which succeeded the seven ages of the world would be that of Christ's second coming. With this association in mind, Christian exegetes read this psalm as foretelling a time of judgment and woe; Cassiodorus and Peter Lombard labelled it as the first penitential psalm. Herbert nods to that tradition but ignores the psalm's eschatological associations.[64] He concentrates instead on the fact that Jewish boys were circumcised eight days after birth and asserts that this psalm would be sung on that occasion, a notion which seems to be original to him.[65]

Another variant introduced by Herbert is the substitution of *in organis* for *in psalmis* (Hebraica)[66] or *in carminibus* (Gallican), together with his explanation that *organum* can refer not only to the name of an instrument but also to musical notation: "Organa vero vocat nunc non instrumentum aliquod; sed notulas psalmi versiculis subscriptas ad quas velud musice psalmus cantari solet." The Hebrew here, as in the title to Psalm 4, is בנגינות (*be-neginot*).[67] Rashi and the rabbis quoted in *Midrash on Psalms* identify this term with 'stringed instruments.' When asserting that it can refer to notation designating musical accompaniment as well as to the name of a specific instrument, Herbert claims the authority of *nonnulli litteratores*.[68] But no source for this assertion has yet been identi-

---

[64] *Midrash on Psalms* interprets the number eight eschatologically, in part: the number signifies Israel's four dispersions under eight kingdoms, from which kingdoms they will be regathered. *Midrash Pss.* I. 94–95

[65] See Jerome, *Comm.in Psalmos* 187:9–11, who mentions the octave separating birth from circumcision. See also *Midrash Pss.* 1:94–95, in particular a passage on 94: "Thinking of circumcision, David said: I shall compose a Psalm concerning it …" which might be the source of Herbert's assertion that this psalm was sung at a *bris*. Note that Andrew of St. Victor also reported on the ritual practices of his Jewish contemporaries. See *Andreae de Sancto Victore Opera IV: Expositionem in Ezechielem*, edited and introduction by Michael A. Signer, CCCM 53E, 1991, "Introduction," xxx–xxi.

[66] The Hexapla records Origen's translation of *neginot* as either φαλμος (psalmos) or υμνος (hymnos); Aquila rendered it as φαλμος (psalmos).

[67] The root נגן means "to strike upon the strings."

[68] In the titulus to Psalm 4, Herbert writes: "Et potest organorum nomine vel instrumentorum nomine esse ut diximus; et secundum non nullos litteratorum; pocius notularum ad quas versiculis psalmorum suscipens; psalmus in synagoga quasi musice

fied; by the mid-twelfth century, in England at least, the term *notula* was used to describe musical notation.[69] Once again, Herbert demonstrates that he is a fearless innovator, ready to adopt a little-known minority opinion concerning the psalm based on his own tests of clarity and precision.

4. Example from Psalm 8 titulus, fol. 10rb–10va

Victori super getiz psalmus david

> Pro quo nostri *Victori super vel pro torcularibus psalmus david* more suo pro interpretato interpretacionem ponentes. Getiz enim ebraice; torcularia sonat latine. Et dicunt nonnulli litteratorum quod sicut de aliis supra in psalmorum titulus positus iam sit et hic nomen getiz nomen instrumenti a loco scilicet geth ad quem fugit david; eo quod ibi repertum fuerit sic appellari ad cuius instrumentati vocem psalmus cantatus fuit. Unde et in titulo psalmi huius instrumenti illius nomen impositum est. Quemad-modum et in aliorum psalmorum titulis instrumentorum nomina ponun-tur ad que cantari a levitis consueverunt.

> Vel sicut alii tradunt accipuntur hic getiz non pro instrumenti illius nomine sed pro torcularibus secundum quod nostri transtulerunt. Et dicunt ideo intitulari psalmum pro torcularibus ad significandum servi-tutis pressuram qua filii esau ydumei pessimi semper israel inimici; tan-dem belli victoria et oppressi sunt. Et hoc per manum ipsius david sicut scriptum est. *Fecit quoque sibi david nomen cum reverteretur capta siria. Et infra. Et facta est universa ydumea serviens david* (2 Sam. 8.13–14) Similiter postea per alios reges de iuda iuxta illud prophete vaticinium, *Et dabo ultionem meam secundum ydumeam per manu populi mei israel* (Ezek. 25.14). Verum de hac torcularis pressura ut psalmi serie nec et mentio sit forte igitur ob id solum intitulatur pro torcularibus; eo quod ipso laudes domino deb-ite rependuntur pro iam dicta super ydumeam torcularis pressura. Que bene sicut inferunt litteratores isti per torcular hic quemadmodum et alibi [*illegible*] super ydumeam pressura nomine torcularis significatur ut

---

cantatur solet. Sicut nunc in ecclesia; in alleluaticis canticis et aliis fit. Et forte illud nunc; in tractum a sinagoga ad ecclesiam. et ita secundum litteratores istos organum aliquando instrumenti; aliquando vero talium notularum nomen est. Super quo talem litteratores dicti adhibendam discrecionem tradunt. Ut si in psalmi titulo habeatur in organis; tunc organorum nomine dictione notule intelligi debeant. Si autem habetur pro vel super organis; tunc organorum nomen instrumentorum musicorum designatum sit …" Fol. 5va.

[69] It may be that Herbert is drawing a parallel between the Massorah, which described how the scriptural text was to be read aloud (with what accents and pauses) and the medieval system of *neumes*, which similarly described accents and patterns of singing in plainchant and polyphony.

in alio propheta sicut scriptum est. *Torcular calcavi solus* (Isa. 63.3). Verum quidquid litterator fingat salva ubique sit super rege nostro messia ecclesiastici interpretacio. Igitur secundum litteratores pro torcularibus sive pressuris super ydumeam debitas domino laudes psalmista rependens; sic inchoat ...

In this selection, Herbert again critiques a long-standing Christian tradition. Since Origen's time, the Hebrew phrase עַל-הַגִּתִּית (*al ha-gitith*) had been interpreted to mean 'winepress,' (*torcular*) in Latin. Herbert, following Rashi, asserts to the contrary that this is a musical term, denoting an instrument manufactured in *geth ad quem fugit david*.

Rashi had acknowledged an alternative explanation given by 'our rabbis' in *Midrash on Psalms*: "[the title] refers to Edom, which in the future will be trod like a winepress (*gath*) in accord with what is stated in the Bible, 'I trod out a vintage alone' (Isa. 63.3)." Rashi rejects this intepretation, however, on the grounds that it does not reflect the psalm's content. As the passage above indicates, Herbert does not share Rashi's scruples on this score. He notes that the translation 'winepresses' is apt in this case, as it reflects Israel's conquest of its ancestral enemy, Edom. His citations to Scripture appear to be more extensive than Rashi's, as he adduced historical examples from 2 Samuel, and the prophecy of Ezekiel applicable to future kings of Judah in addition to the citation from Isaiah 63. Thus Herbert applauds the rabbis' interpretation: "Que bene sicut inferunt litteratores isti per torcular hic; quemadmodum et alibi ... super ydumeam pressura."

The authors of *Midrash on Psalms* regarded the winepress metaphor from an eschatological perspective. The defeat of Israel's historical enemies—Babylon, Greece, Persia, and Edom (meaning Rome)—belonged to a time of future redemption. The harvest preceding the pressing would belong to the messianic age.[70] Interestingly, Herbert is silent on the question of when the prophecies of Ezekiel and Isaiah would be fulfilled. Other Christian exegetes argued that prophetic predictions of Edom's subordination to Israel were actually historical references to David's extraction of tribute from the Idumeans. Thus the future held no prospect for Israel's restoration to power, and as prophecy, these statements applied only to Christianity, *verus Israel*. For Christians as well as Jews, Psalm 8 had powerful eschatological import: the themes of harvest and consummation under Christ were frequently reprised by

---

[70] *Midrash Pss.* 2:119.

Latin exegetes from the time of Hilary of Poitiers.[71] For this reason, perhaps, Herbert concludes his comment with a 'saving' clause. Whatever the *litterator* might say (and however convincing Herbert might find it), the ecclesiastical interpretation must be reasserted: "Salva ubique sit super rege nostro messie ecclesiastici interpretacio."[72]

5. *Example from Psalm 9 titulus*

The text for this last example of Herbert's exegesis of Hebrew terms in the *tituli psalmorum* is too long to include here (the transcription can be found after this discussion). The title under consideration had long perplexed Jewish and Christian commentators; Herbert's version of it reads *Victori almuth labben psalmus david*. Of crucial importance to interpreters was how the Hebrew words עלמות לבן should be pointed (i.e., which vowels should accompany the consonants) and how they should be divided. Jewish and Christian exegetes alike mined the many possibilities afforded by various combinations of spelling and word division to arrive at interpretations that expressed their respective convictions. As we shall see, those convictions were frequently at odds, although Herbert attains a startling reconciliation amongst his authorities.

Herbert's comments on Psalm 9's title canvassed a wide range of opinion. He expounds the possibilities of treating עלמות (*almuth*) as one word or two; likewise with לבן (*laben*). Herbert opens his discussion with the latter case: if לבן is two words, then the second word (*ben*) can have two meanings: 'son' (*filius*) or 'learning' (*doctrina vel eruditio*). Basing his discussion on an unknown source, Herbert claims that part of the title *might* be translated *Victori organa ad discendum*.[73] In this case, he suggests, the 'learning' propounded by the psalmist might be learning to play the musical instrument known as an *almuth*.

---

[71] For instance, Hilary of Poitiers wrote: "Et dignum est hanc ogdoadis perfectam sacramentis coelestibus virtutem in psalmo eo, qui octavo in numero dispositus est, contueri, cui pro torcularibus titulus adjectus est, vasculis in novos fructus praeparatis, et ad ferventis musti calorem continendum innovatis. Et numerus iste ad percipiendos fructus evangelicos, caducis bis corporum nostrorum vasculis reformatis, secundum ogdoadem est evangelicam destinatus. Et hoc psalmi istius textus et sermo testatur ..." *Instructio psalmorum* 13.

[72] See Smalley on Herbert's use *salva* clauses, *RTAM* 18: 60.

[73] A parallel usage is found in the title to Psalm 59[60], *Victori super rosis humilis et perfecti david ad discendum*, Herbert argues. There, the Hebrew is ללמד or *le-lamed*, which Jerome translated as *ad doctrinam* in the Gallican version and *ad docendum* in the Hebraica.

But what if *almuth* were two words? In that case, Jerome's Hebraica reading finds support. Herbert follows Jerome in translating the preposition עַל (*al*) as *pro vel super.* 'Muth' can mean 'death.' Recalling that the second meaning of *ben* is 'son,' the entire phrase might well be understood as Jerome proposed: *victori pro morte filii canticum david.* Herbert adduces support for this position by citing Psalm 47[48]:15: "... [S]icut scriptum est: *Et ipse erit dux noster* almuth quod est *in morte*" (Fol. 51ʳᵇ).

In the exegetical materials on the psalms attributed to Jerome, that author recorded the psalm's traditional title, *In finem pro occultis filii psalmus David* but cautioned, "in hebraico enim habet *alamoth,* quod interpretatur, pro morte."[74] According to him, the Septuagint's translators had suppressed the true meaning of the Hebrew phrase ("the death of the son") so that the Gentiles (Ptolemy, et al.) would not be scandalized by the death of the Son of God. Christians, however, should understand that the entire psalm speaks of the Savior and his death.[75]

Later Christian exegetes commented on the traditional title (*pro occultis filii*). The son's 'hidden things' signified that Jesus's saving work had been hidden from the Jews. Theirs was a providential misunderstanding, according to Augustine: "'For the hidden things of the Son' is not unsuitably understood to be spoken of this advent, in which 'blindness in part happened to Israel, that the fulness of the Gentiles might come in.'" Augustine also noted that the son mentioned in this title was not David's rebellious son Absalom since his name was not mentioned outright—as it is in other psalms.[76] The psalm must be, therefore, about Jesus Christ, David's son *secundum carnem,* as Peter Lombard observed.[77]

By contrast, Herbert says that if the title does indeed mean 'the death of the son,' then the psalm literally is about Absalom. He acknowledges a seeming incongruity, however: the exultant note struck by the word 'victory' and the celebratory tone of the psalm scarcely suits the occasion of Absalom's death—which David bitterly lamented. Herbert suggests instead that in this psalm David exults and gives thanks for the defeat of Ahitofel and Absalom's other counsellors, whom he compares in verse 6 to Gentiles 'uncircumcised of heart:' "Quos pro psalmum gentibus comparat eo quod corde incircumcisi fuissent et

---

[74] Jerome, *Tractatus in Psalmos,* CCSL 78, 28. See also *Commentarioli in Psalmos,* CCSL 72, 191.

[75] Jerome, *Tractatus,* CCSL 78, 28–29.

[76] Augustine, *Enn. in Psalmos, ad. loc.*

[77] In his psalms commentary, *ad loc.,* PL 191.

inmundi quibus poterant consiliis filium adversus patrem instigantes. In signum vero illum tocius factionis auctorem achitofel designans spe- cialiter nomine impii."[78]

Despite the aptness of this version of the title's possible literal mean- ing, Herbert's analysis is not complete. Having demonstrated that both לבן and עלמות can be understood as one or two words, Herbert dis- cusses other interpretations. *Almuth* could refer to a musical instrument, but it might also mean 'infancy' or 'youth.' This latter definition is preferred by Rashi *ad loc.*[79] To support his own preference, Herbert refers to the title of Psalm 45[46], which Jerome had translated as *Vic- tori filiorum core pro iuuentutibus canticum*.[80] By analogy, Herbert suggests, the title to Psalm 9 might read "*Victori pro infancia* vel *iuuentute dealbacio*," because the word *laben* (translated previously as 'to the son') can also mean 'whitening' or 'renewal.'

This discussion of alternatives gives Herbert an opportunity to intro- duce Rashi's exposition of the title, which is markedly eschatological.[81] Rashi had reported that the Massorah glosses *almuth* as 'forever' at Psalm 47[48]:15.[82] He noted that the *poterim* and Dunash had offered interpretations of *almuth*, but he disagrees with them (and leaves them unrecorded). Rashi's own view is derived from the *Pesikta Rav Kahana*, where the psalm is related to the ultimate destruction of Amalek and Edom. When Esau and his progeny are wiped out, Rashi asserts, Israel will be rejuvenated and renewed. Gruber translated Rashi's comment as: "*labben* is a form of *le-labben*, 'to renew.'"[83]

---

[78] It is not clear where Herbert derived this material from. Rashi does not draw this parallel, nor does *Midrash on Psalms*. Christian commentators focused on the Gallican version of the title *pro occultis filii*, which tended to encouragae a meditation on the saving work of the Second Person of the Trinity, which was "hidden" from the Jews. Herbert's mentor Peter Lombard was strident on this topic: the Jews' blindness, of course, prevented them from penetrating the mystery of the incarnation. See Lombard *ad loc.*

[79] Gruber, 74.

[80] There the Hebrew reads על-עלמות (*al-alamoth*), a discrepancy which does not detain Herbert, if indeed he was aware of it.

[81] Gruber suggests that Rashi's interpretation is a response to Christian exegesis which, as we have seen, associated this title with Jesus Christ's advent—and with the reprobation of the Jews. He cites the Hebraica version of the title, however, which was not the version referred to by exegetes other than Herbert. 78, n. 7.

[82] Herbert, in the title to Psalm 5, mentions that *almuth* can be translated as *saeculum*. See also *Midrash Pss.* 1:131.

[83] Gruber, 74. In Biblical Hebrew, the verb means "to whiten."

Herbert adopts Rashi's exegesis, and relates it to his own understanding of Christian eschatology. The cleansing and renewal of Israel
will come at the end of days, as Paul indicated in Romans. To this
traditional Christian assertion, Herbert adds Rashi's hope; the renewal
will occur after the memory of Amalech had been blotted out from
the face of the earth, and after Esau and his progeny have been wiped
out.[84] In effect, Herbert has melded Jewish and Christian eschatological
expectations:

> Sed in fine; ex toto dealbitur. quando omnis israel salvabitur.[85] Quando
> iuxta quod scriptum est; *delebitur memoria amalech de sub celo* (Ex.17:14).
> Et de hac israel dealbacione sive salute et de esau et de seminis eius
> delecione perpetua; secundum litteralem sensum psalmus hic loquitur.
> Unde et david ad ultimam illam israel dealbacionem respiciens. Et in
> persona tocius israel domino gratias agens ...

Herbert constructed this confluence of the two traditions' eschatologies
deliberately, trading on the associations that Rashi had constructed for
the words *almuth* and *lab[b]en*. In so doing, Herbert also adopted a
rehabilitated use of the term *dealbatio*.

In Biblical Hebrew, לבן generally means 'white' as a substantive or
'whiten' as a verb (see Psalm 50[51]:7). Latin exegetes usually translated
this as *candor* or *candidus* and more rarely as *dealbacio*. In a spurious version of the *Book of Hebrew Names* attributed to Origen, the etymology of
Laban is given as *dealbacio*.[86] Subsequent exegetes apparently conflated
the reference to *dealbata sepulchra*, the 'whited sepulchres' or hypocrites
metaphorically decried by Jesus in Matthew 23:27, with the reference
to Laban. For example, Isidore of Seville noted that Laban's presumed
quality of 'whiteness' or purity is apt, given that he was false to Jacob.
By analogy, Laban is allegorized as the Devil who pursues the righteous
man:

> Laban autem consecutus est eum in montem Galaad cum furore, atque
> idola quae Rachel furata erat apud eum requisivit, nec reperit. Quid
> igitur sibi hoc ipsum figuraliter velit, inspiciendum est. Dum Laban
> superius aliam gerat personam, nunc tamen diaboli typum figurat. La-

---

[84] Ex. 17:14; cited in *Midrash on Psalms* and by Rashi at 9.6.

[85] cf. Rom. 11:26; "omnis Israehel salvus fieret"

[86] In Jerome's *Liber Interpretationis Hebraicorum Nominum*, the name's etymology is
candidus. CCSL 72: 68.

ban quippe interpretatur dealbatio. Dealbatio autem diabolus non in-
convenienter accipitur, qui cum sit ex merito tenebrosus, transfigurat se
in angelum lucis.[87]

Dealbatio was wrenched free from associations with Laban and Satan by
the Glossa Ordinaria on Numbers 33:20. There, the glossator discusses
Lebna[88] and explains its etymology as *dealbatio*. But he explicitly departs
from tradition, saying that although the word had had bad associations
it should be understood positively. He cites Psalm 50:7, noting that the
sinner is made clean (whiter than snow). He advances other positive
allusions to *dealbatio* or whiteness. The glossator concludes that the term
refers to the eschatological age, when the purified soul will see God:
"Haec igitur dealbatio ex splendore verae lucis intelligitur provenire, et
ex visionum coelestium claritate descendere."[89]

Herbert affirmed this rehabilitated view of *dealbacio* in his exegesis
of Psalm 9. It connotes the 'glorified' condition of Israel at the end of
time. Commenting on the second verse, *Confitebor domino in toto corde meo;
narrabo omnia mirabilia tua*, he writes:

> *Confitebor domino* id est laudabo dominum. *In toto corde meo narrabo* id
> est narrabo illud mirabile; quod est consummacio omnium mirabilium
> tuorum que pro israele operatus es. Et quod est illud mirabile; hoc est
> israel in fine seculi gloriosa dealbacio et esau et seminis eius sempiterna
> perdicio. Quasi quidem iudeus carnaliter ecclesiasticus vero spiritualiter
> accipet.

Rashi *ad loc.* spoke of the miracles God had done for Israel, preeminently the Exodus. Herbert echoes this thought, and adds to the list of
wonders: at the end of the age, Israel will be glorified and Esau and
his offspring will be destroyed. This prediction is understood by 'the
Jew' carnally and by the 'churchman' spiritually. While this distinction
is typical of Christian exegetes, Herbert remains atypical inasmuch as
he does not disparage these carnal expectations.

---

[87] Isidore of Seville, *Mysticorum in Genesin*, Cap. XXVI, PL 83: 264Dff. There is no
critical edition of this text; the PL reprints the Maurists' text.

[88] Or *Libna*, an unidentified site in the desert, mentioned in the itinerary of the
Hebrews' wanderings.

[89] The relevant passage reads: "Scio in aliis dealbationem culpabiliter poni, ut cum
dicitur paries dealbatus, et monumenta dealbata. Hic autem *dealbatio* est de qua dicitur:
Lavabis me et super nivem dealbabor; et, si fuerint peccata vestra sicut Phoenicium, ut nivem
dealbabo. Et alibi, *Nive dealbabuntur in Selmon*. Et vetusti dierum capilli dicuntur esse
candidi, id est, albi sicut lana. Haec igitur dealbatio ex splendore verae lucis intelligitur
provenire, et ex visionum coelestium claritate descendere." *Liber Numeri*, Cap. XXXIII,
PL113:439C.

Herbert's conflation of Jewish and Christian eschatological expec-
tions was a conscious decision, as is even more apparent in light of
his exegesis of the term *almuth* in those psalms to which he refers for
support for his interpretation of Psalm 9, Psalm 45[46]:1 and Psalm
47[48]:15.

In his discussion of Psalm 45's title, Herbert notes that *almuth* is
thought by some to refer to an instrument. Indeed, that is all Rashi
says of the term *ad loc.*, while referring the reader to 1 Chronicles for
an example. Herbert goes a step further and includes a citation from
1 Chron. 15:19–20: "De quo alibi scriptum est *Porro cantores eman* et
cetera usque *in nablis elamoth*. Sic est in hebreo pro quo nos *in nablis
archana cantabant*. Quod hebreo consonans est" (Fol. 49rb).

Herbert is not an antiquarian; he dispatches the instrument with the
remark that whatever it might have been, its use and form are unknown
apud nos. The translation of *almuth* as *iuventus*, however, intrigues him. He
pursues the exegetical possibilities provided by that alternative, already
present in the Hebraica version of Psalm 45's title: *Victori filiorum core pro
iuventutibus canticum*. Herbert ventures yet again to blend the beliefs and
exegetical methods of the Christian tradition with the eschatologically-
oriented interpretation of Rashi and *Midrash on Psalms*. He notes that
the title is the 'key to the psalm,' a popular Christian trope which
echoes the equally popular conviction that Christ is the key to the
psalter.[90] But in this case, *almuth* (understood as 'youth') is the key; thus
he concludes decisively:

> Almuth vero iuventutem sonat. Unde et transtulerunt hic *pro iuventutibus*
> ubi sicut et in aliis multis pro interpretato interpretatio ponitur. Et secun-
> dum hoc titulus quasi psalmi clavis; psalmi materiam aperit dicens enim
> *pro iuventutibus* indicat quod de israelis redemptione agat que erit in diebus
> novissimus in resurrectione ultima quando renovabitur sicut aquile veri
> israelis iuventus. (Fol. 49rb)

Herbert is remarkably inspecific regarding this Israel whose youth will
be renewed like that of a 'true eagle.' He does not contrast a 'true' or
'spiritual' Israel (meaning Christianity) with a 'carnal' Israel (meaning
contemporary Judaism) here.

Before turning to Psalm 47[48], recall that in his discussion of Psalm
9, Herbert had cited 47[48]:15 in support of the notion that *almuth*
might be read as *al-muth* ('on the death'). In Herbert's actual comments

---

[90] Hilary of Poitiers, *In Librum Psalmorum*; *Instructio* 6.

on verse 15, he notes *mors* as a possible reading.[91] Yet he concentrates once again on *iuventus*. In doing so, he follows Rashi—but not Rashi at 47[48]:15. Rather, Herbert imports the presumption that *almuth* should be translated *iuventus* from Psalm 9, and makes a case for its appropriateness within the context of Psalm 47[48] as Rashi had interpreted it.

Discussing verse 15, Herbert acknowledges that Rashi had read the whole of Psalm 47[48] as an eschatological prophecy, foretelling the messianic era in which the forces ranged against Israel (Gog and Magog) will be defeated by the Messiah, and the 'golden' Jerusalem will be rebuilt: "Litterator psalmum hunc de aurea ierusalem interpretatur quam expectant. In qua dominus magnus apparebit et laudabilis nimis addens de sancti montis specie super quem iuxta ezechielis vaticinum; edificabitur templum in eternum mansurum" (Fol. 51[rb]).

Throughout the passage, Herbert describes the renewal of Israel's youth with references to the rebuilt Temple prophesied by Ezekiel, combined with allusions to the visions of 'new city' of Jerusalem described in the twenty-first chapter of the Book of Revelation. Further evidence of Herbert's impulse to rehabilitate etymology or symbols associated negatively with Judaism is his treatment here of the term *in aurea Jerusalem*. One might assume that to speak of a golden Jerusalem is simply to quote Rev. 21. In fact, the term incurred Christian disapprobation. Jerome[92] and Peter Lombard[93] had lampooned the messianic expectations of Christians (judaizers, per Jerome) and Jews who

---

[91] Together with *absconditus*, the latter probably derived from Jerome: Jerome, *Comm.* 191: 1–5, on Psalm 9: "*In finem pro absconditis filii.* Licet Aquila pro absconditis filii 'adulescentiam filii' posuerit, tamen sciendum in hebraeo haberi 'pro morte filii.' Denique et Symmachus in hunc modum transtulit: 'Pro victoria de morte filii.' Totus igitur psalmus per tropologiam ad Christi pertinet sacramentum."

[92] Jerome attacked the eschatological expectations of Jews and "our Judaizers" in his commentary on Joel 3:17: "Haec Judaei et nostri, ut diximus, judaizantes, ad mille annorum fabulam referunt, quando putant Christum habitaturum in Sion, et in Jerusalem aurea atque gemmata sanctorum populos congregandos, ut qui in isto saeculo oppressi sunt ab universis gentibus, in hoc eodem cunctis imperent nationibus." *Commentariorum in Ioelem*, CCSL 76, 206:313–318.

[93] Lombard on Psalm 43[44]:11: "Haec sperabant Judaei, qui in futuro haec tempora multiplicata sibi exspectant reddi, ut Jerusalem aurea, et hujusmodi. Qui vero ita Deum colit, laudabilis non est, sicut non laudatur in illo jejunium, qui ad luxuriosam coenam servat ventrem suum. Hoc est enim jejunium non continentiae, sed luxuriae. Gratis itaque Deus coli debet, non propter aliud ab eo; et non egredieris Deus evidenter. Non egredieris dico ulterius, o Deus, sicut olim Judaeis faciebas, in virtutibus, id est, in exercitibus nostris. Et per hoc invalidi sumus contra inimicos." PL 191: 431A

believed in a messianic reign of a thousand years in the renewed city, in whose restored Temple sacrifices would once again be conducted. By contrast, when Herbert affirms that Rashi speaks in Psalm 47 of the golden city, he offers no criticism at all of Jewish expectations. Rather, he marries them to Christian symbolism for the end-time. The expectations of Israel for the end of days are extolled, not vilified. According to Herbert, the *litterator* correctly understood the psalm as a prophecy of *novissima redemptione in ierusalem*.

He concludes: "Sequitur 'Ipse erit dux noster in iuventute' id est in novissimo quando deposita vetustate omnes iuvenes erimus. Et quidem super psalmum hunc; litteratoris explanacio haec" (Fol. 49rb): At the end of time, we shall *all* be as youths, as the *litterator* had also explained. Herbert does not distinguish who 'we' are, nor does he discriminate between the fate of a carnal and a spiritual Israel. The implication is that at the end of days (*in novissimo*), the redemption of the world will be achieved for the good of all people.

Herbert concludes his comments on Psalm 9's title by alluding to popular themes from contemporary Christian preaching. His discussion of the *nigredo sponse* recalls Song of Songs 1:4: "I am black yet comely" (*nigra sum sed formosa*) and its resonances in the Christian exegetical tradition. The spouse of the Song was traditionally associated with the Church, whose Bridegroom is Christ. Exegetes like Bernard of Clairvaux exploited the tension in this perceived antithesis: what spouse could be both black and beautiful? Bernard resolved the paradox by asserting that the Church, Christ's spouse, may be outwardly flawed but has nevertheless enjoyed inward renewal—she will in time be made white.

> ... the bride, despite the gracefulness of her person, bears the stigma of a dark skin, but this is only in the place of her pilgrimage. It will be otherwise when the Bridegroom in his glory will take her to himself "in splendor, without spot or wrinkle, or any such thing." But if she were to say now that her color is not black, she would be deceiving herself, and the truth would not be in her.[94]

Individual Christians, interiorly renewed may also lack comeliness; their modesty and humility conceals their true condition:

---

[94] Sermon 25.3, *On the Song of Songs* II, trans. Kilian Walsh, OCSO. Works of Bernard of Clairvaux 3; Cistercian Fathers Series 7 (Kalamazoo, MI: Cistercian Publications, 1976), 52.

... listen to what God promises through His Prophet to those blemished with this kind of blackness, those who seem discolored as by the sun's heat through the lowliness of a penitential life, through zeal for charity. He says: "Though your sins are like scarlet, they shall be made white as snow; though they are red as crimson, they shall be white as wool." The outward blemishes that we may discern in holy persons are not to be condemned, because they play a part in the begetting of interior light, and so dispose the soul for wisdom.[95]

Bernard and other commentators on the Canticle employed another technique to resolve the black-but-beautiful antithesis: the Suffering Servant himself embodied the paradox. Despite his outward appearance, he had "done no iniquity, neither was there deceit in his mouth" (Isa. 53:9). The Servant was in fact the Sun, in whom there is no blemish.[96] Thus, Herbert's phrase *semper enim macula in luna* alludes to the relationship of the Church to Christ as the moon to the sun, also a popular homiletic trope. The Sun is without blemish; whereas the Church which takes its light from Christ will always be prone to failings. This weakness will be eliminated at the end of days. In the age to come, even the 'moon' will be without blemish.[97]

Herbert resituates these classic tropes, understood to reflect a distinctively Christian reality, in a completely different context.

Et ista sunt qui nigredo sponse synagoge tunc; nunc vero ecclesia. Aqua dum hic invitas plene non auferetur nigredo habet. Semper enim macula est in luna. Sed in fine; ex toto dealbitur quando omnis israel salvabitur. Quando iuxta quod scriptum est *delebitur memoria amalech de sub celo* (Ex.17:14).[98]

---

[95] Sermon 25.6, 54. The Latin text reads: "Audi denique quid per Prophetam Deus promittat istiusmodi nigris, quos aut humilitas paenitentiae, aut caritatis zelus, tamquam solis aestus, decolorasse videtur. 'Si fuerint,' ait, 'peccata vestra ut coccinum, quasi nix dealbabuntur; et si fuerint rubra quasi vermiculus, velut lana alba erunt' (Isai. I, 18). Non plane contemnenda in sanctis extera ista nigredo quae candorem operatur internum, et sedem perinde praeparat sapientiae," *Sermones in Cantica Canticorum*, eds. J. Leclercq, C. Talbot, H. Rochais, *Sancti Bernardi Opera*, Vol. 1 (Rome: Editiones Cistercienses, 1957), 166.

[96] A sermon attributed to Peter Damian in the PL but now counted among his dubious works reads: "In sole nulla est macula; et ipse est, qui singulariter ingressus est mundum sine macula, 'qui peccatum non fecit, nec inventus est dolus in ore ejus' (Isa. 53:9)," Peter Damian, *Sermones Ordine Mensium Servato 1–2 Januarius. Sermo Primus: In Epiphania Domini (VI Jan.)* PL 144: 509C.

[97] Peter Lombard on Ps. 84(85).8.

[98] Fol. 11va.

Unique among Christian exegetes, Herbert linked his tradition's eschatological expectations with those of Judaism. Although he asserts that the black spouse was once the synagogue and is now the church, Christianity does not simply cancel out Judaism in his scheme. Both will be cleansed *in fine*. For the Jews, their salvation and purification will be achieved after the destruction of Esau and his progeny.[99] This physical miracle awaits Israel at the consummation of world. Herbert does not suggest that the church's spiritual eschaton will negate this promise. This overview of Psalm 9 and the intertextual relationships Herbert pursues between it and Psalms 45 and 47, shows that he deployed his linguistic abilities—whether great or small—with remarkable consistency on this point. Herbert may disparage aspects of Jewish belief; in some circumstances he may argue that the Jews are blind to the nature of the true Messiah. But he is convinced by the gravity of Israel's suffering in exile and the validity of its faith in God's saving power that the last word spoken in history will not abandon them.[100]

Psalm 9 titulus (fol. 11rb–11va)

Victori almuth laben psalmus david

Pro quo nostri *Victori pro* vel *super morte filii psalmus david*. Nonnulli litteratorum quod hic in titulo hebraice dicitur almuth laben explanaverunt ut latine dicatur ad sensum hunc *victori organa ad discendum*. Et ponitur hic *ad discendum* sicut et in titulo alterius psalmi ubi in titulo habetur sic *Victori super rosis humilis et perfecti david ad discendum*.[101] Et secundum hoc almuth est hic una dictio et instrumenti nomen sicut et alia hebrea nomina supra in psalmorum titulis ad instrumentorum designacionem posita sunt. Ben vero doctrinam vel erudicionem sonat, la articulus est. Est enim ben commune et ad filium et erudicionem. Verum quare

---

[99] This is an extraordinary concession for a Christian who was aware, as Herbert was, that for the Jews, he was among Esau's progeny. See Chapter 6.

[100] Rashi's exegesis of the Suffering Servant motif and of the bride in Song of Songs focused on the two figures as epitomizing Israel's sufferings in Exile. Herbert seems to have been aware of these associations (certainly of the latter). See Psalm 87(88) titulus.

[101] This is a reference to the titulus of Psalm 59[60], which he rendered in part as *Victori super rose testimonio humilis et perfecti David ad discendum* ..., fol. 61rb. The corresponding portion of the title in the Hebraica reads *Victori pro liliis testimonium humilis et perfecti David ad docendum* ...

psalmus sic intituletur scilicet *organa ad discendum* ipsorum qui sic explanant iudicio derelinquo. Nostrorum interpretacioni inherens secundum quos psalmus inscribitur *pro* vel *super morte* pro quo hebreus habet almuth ut fuit dictiones due, al scilicet et muth, al quod est super, muth quod est mors. Et hoc est quod nos hic dicimus *pro* vel *super morte*. Iuxta quod et in fine psalmi quadragesimi sexti sicut scriptum est. *Et ipse erit dux noster* almuth quod est *in morte*. (Ps. 47:15). Ergo addicitur hic filii videri potest david ad litteram hunc psalmum edidisse, pro morte filii sui absolon et complicum suoroum destrucione extulans et gratias agens. Non tam pro filii sui cui post mortem tam miserabilem exhibuit threnum quam pro consiliarii sui achitofel et reliquorum suorum complicum prophano extermino. Quos pro psalmum gentibus comparat eo quod corde incircumcisi fuissent et inmundi quibus poterant consilius filium adversus patrem instigantes. In signum vero illum tocius factionis auctorem achitofel designans specialiter nomine impii. Et secundum hoc psalmi series; prosequenda.

Potest et almuth quod supra duas esse dictiones monstravimus et una dictio esse. Et sonat tunc idem quod infancia vel iuventus. Unde et secundum nonnullos interpretes; talis est psalmi titulus, *Victori pro infancia* vel *iuventibus psalmus david*. Quomodo et in sequenti alius intitulatur psalmus *Deus nobis spes et fortitudo* (Ps 45:2).[102] In illius siquidem psalmi titulo idem verbum hebreum scilicet almuth quo et hic positum est. Erit itaque secundum interpretes hos, titulus psalmi talis *victori pro infancia* vel *iuventute dealbacio psalmus david*. Quod enim illi supra in priori titulo transtulerunt filii, hoc isti intepretati sunt dealbacionem. Et utramque congruit enim. Verbum enim hebreum laben in titulo positum potest esse dictio una. Et est tunc idem quod dealbacio. Potest etiam esse tanquam dictiones une, ben quod sonat filius et la quod tamen non nisi articulus est. Unde ex ambiguitate hac dictionis unius vel dualiter; alii hoc alii illud transtulerunt. Est itaque titulus secundum hos *Victori pro infancia* vel *iuventute dealbacio psalmus david*. Et dicit infanciam vel iuventutem israel iuventutis delicta velud quasdam infancie ipsius sordes. Et ista sunt qui nigredo sponse synagoge tunc nunc vero ecclesia. Aqua dum hic invitas plene non auferetur nigredo habet, semper enim macula est in luna. Sed in fine; ex toto dealbitur quando omnis israel

---

[102] The title to Ps. 45 is *Victori filiorum core pro iuventutibus canticum* in the Hebraica; Herbert's version is missing its title, seemingly due to a scribal error, since the MS *ad loc.* includes a discussion of *almuth* focused on the likelihood that the word names an instrument used to accompany the singing of the psalms; fol. 49[rb].

salvabitur.[103] Quando iuxta quod scriptum est *delebitur memoria amalech de sub celo* (Ex.17:14). Et de hac israel dealbacione sive salute et de esau et de seminis eius delecione perpetua secundum litteralem sensum psalmus hic loquitur. Unde et david ad ultimam illam israel dealbacionem respiciens. Et in persona tocius israel domino gratias agens; sic dicit.

v. 2: Confitebor domino in toto corde meo; narrabo omnia mirabilia tua.

Confitebor domino id est laudabo dominum. *In toto corde meo; narrabo omnia mirabilia tua* id est narrabo illud mirabile; quod est consummacio omnium mirabilium tuorum que pro israele operatus es. Et quod est illud mirabile; hoc est israel in fine seculi gloriosa dealbacio et esau et seminis eius sempiterna perdicio. Quia quidem iudeus carnaliter ecclesiasticus v ero spiritualiter accipet.

---

[103] Cf. Rom. 11:26: "... *omnis Israehel salvus fieret.*"

BIBLIOGRAPHY

I. *Manuscripts*

Herbert of Bosham. *Psalterium cum commento*. MS 2, Cathedral Chapter Library, Saint Paul's Cathedral, London.

Herbert of Bosham. *Prima Pars Psalterii Glosati*. MS B.5.4, Trinity College Library, Trinity College, Cambridge University, Cambridge.

Herbert of Bosham. *Secunda Pars Psalterii*. MS Auct. E inf. 6, Bodleian Library, Oxford University, Oxford.

Ralf Niger. *Phillipicus*. Lincoln Cathedral MS 15, Manuscripts and Special Collections, University of Nottingham Library, Nottingham.

Psalterium Triplex Glosatum (Petri Lombardi). Lincoln Cathedral MS 18, Manuscripts and Special Collections, University of Nottingham Library, Nottingham.

II. *Primary Sources*

Abraham ibn Ezra. *Ibn Ezra's Commentary on the Pentateuch*. Translated and annotated by H. Norman Strickman and Arthur M. Silver. New York: Menorah Publishing, 1988.

Abrahams, Israel, H.P. Stokes, and Herbert Loewe, eds. *Starrs and Jewish Charters Preserved in the British Museum*. 3 vols. Cambridge: Jewish Historical Society, 1930–1932.

Andrew of Saint Victor. *Andreae de Santo Victor Opera II: Expositio hystorica in librum regum*, edited and introduction by Frans van Liere. CCCM 53A,1995.

———. *Andreae de Sancto Victore Opera IV: Expositionem in Ezechielem*, edited and introduction by Michael A. Signer. CCCM 53E, 1991.

Anselm of Canterbury. *Why God Became Man*. Translated by Eugene R. Fairweather. *A Scholastic Miscellany: Anselm to Ockham*. Library of Christian Classics 10. New York: Macmillan, 1956.

Augustine. *De civitate Dei*. CCSL 48.

———. *City of God*. Translated by Henry Bettenson. London: Penguin, 1984.

———. *De doctrina christiana*. CCSL 32.

———. *Ennarationes in Psalmos*. CCSL 38–40.

———. *Epistulae*. CSEL 34.

———. *On Christian Teaching*. Translated by R.P.H. Green. Oxford: Oxford World's Classics, 1997.

———. "In Answer to the Jews." Translated by Marie Liguori Ewald. *Treatises on Marriage and Other Works*, edited by Roy J. DeFerrari. Fathers of the Church

15. Washington: Catholic University Press, 1955.

———. *Tractatus adversus Iudaeos.* PL 42:51–64.

Babylonian Talmud. Hebrew-English edition, under the editorship of Isidore Epstein. London: Soncino Press, 1935–1948.

Bernard of Clairvaux. *Sancti Bernardi opera*, edited by J. Leclercq, C.H. Talbot, and H.M. Rochais. Rome: Editiones Cistercienses, 1957–1977.

———. *On the Song of Songs.* Translated by Kilian Walsh, OCSO. Spencer, MA: Cistercian Publications, 1971–1976.

Biblia Latina cum Glossa Ordinaria: Anastatical Reproduction of the First Printed Edition, Strassburg c. 1480. Edited by K. Froehlich and M. Gibson. Louvain: 1991.

Biblia Sacra Vulgata. Edited by R. Weber. Stuttgart: Deutsche Bibelgesellschaft, 1994

Cassiodorus. *Expositio Psalmorum.* CCSL 97–98.

———. *Explanation of the Psalms.* Translated by P.G. Walsh. Ancient Christian Writers 51–52. New York: Paulist Press, 1990.

Commentarius Cantabrigiensis in Epistolas Pauli e Schola Petri Abelardi. Vol. 2, edited by Arthur Landgraf. Notre Dame, IN: Publications in Medieval Studies, 1939.

Gerhoch of Reichersberg. *Letter to Pope Hadrian on the Novelties of the Day*, edited by Nikolaus M. Häring. Studies and Texts 24. Toronto: Pontifical Institute of Medieval Studies, 1974.

Gilbert Crispin. *The Works of Gilbert Crispin.* Edited by Anna Sapir Abulafia and Gillian R. Evans. London: British Academy, 1986.

Le Glossaire de Leipzig, edited and annotated by Menahem Banitt. Jerusalem: Académie nationale des sciences et des lettres d'Israël, 1995.

Le Guide des Hassidim. Selected and translated by Édouard Gourévitch. Paris: Cerf, 1988.

Herbert of Bosham. *Vita Sancti Thomae. Materials for the History of Thomas Becket, Archbishop of Canterbury*, Vol. 3, edited by James Craigie Robertson. London: Longman et al., 1877.

Hilary of Poitiers. *Tractatus super Psalmos.* CSEL 22.

Hugh of St. Victor. *Didascalicon de studio legendi*, edited by Charles H. Buttimer. Washington: Catholic University Press, 1939.

———. *The* Didascalicon *of Hugh of St. Victor.* Translated by Jerome Taylor. New York: Columbia University Press, 1991.

———. *On the Sacraments of the Christian Faith of Hugh of Saint Victor.* Translated by Roy J. DeFerrari. Medieval Academy of America Publication 58. Cambridge: Medieval Academy of America, 1951.

———. *De Sacramentis Christianae Fidei.* PL 176.

———. *De Scripturis et scriptoribus sacris praenotatiunculae.* PL 175

Isidore of Seville. *Mysticorum in Genesin.* PL 83.

———. *Etymologarium sive Originum Libri XX*, edited by W.M. Lindsay. Oxford: Clarendon Press, 1911.

Jerome. *Commentarioli in Psalmos.* CCSL 72.

———. *Commentariorum in Ioelem.* CCSL 76

———. *Commentariorum in Danielem Libri III (IV).* CCSL 75A.

————. *The Letters of St. Jerome*. Vol. 1. Translated by Charles Christopher Mierow. Ancient Christian Writers 33. Westminster, MD: Newman Press, 1963.

————. *Liber Interpretationis Hebraicorum Nominum*. CCSL 72.

————. *Tractatus in Psalmos*. CCSL 78.

————. *Saint Jérôme Lettres*. 8 vols. Translated and edited by Jérôme Labourt. Paris: Societé d'édition "Les Belles Lettres," 1951.

————. *Sancti Hieronymi Psalterium Iuxta Hebraeos: Édition critique*, edited by Henri de Sainte-Marie. Collectanea Biblica Latina 11. Rome: Libreria Vaticana, 1954.

John of Salisbury. *Letters of John of Salisbury*. 2 vols. Edited by W.J. Millor and C.N.L. Brooke. Oxford: Clarendon Press, 1979.

————. *Metalogicon*. Translated by Daniel McGarry. Berkeley: University of California Press, 1962.

Justin Martyr. *The Dialogue with Trypho*. Translated by A. Lukyn Williams. London: S.P.C.K., 1930.

Kimhi, David. *Commento ai Salmi*. Translated by Luigi Cattani. Rome: Città Nuova Editrice, 1991.

————. *The Commentary of Rabbi David Kimhi on Psalms CXX–CL*, edited and translated by Joshua Baker and Ernest W. Nicholson. Cambridge: Cambridge University Press, 1973.

Kimhi, Joseph. *The Book of the Covenant*. Edited and translated by Frank E. Talmage. Toronto: Pontifical Institute of Medieval Studies, 1972.

Materials for the History of Archbishop Thomas Becket. Edited by J.C. Robertson and J.B. Sheppard. Rolls Series, 1875–1883.

Medieval English Jews and Royal Officials: Entries of Jewish Interest in the English Memoranda Rolls, 1266–1293. Edited, translated, and annotated by Zefira Entin Rokéah. Jerusalem: Hebrew University Magnes Press, 2000.

Midrash on Psalms. Translated by William G. Braude. 2 vols. New Haven: Yale University Press, 1959.

Midrash Rabbah: Exodus. Translated by S.M. Lehrman. London: Soncino.

Midrash Rabbah: Genesis 2. Translated by H. Freedman. London: Soncino, 1939.

Origen. *Homilies on Genesis and Exodus*. Translated by Ronald E. Heine. Fathers of the Church 71. Washington, D.C.: Catholic University of America Press, 1982.

Peter Abelard. *The Letters of Abelard and Heloise*. Translated by Betty Radice. London: Penguin, 1974.

Petri Abaelardi opera, edited by Victor Cousin. Paris: Durand, 1849.

————. *Petri Abaelardi Opera Theologica*, 1: *Commentaria in Epistolam Pauli ad Romanos*. CCCM 11.

Peter Lombard. *Sententiae in IV libris distinctae*, edited with an introduction by Ignatius C. Brady. Grottaferrata: Collegii S. Bonaventurae ad Claras Aquas, 1971–1981.

————. *Petri Lombardi Commentarius in Psalmos Davidicos*. PL 191: 61–1296.

Peter the Venerable. *Adversus Iudeorum inveteratam duritiem*. CCCM 58.

Pseudo-Jerome. *Quaestiones on the Book of Samuel*, edited by Avrom Saltman. Leiden: E.J. Brill, 1975.

R. Samuel ben Meir. *Rabbi Samuel ben Meir's Commentary on* Genesis: *An Annotated Translation*. Translated and annotated by Martin I. Lockshin. Lewiston, NY: Edwin Mellen Press, 1989.

Secundum Salomonem: A Thirteenth Century Latin Commentary on the Song of Solomon, edited and introduction by Sarah Kamin and Avrom Saltman. Ramat-Gan [Israel]: Bar-Ilan University Press, 1989.

Sefer ha-pitronot mi-Bazel. Le glossaire de Bâle, edited and annotated by Menahem Banitt. Jerusalem: Académie nationale des sciences et des lettres d'Israël, 1972.

R. Solomon ben Isaac of Troyes. *Rashi's Commentary on Psalms 1–89 (Books I–III),* edited, translated and introduction by Mayer I. Gruber. Atlanta: Scholars Press, 1998.

The Targums of Onkelos and Jonathan ben Uzziel on the Pentateuch with the Fragments of the Jerusalem Targum. Translated by J.W. Etheridge. NY: KTAV, reprint 1968.

Theodore of Mopsuestia. *Le Commentaire de Théodore de Mopsueste sur les Psaumes,* edited by Robert Devreesse. Studi e Testi 93. Vatican City: Biblioteca Apostolica Vaticana, 1939.

Walter Daniel. *Life of Ailred of Riveaulx,* edited and translated by F.M. Powicke. London: Thomas Nelson, 1950.

William FitzStephen. *Vita Sanctae Thomae. Materials for the History of Thomas Becket, Archbishop of Canterbury.* Vol. 3, edited by James Craigie Robertson. London: Longman et al., 1877.

William of St. Thierry. *Exposition on the Epistle to the Romans.* Translated by J.B. Hasbrouck, edited by John D. Anderson. Cistercian Fathers Series 27. Kalamazoo, MI: Cistercian Publications, 1980.

[Odo]. *Ysagoge in Theologiam.* Latin text published by Arthur Landgraf, *Ecrits Theologiques de l'Ecole d'Abelard: Textes Inedits.* Spicilegium Sacrum Lovaniense Etudes et Documents 14. Louvain: Spicilegium Sacrum Lovaniense, 1934.

III. *Secondary Sources*

Abulafia, Anna Sapir. *Christians and Jews in the Twelfth-Century Renaissance.* London: Routledge, 1995.

——. "Christians Disputing Disbelief: St. Anselm, Gilbert Crispin and Pseudo-Anselm." In *Religionsgesprache im Mittelalter.* Wolfenbuttler Mittelalter-Studien 4, edited by B. Lewis and F. Niewoehner. Wiesbaden: Harrassowitz, 1992.

——. "Jewish Carnality in Twelfth-Century Renaissance Thought." In *Christianity and Judaism,* edited by Diana Wood. Oxford: Basil Blackwell, 1992.

——. "Jewish-Christian Disputations and the Twelfth-Century Renaissance." *Journal of Medieval History* 15 (1989): 105–125.

——. "Twelfth-Century Christian Expectations of Jewish Conversion: A Case Study of Peter of Blois." *Aschkenas: Zeitschrift für Geschichte und Kultur der Juden* 8 (1998): 45–70.

——. "Twelfth-Century Renaissance Theology and the Jews." In *From Witness to Witchcraft: Jews and Judaism in Medieval Christian Thought*, edited by Jeremy Cohen. Wiesbaden: Harrassowitz, 1996.

Adler, William. "Jews as Falsifiers: Charges of Tendentious Emendation in Jewish-Christian Polemic." In *Translation of Scripture*, edited by David M. Goldenberg. Philadelphia: Jewish Quarterly Review Supplement, 1990.

Baldwin, John W. *Masters, Princes, and Merchants: The Social Views of Peter the Chanter and His Circle*. 2 vols. Princeton: Princeton University Press, 1970.

———. "Masters at Paris from 1179 to 1215: A Social Perspective." In *Renaissance and Renewal in the Twelfth Century*, edited by Robert L. Benton, Giles Constable, and Carol D. Lanham. Toronto: Medieval Academy Reprints for Teaching 26, 1991.

Balfour, David. "The Origins of the Longchamp Family." *Medieval Prosopography* 18 (1997): 73–92.

Banitt, Menahem. "The *La'azim* of Rashi and of the French Biblical Glossaries." In *World History of the Jewish People: The Dark Ages 711–1096*, edited by Cecil Roth. New Brunswick, NJ: Rutgers University Press, 1966.

———. "Les Poterim." *Revue des Études Juives* 125 (1966): 21–33.

Barlow, Frank. *Thomas Becket*. London: Weidenfeld and Nicolson, 1986.

Barrow, Julia. "Education and the Recruitment of Cathedral Canons in England and Germany 1100–1225." *Viator* 20 (1989): 117–137.

Baskin, Judith R. *Pharoah's Counsellors: Job, Jethro and Balaam in Rabbinic and Patristic Tradition*. Brown Judaic Studies 47. Chico, CA: Scholars Press, 1983.

Bauman, Zygmunt. "Allosemitism: Premodern, Modern, Postmodern." In *Modernity, Culture, and "the Jew,"* edited by Bryan Cheyette and Laura Marcus. Stanford: Stanford University Press, 1998.

Bautier, Robert-Henri. "Les origines et les premiers développements de l'abbaye de Saint-Victor de Paris." In *L'abbaye parisienne de Saint-Victor au Moyen Age*. Bibliotheca Victorina 1, edited by Jean Longère. Paris: Brepols, 1991.

Bautier, Robert-Henri. "Les premières relations entre le monastère de Pontigny et la royauté anglaise." In *Thomas Becket: actes du colloque international de Sédières, 19–24 août 1973*, edited by Raymonde Foreville. Paris: CNRS & Beaushesne, 1975.

Bedos-Rezak, Brigitte. "The Confrontation of Orality and Textuality: Jewish and Christian Literacy in Eleventh- and Twelfth-Century Northern France." In *RASHI 1040–1990: Hommage à Ephraim E. Urbach*. Patrimoines Judaisme, edited by Gabrielle Sed-Rajna. Paris: Cerf, 1993.

Beit-Arié, Malachi. *The Earliest Dated Anglo-Hebrew Manuscript Written in England (1189 CE)*. London: Valmadonna Trust Library, 1985.

Bell, David. "*Agrestis et infatua interpretatio*: The Background and Purpose of John of Forde's Condemnation of Jewish Exegesis." In *A Gathering of Friends: The Learning and Spirituality of John of Forde*. Cistercian Studies Series 161, edited by Hilary Costello and Christopher Holdsworth. Kalamazoo, MI: Cistercian Publications, 1996.

Benin, Stephen D. "Jews and Christian History: Hugh of St. Victor, Anselm of Havelberg and William of Auvergne." In *From Witness to Witchcraft: Jews and Judaism in Medieval Christian Thought*, edited by Jeremy Cohen. Wiesbaden: Harrassowitz, 1996.

Benton, John L. "The Court of Champagne as a Literary Center." *Speculum* 36 (1961): 551–591.

Benton, Robert L. and Giles Constable, eds. *Renaissance and Renewal in the Twelfth Century*. Medieval Academy Reprints for Teaching 26. Toronto: University of Toronto Press, 1991.

Berger, David. *The Jewish-Christian Debate in the High Middle Ages*. Philadelphia: JPS, 1979.

Berman, Constance Hoffman. *The Cistercian Evolution: The Invention of a Religious Order in Twelfth-Century Europe*. Philadelphia: University of Pennsylvania Press, 2000.

Berndt, Rainer. *André de Saint-Victor: Exégète et Théologien*. Bibliotheca Victorina 2. Paris: Brepols, 1991.

——. "La pratique exégétique d'André de Saint-Victor: Tradition victorine et influence rabbinique." In *L'Abbaye Parisien de Saint-Victor au Moyen Âge*. Bibliotheca Victorina 1, edited by Jean Longère. Paris: Brepols, 1991.

——. "L'Influence de Rashi sur l'Exégèse d'André de Saint-Victor." In *Rashi Studies*, edited by Zvi Arie Steinfeld. Ramat-Gan [Israel]: Bar-Ilan University Press, 1993.

Bhabha, Homi. *The Location of Culture*. London and New York: Routledge, 1994.

Biddick, Kathleen. "The ABC of Ptolemy: Mapping the World with the Alphabet." In *Text and Territory: Geographical Imagination in the European Middle Ages*, edited by Sylvia Tomasch and Sealy Gilles. Philadelphia: University of Pennsylvania Press, 1998.

——. "Coming out of Exile: Dante on the Orient[alism] Express." *American Historical Review* (October 2000): 1234–1249.

Blumenkranz, Bernhard. "La Synagogue de Rouen." In *Art et archéologie des Juifs en France mediévale*. Toulouse: Privat, 1980.

Bouchard, Constance Brittain. "The Cistercians and the *Glossa Ordinaria*." *Catholic Historical Review* 86 (2000): 183–192.

Boyarin, Daniel. "Justin Martyr Invents Judaism." *Church History*, 70:3 (2001) 427–462.

Brady, Ignatius C. "Peter Manducator and the Oral Teachings of Peter Lombard." *Antonianum* 41 (1966): 454–490.

Brandin, Louis and Mayer Lambert. *Glossaire hébreu-français du XIIIe siècle*. Geneva: Slatkine Reprints, 1977.

Bredero, Adriaan H. "Thomas Becket et la Canonisation de Saint Bernard." In *Thomas Becket: actes du colloque international de Sédières, 19–24 août 1973*, edited by Raymonde Foreville. Paris: CNRS & Beauchesne, 1975.

Brooke, C.N.L. "Gregorian Reform in Action: Clerical Marriage in England, 1050–1200." *Cambridge Historical Review* 12 (1956): 1–21.

Brown, Dennis. *Vir Trilinguis: A Study in the Biblical Exegesis of Saint Jerome*. Kampen: Kok Pharos, 1992.

Bruns, Gerald A. *Hermeneutics Ancient and Modern*. New Haven: Yale University Press, 1992.

Carruthers, Mary J. *The Book of Memory: A Study of Memory in Medieval Culture*, Cambridge: Cambridge University Press, 1990.

Châtillon, Jean. "La Bible dans les écoles du XIIe siècle." In *Le Moyen Age et la Bible*. Bible de tous les temps 4, edited by Pierre Riché and Guy Lobrichon. Paris: Beauchesne, 1984.

——. *Le Mouvement Canonial au Moyen Age: Réforme de l'église, spiritualité, et culture*, edited by Patrice Sicard. Bibliotheca Victorina 3. Paris: Brepols, 1992.

Chazan, Robert. "The Blois Incident of 1171: A Study in Jewish Intercommunal Organization." *Proceedings of the American Academy for Jewish Research* 36 (1968): 13–31.

——. *European Jewry and the First Crusade*. Berkeley: University of California, 1987.

——. *Medieval Jewry in Northern France*. Baltimore: Johns Hopkins University Press, 1973.

Cheney, C.R. *Hubert Walter*. London: Nelson, 1967.

Chenu, Marie-Dominique. *Nature, Man and Society in the Twelfth Century*, trans. Jerome Taylor and Lester K. Little. Medieval Academy Reprints for Teaching 37. Toronto: University of Toronto Press, 1997.

——. *La théologie au douzième siècle*. 2nd ed. Études de Philosophie Médiévale 45. Paris: Vrin, 1966.

Clanchy, M.T. *From Memory to Written Record: England 1066–1307*. Cambridge: Harvard University Press, 1979.

Classen, Peter. "*Res Gestae*, Universal History, Apocalypse: Visions of Past and Future." In *Renaissance and Renewal*, edited by Robert L. Benson and Giles Constable with Carol D. Lanham. Toronto: Medieval Academy Reprints for Teaching 26, 1991.

Cluse, Christoph. "Jewish Elementary Education in Medieval Ashkenaz." In *Seriis Intendere: A Collection of Essays Celebrating the Twenty-fifth Anniversary of the Centre for Medieval Studies*, edited by Sharon A. Hanen. Leeds, 1994.

Cohen, Gerson D. "Esau as Symbol in Early Medieval Thought." In *Jewish Medieval and Renaissance Studies*, edited by Alexander Altman. Cambridge: Harvard University Press, 1967.

——. "Messianic Postures of Ashkenazim and Sephardim (Prior to Sabbethai Zvi)." In *Studies of the Leo Baeck Institute*, edited by Maz Kreutzberger. New York: Frederick Ungar Publishing, 1967.

Cohen, Jeremy. *The Friars and the Jews*. Ithaca: Cornell University Press, 1982.

——. *Living Letters of the Law: The Idea of the Jew in the Medieval Christianity*. Berkeley: University of California Press, 1999.

——. "Scholarship and Intolerance in the Medieval Academy: the Study and Evaluation of Judaism in European Christendom." *American Historical Review* 91(1986): 592–613.

——. "*Synagoga conversa*: Honorius Augustodunensis, the Song of Songs, and Christianity's 'Eschatological Jew.'" *Speculum* 79 (2004): 309–340.

Coleman, Janet. *Ancient and Medieval Memories: Studies in the Reconstruction of the Past*. Cambridge: Cambridge University Press, 1991.

Colish, Marcia. *Peter Lombard*. 2 vols. Leiden: E.J. Brill, 1994.

Constable, Giles. *The Reformation of the Twelfth Century*. Cambridge: Cambridge University Press, 1996.

Contreni, John J. "Carolingian Biblical Studies." In *Carolingian Essays*, edited by Ute-Renate Blumenthal. Washington: Catholic University of America Press, 1983.

Crosby, Everett U. *Bishop and Chapter in Twelfth-Century England: A Study of the Mensa Episcopalis*. Cambridge: Cambridge University Press, 1994.

Crozet, Rene. "L'episcopat de France et l'Ordre de Cîteaux au XIIe Siècle." *Cahiers de civilisation médiévale* 18 (1975): 263–268.

Culler, Jonathan. *Structuralist Poetics: Structuralism, Linguistics and the Study of Literature*. Ithaca, New York: Cornell University Press, 1975.

Dahan, Gilbert. *Les intellectuels chrétiens et les Juifs au Moyen Âge*. Paris: Cerf, 1991.

———. "La connaissance de l'hébreu dans les correctoires de la Bible du XIIIe siècle." In *RASHI 1040–1990: Hommage à Ephraim E. Urbach*. Patrimoines Judaisme, edited by Gabrielle Sed-Rajna. Paris: Cerf, 1993.

———. "Juifs et chrétiens en occident médiéval: la rencontre autour de la Bible (XIIe–XIVe siècles)." *Révue de Synthèse* 4 (1989): 3–31.

———. Gérard Nahon, Elie Nicolas, eds. *Rashi et la culture juive en France du Nord au Moyen Âge*. Collection de la Revue des Études Juives. Paris-Louvain: Peeters, 1997.

De Bruyne, Donatien. "Le problème du psautier romain." *Revue Bénédictine* 42 (1930): 101–126.

De Hamel, Christopher. *Glossed Books of the Bible and the Origins of the Paris Book Trade*. Dover, NH: D.S. Brewer, 1984.

De Jonge, Mayke. "Old Law and New-Found Power: Hrabanus Maurus and the Old Testament." In *Centres of Learning: Learning and Location in Pre-Modern Europe and the Near East*, edited by Jan Willem Drijvers and Alasdair A. MacDonald. Leiden: E.J. Brill, 1995.

De Lubac, Henri. *Exégèse Médiévale*. Paris: Aubier, 1961.

———. *Medieval Exegesis I: The Four Senses of Scripture*. Translated by Mark Sebanc. Grand Rapids, MI: Eerdmans, 1998.

De Visscher, Eva S. "The Jewish-Christian Dialogue in Twelfth-Century Western Europe: Herbert of Bosham's *Commentary on the Psalms*." Ph.D. thesis, School of Theology and Religious Studies, University of Leeds, 2003.

Delhaye, Philippe. "L'organisation scolaire au XIIe siècle." *Traditio* 5 (1947): 211–268.

Denifle, H. "Die Handschriften der Bibel-Correctorien des 13. Jahrhunderts." *Archiv für Literatur und Kirchengeschichte des Mittelalters* 4 (1888): 270–276.

Dimier, Marie-Anselme. "Henri II, Thomas Becket, et les Cisterciens." In *Thomas Becket: actes du colloque international de Sédières, 19–24 août 1973*, edited by Raymonde Foreville. Paris, CNRS & Beauchesne, 1975.

Dobson, R.B. "The Jews of Medieval York and the Massacre of March 1190." Borthwick Papers No. 45. York: St. Anthony's Press, 1974.

———. "The Medieval York Jewry Reconsidered." In *Jews in Medieval Britain*, edited by Patricia Skinner. Woodbridge, Suffolk: Boydell Press, 2003.

Dodwell, C.R. *The Canterbury School of Illumination*. Cambridge: Cambridge University Press, 1954.

Duggan, Anne J. *The Correspondence of Thomas Becket*. 2 vols. Oxford: Clarendon Press, 2000.

——. *Thomas Becket*. London: Arnold; distributed by Oxford University Press, New York, 2004.

Dutton, Marsha L. "The Conversion and Vocation of Aelred of Rievaulx: A Historical Hypothesis." In *England in the Twelfth Century: Proceedings of the 1988 Harlaxton Symposium*, edited by Daniel Williams. Woodbridge, UK: Boydell Press, 1990.

The Eadwine Psalter, edited by Margaret Gibson, T.A. Heslop, and Richard Pfaff. London: Modern Humanities Research Association,1992.

Einbinder, Susan L. "Pucellina of Blois: Romantic Myths and Narrative Conventions." *Jewish History* 12 (1998): 29–46.

Estin, Colette. *Les psautiers de Jérôme à la lumière des traductions juives antérieures*. Collectanea Biblica Latina 15. Rome: San Girolamo, 1984.

Evans, G.R. *Old Arts and New Theology*. Oxford: Clarendon Press, 1980.

Ferruolo, Stephen C. *Origins of the University: The Schools of Paris and their Critics, 1110–1215*. Stanford: Stanford University Press, 1985.

Field, Frederick. *Origenis Hexaplorum*. Hildesheim: Georg Olms, reprint 1964.

Flahiff, G.B. "Ralph Niger: an introduction to his life and works." *Mediaeval Studies* [Toronto] 2 (1940): 104–136.

Flint, Valerie I.J. "Some notes on the early Twelfth-Century Commentaries on the Psalms." *RTAM* 38 (1971): 80–88.

——. "World History in the Twelfth Century; the 'Imago Mundi' of Honorius Augustodunensis." In *The Writing of History in the Middle Ages: Essays Presented to Richard William Southern*, edited by R.H.C. Davis and J.M. Wallace-Hadrill.

Foucault, Michel. *The Archaeology of Knowledge*, trans. A.M. Sheridan Smith. New York: Pantheon, 1972.

Foreville, Raymonde. "Liminaire." In *Thomas Becket: actes du colloque international de Sédières, 19–24 août 1973*, edited by Raymonde Foreville. Paris: CNRS & Beauchesne, 1975.

Fredriksen, Paula. "*Excaecati occulta iustitia Dei*: Augustine on the Jews and Judaism." *Journal of Early Christian Studies* 3 (1995): 299–324.

Friedman, Yvonne. "An Anatomy of Anti-Semitism: Peter the Venerable's Letter to Louis VII, King of France (1146)." In *Bar-Ilan Studies in History*, edited by Pinhas Artzi. Ramat-Gan [Israel]: Bar-Ilan University Press, 1978.

Funkenstein, Amos. "Basic Types of Christian anti-Jewish Polemic in the later Middle Ages." *Viator* 2:373–382.

——. "Changes in Christian Anti-Jewish Polemics in the Twelfth Century." In *Perceptions of Jewish History*. Berkeley: University of California Press, 1993.

——. "Scripture Speaks the Language of Man: the Uses and Abuses of the Medieval Principle of Accomodation." In *L'homme et son univers* 1, edited by C. Wenin. Louvain-la-Neuve, 1986.

Gelles, Benjamin J. *Peshat and Derash in the Exegesis of Rashi*. Leiden: E.J. Brill, 1981.

Giard, Luce. "Hugues de Saint-Victor: Cartographe du Savoir." In *L'Abbaye Parisienne de Saint-Victor au Moyen Age*, edited by Jean Longère. Paris: Brepols, 1991.

Gibson, Margaret T. "The Place of the *Glossa ordinaria* in Medieval Exegesis." In *Ad Litteram: Authoritative Texts and Their Medieval Readers*, edited by Mark D. Jordan and Kent Emery, Jr. Notre Dame, IN: University of Notre Dame Press, 1992.

———. *The Bible in the Latin West*. Notre Dame, IN: University of Notre Dame Press, 1993.

———. "The Twelfth-Century Glossed Bible." In *The* Artes *and Bible in the Medieval West*. London: Variorum, 1993.

Glunz, H.H. *The History of the Vulgate in England from Alcuin to Roger Bacon*. Cambridge: Cambridge University Press, 1933.

Goetz, Hans-Werner. "Historical Consciousness and Institutional Concern in European Medieval Historiography (11th and 12th Centuries)." Paper presented at the 19th International Congress of Historical Sciences, Oslo, August 6–13, 2000.

Golb, Norman. "Les Écoles Rabbiniques en France au Moyen Age." *Revue de l'histoire des religions* 102 (1985): 243–265.

Goodwin, Deborah L. "A Study of Herbert of Bosham's Psalms Commentary (c. 1190)." Ph.D. dissertation, University of Notre Dame, 2001.

———. "Herbert of Bosham and the Horizons of Twelfth-Century Exegesis." *Traditio* 58 (2003), 133–173.

Gorday, Peter. *Principles of Patristic Exegesis: Romans 9–11 in Origen, John Chrysostom, and Augustine*. Studies in the Bible and Early Christianity 4. New York: Edwin Mellen Press, 1983.

Grabmann, Martin. *Geschichte der Scholastische Method*. 2 vols. Freiburg: Herdersche Verlagshandlung, 1911.

Grabois, Aryeh. "The *Hebraica Veritas* and Jewish-Christian Intellectual Relations in the Twelfth Century." *Speculum* 50 (1975): 613–634.

Gross, Henri. *Gallia Judaica: dictionnaire géographique de la France d'après les sources rabbiniques*. Amsterdam: Philo Press, reprint 1969.

Gross-Diaz, Theresa. *The Psalms Commentary of Gilbert of Poitiers: From* Lectio Divina *to the Lecture Room*. Leiden: E.J. Brill, 1996.

———. "What's a Good Solider to Do? Scholarship and Revelation in the Postills on the Psalms." In *Nicholas of Lyra: The Senses of Scripture*. Studies in the History of Christian Thought 90, edited by Philip D.W. Krey and Lesley Smith. Leiden: E.J. Brill, 2000.

Hailperin, Herman. *Rashi and the Christian Scholars*. Pittsburgh: University of Pittsburgh Press, 1963.

Harden, J.M., ed. *Psalterium Iuxta Hebraeos Hieronymi*. London: S.P.C.K., 1922.

Hay, David M. *Glory at the Right Hand: Psalm 110 in Early Christianity*. Nashville: Abingdon Press, 1973.

Heschel, Susannah. "Revolt of the Colonized: Abraham Geiger's *Wissenschaft des Judentums* as a Challenge to Christian Hegemony in the Academy." *New German Critique* 77 (1999), 61–85.

Holtz, Louis. "A l'école de Donat, de Saint Augustin à Bede." *Latomus* 36 (1977):522–538.

Hunt, R.W. "The Disputation of Peter of Cornwall against Symon the Jew." In *Studies in Medieval History Presented to Frederick Maurice Powicke*. Oxford: Clarendon Press, 1948: 143–156.

———. "English Learning in the Late Twelfth Century." In *Essays in Medieval History*, edited by R.W. Southern. London: Macmillan, 1968.

———. "The Introductions to the '*Artes*' in the Twelfth Century." In *Studia Mediaevalia in honorem Raymondi Josephi Martini*. Bruges: De Tempel, 1948.

———. *The Schools and the Cloister: The Life and Writings of Alexander Nequam*, edited and revised by Margaret Gibson. Oxford: Clarendon Press, 1984.

Irvine, Martin. *The Making of Textual Culture: 'Grammatica' and Literary Theory, 350–1100*. Cambridge: Cambridge University Press, 1994.

Jacobs, Joseph. *The Jews of Angevin England: Documents and Records*. London: David Nutt, 1893.

Jaeger, C. Stephen. *The Envy of Angels: Cathedral Schools and Social Ideals in Medieval Europe, 950–1200*. Philadelphia: University of Pennsylvania Press, 1994.

James, M.R. "The Salomites." *Journal of Theological Studies* 35 (1934): 287–297.

Jordan, William Chester. *The French Monarchy and the Jews*. Philadelphia: University of Pennsylvania Press, 1989.

Kaczynski, Bernice M. "Edition, Translation and Exegesis: The Carolingians and the Bible." In *The Gentle Voices of Teachers: Aspects of Learning in the Carolingian Age*, edited by Richard E. Sullivan. Columbus: Ohio State University Press, 1995.

Kamesar, Adam. *Jerome, Greek Scholarship, and the Hebrew Bible*. Oxford: Clarendon Press, 1993.

Kamin, Sarah. "Affinities Between Jewish and Christian Exegesis in Twelfth Century Northern France." In *Proceedings of the Ninth World Congress of Jewish Studies*, edited by M. Goshen-Gottstein and D. Assaf. Jerusalem: Magnes Press, 1988.

———. "Rashi's Exegetical Categorization with Respect to the Distinction between *Peshat* and *Derash*." *Immanuel* 11 (1980): 16–32.

———. "The Theological Significance of the *Hebraica Veritas* in Jerome's Thought." In *Sha'arei Talmon*, edited by Michael Fishbane et al. Winona Lake, IN: Eisenbrauns, 1992.

Kanarfogel, Ephraim. *Jewish Education and Society in the High Middle Ages*. Detroit: Wayne State University Press, 1993.

Katz, Jacob. *Exclusiveness and Tolerance: Studies in Jewish-Gentile Relations in Medieval and Modern Times*. W. Orange, NJ: Behrmann, 1983.

Kelly, J.N.D. *Jerome: His Life, Writings, and Controversies*. NY: Harper and Row, 1975.

Ker, N.R. *Medieval Manuscripts in British Libraries I: London*. Oxford: Clarendon, 1969.

Kinder, Terryl N. *Architecture of the Cistercian Abbey of Pontigny: The Twelfth-Century Church*. Ph.D. dissertation, Indiana University, 1982. Ann Arbor: University Microfilms, 1982.

Klausner, Joseph. *The Messianic Idea in Israel*. Translated by W.F. Stinespring. New York: Macmillan, 1955.

Klepper, Deanna. "Nicholas of Lyra and Franciscan Interest in Hebrew Scholarship." In *Nicholas of Lyra: The Senses of Scripture*. Studies in the History of Christian Thought, vol. 90, edited by Philip D.W. Krey and Lesley Smith, Leiden: E.J. Brill, 2000.

Knowles, David. *Episcopal Colleagues of Archbishop Thomas Becket.* Cambridge: Cambridge University Press, 1951.

Kuczynksi, Michael P. *Prophetic Song: The Psalms as Moral Discourse in Late Medieval England.* Philadelphia: University of Pennsylvania Press, 1995.

La Bonnardière, A.-M. "Augustin a-t-il utilisé la 'Vulgate' de Jérôme?" *St Augustin et la Bible*, edited by A.-M. La Bonnardière. Bible de tous les temps 3. Paris: Beauchesne, 1986.

Langmuir, Gavin. *History, Religion and Anti-Semitism.* Berkeley: University of California Press, 1990.

———. *Toward a Definition of Anti-Semitism.* Berkeley: University of California Press, 1990.

LeMoine, Michel. "Abélard et les Juifs." *Revue des études juives* 153/3–4 (1994): 253–267.

Leroquais, Victor. *Les Psautiers manuscrits latins des bibliothèques publique de France.* Macon: Protat Freres, 1940–1941.

Levy, Raphael. "The Use of Hebrew Characters for Writing Old French." In *Mélanges de Langue et de Littérature du Moyen Age et de la Renaissance offerts à Jean Frappier.* Geneva: Librairie Droz, 1970.

Lieftinck, G.I. "The 'Psalterium Hebraycum' from St. Augustine's Canterbury Rediscovered in the Scaliger Bequest at Leiden." *Transactions of the Cambridge Bibliographical Society* 2:2 (1955): 97–104.

Light, Laura. "Versions et révisions du texte biblique." In *Le Moyen Age et la Bible*, edited by Pierre Riché and Guy Lobrichon. Bible de tous les temps 4. Paris: Beauchesne, 1984.

Little, Lester K. *Religious Poverty and the Profit Economy in Medieval Europe.* Ithaca, NY: Cornell University Press, 1978.

Loewe, Raphael. "Alexander Neckam's Knowledge of Hebrew." *Mediaeval and Renaissance Studies* 4 (1958): 17–34.

———. "The Medieval Christian Hebraists of England: Herbert of Bosham and Earlier Scholars." *Transactions of the Jewish Historical Society of England* 17 (1953): 225–249.

———. "The Medieval Christian Hebraists of England: The *Superscriptio Lincolniensis.*" Hebrew Union College Annual 28 (1957): 205–252.

———. "Herbert of Bosham's Commentary on Jerome's Hebrew Psalter." *Biblica* 34 (1953): 44–77, 159–192, 275–298.

Lotter, Friedrich. "The Position of the Jews in Early Cistercian Exegesis and Preaching." In *From Witness to Witchcraft: Jews and Judaism in Medieval Christian Thought*, edited by Jeremy Cohen. Wiesbaden: Harrassowitz, 1996.

Luscombe, David E. "The Authorship of the *Ysagoge in Theologiam.*" *Archives d'Histoire Doctinale et Litteraire du Moyen Age* 35 (1968): 7–16.

Marcus, Ivan G. *Piety and Society: The Jewish Pietists of Medieval Germany.* Leiden: E.J. Brill, 1981.

———. *Rituals of Childhood: Jewish Acculturation in Medieval Europe.* New Haven: Yale University Press, 1996.

McCarthy, David Paul. "Saint Jerome's Translation of the Psalms: the Question of Rabbinic Tradition." In *Open thou mine eyes*, edited by H. Blumberg. Hoboken, NJ: KTAV, 1992.

McGinn, Bernard. *Visions of the End: Apocalyptic Traditions in the Middle Ages*. New York: Columbia University Press, 1998.

McKane, William. *Selected Christian Hebraists*. Cambridge: Cambridge University Press, 1989.

Milhau, Marc. "Sur la division tripartite du Psautier: Hilaire de Poitiers." In *Le Psautier chez les Pères*. Cahiers de Biblia Patristica 4, edited by J. Irigoin. Strassbourg: Centre d'Analyse et de Documentation Patristiques, 1994.

Minnis, A.J. "Discussions of 'Authorial Role' and 'Literary Form' in Late-Medieval Scriptural Exegesis." *Beitraege zur Geschichte der Deutschen Sprache und Litteratur* 99 (1977): 37–65.

——. and A.B. Scott. *Medieval Literary Theory and Criticism, c. 1100-c. 1375*. Oxford: Oxford University Press,1991.

——. *Medieval Theory of Authorship*. 2ⁿᵈ ed. Aldershot, UK: Wildwood House, 1988.

Mitchell, David C. *The Message of the Psalter: An Eschatological Programme in the Book of Psalms*. Journal for the Study of the Old Testament Supplement Series 252. Sheffield: Sheffield Academic Press, 1997.

Moore, Rebecca. *Jews and Christians in the Life and Thought of Hugh of St. Victor*. University of South Florida Studies in the History of Judaism 138. Atlanta: Scholars Press, 1998.

——. "The Jews in World History according to Hugh of St Victor." *Medieval Encounters* 3 (1997):1–19.

Moore, R.I. *The Creation of a Persecuting Society*. Oxford: Oxford University Press, 1987.

——. "Literacy and the Making of Heresy." In *Heresy and Literacy, 1000–1530*. Edited by Peter Biller and Anne Hudson. Cambridge: Cambridge University Press, 1994.

Moore-Gilbert, Bart. *Postcolonial Theory*. London: Verso, 1997.

Morey, Adrian. *Bartholomew of Exeter, Bishop and Canonist*. Cambridge: Cambridge University Press, 1937.

Mortimer, Richard. *Angevin England 1154–1248*. A History of Medieval Britain 2. Oxford: Blackwell, 1994.

Mundill, Robert. *England's Jewish Solution: Experiment and Expulsion, 1262–1290*. Cambridge: Cambridge University Press, 1998.

Newman, Martha G. *The Boundaries of Charity: Cistercian Culture and Ecclesiastical Reform, 1098–1180*. Stanford: Stanford University Press, 1966.

Nirenberg, David. *Communities of Violence*. Princeton, NJ: Princeton University Press, 1996.

Olszowy-Schlanger, Judith. "The Knowledge and Practice of Hebrew Grammar among Christian Scholars in Pre-expulsion England: the Evidence of 'Bilingual' Hebrew-Latin Manuscripts." In *Hebrew Scholarship and the Medieval World*, edited by Nicholas de Lange. Cambridge: Cambridge University Press, 2001.

——. "A Thirteenth-Century Glossary of Hebrew, Latin, French, and English Words." Paper presented at the Fortieth International Congress on Medieval Studies, Western Michigan University, Kalamazoo, MI, May 7, 2005.

Orme, Nicolas. *Education and Society in Medieval and Renaissance England.* London: Hambledon, 1989.

Paré, G., A. Brunet, and P. Tremblay. *La Renaissance du XIIe Siècle: Les Écoles et L'Enseignement.* Paris: Vrin, 1933.

Partner, Nancy F. *Serious Entertainment: The Writing of History in Twelfth-Century England.* Chicago: University of Chicago Press, 1977.

Pastan, Elizabeth Carson. "Fit for a Count: The Twelfth-Century Stained Glass Panels from Troyes." *Speculum* 64 (1989):338–378.

Patai, Raphael. *The Messiah Texts.* Detroit: Wayne State University Press, 1979.

Peri, Vittorio. "Correctores immo corruptores: Un Saggio di Critica Testuale nella Roma del XII Secolo." *Italia Mediovale e Umanistica* 20 (1977): 19–125.

———. *Omelie Originiane sui Salmi: Contributo all'identificazione del testo latino.* Citta del Vaticano: Biblioteca Apostolica Vaticana, 1980.

Post, Gaines. "Alexander III, the *Licentia Docendi*, and the Rise of the Universities." In *Anniversary Essays in Medieval History*, edited by C.H. Taylor. Freeport, NY: Books for Libraries, reprint 1967.

Principe, Walter H. *William of Auxerre's Theology of the Hypostatic Union.* Toronto: Pontifical Institute of Medieval Studies, 1963.

Ray, Roger. "Medieval Historiography through the Twelfth Century: Problems and Progress of Research." *Viator* 5 (1974): 33–59.

Ricoeur, Paul. *Essays in Biblical Hermeneutics*, edited by Lewis A. Mudge. Philadelphia: Fortress, 1980.

———. "Toward a Narrative Theology: Its Necessity, Its Resources, Its Difficulties." In *Figuring the Sacred: Religion, Narrative, and Imagination.* Translated by David Pellauer. Minneapolis: Fortress, 1995.

———. "Philosophical and Theological Hermeneutics: Ideology, Utopia and Faith." In *Protocol of the Seventeenth Colloquy* [November 4, 1975], edited by W. Wuellner. Berkeley: Center for Hermeneutical Studies in Hellenistic and Modern Culture at the Graduate Theological Union and the University of California, 1976.

Rondeau, Marie-Josèphe. *Les commentaires patristiques du Psautier IIIe–Ve siècles.* Rome: Pont. Inst. Studiorum Orientalium, 1982.

Rosenthal, E.I.J. "Anti-Christian Polemic in Medieval Bible Commentaries." *Journal of Jewish Studies* 11 (1960): 115–135.

Rouse, Richard and Mary. "*Statim Invenire*: Schools, Preachers, and New Attitudes to the Page." In *Renaissance and Renewal in the Twelfth Century*, edited by Robert L. Benson and Giles Constable with Carol D. Lanham. Medieval Academy Reprints for Teaching 26. Toronto: University of Toronto Press, 1991.

Rowley, H.H. *Darius the Mede and the Four World Empires in the Book of Daniel: A Historical Study of Contemporary Theories.* Cardiff: University of Wales Press, 1964.

Said, Edward W. *Orientalism.* New York: Pantheon, 1978.

Salmon, Pierre. *Les* Tituli Psalmorum *des Manuscrits Latins.* Collectanea Biblica Latina 12. Paris: Cerf, 1959.

Saltman, Avrom. "John of Salisbury and the World of the Old Testament."

In *The World of John of Salisbury*, edited by Michael Wilks. Oxford: Basil Blackwell, 1984.

——. "Supplemental Notes on Ralph Niger." In *Bar-Ilan Studies in History*, edited by Pinhas Artzi. Ramat Gan, Israel: Bar-Ilan University Press, 1978.

Shereshevsky, Esra. "Rashi's and Christian Interpretations." *Jewish Quarterly Review* 61 (1970–1971): 76–86.

Signer, Michael A. "From Theory to Practice: the *De doctrina christiana* and the Exegesis of Andrew of St. Victor." In *Reading and Wisdom: the* De doctrina christiana *of Augustine in the Middle Ages*, edited by Edward D. English. Notre Dame: University of Notre Dame Press, 1995.

——. "The *Glossa Ordinaria* and the Transmission of Medieval Anti-Judaism." In *A Distinct Voice: Medieval Studies in Honor of Leonard E. Boyle, O.P*, edited by Jacqueline Brown and William P. Stoneman. Notre Dame: University of Notre Dame Press, 1998.

——. "God's Love for Israel: Apologetic and Hermeneutical Strategies in Twelfth-Century Biblical Exegesis." In *Jews and Christians in Twelfth-Century Europe*, edited by Michael A. Signer and John Van Engen. Notre Dame: University of Notre Dame Press, 2001.

——. "How the Bible Has Been Interpreted in Jewish Tradition." *New Interpreter's Bible*. Vol. 1. Nashville: Abingdon Press, 1994.

——. "King/Messiah: Rashi's Exegesis of Psalm 2." *Prooftexts* 3 (1983): 273–284.

——. "*Peshat, Sensus Litteralis*, and Sequential Narrative." *In Frank Talmage Memorial Volume*, edited by Barry Walfish. Haifa: University of Haifa Press, 1993.

——. "Polemics and Exegesis: The Varieties of Twelfth Century Christian Hebraism." In *Hebraica Veritas? Christian Hebraists and the Study of Judaism in Early Modern Europe*, edited by Allison Coudert. Philadelphia: University of Pennsylvania Press, 2004.

——. "Rashi as Narrator." In *Rashi et la culture juive en France du Nord au moyen âge*, edited by G. Nahon and C. Touati. Paris-Louvain: Peeters, 1997.

——. "St. Jerome and Andrew of St. Victor: Some Observations." *Studia Patristica* 17, vol. 1, edited by E. Livingstone. Oxford: Pergamon Press, 1982.

Siker, Jeffrey S. *Disinheriting the Jews: Abraham in Early Christian Controversy*. Louisville, KY: Westminster/John Knox Press, 1991.

Simon, Uriel. *Four Approaches to the Book of Psalms: From Saadiah Gaon to Abraham ibn Ezra*. Translated by Lenn J. Schramm. Albany: State University of New York Press, 1991.

Smalley, Beryl. "Andrew of St. Victor: A Twelfth-Century Christian Hebraist?" *RTAM* 10 (1938): 358–373.

——. *The Becket Conflict and the Schools*. Totowa, NJ: Rowman and Littlefield, 1973.

——. "The Bible in the Medieval Schools." In *Cambridge History of the Bible*. Vol. 2, *The West from the Fathers to the Reformation*, edited by G.W.H. Lampe. Cambridge: Cambridge University Press, 1969.

——. "Les commentaires bibliques de l'époque romane: glose ordinaire et gloses périmées." *Cahiers de civilisation médiévale* 4 (1961).

———. "A Commentary on the *Hebraica* by Herbert of Bosham." *RTAM* 18 (1951): 29–65.

———. "An Early Twelfth-Century Commentator on the Literal Sense of Leviticus." *RTAM* 36 (1969): 78–99.

———. "Gilbert Universalis, Bishop of London (1128–1134), and the Problem of the *Glossa Ordinaria*." *RTAM* 8 (1936): 24–60.

———. "Glossa Ordinaria." *Theologische Realenzyklopaedie* 13 (1984).

———. "Stephen Langton and the Four Senses of Scripture." *Speculum* 6:1 (1931): 60–76

———. *The Study of the Bible in the Middle Ages.* 3rd ed. Notre Dame: University of Notre Dame Press, 1978.

Somerville, Robert. *Pope Alexander III and the Council of Tours (1163): A Study of Ecclesiastical Politics and Institutions in the Twelfth Century.* Berkeley: University of California Press, 1977.

Southern, R.W. "Aspects of the European Tradition of Historical Writing: 2. Hugh of St Victor and the Idea of Historical Development." *Transactions of the Royal Historical Society* 21 (1971): 159–179.

———. *Medieval Humanism and Other Studies.* Oxford: Basil Blackwell, 1970.

———. *Saint Anselm: A Portrait in a Landscape.* Cambridge: Cambridge University Press, 1990.

———. *Robert Grosseteste: The Growth of an English Mind in Medieval Europe.* Oxford: Clarendon Press, 1992.

———. *Scholastic Humanism and the Unification of Europe.* Oxford: Blackwell, 1995.

———. "The Schools of Paris and the Schools of Chartres." In *Renaissance and Renewal in the Twelfth Century*, edited by Robert L. Benton, Giles Constable, and Carol D. Lanham. Medieval Academy Reprints for Teaching 26. Toronto: University of Toronto Press, 1991.

Sparks, H.F.D. "Jerome as Biblical Scholar." In *Cambridge History of the Bible.* Vol. 1, *From the Beginnings to Jerome*, edited by P.R. Ackroyd and C.F. Evans. Cambridge: Cambridge University Press, 1970.

Spicq, C. *Esquisse d'Une Histoire de l'Exégèse Latine au Moyen Age.* Paris: Vrin, 1944.

Spiegel, Gabrielle M. "History, Historicism, and the Social Logic of the Text." *Speculum* 65 (1990): 59–86

Stirnemann, Patricia. "Où ont été fabriqués les livres de la glose ordinaire dans la première moitié du XIIe siècle?" *Le XIIe siècle: Mutations et renouveau en France dans la première moitié du XIIe siècle.* Léopard d'Or: Paris, 1994.

Stock, Brian. *The Implications of Literacy.* Princeton: Princeton University Press, 1983.

Strack, H.L. and G. Stemberger, *Introduction to Talmud and Midrash.* Translated by Markus Bockmuehl. Edinburgh: T. & T. Clark, 1991.

Talbot, C.H. "Notes on the Library of Pontigny." *Analecta Sacri Ordinis Cisterciensis*, 10 (1954): 106–168.

Talmage, Frank Ephraim. *David Kimhi: The Man and the Commentaries.* Cambridge: Harvard University Press, 1975.

Thiel, Matthias. "Grundlagen und Gestalt der Hebräischkenntnisse des frühen Mittelalters." *Studi Medievali* 4 (1973): 3–212.

Thomson, Rodney M. "England and the Twelfth-Century Renaissance." In

England and the Twelfth-Century Renaissance. Aldershot, U.K.: Variorum, 1998. 3–21.

———. *Manuscripts from St. Albans Abbey, 1066–1235.* Oxford: D.S. Brewer for the University of Tasmania, 1985.

———. "What is the *Entheticus?*" *The World of John of Salisbury,* edited by Michael Wilks. Oxford: Basil Blackwell, 1984. Ecclesiastical History Society. 287–301.

Timmer, David E. "Biblical Exegesis and the Jewish-Christian Controversy in the Early Twelfth Century." *Church History* 58 (1989): 309–321.

Tolan, John. *Petrus Alfonsi and his Medieval Readers.* Gainesville: University Press of Florida, 1993.

Tomasch, Sylvia. "Postcolonial Chaucer and the Virtual Jew." In *The Postcolonial Middle Ages,* edited by Jeffrey Jerome Cohen. New York: Palgrave, 2000.

Turner, Ralph V. *Men Raised from the Dust: Administrative Service and Upward Mobility in Angevin England.* Philadelphia: University of Pennsylvania Press, 1988.

Unterseher, Lisa A. "The Mark of Cain and the Jews: Augustine's Theology of the Jews." *Augustinian Studies* 33 (2002): 99–121.

Urbach, E.E. *The Sages: Their Concepts and Beliefs.* Translated by Israel Abrahams. Jerusalem: Magnes Press, 1975.

Van der Heide, A. "Rashi's Biblical Exegesis: Recent Research and Developments." *Bibliotheca Orientalis* 41 (1984): 292–318.

Van Engen, John. "Ralph of Flaix: the Book of Leviticus Interpreted as Christian Community." In *Jews and Christians in Twelfth Century Europe,* edited by Michael A. Signer and John Van Engen. Notre Dame: University of Notre Dame Press, 2001.

Van Liere, F[rans]. "Andrew of St. Victor's Commentary on Samuel and Kings: Edited with a Study of Sources and Methods." Ph.D. dissertation, Groningen, 1995.

———. "Andrew of St Victor (d. 1175): Scholar between Cloister and School." In *Centres of Learning: Learning and Location in Pre-Modern Europe and the Near East,* edited by Jan Willem Drijvers and Alasdair A. MacDonald. Leiden: E.J. Brill, 1995.

———. "Twelfth-Century Christian Scholars and the Attribution of the Talmud." *Medieval Perspectives* 17:2 (2002), 93–104.

Van Zwieten, J.W.M. "Jewish Exegesis within Christian Bounds." *Bijdragen: tijdschrift voor filosofie en theologie* 48 (1987): 327–335.

———. "Scientific and Spiritual Culture in Hugh of St Victor." In *Centres of Learning: Learning and Location in Pre-Modern Europe and the Near East,* edited by Jan Willem Drijvers and Alasdair A. MacDonald. Leiden: E.J. Brill, 1995.

Vessey, Mark. "Conference and Confession: Literary Pragmatics in Augustine's '*Apologia contra Hieronymum*'." *Journal of Early Christian Studies* 1:175–213.

Wacholder, Ben Zion. "Cases of Proselytizing in the Tosafist Responsa." *Jewish Quarterly Review* 51(1960): 288–315.

Ward, Benedicta, SLG. *The Sayings of the Desert Fathers.* Kalamazoo, MI: Cistercian Publications, 1984.

Weber, Robert. "Deux préfaces au Psautier dues à Nicolas Maniacoria." *Révue Bénédictine* 63 (1953): 3–17.

White, Caroline. *The Correspondence (394–419) between Jerome and Augustine of Hippo.* Lewiston, NY: Edwin Mellen Press, 1990.

Williams, John R. "William of the White Hands and the Men of Letters." In *Haskins Anniversary Essays in Mediaeval History*, edited by C.H. Taylor. Freeport, NY: Books for Libraries Press, reprinted 1969.

Wilmart, A. "Nicolas Manjacoria: Cistercien à Trois-Fontaines." *Révue Bénédictine* 33 (1921): 136–143.

Yerushalmi, Yosef Hayim. "Response to Rosemary Radford Ruether." In *Auschwitz: Beginning of a New Era?* Edited by Eva Fleischner. New York: KTAV, 1977.

Young, Frances. "Typology." In *Crossing the Boundaries: Essays in Biblical Interpretation in Honour of Michael D. Goulder*, edited by Stanley E. Porter, Paul Joyce and David E. Orton. E.J. Brill: Leiden 1994.

Young, Robert J.C. *Colonial Desire: Hybridity in Theory, Culture, and Race.* New York: Routledge, 1995.

Zinn, Grover A. "*Historia fundamentum est*: the Role of History in the Contemplative Life According to Hugh of St. Victor." In *Contemporary Reflections on the Medieval Christian Tradition: Essays in Honor of Ray C. Petry*, edited by George H. Shriver. Durham, NC: Duke University Press, 1974.

———. "History and Interpretation: 'Hebrew truth,' Judaism, and the Victorine Exegetical Tradition." In *Jews and Christians*, edited by James Charlesworth. NY: Crossroad, 1990.

———. "Hugh of St. Victor's *De Scripturis et scriptoribus sacris* as an *Accessus* Treatise for the Study of the Bible." *Traditio* 52 (1997): 111–134.

———. "The Influence of Augustine's *De doctrina christiana* upon the Writings of Hugh of St. Victor." In *Reading and Wisdom: The* De doctrina christiana *in the Middle Ages*, edited by Edward D. English. Notre Dame: University of Notre Dame Press, 1995.

———. "The Influence of Hugh of St. Victor's *Chronicon* on the *Abbreviationes chronicorum* by Ralph of Diceto." *Speculum* 52 (1977): 38–61.

Ziolkowski, Jan. "Put in No-Man's-Land: Guibert of Nogent's Accusations against a Judaizing and Jew-Supporting Christian." In *Jews and Christians in Twelfth-Century Europe*, edited by Michael A. Signer and John Van Engen. Notre Dame: University of Notre Dame Press, 2001.

INDEX